Criminal Law, Procedure, and Evidence

Providing a complete view of U.S. legal principles, this book addresses distinct issues as well as the overlays and connections between them. It presents as a cohesive whole the interrelationships between constitutional principles, statutory criminal laws, procedural law, and common-law evidentiary doctrines. This fully revised and updated new edition also includes discussion questions and hypothetical scenarios to check learning.

Constitutional principles are the foundation upon which substantive criminal law, criminal procedure law, and evidence laws rely. The concepts of due process, legality, specificity, notice, equality, and fairness are intrinsic to these three disciplines, and a firm understanding of their implications is necessary for a thorough comprehension of the topic. This book examines the tensions produced by balancing the ideals of individual liberty embodied in the Constitution against society's need to enforce criminal laws as a means of achieving social control, order, and safety. Relying on his first-hand experience as a law enforcement official and criminal defense attorney, the author presents issues that highlight the difficulties in applying constitutional principles to specific criminal justice situations. Each chapter of the text contains a realistic problem in the form of a fact pattern that focuses on one or more classic criminal justice issues to which readers can relate. These problems are presented from the points of view of citizens caught up in a police investigation and of police officers attempting to enforce the law within the framework of constitutional protections.

This book is ideal for courses in criminal law and procedure that seek to focus on the philosophical underpinnings of the system.

Walter P. Signorelli is Lecturer and Adjunct Professor of Law and Police Science at John Jay College of Criminal Justice at the City University of New York (CUNY), USA, and a practicing criminal defense attorney. Signorelli was a member of the New York City Police Department for more than thirty years. He retired as an Inspector in the Detective Division having been the commanding officer of precincts in Brooklyn and Manhattan, in the Organized Crime Control Bureau, and in the Narcotics Division. He is a graduate of St. John's University School of Law, cum laude, and the Columbia University Police Management Institute. He is the author of *The Crisis of Police Liability Lawsuits: Prevention and Management* (2006), *The Constable Has Blundered: The Exclusionary Rule, Crime, and Corruption* (2010), *Rome and America: The Great Republics: What the Fall of the Roman Republic Portends for the United States* (2018), and *Tiberius Bound* (2022).

Criminal Law, Procedure, and Evidence

Second Edition

Walter P. Signorelli

Routledge
Taylor & Francis Group

NEW YORK AND LONDON

Designed cover image: ©Getty Images

Second edition published 2024
by Routledge
605 Third Avenue, New York, NY 10158

and by Routledge
4 Park Square, Milton Park, Abingdon, Oxon, OX14 4RN

Routledge is an imprint of the Taylor & Francis Group, an informa business

© 2024 Walter P. Signorelli

First edition published by Routledge 2011

Library of Congress Cataloging-in-Publication Data
Names: Signorelli, Walter P., author.
Title: Criminal law, procedure, and evidence / Walter P. Signorelli.
Description: Second edition. | New York, NY : Routledge, 2024. |
Includes bibliographical references and index. |
Identifiers: LCCN 2023022056 (print) | LCCN 2023022057 (ebook) |
ISBN 9781032540849 (hardback) | ISBN 9781032539096 (paperback) |
ISBN 9781003415091 (ebook)
Subjects: LCSH: Criminal law–United States. |
Criminal procedure–United States.
Classification: LCC KF9219 .S56 2024 (print) |
LCC KF9219 (ebook) | DDC 345.73–dc22
LC record available at https://lccn.loc.gov/2023022056
LC ebook record available at https://lccn.loc.gov/2023022057

ISBN: 978-1-032-54084-9 (hbk)
ISBN: 978-1-032-53909-6 (pbk)
ISBN: 978-1-003-41509-1 (ebk)

DOI: 10.4324/9781003415091

Typeset in Sabon
by Newgen Publishing UK

Access the Support Material: www.routledge.com/9781032539096

This book is dedicated to all my students and colleagues with whom I have had so much fun over the years, and to those who played a part in the development of this book. Thank you, all.

Contents

Preface   xv

SECTION I
Overview   **1**

1   Balancing Law Enforcement and Individual Rights   3
    Problem 5
       Questions 6
       Discussion 6
    References 9

2   Social Control in a Free Society   10
    Constitutional Requirements 16
    Problem 17
       Questions 17
    Applications to White-collar Crime 17
    References 19

3   A Bill of Rights Summary   20
    First Amendment 21
    Second Amendment 22
    Third Amendment 22
    Fourth Amendment 23
    Fifth Amendment 25
    Sixth Amendment 26
    Seventh Amendment 27
    Eighth Amendment 27
    Ninth Amendment 28
    Tenth Amendment 28
    Rejected Amendment 28
    Problem 29
       Questions 29
    References 30

SECTION II
Crime and Due Process Protections   **31**

4   Development of Due Process Protections   33
    Fourteenth Amendment 33
    Federalism and the Dual Court System 34
    Applying Due Process to the States 34
    Brown v. Mississippi *35*
    Rochin v. California *37*
    Selective Incorporation of Federal Rights into the Fourteenth
        Amendment 38
    Trial by Jury 39
    Unanimous Verdicts 40
    Self-incrimination 40
    Right to Remain Silent and Presumption of Innocence 41
    Problem 41
        Questions 43
    Warren Court Criminal Procedure Decisions 44
    Right to Keep and Bear Arms 45
    References 48

5   Principles of Criminal Law   49
    Actus Reus 50
    Mens Rea 51
    Causation 53
    Felony Murder 55
    Accomplice Liability 56
    Death of Accomplice 57
    Strict Liability Crimes 57
    Problem 58
        Questions 58
    References 59

6   Crimes and Punishments   60
    Assault and Self-defense 60
    Self-defense 61
    Homicide 61
    Manslaughter 63
    Justification 63
    Citizen's Arrest 64
    Negative and Affirmative Defenses 66
    Mistake of Fact and Factual Impossibility 67
    Problem 68
        Questions 69
    Death Penalty 69

Rape 72
Larceny 74
Three Strikes 75
Federal Crimes 76
Double Jeopardy 77
Felon in Possession of Firearm Act 78
Patterson v. New York 79
Reference 84

7   The Exclusionary Rule and the Fourth Amendment   85
Wolf v. Colorado 87
Mapp v. Ohio 88
Payton v. New York 89
How Far Does the Exclusionary Rule Go? 89
Independent Source Exception 91
Problem 92
  Questions 92
References 93

SECTION III
Search and Seizure   **95**

8   Search Warrants   97
Oath or Affirmation 97
Probable Cause and Particularity 98
Confidential Informants 99
Challenging the Truthfulness of a Warrant Application 102
Problem 102
  Questions 104
Anticipatory Warrants and Controlled Deliveries 104
Procedures and Statutory Rules 105
Knock-and-Announce Rules 106
Administrative Warrants 108
Special Needs Searches 110
  Border and Airport Searches 110
  Prison, Parole, and Probation Supervision 111
  Schools and Students 111
References 113

9   The Law of Arrest   114
Probable Cause 115
Arrest Warrants 116
Elements of an Arrest 117
Florida v. Royer 118

Questions Raised by Florida v. Royer *120*
Good Judgment and Discretion 121
Hearsay 122
Confidential Informants 123
Use of Force to Arrest 123
Problem 124
    Questions 125
Prosecution 126
References 127

10 Searches without Warrants   128
Plain View 128
Searches Incidental to a Lawful Arrest: Chimel v. California *129*
Telephone and Computer Files 131
The Emergency Exception 131
Hot Pursuits 132
Exigent Circumstances 133
Brigham City, Utah v. Stuart *134*
Questions Raised by Brigham City, Utah v. Stuart *137*
Protective Sweeps 138
Problem 138
    Questions 139
Open Fields 140
References 141

11 A Not So Uncommon Police/Citizen Encounter   142
Problem 142
    Questions 149
    Discussion 150
References 151

12 Stop, Question, and Frisk   152
Reasonable Suspicion 153
Time and Place 154
The Frisk 154
Use of Force 155
Problem 156
    Questions 158
Anonymous Tips 158
Inquiries on Less than Reasonable Suspicion 159
Summary 163
References 164

13 Consent Searches   165
    Voluntary Consent 165
    Problem 166
        Questions 167
    Third-party Consent 167
    Georgia v. Randolph 168
    Questions Raised by Georgia v. Randolph 173
    Good-faith Mistakes 173
    Abandoned Property 174
    California v. Greenwood 174
    Questions Raised by California v. Greenwood 176
    Induced Abandonment 177
    References 178

14 Search and Seizure of Vehicles and Occupants   179
    Mobility and the Automobile Exception 179
    Lesser Expectation of Privacy 181
    Closed Containers 181
    Occupants 181
    Searches Incidental to Arrest 182
    Stop and Frisk In and Around Automobiles 183
    Traffic Stops 183
    Problem 184
        Questions 185
    Detention of Drivers and Passengers 186
    Traffic Violations as a Pretext to Stop, Frisk, or Search 187
    Roadblocks and Safety Checks 188
    Inventory Searches 188
    Standing to Challenge Searches 188
    Summary 189
    References 191

SECTION IV
The Individual as the Subject of Government Investigation   193

15 The Privilege against Compelled Self-incrimination and
    Miranda v. Arizona   195
    Confessions 196
    False Confessions 198
    Supervision of Police Interrogation Practices 199
    Problem 199
        Questions 201
    Miranda v. Arizona 202

16 Refining *Miranda*   207
    Questions Raised by Miranda *207*
    Problem 210
        Questions 210
    Suppressing Confessions to Enforce the Fourth Amendment 211
    Exceptions to Miranda *211*
        Public Safety 211
        Traffic Enforcement 211
        Attenuation 212
        Waiver 212
    Diluting the Poisonous-Tree Doctrine 213
    Congressional Attempt to Overrule Miranda *215*
    The Court's Response 216
    Severing a Branch of the Poisonous Tree 217
    References 218

17 The Right to Counsel   219
    Indirect Questioning 222
    Inevitable Discovery Exception 222
    Problem 223
        Questions 224
    Jailhouse Informants 225
    Offense-specific Variations 226
    Right to Counsel for Factually-related Cases 227
    Interminable Right to Counsel 229
    Exceptions to Miranda, *the Right to Counsel, and the*
        Fruits-of-the-Poisonous-Tree Doctrine 230
    Interconnectivity of Rights 230
    Problem 230
        Questions 232
    References 233

18 Evidence and Due Process   234
    Relevant, Material, and Competent 234
    Too Prejudicial 237
    Circumstantial Evidence 238
    Character Evidence 240
    Credibility 240
    The MIMIC Rule 241
    Presumptions 242
    Problem 243
        Questions 245
    References 246

19 Identifications and Due Process 247

Lineups 247
Show-ups 249
Point-outs During a Canvas 249
Photographs 249
In-court Identifications 250
Bolstering In-court Testimony with Prior Identifications 250
Right to Counsel at Lineups 251
Confirmatory Identifications by Police Officers 252
Corroboration 252
Identifications without Eyewitnesses 253
Self-incrimination by Physical Evidence 253
Problem 256
  Questions 258
References 259

20 The Right of Confrontation 260

Hearsay 260
Non-hearsay 261
Hearsay Exceptions 262
Dying Declarations 262
Confessions 263
Admissions 263
Excited Utterances and Spontaneous Statements 264
Prior Inconsistent Statements 265
Defendant's Prior Inconsistent Statements 265
Prior Testimony 268
Declarations against Interest 268
Problem 270
  Questions 270

21 Government Surveillance 272

Omnibus Crime Control and Safe Streets Act of 1968 275
Strict Requirements 276
E-mail and Text Messages 277
Pen Registers and Trap-and-Trace Devices 277
Tracking a Person's Movements 278
X-rays, Metal Detectors, Thermal Imaging, and Video 281
Dogs 282
Problem 282
  Questions 284
References 285

22 Terrorism and the Patriot Act   286
    Problem 289
      Questions 291
    References 292

    Case Index   293
    Subject Index   297

Preface

Criminal Law, Procedure, and Evidence was published in 2011. It was up-to-date at that time, but society, criminal justice, and the law have continued to evolve. New technologies and developments have generated new issues and controversies for courts and the law to address. By and large, our courts have effectively resolved these new issues, making changes when necessary, but adhering to the fundamental principles of our law, our democratic values, and the spirit of our Constitution.

This edition updates the law, and includes recent important cases that show how our courts have continued to carry the flame of constitutional rights and protections that was lit in earnest a century ago.

Since the spark was lit by the Supreme Court in the early twentieth century, particularly by Justices John Harlan I, Oliver Wendell Holmes, Jr., Louis Brandeis, Benjamin Cardozo, and Hugo Black, the application of constitutional principles to public and private life has continued to grow. Most profound has been the application of constitutional principles to substantive and procedural criminal law—and, in recent years, to evidence law. Consequently, the usually distinct subjects of criminal law, procedure, and evidence can no longer be studied effectively without relating them to the constitutional principles of due process, legality, equality, and fairness.

The goal of this book is to provide a comprehensive understanding of criminal law, procedure, and evidence, with a focus on how constitutional law interacts with and affects these disciplines. The book addresses distinct issues, such as probable cause, search and seizure, stop and frisk, confessions, *Miranda* warnings, the right to counsel, lineups, the exclusionary rule, criminal law principles, proportionate sentencing, competent evidence, standards of proof, and the right to confront accusers, but also the overlays and connections between these issues, thereby providing a complete view of American legal principles.

In our federal system, laws vary from one state to another, and significant differences exist between state and federal law; however, the mandates of the U.S. Constitution impose general principles that each jurisdiction must follow. The challenge for practitioners is to apply these constitutional principles to specific situations in a manner that produces just and fair results. To describe how the process works, this book draws on a wide array of cases and relates those cases to the kind of encounters between citizens and police that regularly occur throughout the nation. While covering the landmark cases, this book emphasizes the cases and issues that are less settled and more pertinent to current conditions; for example, extensive coverage is provided of the various and fluid situations that might arise when the police stop an automobile. In such a situation, it is important for individuals to understand their rights and the powers of the police, while it is equally, or perhaps more, important for the police to understand the limits of their powers. The roles of the police, prosecutors, defense attorneys, and judges are explained, and critical issues such as false confessions and misidentifications are thoroughly explored.

Most readers have a sense that in our constitutional society individuals have a "right to be let alone," yet they also understand that law enforcement officers must sometimes infringe on that right. The balance between individual rights and police power is a major theme of this book, and, in the context of a society gripped by threats of terrorism, keeping the right balance is crucial. While recognizing the importance of police efficiency and effectiveness, restricting police authority is equally important for a free society. Setting ground rules for police to follow in their routine functions establishes boundaries that tend to prevent extreme police conduct. Limiting police authority creates a bulwark against unlimited police oppression. As Justice Louis Brandeis wrote in a case that involved federal agents breaking state laws:[1]

> Decency, security, and liberty alike demand that government officials shall be subjected to the same rules of conduct that are commands to the citizen. In a government of laws, existence of the government will be imperiled if it fails to observe the law scrupulously. Our government is the potent, omnipresent teacher. For good or ill, it teaches the whole people by its example. Crime is contagious. If the government becomes a law-breaker, it breeds contempt for the law; it invites every man to become a law unto himself; it invites anarchy. To declare that in the administration of criminal law the end justifies the means—to declare that the government may commit crimes in order to secure the conviction of a private criminal—would bring terrible retribution. Against that pernicious doctrine this court should resolutely set its face.

Notwithstanding the need for restrictions, law enforcement officers must be granted a substantial degree of discretion to perform their duties. They often face dangerous and quickly changing circumstances that require them to act expeditiously without the benefit of complete information. Substantive and procedural law authorizes officers to act, but then courts review their actions and, if necessary, correct them. An escalating set of standards provides checks and balances at each stage of the criminal justice process. Consequently, an arrest of a particular individual may be justified by circumstances, while a jury acquittal of the same individual for the same conduct may be equally justified.

Each chapter of the text contains a problem in the form of a fact pattern that highlights one or more classic criminal justice issues to which students can relate, such as an automobile stop, a family dispute, or a police interrogation. These problems are presented from the points of view of citizens caught up in a police investigation and of police officers attempting to enforce the law within the framework of constitutional protections. After each problem, questions are posed, and the reader is asked to play the role of a decision-maker—a citizen, police officer, prosecutor, defense attorney, or judge.

Some of the questions have obvious answers; the reader, even without any legal training but just by applying instinct and common sense, should recognize the generally accepted answer. Other questions raise conflicting issues that do not lend themselves to easy answers; there may be diametrically opposed answers for both of which valid and rational supporting arguments are conceivable.

Contradictory answers most often arise because of differences in the weight and credibility given to the specific facts of a case, and differences in the application of general principles to specific facts. Contradictory answers also arise because of the different weight given to competing interests within society. The debate is healthy. Our justice system is alive and adapts to changing circumstances and persuasive advocacy, and adversarial debate is the process by which our justice system progresses. Because the law is continually changing, readers with an interest in the subject, particularly students and criminal justice practitioners, must do more than memorize the results of a list of cases; they must endeavor to gain an understanding of legal history, principles, and purposes.

Highlighted are the recent right-to-privacy cases—*Riley v. California*, *United States v. Jones*, and *Carpenter v. United States*; the double jeopardy case, *Gamble v. United States*; the unanimous verdict case, *Ramos v. Louisiana*; the right to counsel case, *Maryland v. Shatzer*; the right of confrontation case, *Crawford v. Washington*; and the right to bear arms case, *New York State Rifle and Pistol Association v. Bruen*, 597 U.S. ... (2022), 142 S.Ct. 2111 (2022).

Accounts are included of the widely-publicized trials of the California police officers in the Rodney King case; the confessions of the teenagers in the Central Park jogger case; and the trial of three Florida men accused of the murder of Ahmaud Arbery. These examples illustrate clearly how legal principles were applied to the facts of well-known and complex cases.

Law enforcement officers who study this book will gain a broad working knowledge of criminal law and procedure and the evidentiary standards that will help them to make better decisions and to explain in court the reasons for their decisions. Fully developed and competent explanations by trained officers of their actions help the courts to assess the what, how, and why of police actions and whether they were lawful or justified. The material presented will help students and others assessing police performance and the effectiveness of the criminal justice system to apply a broader perspective to specific situations they may encounter.

The ultimate goal of the book is to educate readers regarding liberty and security issues so that they may apply critical thinking when they are confronted with such issues in life or in the media. With a more developed understanding of criminal justice and constitutional principles, the reader will have the background information to intelligently analyze the issues and to confidently provide valid and reasonable arguments for any positions that they choose to adopt or advocate.

Note

1 Dissenting, *Olmstead v. United States*, 277 U.S. 438 (1928).

Section 1

Overview

Chapter 1

Balancing Law Enforcement and Individual Rights

The American sense of liberty and individual rights springs from the U.S. Constitution and the Bill of Rights. These documents provide the guidelines for all federal, state, and local laws; they guarantee that the United States will remain a nation governed by the rule of law. They also balance society's need to achieve social control, order, and safety against the individual's right to life, liberty, and property. Although, as Americans, we are aware that we have certain rights, we often take those rights for granted. At work and school, and in other endeavors, we generally expect to be treated fairly and equally. However, when we become the subject of a government investigation or the accused in a criminal prosecution, our rights become paramount in our minds, and we fully appreciate their crucial importance and the need for an impartial criminal justice system.

The values of freedom and individual rights emerged early in our nation's history and traditions, and Americans have internalized what Thomas Jefferson expressed in the Declaration of Independence:

> We hold these truths to be self-evident: that all men are created equal, that all men are endowed by their Creator with certain unalienable rights, that among these are life, liberty, and the pursuit of happiness.

When James Madison wrote the Bill of Rights, he transformed Jefferson's "life, liberty, and the pursuit of happiness" into "No person shall be... deprived of life, liberty, or property, without due process of law." This historic clause can be traced back to the English Magna Carta of 1215. It is contained in the Fifth and Fourteenth Amendments and in state constitutions.

Due process of law encompasses many concepts, including the right to notice of charges and the opportunity to be heard. It requires that a law or regulation imposed on an individual may not be unreasonable, arbitrary, capricious, or *ex post facto* (criminalizing an act after it has been committed), and it requires that the means selected to enforce a law must have a real and substantial relation to the objective of the law.

The Constitution provides that Congress shall make the laws, the executive branch shall enforce the laws, and the judiciary shall interpret the laws. The Bill of Rights is a counterweight and sets forth limitations on the kind of laws that may be enacted and the methods by which laws may be enforced. For example, the First Amendment limits the kind of laws that may be passed. It limits the use of criminal or civil law to abridge the rights of freedom of speech, freedom of religion, and peaceful assembly. The Fourth, Fifth, Sixth, and Eighth

DOI: 10.4324/9781003415091-2

Amendments limit the methods by which the government may enforce criminal laws. These amendments are the heart of criminal procedure law. They prohibit unreasonable searches and seizures, compelled self-incrimination, unfair trials, cruel and unusual punishments, and other oppressive government conduct.

Criminal procedure law puts into practice the ideals of the Constitution, and safeguards the rights of all persons by defending the rights of suspects and defendants. Because circumstances can make anyone a suspect or a defendant, criminal procedure law protects us all by governing the methods by which law enforcement agencies investigate and prosecute crime. It mandates that law enforcement officers ensure that individuals under investigation or accused of crimes are treated fairly and afforded their rights. The methods and procedures allowed by the law for pursuing criminals determine the nature and tenor of our society and whether we live in a free or an oppressive nation.

The main actors in the criminal justice process are police officers, prosecutors, defense attorneys, judges, and, ultimately, jurors; however, the police play the largest role. Far more crimes are reported to the police than are referred to prosecutors and the court system. The police question, frisk, or search far more people than they arrest, and, when arrests are made, relatively few of these cases progress through the criminal justice process to an actual trial. Therefore, much of criminal procedure law pertains to the conduct of police.

Traditional criminal procedure law developed from many sources, including the common law, the Constitution, statutory law, and customary police practices. In recent decades, however, courts have actively reshaped this area of law. Emphasizing constitutional principles, they have overridden statutes and customary police practices, and judges have become the predominant arbiters of what are acceptable or unacceptable law enforcement practices. For the most part, they have achieved a reasonable balance between the rights of the individual and the needs of the government to control crime and maintain order. This ideal balance might be called "ordered liberty."[1] However, the balance constantly shifts because of the competing interests and opinions of those on the law enforcement side of the scales and those on the individual rights side. Advocates of strict law enforcement generally place a high value on the repression of criminal conduct through aggressive police tactics and the imposition of swift and certain punishments. Conversely, advocates of protection for individual rights place a higher value on due process for the accused and limitations on law enforcement authority. This does not mean that most of those who favor strict law enforcement are against protecting individual rights—in fact, they have often taken the lead in protecting these rights—nor does it mean that most advocates of due process rights are against appropriate punishments when defendants have been fairly convicted of crimes.

Law enforcement officers are charged with the responsibility for investigating crime, apprehending criminals, and obtaining the necessary evidence for a prosecution. These are difficult and formidable tasks and often must be carried out in complex or dangerous circumstances. Nevertheless, they must be accomplished within a framework of established rules. Neither police officers investigating common crimes nor federal investigators pursuing white-collar criminals can arbitrarily make arrests or conduct searches. Moreover, district attorneys cannot continue prosecutions unless they have probable cause and sufficient credible evidence. Law enforcement decisions must be justified on a rational, objective basis and must comport with the rule of law as established by the Constitution, Congress, and the courts.

It is unlikely that most police officers will know all the complexities and nuances of criminal procedure law, but they must possess a substantial working knowledge of its essential elements so that they can effectively perform their duties without compromising law enforcement objectives. A violation of established criminal procedure rules, whether done willfully or negligently, may have adverse consequences for the individual officer, other officers, and the prosecution of the criminal case. Violations of the rules can result in civil lawsuits against officers for false arrest, assault, trespass, malicious prosecution, or civil rights violations. Occasionally, law enforcement officers who commit serious violations are prosecuted under state or federal criminal laws. More often, violations invoke the exclusionary rule.

The *exclusionary rule* is the primary means by which courts enforce constitutional restraints on law enforcement. The rule prohibits the use in a criminal trial of evidence obtained in violation of constitutional protections. When the police conduct an unlawful arrest, search, or interrogation, any physical evidence, confession, or information directly obtained from the unlawful conduct will be inadmissible against the defendant whose rights were violated. The theory of the rule is that, if the suppression of evidence is the remedy for a police violation, the police will be deterred from committing the same kind of violations in the future. It is not a cost-free remedy. The suppression of evidence can undermine otherwise viable prosecutions and can often result in guilty defendants being released and victims of a crime losing their opportunity for justice. Therefore, it is crucial that law enforcement officers understand the rules and, as far as reasonably possible, perform their functions in accordance with them. They must be aware that handling even the most common police problems can raise serious criminal procedure and exclusionary rule issues.

In our adversarial justice system, defense attorneys, in addition to arguing the guilt or innocence of the defendant, routinely challenge the appropriateness and lawfulness of police actions. The most common challenges to pre-arrest police conduct pertain to probable cause for arrest, unreasonable search and seizure, and identification procedures. The most common challenges to post-arrest police conduct pertain to the right against compelled self-incrimination, the right to counsel, and the right to a fair trial. Judges decide the merits of these challenges. When they deem them meritorious, they decide whether the evidence should be suppressed. The following is a typical problem that arises every day across the nation.

Problem

Officers Able and Barker respond to a 911 call regarding a domestic incident at a private house. They meet Mrs. Warner, a middle-aged woman, in front of the house. Warner tells the officers that her 20-year-old daughter, Joan, who lives in the house off and on with her boyfriend, Charles Samson, called her yesterday and told her that Samson had hit her and threatened to shoot her. Warner says she has not heard from her daughter since and is worried about her. Warner also recounts that Samson, a male of about 40 years of age, 6 feet tall, and weighing 250 pounds, has abused her daughter in the past and threatened that if the daughter ever tried to leave him he would kill her. She also says Samson keeps a gun somewhere in the house; she knows this because she saw him with it once.

The officers knock on the front door, and Samson comes to the door but does not open it. Speaking through the door, Samson denies that he threatened Joan and refuses to allow the officers to enter the residence to search for her. He further states that Joan left the house yesterday and went to her girlfriend's house. He does not know the address, but he gives them Joan's cell phone number.

The officers call the cell phone number, but the line is temporarily disconnected. Again they knock on the door, and when Officer Barker asks Samson whether Joan is inside, he replies, "None of your goddamn business. And get off my property."

Barker shouts, "Open the door, or we'll break it down."

Samson shouts, "Go to hell!"

Questions

1. Do the officers have lawful authority to demand that Samson open the door?
2. Do the officers have a reasonable belief that a life-threatening emergency exists in the house?
3. Should the officers make further efforts to contact Joan before taking further action?
4. Should the officers forcibly enter the house to search for Joan?
5. Should the officers forcibly enter the house to search for the gun?
6. Should they get a search warrant before entering the house to search for Joan?
7. Should they get a search warrant before entering the house to search for the gun?
8. In either case, do they have probable cause to support the issuance of a search warrant?
9. Should they arrest Samson?
10. If they decide to arrest him, should they forcibly enter the house to do so?
11. Should they arrest Samson on the basis of the allegations of past abuse of Joan?
12. If they decide to arrest him, should they get an arrest warrant before entering the house?
13. If they arrest him in the house, should they search the house for Joan?
14. If they arrest him in the house, should they search the house for the gun?

Discussion

In situations such as that in the foregoing problem, whatever actions the officers take will have consequences. They have to make on-the-scene decisions on the basis of incomplete information while balancing safety concerns against civil rights protections. They have to decide whether to forcibly enter the residence, arrest Samson, search the house without a warrant, or obtain a search warrant.

It might seem that a judicious approach would be to continue investigating and, if further evidence develops, apply for a search warrant. Such an approach would clearly avoid violating constitutional rights; however, other considerations are pertinent, such as the possible destruction of evidence or danger to other persons. Depending on their on-the-scene assessment of Mrs. Warner's credibility, the available background information about Samson, or other information from witnesses, the officers will make their decision. What they choose to do and how they proceed might result in a proper adjudication of the matter, or it might result in a miscarriage of justice. If they recover a gun, it might prevent violence and lead to Samson's conviction. On the other hand, the recovered gun might be suppressed at trial because the court determines that the officers' actions violated constitutional rights. A court reviewing the officers' actions will need to hear testimony from witnesses describing the incident in detail and will need to ascertain all the information that the officers possessed at the time they made their decisions.

The officers' decisions and actions are assessed throughout the criminal justice process. In a typical case, after the police make an arrest and the prosecution consents to go forward by filing a formal complaint with the court, the defendant will be arraigned. At the arraignment, the judge may release the defendant, set bail, or remand into custody without setting bail. When the defendant cannot post bail or has been remanded, the court must conduct a preliminary hearing within five days for a misdemeanor or seven days for a felony (unless waived by the defendant) to determine whether legally sufficient evidence has been presented to hold him for trial. If the prosecution cannot present legally sufficient evidence, the defendant must be released without bail. The prosecution can circumvent this process by obtaining a grand jury indictment.

Most cases are adjudicated by plea bargains in which the defendant enters a plea of guilty to the crime charged or to a lesser charge in exchange for a negotiated sentence. In cases that proceed toward trial, hearings are held regarding the admissibility of evidence and at these hearings judges make decisions that often affect the outcome of the case. Judges have been called gatekeepers: they must decide what evidence will be let through the gate, what will be kept out, and what will go forward to the next gate. The oft-quoted maxim that judges decide questions of law and juries decide questions of fact can be misleading. The maxim may apply to jury trials, but juries are not present at preliminary hearings, and judges must be both fact finders and arbiters of the law. They apply the facts to the legal standards that must be met to justify government actions.

Some of the standards that courts have applied are set forth below. They are not all-inclusive, and some courts have used variations:

Stop and question

Reasonable suspicion—Facts and circumstances that would lead an officer of ordinary intelligence, judgment, and experience to believe that criminal activity is afoot

Arrest

Probable cause—Facts and circumstances to warrant a person of ordinary intelligence, judgment, and experience to believe that an offense has been or is being committed by a particular person

Search with a warrant

Probable cause and particularity—Facts and circumstances to warrant an officer of reasonable intelligence and experience to believe that particular articles subject to seizure are located at a particular location[2]

Search without a warrant

Recognized exception to the warrant requirement—A life-threatening emergency, hot pursuit, or other circumstances requiring urgent action

Prosecution

Legally sufficient evidence—Evidence of a non-hearsay nature supporting each and every element of the crime charged

Prosecution's direct case

Prima facie evidence—Evidence presented in court which, if left unexplained or uncontradicted, is sufficient to sustain a judgment in favor of the charge it supports

Affirmative defenses

Preponderance of the evidence—Evidence that is of greater weight or more convincing than the evidence that is offered in opposition to it

Conviction

Proof beyond a reasonable doubt—Facts and circumstances that would lead a juror of ordinary intelligence, common sense, and experience to be firmly convinced that the defendant is guilty; the juror's conclusion must be based on reason and common sense and must be of such a convincing character that the juror would be willing to rely and act upon it unhesitatingly

Failure to meet one or more of the above standards, depending on the stage of the proceedings, may result in suppression of evidence, dismissal of the charges, a directed verdict of acquittal, or a jury verdict of not guilty. Meeting the above standards may result in a verdict of guilty; however, the proof beyond a reasonable doubt standard for a guilty verdict is the most difficult to meet and, consequently, in a substantial number of cases truly guilty defendants are found not guilty. A not guilty verdict does not necessarily mean that the defendant was innocent; it means that the prosecution did not meet its burden to prove the case and to overcome the defendant's presumption of innocence.

A consensus on an exact definition of proof beyond reasonable doubt has not been reached, and the instructions that judges give to juries about its meaning vary from court to court. The U.S. Supreme Court has not provided a precise definition, and in *Victor v. Nebraska*, 511 U.S. 1 (1994), the Court held only that "taken as a whole, the instructions must properly convey the concept of reasonable doubt." The Court suggested that it would approve the following jury instructions:

> The government has the burden of proving the defendant guilty beyond a reasonable doubt. Some of you may have served as jurors in civil cases, where you were told that it is only necessary to prove that a fact is more likely than not true. In criminal cases, the government's proof must be more powerful than that. It must be beyond a reasonable doubt.
>
> Proof beyond a reasonable doubt is proof that leaves you firmly convinced of the defendant's guilt. There are very few things in this world that we know with absolute certainty, and in criminal cases the law does not require proof that overcomes every possible doubt. If, based on your consideration of the evidence, you are firmly convinced that the defendant is guilty of the crime charged, you must find him guilty. If, on the other hand, you think there is a real possibility that he is not guilty, you must give him the benefit of the doubt and find him not guilty.

Due process of law does not require that a jury acquit a defendant on a mere possibility of doubt, but it requires a higher degree of proof than the preponderance of evidence standard that is used in civil lawsuits.[3] Due process requires jurors to deliberate impartially and in an environment in which coercion is absent.

A jury instruction that violated due process was given in the murder trial of Benjamin Feldman. Regarding reasonable doubt, the trial judge instructed the jury:

It is not a doubt based upon sympathy or whim or prejudice or bias or a caprice, or a sentimentality, or upon a reluctance of a weak-kneed, timid, jellyfish of a juror who is seeking to avoid the performance of a disagreeable duty, namely, to convict another human being of the commission of a serious crime.

The New York Court of Appeals in *People v. Feldman*, 296 N.Y. 127 (1947), disapproved of the instruction and reversed the defendant's conviction, ruling that the judge's instruction was not conducive to a fair and impartial consideration of the evidence.

Our society adheres to the proof beyond a reasonable doubt standard to reduce the risk of erroneously punishing an innocent person. Simply, our value system holds that we should not condemn a person when there is a reasonable doubt about their guilt: "It is far worse to convict an innocent man than to let a guilty man go free."[4]

The question of how far we should tip the scales of justice in favor of an accused in order to avoid mistakes has been debated ever since Lord Blackstone made his comment, "It is better that ten guilty persons escape, than that one innocent suffer."[5] His comment has raised questions. Is there a point at which too many rights and protections for an accused will make it too difficult to obtain a conviction? At what point will acquittals of too many guilty defendants lead to disorder and unlawfulness? Should we tolerate the possibility of a small percentage of wrongful convictions of innocent persons in order to maintain the ability of the system to convict guilty persons?

The principal questions underlying Blackstone's comment pertain not just to questions of guilt or innocence, but to every stage of the criminal justice process. What should the balance be between police and prosecutorial authority on the one hand and the rights and protections of the individual on the other? At what point will too much police and prosecutorial authority turn our nation into a totalitarian state? At what point will too much support and enforcement of individual liberties prevent law enforcement from effectively performing its functions?

These are but a few of the many questions about our criminal procedure law that are under continual debate. They are the kind of difficult questions that will be asked in the chapters that follow, questions that affect us in important ways both as individuals and as a society.

Notes

1 *Palko v. Connecticut*, 302 U.S. 319 (1937).
2 *Carroll v. United States*, 267 U.S. 132 (1925); *Brinegar v. United States*, 338 U.S. 160 (1949); *Draper v. United States*, 358 U.S. 307 (1959); *Beck v. Ohio*, 379 U.S. 89 (1964).
3 *People v. Sandoval*, 34 N.Y.2d 971 (1974).
4 *In re Winship*, 397 U.S. 358, 90 S.Ct. 692 (1970), J. Harlan, concurrence.
5 Blackstone, *Commentaries on the Laws of England* (1765), 2 Bl.Com.c.27, p.358.

References

Brigham City, Utah v. Stuart, 547 U.S. 398,126 S.Ct. 1943 (2006).
Georgia v. Randolph, 547 U.S. 103, 126 S.Ct. 1515 (2006).
Illinois v. Rodriguez, 497 U.S. 177, 110 S.Ct. 2793 (1990).
Payton v. New York, 445 U.S. 573, 100 S.Ct. 1371 (1980).
United States v. Matlock, 415 U.S. 164 (1974).

Chapter 2

Social Control in a Free Society

Liberty and freedom are elements of the American national identity, but liberty and freedom require a satisfactory level of order and security. Criminal law, its enforcement, and the threat of its enforcement are the principal means by which the government protects citizens against harm to their persons and property, and thereby provides the necessary environment for the exercise of liberty and freedom. Criminal law sets the outer boundaries of acceptable conduct and draws the line between the individual's exercise of freedom and the infringement of the rights of others. As with all laws, criminal laws tell people what they must or must not do.

Not all antisocial, injurious, or wrongful behavior is criminal; only acts deemed substantially harmful to the foundations of society or detrimental to its efficient functioning are defined as criminal. A crime is a social harm caused by conduct that is defined and made punishable by law.

The social harm caused by a crime justifies the imposition of punishment for the general deterrence of the public and also for the specific deterrence, incapacitation, or rehabilitation of the individual. Moreover, in some particularly heinous cases, arguably, it justifies punishment as a means of retribution. Punishments can include fines, probation, incarceration, and, in some states, execution. While the severity of the harm caused is the primary determinant of the severity of the punishment imposed, the background of the convicted person also influences decisions about punishment. In most cases, a first-time offender will receive a lesser punishment than a repeat offender for the same crime.

Deterrence also arises because of the social stigma attached to a criminal conviction. Crimes are distinguishable from private wrongs not only because of the possibility of state-sanctioned punishment, but also because conviction for a crime is accompanied by community condemnation.

> The essence of punishment for moral delinquency lies in the criminal conviction itself. One may lose more money on the stock market than in a court-room; a prisoner of war camp may well provide a harsher environment than a state prison; death on the field of battle has the same physical characteristics as death by sentence of law. It is the expression of the community's hatred, fear, or contempt for the convict which alone characterizes physical hardship as punishment.[1]

The stigma of a criminal conviction can adversely affect the remainder of a person's life by making him or her ineligible for certain jobs, occupations, or licenses. Furthermore, a convicted felon is ineligible to vote.

DOI: 10.4324/ 9781003415091-3

Throughout history, and across all societies, some acts have consistently been deemed criminal. Murder, atrocious assault, forcible rape, robbery, burglary, grand larceny, and arson have been considered *malum in se*, or bad in themselves, and every society throughout every era has punished these acts. Other acts have been considered merely *malum prohibitum*, or crimes only because they have been defined by law as such. These have varied from society to society and from era to era. Each society and each generation has reached a judgment that certain kinds of conduct, although not inherently or universally wrong, are detrimental to the public good and should therefore be deterred by the threat of punishment.

An understanding of modern criminal law requires a look back in history at the moral, religious, cultural, economic, and political influences that led to the formation of our present system. In many aspects, the principles of modern criminal law can be traced to the laws of ancient societies; in other aspects, the contrasts between modern criminal law and the laws of earlier societies are striking. Statutory law can be traced to the Code of Hammurabi, a set of laws from the ancient kingdom of Babylon, which thrived for hundreds of years in the area of modern-day Iraq. Named after King Hammurabi, who ruled around 1792 to 1750 B.C., the Code was found inscribed on a stone pillar about eight feet high and five feet in circumference, near the ruins of the city of Susa.[2] It enumerated crimes and punishments for matters pertaining to property, theft, sexual relationships, and violence. Like modern law, the Code provided notices, instructions, and warnings to citizens. In contrast to modern law, the Code dispensed justice in unequal terms, with outcomes and punishments determined by the social status of the violator and the victim. Examples of its pronouncements are as follows:

7. If any one buy from the son or the slave of another man, without witnesses or a contract, silver or gold, a male or female slave, an ox or a sheep, an ass or anything, or if he take it in charge, he is considered a thief and shall be put to death.
129. If a man's wife be surprised with another man, both shall be tied and thrown into the water, but the husband may pardon his wife and the king his slaves.
145. If a man takes a wife, and she bear him no children, and he intend to take another wife: if he take this second wife, and bring her into the house, this second wife shall not be allowed equality with his wife.
195. If a son strike his father, his hands shall be hewn off.
196. If a man put out the eye of another man, his eye shall be put out.
198. If he put out the eye of a freed man, or break the bone of a freed man, he shall pay one gold mina.
199. If he put out the eye of a man's slave, or break the bone of a man's slave, he shall pay one-half of its value.
200. If a man knock out the teeth of his equal, his teeth shall be knocked out.[3]

Without more information about the culture of Babylonian society, it is difficult to gauge how strictly the Code and its punishments were enforced. It is also difficult to judge the morality of such laws without a fuller understanding of the circumstances that produced them.

For Greek and Roman laws, we have more information on which to make judgments. In 621 B.C., the first written code of laws for the Greek city-state of Athens was promulgated by Draco, a statesman of Athens. The word "draconian" derives from his name and the severity of the punishments he imposed on his subjects. The Athenian code was liberalized significantly by the statesman Solon (638–558 B.C.), who was appointed chief executive magistrate in the hope that he would reconcile disputes between the nobles and the commoners. He promulgated laws that gave commoners a greater share of wealth and power, the right to bring lawsuits against nobles, and the right to appeal to the jury-court, which handled both public and private disputes.[4]

> He gave every citizen the privilege of entering suit in behalf of one who had suffered wrong. If a man was assaulted, and suffered violence or injury, it was the privilege of any one who had the ability and the inclination to indict the wrongdoer and prosecute him. The lawgiver in this way rightly accustomed the citizens, as members of one body, to feel and sympathize with one another's wrongs.[5]

Greek philosophers delved into the justification for law and the right to punish. Both Plato and Aristotle pontificated about the nature of law and the imperative that man's laws be based on divine or natural law. In general and abstract terms, they concluded that laws incompatible with divine or natural law were unjust.[6]

It is believed that a commission from Rome traveled to Athens to study the Athenian laws. Early Roman law was memorialized in the Twelve Tables, which set forth basic rules relating to family, religious, and economic life. In about 450 B.C., the Tables were engraved on bronze tablets, which were then erected in the Roman Forum. Although only fragments have survived, much of their contents have been reconstructed from other records. The Tables were comprehensive but required interpretation. Consequently, *pontifices*, or priests, interpreted the Tables for their application to particular cases; for example, the law of arson stated:

> Any person who destroys by burning any building or heap of corn deposited alongside a house shall be bound, scourged, and put to death by burning at the stake, provided that he has committed the said misdeed with malice aforethought.[7]

The term "malice aforethought" had to be interpreted, and defining, applying, and proving it were critical matters that, then as now, required good judgment and understanding.

At a critical time for the Roman Republic, Marcus Tullius Cicero (106–43 B.C.), a powerful statesman, jurist, and philosopher, described the ideals of law. His thoughts were a culmination of Greek and Roman philosophy, and they foreshadowed the natural law tenets of the European Enlightenment and the American revolutionary period:

> True Law is Reason, right and natural, commanding people to fulfill their obligations and prohibiting and deterring them from doing wrong. Its validity is universal; it is immutable and eternal. Its commands and prohibition apply effectively to good men, and those uninfluenced by them are bad. Any attempt to supersede this law, to repeal any part of it, is sinful; to cancel it entirely is impossible. Neither the Senate nor the assembly can exempt us from its demands; we need no interpreter or expounder of it but ourselves. There will not be one law at Rome, one at Athens, or one now and one later, but all nations will be subject all the time to this one changeless and everlasting law.[8]

Near the end of the Roman Empire, from 527 to 565 A.D., the Emperor Justinian I ruled the eastern half of the empire from the capital city of Constantinople (today's Istanbul). The emperor ordered a compilation of Roman law—the *Corpus Juris Civilis*—which came to be known as the Justinian Code. This delineated public law and private law. Public law dealt with the organization of the Roman state, its senate, and government offices; private law dealt with contracts, property, and the legal status of citizens, free persons, slaves, freedmen, husbands, and wives. It also provided remedies for wrongs and injuries. Written roughly 2000 years after the Code of Hammurabi, the Justinian Code had differences from and similarities with the Code of Hammurabi. Like the Code of Hammurabi, the Justinian Code provides a view of the class structure and inequalities of an ancient society. Unlike the Code of Hammurabi, it places great weight on a potential wrongdoer's state of mind in conjunction with his actions. The emphasis on the actor's state of mind demonstrates the development of social complexity and the advancement of critical legal analysis. The following are examples from Book 4 of the Justinian Code:

Part I, Section 7. A person, however, who borrows a thing, and applies it to a purpose other than that for which it was lent, only commits theft if he knows that he is acting against the wishes of the owner, and that the owner, if he were informed, would not permit it; for if he really thinks the owner would permit it, he does not commit a crime; and this is a very proper distinction, for there is no theft without the intention to commit a theft.

Part I, Section 18. It should be observed that the question has been asked whether, if a person under the age of puberty, takes away the property of another, he commits a theft. The answer is that it is the intention that makes the theft; such a person is only bound by the obligation springing from the delinquency if he is near the age of puberty, and consequently understands that he commits a crime.

Part III, Section 2. To kill wrongfully is to kill without any right; consequently, a person who kills a thief is not liable to this action, that is, if he could not otherwise avoid the danger with which he was threatened.

Part III, Section 3. Nor is a person made liable by this law who has killed by accident, provided there is no fault on his part, for this law punishes fault as well as willful wrong-doing.

"Justice is the constant and perpetual wish to render everyone his due" was a noteworthy pronouncement of the Justinian Code. Though Roman law had merits over and above some other systems, to the modern mind, the Roman idea of justice is critically flawed. Modern democratic values do not countenance qualifying a person's "due" according to his or her social status. The following examples from the Code are illustrative:

Part III, Section 4. Consequently, if anyone playing or practicing with a javelin, pierces with it your slave as he goes by, there is a distinction made; if the accident befalls a soldier while in the camp, or other places appropriate to military exercises, there is no fault in the soldier, but there would be in anyone besides a soldier, and the soldier himself would be in fault if he inflicted such an injury in any other place than one appropriated to military exercises.

Part IV, Section 3. An injury cannot, properly speaking, be done to a slave, but it is the master who, through the slave, is considered to be injured; not, however, in the same way as through a child or wife, but only when the act is of a character grave enough to make it a manifest insult to the master, as if a person has flogged severely the slave of another, in which case this action is given against him. But a master cannot bring an action against a person who has collected a crowd round his slave, or struck him with his fist.

After the fall of Constantinople and the end of the Eastern Roman Empire in 1453 A.D., the Justinian Code lost its authority. However, many of its principles were adopted in the

West by the Holy Roman Empire and later by the monarchies in Austria, Germany, France, and Spain.

In 1791, during the French Revolution, the National Constituent Assembly enacted a new penal code that emphasized the ideals of rationalism. The new penal code eliminated "phony offenses, created by superstition, feudalism, the tax system, and despotism," including such offenses as blasphemy, heresy, sacrilege, and witchcraft. The Assembly also eliminated the disparate criminal punishments imposed due to a person's status. In keeping with its motto of liberty, fraternity, and equality, and also in keeping with those stark and brutal times, the Assembly ruled that all citizens would be entitled to the same method of execution. No longer would aristocrats have the benefit of being beheaded while peasants suffered crueler forms of death: all condemned citizens would be guillotined, not only the aristocrats.

In 1804, Napoleon Bonaparte ordered the writing of a new Civil Code that followed the traditional Roman civil law traditions but also reflected the egalitarian principles of revolutionary France. Known as the Napoleonic Code, the new law was designed to reduce the power and independence of judges, who in pre-revolutionary France were arms of the king. Statutory law would be primary, and judges were only to discover the applicable statutes and apply them to cases without interposing their own opinions. However, the reality has always been that a code cannot predict every problem, and judges invariably must interpret the law and express opinions in order to apply a statute correctly.

In England, judges not only interpreted the law but also made the law. In early English history, Anglo-Saxon tribal leaders and judges settled disputes, and as a result wide variations among localities militated against uniformity in the law. Then, in 1066, William the Conqueror, the Norman king, invaded England from Normandy in France and defeated the Anglo-Saxons at the Battle of Hastings. To consolidate his rule, he sent commissioners to ascertain the varying judge-made laws and rulings of the local communities and to consolidate the best of these into a single body of general principles. These principles and decisions have come to be known as the common law.

Although England did not adopt the Roman civil law model, the Normans integrated some concepts of Roman law into English common law, and this is the source of the extensive use of Latin phrases in English law. The Latin rubric *stare decisis et non quieta movere*, or "stand by the decision and do not disturb what is settled," is an important principle of common law.

Under the common-law system, decided cases became precedents for subsequent cases that had similar facts or issues, and, in order to promote uniformity and stability in the law, judges bound themselves to decide cases according to the established precedents. To facilitate adherence to precedents, the decisions of judges were written and compiled in source books. In 1765, William Blackstone published *Commentaries on the Laws of England*, the most comprehensive written source of common law, and this became the primary sourcebook for subsequent English and American law.

American courts follow the common-law procedure of adherence to precedents. For state and non-federal issues, American state courts are only bound by decisions within the state jurisdiction. Thus, a Texas court is not bound by a California court opinion, although the Texas court could voluntarily adopt the reasoning of the California opinion. For federal issues, state courts have to follow the precedents of the U.S. Supreme Court and the federal Circuit Courts of Appeal.

Although the common-law system provides uniformity and stability, it is flexible enough to adapt to changing circumstances and evolving standards and values. A court may overrule its own precedent, or a higher court may reverse a lower court. More often, rather than expressly overruling an established precedent, a court might distinguish the instant case on the grounds that the facts and circumstances are not exactly the same as the precedent case and therefore require a different outcome.

However, in some cases the common-law rule must be overturned entirely. As Justice Oliver Wendell Holmes opined:

> It is revolting to have no better reason for a rule of law than that so it was laid down in the time of Henry IV. It is still more revolting if the grounds on which it is laid down have vanished long since, and the rule simply persists from blind imitation of the past. ("The Path of the Law," 10 Harv L. Rev. 457, 469 (1897)).

Overruling a precedent because of changing circumstances might occur after the development of more sophisticated technology; for example, at common law, a conviction for murder required that the death must have resulted within a year and a day from the date of the inflicted injury. The rule stated:

> If death did not take place within a year and a day of the time of receiving the wound, the law draws the conclusion that it was not the cause of death; and neither the court nor jury can draw a contrary one.[9]

The rationale for this rule was simply the uncertainty of proof of direct causation between the injury and the death after such a long passage of time. However, with advancements in medical science and a greater ability to track causation, some courts have abandoned the old rule and have allowed such homicide prosecutions to proceed and convictions to stand.[10]

In *People v. Brengard*, the New York Court of Appeals overturned the year-and-a-day rule. In that case, on July 22, 1928, Nassau County Police Officer John Kennedy was ambushed and shot several times. A bullet entered his spine, causing paralysis to his legs and other injuries.

Brengard was arrested and charged with first-degree assault and other charges.

Officer Kennedy was hospitalized and had to undergo several operations over a period of four years. On April 28, 1932, his right leg had to be amputated. On July 13, 1932, he died, with the cause of death listed as bullet wound to the spinal column.

In July 1932, the defendant was charged with Kennedy's murder, and raised the common-law "year-and-a-day rule" defense. Nevertheless, he was convicted. His appeal was denied by the Court of Appeals, which abandoned the year-and-a-day rule, and pointed out that when the legislature abolished common-law crimes and replaced them with the penal law statutes, it did not include time as a factor in the definition of murder.

After the American Revolution, the substantive common-law crimes were gradually superseded by legislatively defined crimes in the form of statutes. Some states maintain the ability to enforce common-law crimes; other states have entirely abolished them. However, despite legislative intent to replace common-law crimes with legislatively enacted crimes, common-law principles and definitions are nonetheless relied upon to interpret the meaning of statutes. How a court applies a common-law definition to a statute can drastically change the outcome of a criminal case. At common law, homicide was conduct causing the death of a person who has been born and is alive. Consequently, in *Keeler v. Superior Court*, 470 P.2d 617 (Cal. 1970), a case in which the defendant stomped on a pregnant woman's abdomen, thereby causing the death of her fetus, the court held that the killing of an unborn fetus was not murder, since "a killing cannot be a criminal homicide unless the victim is a living human being."

The California legislature responded to *Keeler* by amending the murder statute to read: "Murder is the unlawful killing of a human being, or a fetus, with malice afore-thought."[11] Thirteen other states made similar changes to their homicide laws. In 2003, this issue received national news media attention after the arrest and conviction of Scott Peterson for the murder of his pregnant wife, Laci Peterson. He was convicted of the mur-ders of both his wife and the unborn child.[12]

Other states have not changed the law, and their courts adhere to the common-law def-inition. For example, in *People v. Joseph*, 130 Misc.2d 377, 496 N.Y.S.2d 328 (1985), the defendant was charged with two counts of vehicular homicide for causing a collision that caused the death of a woman and the subsequent stillbirth of her child. The New York court dismissed the charges pertaining to the stillborn child, holding that for the purpose of defining homicide, a "person" is someone born and alive. Until the legislature changes the common-law definition, New York courts will adhere to this.

Constitutional Requirements

In addition to the interplay between common law and statutory law, constitutional due process doctrines affect both substantive and procedural criminal law. A statute that is too vague or broad will be voided as unconstitutional. The basis for this constitutional prohib-ition is the principle of legality, which requires criminal offenses to be as precisely defined as possible so that it can be known with reasonable certainty beforehand what acts are criminal and what acts are not. Criminal statutes must be sufficiently definite to give per-sons of ordinary intelligence fair warning that their contemplated conduct is prohibited; statutes must provide explicit standards for those who apply them, to avoid arbitrary and capricious enforcement. Vague and overly broad statutes fail to warn individuals of what the law forbids, and such statutes leave too much discretion in the hands of government officials.

The police are the means by which society enforces the law and maintains order so that people may live safely and go freely about their business; however, unless police powers are contained within understandable parameters, liberty and freedom will be threatened by arbitrary and capricious exercises of authority. For example, the city of Cincinnati, as many states and localities had done, passed an ordinance that made it unlawful for "three or more persons to assemble… on any sidewalks and there conduct themselves in a manner annoying to persons passing by." The term "assemble" was not defined. Could it include three people having a conversation? Moreover, who is to decide what conduct is "annoying"?

In *Coates v. City of Cincinnati*, 402 U.S. 611 (1971), the Supreme Court found this ordinance unconstitutional because "men of common intelligence must necessarily guess at its meaning." As a result of *Coates*, similar laws across the country were found unconsti-tutional, and many vagrancy and loitering laws were voided. The need for such laws, how-ever, caused legislatures to attempt to rewrite them in a manner that would be acceptable under the principles of legality and constitutional due process of law.

In response to an increase in violent street gang activity, the City of Chicago passed the Gang Congregation Ordinance, which made it a crime for gang members to loiter with one another in a public place with no apparent purpose. This ordinance was more specific than the Cincinnati ordinance and contained an element that the defendants did not promptly disperse when ordered to do so by a police officer; nevertheless, the Supreme Court, in *City of Chicago v. Morales*, 527 U.S. 41 (1999), ruled that the ordinance was unconstitutional because it "affords too much discretion to the police and too little notice to citizens who wish to use the public streets."

Problem

A police department received a 911 call from a person who stated that a man was exposing himself from a window. An officer who responded to the location observed a man, who appeared not to be wearing clothes, standing in a second-floor window of an apartment building. As the officer parked his car, a pedestrian approached him and stated that every day when she walked her dog on this street the man coincidentally appeared naked in the window. The officer, on the basis of the pedestrian's assertion and his observation, went to the second-floor apartment and, after speaking with the occupant, arrested him. The officer charged the man with violation of a statute that read:

> It shall be unlawful for any person to commit any indecent, immodest or filthy act in a public place or in such a situation that persons passing in a public place might ordinarily see the same.

Questions

1. On the basis of the plain meaning of the words in the statute, did the defendant violate the statute?
2. Did the defendant have fair notice that his conduct was prohibited by law?
3. Should criminal laws encompass indecent or immoral conduct?
4. Did the defendant have to know such a law existed in order for him to be found guilty?
5. Could the defendant be successfully prosecuted on the basis of the police officer's observations alone?
6. Would it be necessary for the pedestrian to testify about her observations?
7. Did the fact that the defendant was in his own apartment preclude a prosecution under the statute?
8. Should a court or jury find that the defendant's conduct did not constitute an indecent, immodest, or filthy act?
9. Should a court rule that the statute, as applied, violated the defendant's rights?
10. Should a court rule that the statute on its face was unconstitutional?

Applications to White-collar Crime

As the criminal statute books grow ever more complex and reach into business activities that traditionally were subject to the doctrine of *caveat emptor*, or "buyer beware," the constitutional doctrines of overbreadth and vagueness grow in importance as protections for the individual against government prosecutions that sometimes overreach. After the 2001 Enron scandal that precipitated a severe stock market downturn, the U.S. Department of Justice indicted dozens of prominent business and political leaders. Each such leader was indicted on a long list of charges related to alleged unscrupulous business or political practices. Some commentators have contended that, after a scandal that precipitates public outrage, prosecutors invariably go after high-profile defendants connected to the scandal for whom there is no sympathy, in order to convict them of *something*.

Three of the people indicted after the Enron scandal, Jeffrey Skilling, Conrad Black, and Bruce Weyhrauch, were convicted of numerous charges. Their cases involved separate matters, but each of the defendants was convicted under a 1988 law, 18 U.S.C. § 1346, which makes it a crime to deprive someone of "the intangible right of honest services" by misusing his position for private gain and knowingly and intentionally breaching his duty of loyalty. This statute had become a favorite of prosecutors in white-collar cases as a kitchen-sink charge against politicians and business leaders.

On June 24, 2010, the Supreme Court unanimously overturned the three convictions because the "honest services" statute was overbroad and too vague: "To satisfy due process, a penal statute must define the criminal offense [1] with sufficient definiteness that ordinary people can understand what conduct is prohibited and [2] in a manner that does not encourage arbitrary and discriminatory enforcement." The Court held that Section 1346 does not meet either of these two due process essentials. First, the phrase "the intangible right of honest services" does not adequately define what behavior it bars. Second, the broad sweep of the statute allows government agents, prosecutors, and juries to pursue their personal predilections, thereby facilitating opportunistic and arbitrary prosecutions.[13]

In the most prominent of the three cases, the government had charged Skilling with conspiring to defraud Enron's shareholders by misrepresenting the company's fiscal health, thereby artificially inflating its stock price. It was the government's trial theory that Skilling profited from the fraudulent scheme through the receipt of salary and bonuses and through the sale of approximately $200 million in Enron stock, which netted him $89 million. The government did not, at any time, allege that Skilling solicited or accepted side payments from a third party in exchange for making these misrepresentations.

With the majority opinion written by Justice Ruth Bader Ginsburg, the Court held that the use of the "deprivation of honest services" theory adversely affected the conspiracy charges against Skilling and that his conspiracy convictions were premised on the improper theory of deprivation of honest services. While the Court did not invalidate the statute entirely, it held that it was meant to apply to bribery and kickback schemes in which someone was deprived of money or property. Because it was not shown that Skilling had deprived a particular victim of money or property, the statute could not be used as a basis to convict him for his role in the Enron scandal.

Although the Court's decision was unanimous, three of the justices would have gone further and would have invalidated the entire law rather than ruling only that it could not be used against Skilling. The Court held that Skilling did not commit honest-services fraud; therefore, his interrelated convictions for wire fraud and securities fraud were also flawed.

Undoubtedly, while some citizens will take a cynical view of the vacating of these convictions, the due process principles of fair notice and specificity that the Supreme Court unanimously upheld are applicable to all citizens and are applicable to all categories of crime, including crimes pertaining to speech, conspiracy, association, morals, obscenity, and other public and private conduct.

Allowing the government, in response to economic, financial, environmental, or other disasters, to single out individuals for punishment on the basis of overbroad statutes that encompass almost any inappropriate conduct would, in effect, be comparable to allowing *ex post facto* laws, which are barred by the Constitution. Moreover, the Constitution bars Congress from passing Bills of Attainder, which are laws that target an individual or a particular group and which do not apply to all citizens. Overbroad statutes allow the executive branch to circumvent the Bill of Attainder prohibition against singling out individuals or particular groups for punishment.[14]

Notes

1 Gardner, George K., *Bailey v. Richardson* and the Constitution of the United States, *Boston University Law Review*, 33, 193, 1953.
2 Harper, Robert Francis, *The Code of Hammurabi*, Chicago University Press, 1904.
3 *Ibid.*
4 Aristotle, *The Athenian Constitution*, 9.1, translated by P.J. Rhodes, Penguin Books, New York, 2002, p. 50.
5 Plutarch, *Solon and Publicola*, 18.5, Vol. 46, Loeb Classical Library, 1914, p. 453.
6 Hall, Jerome, Plato's legal philosophy, *Indiana Law Journal*, 31, 204, 1955–1956; Romnen, Heinrich, *The Natural Law: A Study in Legal and Social History and Philosophy*, Liberty Fund, Indianapolis, IN, 1998.
7 *The Law of the Twelve Tables*, 8.10, Vol. 329, Loeb Classical Library, 1938, p. 481.
8 Cicero, *The Republic*, 3, ssii.211, Harvard University Press, Cambridge, MA.
9 *State v. Orrell*, 12 N.C. 139 (1826).
10 *People v. Brengard*, 265 N.Y. 100 (1934).
11 California Penal Code, Section 187(a).
12 Murphy, Dean E., Scott Peterson sentenced to death for killing pregnant wife, *The New York Times*, March 17, 2005.
13 Slip Opinions, June 24, 2010: *Black v. United States*, 561 U.S. 465 (2010), *Weyhrauch v. United States*, 08-1196, *United States v. Skilling*, 561 U.S. 358 (2010).
14 U.S. Constitution, Article I, Section IX.

References

Kolender v. Lawson, 4671 U.S. 352 (1983).
Lanzetta v. New Jersey, 306 U.S. 451 (1939).
Papachristou v. City of Jacksonville, 405 U.S. 156 (1972).
Rose v. Locke, 423 U.S. 48 (1975).
Smith, Sheriff, v. Goguen, 415 U.S. 566 (1974).
State v. Metzger, 319 N.W.2d 459 (Neb. 1982).

Chapter 3

A Bill of Rights Summary

The primary source of current American criminal procedure law is the U.S. Constitution and the Bill of Rights contained therein. This has been true in federal courts since the founding of the nation; however, in state courts, where most criminal actions are brought, it has not always been the case.

By April 30, 1789, when George Washington was sworn in as the first president, only 11 of the 13 states had ratified the Constitution and agreed to join the union. North Carolina and Rhode Island held back, primarily because they believed the newly formed central government had been granted too much power.

On September 25, 1789, the first Congress of the United States was seated. In response to complaints of too much centralized power and too few protections for individual citizens, the members passed ten amendments to the Constitution. These amendments induced North Carolina and Rhode Island to join the union, and the unification of all 13 states into one nation was complete.

On December 15, 1791, the ten amendments were ratified by the 13 states and became known as the Bill of Rights. Without the Bill of Rights, it is unlikely that our nation would have remained unified. The colonists had rebelled against what they viewed as the unchecked power of the English king and parliament, and they feared creating another powerful central government. The original Constitution of 1789 established the checks and balances system; however, it provided only five specific protections for the individual who might face criminal prosecution by the government, and it left out many rights that English subjects possessed under common law. The Constitution of 1789 did not include basic individual rights such as freedom of speech, freedom of the press, freedom of religion, the right against unreasonable searches or seizures, the right to counsel, the right against self-incrimination, and the right to confront accusers.

Viewed from the present, it may seem surprising that the original Constitution did not have the provisions enunciated in the Bill of Rights. Only a few provisions of the original Constitution addressed issues of due process for citizens:

1. Habeas corpus, the right to petition a court for release from unlawful imprisonment, was protected (except in times of rebellion or invasion).[1]
2. Bills of Attainder were prohibited. Such bills are special acts of a legislature, either federal or state, that declare that specific persons or groups have committed a crime and can be punished without a judicial trial.[2]
3. *Ex post facto* laws, by either federal or state legislatures, were prohibited. Such laws retroactively punish previously committed acts that were lawful at the time committed, or they increase the punishment for previously committed acts.[3]

DOI: 10.4324/9781003415091-4

4. Crimes were to be tried by jury and held in the state in which the crime was committed.[4] This was of major importance to the colonists because the British government had repeatedly avoided local jury trials for colonists by shifting cases to the juryless admiralty or chancery courts, or by authorizing trials in England for crimes committed in America.[5]

5. Treason against the United States was defined, and a prosecution for treason required a high evidentiary standard for conviction. Testimony of two witnesses or confession in open court was required to convict.[6]

The original Constitution did not guarantee many of the rights that individual state governments had provided for their citizens, and many state representatives voiced dissatisfaction with the lack of federal due process protections for individuals. James Madison, who later became the fourth president of the United States, was also dissatisfied. The Americans had thrown off the oppressive British regime, which had trampled on their rights, and Madison did not want an oppressive American central government replacing the British. To help prevent this, he wrote the Bill of Rights and advocated the adoption of each amendment.

First Amendment

The language of the First Amendment clearly imparted the purpose and philosophy embodied in the Bill of Rights:

> Congress shall make no law respecting an establishment of religion, or prohibiting the free exercise thereof; or abridging the freedom of speech, or of the press; or the right of the people peaceably to assemble, and to petition the Government for a redress of grievances.

The Bill of Rights, at first, was a restraint on the federal government, not on the state governments. The opening phrase, "Congress shall make no law," referred to the U.S. Congress, not to the state legislatures.

The words of the Amendment seem definitive; however, they are not absolute. Certain kinds of speech can be prohibited. Justice Oliver Wendell Holmes famously wrote, "The most stringent protection of free speech would not protect a man in falsely shouting fire in a theatre and causing a panic."[7]

The free speech clause does not protect obscenity or defamation. It does not protect fighting words, incitement to riot, sedition, or hate speech when there is a clear and present danger that the speech will result in violence.[8]

In *Schenk v. United States*, 249 U.S. 47 (1919), the U.S. Supreme Court upheld the defendant's conviction for speech that violated the Espionage Act of 1917 that had been passed during World War I. Schenk was a Communist Party leader who had distributed leaflets to military draftees urging them to resist the draft during time of war. The Court affirmed his conviction as a clear and present danger to the war effort and the safety of the nation. Justice Holmes wrote, "The question in every case is whether the words used are used in such circumstances and are of such a nature as to create a clear and present danger that they will bring about the substantive evils that Congress has a right to prevent."

In 1951, during the period known as the McCarthy era, the Supreme Court, in *Dennis v. United States*, 341 U.S. 494 (1951), upheld the conviction of Communist Party leaders for organizing, advocating, and teaching the violent overthrow of the government. Although the facts of the case did not show an imminent clear and present danger of violence, the

Court noted that the extreme seriousness of a threat can compensate for the lack of immediacy. The Court differentiated the isolated speech of individuals or small groups from the speech of large-scale conspiratorial movements. The clear and present danger test would apply to the former, while a new "sufficient danger of substantive evil" test would apply to the latter.

In the 1960s, the Warren Court initiated a period of more leeway for free speech. In *United States v. O'Brien*, 391 U.S. 367 (1968), the Court reversed the convictions of protesters who had burned their draft cards in symbolic speech to express opposition to the Vietnam War. It is established jurisprudence that statutes or other government orders that restrict free speech must be examined under a strict scrutiny standard that gives preference to the expression of ideas over the restraint of speech. The content and ideas expressed in speech are almost never restrained unless violence is contemplated or there exists a compelling state interest to do so.

In a flag-burning case in which the symbolic burning of the American flag was held to be protected by the First Amendment, the Supreme Court explained:

> The First Amendment literally forbids the abridgement only of "speech," but we have long recognized that its protection does not end at the spoken or written word. While we have rejected "the view that an apparently limitless variety of conduct can be labeled 'speech' whenever the person engaging in the conduct intends thereby to express an idea," we have acknowledged that conduct may be sufficiently imbued with elements of communication to fall within the scope of the First and Fourteenth Amendments.[9]

A bedrock principle underlying the First Amendment is that the government may not prohibit speech simply because it finds the ideas expressed offensive or disagreeable.

Second Amendment

The Second Amendment limited the powers of the federal government and confirmed the authority of the states:

> A well-regulated Militia, being necessary to the security of *a free State*, the right of the people to keep and bear Arms shall not be infringed.

Whether the right to bear arms pertained to state militias or to individual citizens remained an unresolved question until June 26, 2008, when the Supreme Court in *District of Columbia v. Heller*[10] ruled that the Second Amendment protects an individual's right to possess a firearm for traditionally lawful purposes, such as self-defense within the home. This right is unconnected with service in the militia. Although the Court rejected a blanket prohibition on the ownership of handguns, the Court did not prohibit reasonable regulations pertaining to felons, mentally incompetent persons, or the possession of handguns outside of the home.

Third Amendment

> No Soldier shall, in time of peace be quartered in any house, without the consent of the Owner, nor in time of war, but in a manner to be prescribed by law.

Fortunately, citizens of our nation, at least since the Civil War, have rarely had to invoke the Third Amendment.

Fourth Amendment

Madison wrote the Fourth Amendment to prevent recurrences of the British use of general warrants and writs of assistance that, in effect, allowed agents of the government to search anyone, wherever and whenever they wished. The Fourth Amendment placed substantial restraints on the new American central government and granted significant rights to individuals:

> The right of the people to be secure in their persons, houses, papers, and effects, against unreasonable searches and seizures, shall not be violated, and no Warrants shall issue, but upon probable cause, supported by Oath or affirmation, and particularly describing the place to be searched, and the persons or things to be seized.

Probable cause is a foundational concept of the Fourth Amendment and of all American criminal procedure law. It is an essential element of the concept of due process of law, and its development has been concurrent with the development of individual liberty and democratic principles. Probable cause has its roots in the Magna Carta (or Great Charter) which the king of England was forced to sign in 1215. The document proclaimed that, "No freeman shall be taken, imprisoned... except by lawful judgment of his peers or the laws of the land." It established that no one could be taken into custody on mere suspicion, on a whim, or without good cause. The Fourth Amendment extended the probable cause protection from the governmental seizure of a person to the search and seizure of his property.

A search occurs when government agents intrude into a person's zone of privacy, whether it is his or her physical person, clothing, property, home, or communications. Until the twentieth century, for a search to be deemed a violation, an actual physical trespass had to occur. When wiretapping, electronic eavesdropping, and other technologies became feasible, courts recognized that unlawful searches could occur without an actual physical trespass when the government electronically intercepted communications or used other sensory devices to detect movements and activity inside a private premises.[11] A seizure occurs when a government officer impounds an object, intercepts a communication, or takes a person into custody.

Courts prefer that the government obtain a warrant before conducting an arrest or a search and seizure, but a warrant is not always required. Reasonable exceptions are allowed, and, in fact, the vast majority of arrests and searches are made without warrants. In either case, with or without a warrant, an arrest always, and a search generally, requires probable cause.

Arrest warrants and search warrants can only be issued on the basis of sworn affidavits or testimony establishing probable cause to arrest or search, and the requirements to satisfy probable cause vary depending on the facts and circumstances of each particular case. The term *probable cause* was written in the Fourth Amendment, but it was not defined there. Case law and statutes have attempted to define the term. Although it has proved difficult, general definitions have been developed and accepted in the context of both arrests and searches.

Probable cause to arrest exists when the facts and circumstances within the officers' knowledge and of which they have reasonably trustworthy information are sufficient to warrant a man of reasonable caution to believe that an offense has been or is being committed by a particular person. Probable cause to search exists when the facts and circumstances within the officers' knowledge and of which they have reasonably trustworthy information are sufficient to warrant a man of reasonable caution to believe that impoundable articles are located at a particular location.[12]

As with any general definition, the difficulty is in its application to specific situations—and this is especially true for probable cause, because its inexact and open-ended nature leaves room for widely divergent interpretations and applications. The level and kind of probable cause required for an arrest might be different from that required for a search, and the probable cause for an action with a warrant might be different from the probable cause for an action without a warrant. "Courts generally exercise a higher level of scrutiny when reviewing probable cause determinations made by police acting without a warrant than when reviewing determinations made by a detached and neutral magistrate. Indeed, it is frequently said that a lower quantum of evidence of probable cause is sufficient to sustain a search or arrest authorized by a warrant."[13]

Despite the difficulties in its interpretation and application, the Supreme Court has recognized probable cause as the best means of balancing competing interests. The Court wrote:

> These long-prevailing standards seek to safeguard citizens from rash and unreasonable interferences with privacy and from unfounded charges of crime. They also seek to give fair leeway for enforcing the law in the community's protection. Because many situations which confront officers in the course of executing their duties are more or less ambiguous, room must be allowed for some mistakes on their part. But the mistakes must be those of reasonable men, acting on the facts leading sensibly to their conclusions of probability. The rule of probable cause is a practical, non-technical conception affording the best compromise that has been found for accommodating these often opposing interests. Requiring more would unduly hamper law enforcement. To allow less would be to leave law-abiding citizens at the mercy of the officers' whim or caprice.[14]

When courts review government arrest and search and seizure actions, they employ an objective standard to determine whether or not probable cause existed. They review the circumstances of the action from the viewpoint of an objective and reasonably prudent person, not from the subjective mindset of the particular officer who took the action. Nonetheless, courts consider the training and experience of the police officer as an objective factor when assessing whether the officer had probable cause.

On the basis of observations of the same facts and circumstances, a trained and experienced police officer might be able to establish probable cause more readily than a layman unfamiliar with criminal offenses and behavior. As a federal Circuit Court of Appeals observed in *Bell v. United States*, 254 F.2d 81 (1958):

> A fact which spells reasonable cause to a doctor may make no impression on a carpenter, and *vice versa*.... An officer experienced in the narcotics traffic may find probable cause in the smell of drugs and the appearance of paraphernalia which to the lay eye is without significance. His action is not measured by what might be probable cause to an untrained civilian passerby.... The question is what constituted probable cause in the eyes of a reasonable, cautious and prudent peace officer under the circumstances of the moment.

Probable cause to arrest "need not be supported by information and knowledge which, at the time, excludes all possibility of innocence and points to the defendant's guilt beyond a reasonable doubt. As the very name suggests, probable cause depends upon probabilities, not certainty."[15]

To make an arrest, an officer must have more than suspicion. Suspicion is uncertain and often based on misinterpretation, conjecture, or unreliable information. Suspicion does not justify an arrest or the detention of a person against their will.

Reasonable suspicion, which has a higher level of reliability than mere suspicion, allows an officer to stop and question a suspect for a brief period of time. It is based on facts and circumstances that would lead a reasonable police officer to conclude that criminal activity has occurred, is occurring, or will occur. The important distinction between probable cause and reasonable suspicion is that reasonable suspicion alone, without more evidence of criminal activity, does not justify an arrest, and it does not justify a full-blown search of a suspect. However, when officers stop a person on the basis of reasonable suspicion and they have an additional reasonable fear for their safety, they may conduct a frisk or pat-down of the suspect, which is a far less intrusive act than a search.[16]

Applying the principles of search and seizure law to specific factual situations can be a difficult matter of judgment. To perform their roles properly, law enforcement officers must acquire a high degree of knowledge in the areas of probable cause and search and seizure law. Such knowledge is essential for making appropriate decisions and properly explaining their actions to the court. The distinctions between probable cause, reasonable suspicion, and mere suspicion will be covered extensively in subsequent chapters.

Fifth Amendment

The Fifth Amendment proclaimed the rights of persons accused of and prosecuted for crimes. It included the rights against compulsory self-incrimination and double jeopardy, and the cornerstone right to due process of law:

> No person shall be held to answer for a capital, or otherwise infamous, crime, unless on presentment or indictment of a Grand Jury, except in cases arising in the land or naval forces, or in the Militia, when in actual service in time of War or public danger; nor shall any person be subject for the same offence to be twice put in jeopardy of life or limb; nor shall be compelled in any criminal case to be a witness against himself, nor be deprived of life, liberty, or property, without due process of law; nor shall private property be taken for public use, without just compensation.

The most ubiquitous principle of criminal procedure law is the right to due process of law. In addition to the Fifth and Fourteenth Amendments, every American state constitution has similar provisions that prohibit the government from taking a person's life, liberty, or property, whether as a criminal or civil punishment, without due process of law. Due process procedural rights refer to safeguards that are deemed "implicit in the concept of ordered liberty" and "so rooted in the traditions and conscience of our people as to be ranked as fundamental."[17] These rights encompass not only rights enunciated in constitutions but also traditional rights dating from before the Constitution, such as the presumption of innocence and the proof beyond a reasonable doubt standard for a criminal conviction.[18]

Justice Felix Frankfurter in *Wolf v. Colorado*, 338 U.S. 25 (1949), instructed:

> Due process of law thus conveys neither formal nor fixed nor narrow requirements. It is the compendious expression for all those rights, which the courts must enforce because

they are basic to our free society. But basic rights do not become petrified as of any one time, even though, as a matter of human experience, some may not too rhetorically be called eternal verities. It is of the very nature of a free society to advance in its standards of what is deemed reasonable and right. Representing as it does a living principle, due process is not confined within a permanent catalogue of what may at a given time be deemed the limits or the essentials of fundamental rights.

Sixth Amendment

The Sixth Amendment pronounced the rights of an accused person during his or her criminal trial:

> In all criminal prosecutions, the accused shall enjoy the right to a speedy and public trial, by an impartial jury of the State and district wherein the crime shall have been committed, which district shall have been previously ascertained by law, and to be informed of the nature and cause of the accusation; to be confronted with the witnesses against him; to have compulsory process for obtaining Witnesses in his favor, and to have the Assistance of Counsel for his defense.

The Sixth Amendment right to a public trial belongs to the defendant rather than the public. It applies to criminal trials, not civil trials. It covers the entire trial, including jury selection, opening statements, testimony of witnesses, closing arguments, the judge's instructions to the jury, the return of the verdict, and sentencing. It also covers pretrial hearings.[19]

The importance of this right is that it acts as "a safeguard against any attempt to employ our courts as instruments of persecution. The knowledge that every criminal trial is subject to contemporaneous review in the forum of public opinion is an effective restraint on possible abuse of judicial power."[20] Public trials can encourage unknown witnesses to come forward; they tend to discourage perjury by inducing fear in witnesses that any false testimony they give will be observed and uncovered; and they influence prosecutors to carry out their duties fairly and responsibly. The right to a public trial is not absolute, and courts have balanced the right against other important interests, such as the protection of the identity of an undercover police officer during a hearing or of the dignity of a rape victim during her testimony.[21]

The Sixth Amendment right to confront witnesses was of crucial importance to the development of the American system of criminal justice. It established our adversarial criminal justice system and precluded the inquisitorial system that had been employed at times in Britain and is still employed on the European continent. During the colonial period, the American colonists complained that the British prosecuted them on the basis of secret *ex parte* affidavits, and denied them the opportunity to cross-examine their accusers. The well-known case of Sir Walter Raleigh fueled the American determination.

Raleigh was a famous explorer and had established British colonies in the New World. In 1603, he was tried for treason against the Crown on the basis of a letter written by an alleged accomplice, Lord Cobham, and Cobham's confession that implicated Raleigh. Cobham's confession was likely obtained by coercion during an inquisitorial interrogation. In Cobham's absence, his hearsay letter and hearsay statements were admitted in evidence at Raleigh's trial. Raleigh demanded, "Let Cobham be here, let him speak it. Call my accuser before my face." However, the court refused to bring Cobham to testify, and Raleigh was convicted, sentenced to death, and eventually executed. Too many American colonists had suffered fates similar to Raleigh's, and the Sixth Amendment right to confront witnesses was reinforced to prevent such injustices.

A corollary to the right to confront witnesses was the right to assistance of counsel. This right was also considered essential to correcting the abuses of the British system. In England, until the Glorious Revolution of 1688, persons charged with a felony or treason against the Crown had no right to assistance of counsel. Persons charged with misdemeanors or persons involved in civil suits, however, were allowed to retain counsel.

After the 1688 revolution, the English rule denying counsel in treason cases was abolished, but restrictions on counsel in felony cases continued until 1836. To the Americans, the English practice of allowing counsel in less serious cases but denying counsel in more serious cases seemed counterintuitive.

In the courts of the American colonies, counsel was allowed in local cases, and Madison wanted to ensure that counsel would be allowed in federal cases brought by the new central government. On the basis of this constitutional support, defense attorneys acquired the authority to challenge the government and to develop and steward the American adversarial system.

Seventh Amendment

The original Constitution had provided a right to a jury trial in criminal prosecutions, but not for civil lawsuits. The Seventh Amendment extended the right to a jury trial to civil common-law cases:

> In Suits at common law, where the value in controversy shall exceed twenty dollars, the right of trial by jury shall be preserved, and no fact tried by a jury, shall be otherwise re-examined in any Court of the United States, than according to the rules of the common law.

The proponents of the Bill of Rights were primarily concerned with protecting the rights of the individual against the potentially oppressive actions of the government. They recognized that a citizen's common-law right to bring suit against the government for unlawful acts of oppression or trespass would be more effectively enforced when tried before a jury of the citizen's peers, rather than before a judge employed by the government. During the colonial period, suits against the government that were tried or reviewed by judges had produced unsatisfactory results, and the Seventh Amendment was seen as the necessary and primary means by which individuals could obtain redress for government abuses.

Eighth Amendment

The Eighth Amendment reinforced the restraints on governmental power, banned barbaric punishments that had been used in the past, and furthered the ideals of human dignity:

> Excessive bail shall not be required, nor excessive fines imposed, nor cruel and unusual punishments inflicted.

The excessive bail clause applies only in the federal courts, for the Supreme Court has never imposed the excessive bail clause on the states. As will be noted for each of the clauses in the Bill of Rights, what may seem like an absolute always has qualifiers. In 1984, the U.S. Congress enacted the Bail Reform Act, which permits federal judges to refuse to set bail and to preventively detain suspects who, according to certain objective criteria, are determined to pose a potential menace to the community. This Act cured the somewhat disingenuous practice of setting bail in amounts far above the resources of a defendant, which, in effect, constituted preventive detention.

In recent decades, cruel and unusual punishment has been a major subject for Supreme Court review, particularly as regards the death penalty. However, there is no serious debate as to whether the death penalty was an accepted form of punishment when the Constitution was adopted. When the Eighth Amendment was written, execution was an expected and regular form of punishment. The Constitution expressly refers to the death penalty. The Fifth Amendment states that no person shall be deprived of "life" without due process of law and ensures that no person shall be held for a "capital crime" (one for which the sentence would be the death penalty) without a grand jury indictment.

These references clearly establish that the death penalty was not one of the cruel and unusual punishments prohibited by the Eighth Amendment. However, under what circumstances and to whom the death penalty may be applied has been a major area of litigation.

Ninth Amendment

The Ninth Amendment ensured that the failure to enumerate a fundamental right (many such rights had already been established at common law) did not mean that such rights were abrogated and that the government could arbitrarily disregard them:

> The enumeration in the Constitution, of certain rights, shall not be construed to deny or disparage others retained by the people.

The right to privacy, the right to be free of arbitrary and capricious treatment by government officials, and other recognizable rights exist under the broad umbrella of this amendment even though they were not specifically written into the Constitution.[22] The Ninth Amendment supports the idea of the Constitution as a living document that changes with the needs of modern times.

Tenth Amendment

The Tenth Amendment limited federal government power to only those powers specifically granted to the federal government, and retained all other government powers within the states:

> The powers not delegated to the United States by the Constitution, nor prohibited by it to the States, are *reserved to the States* respectively, or to the people.

In effect, the Tenth Amendment restricted central government authority, but it left open the amount and type of authority that states might impose on their citizens, including the enforcement of criminal laws and the procedures to prosecute and adjudicate criminal charges.

Rejected Amendment

Congress did not apply the restraints and protections enunciated in the Bill of Rights to the states. Madison had written an amendment that proposed that the states be prohibited from abridging freedom of expression, freedom of religion, and the right to criminal jury trials. The House of Representatives passed the amendment, but the Senate rejected it, and it was not sent to the states for ratification.[23]

Consequently, between the ratification of the Bill of Rights and the Civil War, each sovereign state, free of federal control, developed and applied its own set of criminal procedures and practices. Although most states had provisions in their constitutions that were similar to those of the U.S. Constitution, the interpretations and applications of these provisions were widely divergent, and consistency between the states was lacking.

Problem

Police Officers Cruise and Pryor responded to an automobile collision. When they arrived at the scene, they found that there had been a serious collision in which the driver of the first vehicle had been severely injured. Officer Cruise rendered first aid to the driver until an ambulance arrived.

The driver of the second vehicle did not appear to be as severely injured as the first driver. He remained seated in his car. Officer Pryor approached him and asked whether he was okay. His response was mostly unintelligible, but he said his name was Carter. The officer noticed that Carter's eyes were glassy and his speech was slurred. The officer did not smell alcohol on Carter's breath, so he suspected the influence of drugs. He asked him to step out of the car. As Carter got out, the officer noticed three red and blue capsules on the front seat of the car. When he asked what they were, Carter reached for the capsules and put them in his mouth. The officer grabbed Carter by the throat and tried to prevent him from swallowing the capsules, but to no avail.

Pryor placed Carter under arrest for driving under the influence of drugs, and he took him to a nearby hospital where he instructed the emergency room personnel to pump Carter's stomach to retrieve the capsules, which would be evidence. During the procedure, the capsules were recovered; however, Carter slipped into a semiconscious state. At that point, Pryor asked the nurse take a sample of Carter's blood, which she did.

After Carter recovered, he was arraigned for driving while impaired by drugs and for vehicular manslaughter because the driver of the first car died as a result of the collision. Laboratory analysis disclosed that the capsules recovered from Carter's stomach were barbiturates, and the blood sample disclosed that he had a high level of barbiturates, cocaine, and marijuana in his bloodstream. Carter's attorney moved for suppression of the capsules and the blood analysis on the grounds of unreasonable search and seizure.

Questions

1. Did Officer Pryor have probable cause to believe that evidence of the crime was in Carter's stomach?
2. Did Officer Pryor need to obtain a search warrant signed by a judge to order the hospital to pump Carter's stomach?
3. Did Officer Pryor need to obtain a search warrant signed by a judge to order the hospital to extract the blood sample?
4. Did the exigent circumstances exception to the search warrant requirement allow the efforts to retrieve the capsule and blood evidence?
5. Should the judge exclude the capsules from evidence?
6. Should the judge exclude the blood sample results from evidence?

7. Assuming, for argument's sake, that a judge did sign a search warrant for the capsules in Carter's stomach, would an appellate court, nevertheless, exclude that evidence?

Notes

1 U.S. Constitution, Article I, Section 9.
2 U.S. Constitution, Article I, Section 9, Clause 3; Article I, Section 10, Clause 1.
3 *Ibid.*
4 U.S. Constitution, Article III, Section 2.
5 Amar, Akhil Reed, *America's Constitution: A Biography*, Random House, New York, 2005, p. 329.
6 U.S. Constitution, Article III. Section 3, Clause 1.
7 *Schenk v. United States*, 249 U.S. 47 (1919).
8 *Chaplinsky v. New Hampshire*, 315 U.S. 568 (1942).
9 *Texas v. Johnson*, 491 U.S. 397 (1989).
10 *District of Columbia v. Heller*, 554 U.S. 570 (2008).
11 *Katz v. United States*, 389 U.S. 347 (1967); *Kyllo v. United States*, 533 U.S. 27 (2001).
12 *Carroll v. United States*, 267 U.S. 132 (1925); *Brinegar v. United States*, 338 U.S. 160 (1949); *Draper v. United States*, 358 U.S. 307 (1959); *Beck v. Ohio*, 379 U.S. 89 (1964).
13 *People v. Bigelow*, 66 N.Y.2d 417 (1985).
14 *Brinegar v. United States*, 338 U.S. 160 (1949).
15 *People v. Sanders*, 70 A.D.2d 688, 433 N.Y.S.2d 630 (1985).
16 *Terry v. Ohio*, 392 U.S. 1 (1968).
17 *Palko v. Connecticut*, 302 U.S. 319 (1937).
18 *In re Winship*, 397 U.S. 358 (1970); *Commonwealth v. Webster*, 59 Mass. 295 (1850).
19 *Waller v. Georgia*, 467 U.S. 29 (1984).
20 *In re Oliver*, 333 U.S. 257 (1948).
21 *Latimore v. Sielaff*, 561 F.2d 691 (7th Cir. 1977).
22 No major Supreme Court case has been decided solely on the basis of the Ninth Amendment, but it has been relied on in combination with other rights—notably, in *Griswold v. Connecticut*, 381 U.S. 479 (1965), which was the precursor to *Roe v. Wade*, 410 U.S. 113 (1973).
23 Amar, Akhil Reed, *America's Constitution: A Biography*, Random House, New York, 2005.

References

Breithaupt v. Abram, 352 U.S. 432 (1957).
Rochin v. California, 342 U.S. 165 (1952).
Schmerber v. California, 384 U.S. 757 (1966).

Crime and Due Process Protections

Chapter 4

Development of Due Process Protections

The Civil War (1861–1865) brought sudden and dramatic changes but also sparked evolutionary changes that have progressed for more than a century. When the southern states tried to secede from the Union, President Abraham Lincoln and the North went to war to prevent the dissolution of the nation. After the North won the war, Union armies occupied the South, and northern administrators were sent to oversee the dismantling of slavery.

In 1865, the Thirteenth Amendment abolishing slavery was passed and ratified. The Amendment proclaimed that "neither slavery nor involuntary servitude... shall exist within the United States, or any place subject to their jurisdiction." However, southern resistance to equal rights for the newly freed slaves was persistent and formidable. Senator Charles Sumner (1811–1874), an unwavering abolitionist, led the movement to compel the South to comply with the new, more inclusive Constitution. He was instrumental in the passage of the Fourteenth Amendment, which clearly imparted the rights of citizenship to the freed slaves and mandated equality and due process of the law for all citizens.

Fourteenth Amendment

The Fourteenth Amendment was proposed in 1866 and ratified in 1868. The first and fifth sections of the Amendment held profound consequences for American civil rights and criminal procedure law:

> **Section 1.** All persons born or naturalized in the United States and subject to the jurisdiction thereof, are citizens of the United States and of the State wherein they reside. *No State shall make or enforce* any law which shall abridge the privileges and immunities of citizens of the United States; nor shall any State deprive any person of life, liberty, or property, without due process of law; nor deny to any person within its jurisdiction the equal protection of the laws....
>
> **Section 5.** *The Congress shall have the power to enforce*, by appropriate legislation, the provisions of this article.

The reversal in form and substance from the First Amendment's "Congress shall make no law..." to the Fourteenth Amendment's "Congress shall have the power to enforce..." changed the fundamental structure of the nation. In principle, it empowered the federal government to protect citizens from illegal actions of their own states.

In 1870, the Fifteenth Amendment was ratified. It ensured voting rights for all male citizens, including freed slaves, completing the trilogy of the nation-changing amendments. Were history delivered in a neat package, the burgeoning of civil rights and equality before the

DOI: 10.4324/9781003415091-6

law would have followed the implementation of this trilogy of amendments. However, the actual exercise of federal power within states met strong resistance, and it took more than a century to fulfill, or nearly fulfill, the promise of these amendments.

Federalism and the Dual Court System

The United States is comprised of the national government with its laws and court system and also the individual sovereign states with their own sets of laws and courts. It is too simplistic to generalize by saying that the state courts deal with local issues and problems while the federal courts deal only with issues that affect the nation as a whole, as the division and demarcation of responsibilities is often not clear. State and federal courts share judicial powers, and cases that affect both jurisdictions may move from a state court to a federal court and, in turn, from a federal court back to a state court.

Because the U.S. Constitution is an umbrella over all of the states, litigants may appeal a final state ruling on a federal constitutional issue to the U.S. Supreme Court. In fact, not only may a convicted defendant file such an appeal, but a state prosecutor also may appeal a ruling that favored a defendant. In addition, persons incarcerated in state institutions may file a writ of habeas corpus in a federal district court challenging the incarceration. Although there are restrictions on the right of a state inmate to file a federal habeas corpus petition (namely, that all state remedies have been exhausted), if the case is heard, the petitioner may appeal an adverse ruling in the federal district court to the federal Circuit Court of Appeals, and from there the petitioner may appeal to the Supreme Court. Although there is a rather low probability that the Supreme Court will issue a writ of certiorari agreeing to hear the case, it is possible that the Court will accept a case that has important national implications.

Applying Due Process to the States

The Fifth Amendment's language "No person shall be… deprived of life, liberty, or property, without due process of law" pertained to the federal government. Similar language in the Fourteenth Amendment, "nor shall any State deprive any person of life, liberty, or property, without due process of law," pertained to the states. The meaning and the relationship of these "due process of law" clauses have been debated for 150 years and have undergone a long evolutionary process to reach today's understanding. During most of those years, until the 1960s, advocates for states' rights successfully resisted the proposition that the states must apply the clause in the same manner as the federal government. They argued that states could administer their criminal justice systems as they saw fit. Over the course of the twentieth century, however, they lost their argument, as the federal courts gradually began to use their authority to protect the rights of individuals against abusive state actions.[1]

In 1932, the Supreme Court's intervention in state criminal procedure practices took a dramatic step in *Powell v. Alabama*, 287 U.S. 45, the infamous Scottsboro Boys case, in which nine African-American teenage defendants were convicted of rape within days of their arrests and faced the death penalty. During their so-called trials, they were not assigned competent counsel to represent them. The Supreme Court, using the Fourteenth Amendment due process clause, reversed the convictions, ruling that competent counsel was required in death penalty cases:

The right to be heard would be, in many cases, of little avail if it did not comprehend the right to be heard by counsel. Even the intelligent and educated layman has small and sometimes no skill in the science of law. If charged with crimes, he is incapable, generally of determining for himself whether the indictment is good or bad. He is unfamiliar with the rules of evidence. Left without the aid of counsel he may be put on trial without a proper charge, and convicted upon incompetent evidence, or evidence irrelevant to the issue or otherwise inadmissible. He lacks both the skill and knowledge adequately to prepare his defense.

Although *Powell* was decided by justices of a conservative court who generally supported states' rights, the necessity and justice of their decision overrode their political ideology. In later years, when the makeup and the ideology of the Court shifted as a result of political maneuvering over President Franklin Delano Roosevelt's New Deal legislation, support for states' rights diminished significantly. The federal government assumed far greater powers than ever before, and several landmark cases convincingly established federal oversight of state practices.

Brown v. Mississippi

The egregious case of *Brown v. Mississippi*, 297 U.S. 278 (1936), following the Scottsboro Boys case, set the federal courts and much of the nation on a quest to eliminate state violations of fundamental civil rights, particularly the rights of disenfranchised minorities. The question in *Brown* was whether convictions that rested solely upon confessions extorted by officers of the state by brutality and violence were consistent with the due process of law required by the Fourteenth Amendment.

Brown and his two co-defendants were indicted and arraigned for murder. The primary evidence against the defendants was their confessions. Although attorneys were appointed by the court to defend them, little time was afforded for them to prepare a defense. The trial began the morning after the arraignment and concluded a day later. The defendants were found guilty and sentenced to death.

Brown appealed through the state courts, which astonishingly upheld his conviction. He then appealed to the Supreme Court, which granted a writ of certiorari. The best argument for the Court's ultimate decision was its recounting of the circumstances in which the confessions were obtained:

The crimes with which these defendants... are charged were discovered about one o'clock p.m. on Friday, March 30, 1934. On that night, one Dial, a deputy sheriff, accompanied by others, came to the home of Ellington, one of the defendants, and requested him to accompany them to the house of the deceased, and there a number of white men were gathered, who began to accuse the defendant of the crime. Upon his denial they seized him, and with the participation of the deputy they hanged him by a rope to the limb of a tree, and having let him down, they hung him again, and when he was let down the second time, and he still protested his innocence, he was tied to a tree and whipped, and still declining to accede to the demands that he confess, he was finally released and he returned with some difficulty to his home, suffering intense pain and agony. The record of the testimony shows that the signs of the rope on his neck were plainly visible during the so-called trial. A day or two thereafter the said deputy, accompanied by another, returned to the home of the said defendant and arrested him, and departed with the prisoner towards the jail in an adjoining county, but went by a route which led into the State of Alabama; and while on the way, in that State, the deputy stopped and again severely whipped the defendant, declaring that he would continue the whipping until he confessed, and the defendant then agreed to confess to such a statement as the deputy would dictate, and he did so, after which he was delivered to jail.

The other two defendants, Ed Brown and Henry Shields, were also arrested and taken to the same jail. On Sunday night, April 1, 1934, the same deputy, accompanied by a number of white men, one of whom was also an officer, and by the jailer, came to the jail, and the two last named defendants were made to strip and they were laid over chairs and their backs were cut to pieces with a leather strap with buckles on it, and they were likewise made by the said deputy definitely to understand that the whipping would be continued unless and until they confessed, and not only confessed, but confessed in every matter of detail as demanded by those present; and in this manner the defendants confessed the crime, and as the whippings progressed and were repeated, they changed or adjusted their confession in all particulars of detail so as to conform to the demands of their torturers. When the confessions had been obtained in the exact form and contents as desired by the mob, they left with the parting admonition and warning that, if the defendants changed their story at any time in any respect from that last stated, the perpetrators of the outrage would administer the same or equally effective treatment.

Further details of the brutal treatment to which these helpless prisoners were subjected need not be pursued. It is sufficient to say that in pertinent respects the transcript reads more like pages torn from some medieval account than a record made within the confines of a modern civilization which aspires to an enlightened constitutional government.

All this having been accomplished, on the next day, that is, on Monday, April 2, when the defendants had been given time to recuperate somewhat from the tortures to which they had been subjected, the two sheriffs, one of the county where the crime was committed, and the other of the county of the jail in which the prisoners were confined, came to the jail, accompanied by eight other persons, some of them deputies, there to hear the free and voluntary confession of these miserable and abject defendants. The sheriff of the county of the crime admitted that he had heard of the whipping, but averred that he had no personal knowledge of it. He admitted that one of the defendants, when brought before him to confess, was limping and did not sit down, and that this particular defendant then and there stated that he had been strapped so severely that he could not sit down, and, as already stated, the signs of the rope on the neck of another of the defendants were plainly visible to all. Nevertheless the solemn farce of hearing the free and voluntary confessions was gone through with, and these two sheriffs and one other person then present were the three witnesses used in court to establish the so-called confessions....

The defendants were brought to the courthouse of the county on the following morning, April 5th, and the so-called trial was opened and was concluded on the next day, April 6, 1934, and resulted in a pretended conviction with death sentences. The evidence upon which the conviction was obtained was the so-called confessions.

The Supreme Court unanimously reversed the conviction, ruling:

The state is free to regulate the procedure of its courts in accordance with its own conceptions of policy, unless in so doing it "offends some principle of justice so rooted in the traditions and conscience of our people as to be ranked as fundamental." The State may abolish trial by jury. It may dispense with indictment by a grand jury and substitute complaint or information. But the freedom of the State in establishing its policy is the freedom of constitutional government and is limited by the requirement of due process of law. Because a State may dispense with a jury trial, it does not follow that it may substitute trial by ordeal. The rack and torture chamber may not be substituted for the witness stand.... The due process clause requires "that state action, whether through one agency or another, shall be consistent with the fundamental principles of liberty and justice which lie at the base of all our civil and political institutions." It would be difficult to conceive of methods more revolting to the sense of justice than those taken to procure the confessions of these petitioners, and the use of the confessions thus obtained as the basis for conviction and sentence was a clear denial of due process.

... Coercing the supposed state's criminals into confessions and using such confessions so coerced from them against them in trials has been the curse of all countries. It was the chief inequity, the crowning infamy of the Star Chamber, and the Inquisition, and other similar institutions. The constitution recognized the evils that lay behind these practices and prohibited them in this country.... The duty of maintaining constitutional rights of a person on trial for his life rises above mere rules of procedure and wherever the court is clearly satisfied that such violations exist, it will refuse to sanction such violations and will apply the corrective. [internal citations omitted]

Brown provided indisputable evidence of the need for federal intervention into the continuing and prevalent denial of fundamental rights to African-American citizens in the southern states. It also provided a powerful motivation for the civil rights movement that was taking shape and that would achieve significant milestones in 1954 in *Brown v. Board of Education,* 347 U.S. 483, the landmark desegregation case, and the Civil Rights Act of 1964.

Rochin v. California

Rochin v. California, 342 U.S. 165 (1952), established the Fourteenth Amendment due process clause as a kind of visceral, non-intellectual check on the methods that states employed to enforce their criminal laws. Fourth Amendment jurisprudence allows the state to obtain physical evidence from defendants, such as fingerprints and blood or hair samples. The state can use force if necessary to obtain this evidence, but *Rochin* placed limits on the amount and kind of force that could be employed.

In *Rochin*,

Three deputy sheriffs of the County of Los Angeles, on the morning of July 1, 1949, made for the two-story dwelling house in which Rochin lived with his mother, common-law wife, brothers, and sisters. Finding the outside door open, they entered and then forced open the door to Rochin's room on the second floor. Inside they found petitioner sitting partly dressed on the side of the bed, upon which his wife was lying. On a nightstand beside the bed the deputies spied two capsules. When asked 'Whose stuff is this?' Rochin seized the capsules and put them in his mouth. A struggle ensued, in the course of which the three officers jumped upon him and attempted to extract the capsules. The force they applied proved unavailing against Rochin's resistance. He was handcuffed and taken to a hospital. At the direction of one of the officers a doctor forced an emetic solution through a tube into Rochin's stomach against his will. This stomach pumping produced vomiting. In the vomited matter were found two capsules, which proved to contain morphine.

The two capsules of morphine were admitted into evidence against Rochin, and he was convicted. The Supreme Court granted certiorari because a serious question was raised as to the limitations that the due process clause of the Fourteenth Amendment could impose on state criminal proceedings. The Court explained that due process of law is a summarized constitutional guarantee of respect for those personal immunities that are "so rooted in the traditions and conscience of our people as to be ranked as fundamental," or are "implicit in the concept of ordered liberty."

In reversing the defendant's conviction, the Court stated:

> Applying these general considerations to the circumstances of the present case, we are compelled to conclude that the proceedings by which this conviction was obtained do more than offend some fastidious squeamishness or private sentimentalism about combating crime too energetically. This is conduct that *shocks the conscience* [emphasis added]. Illegally breaking into the privacy of the petitioner, the struggle to open his mouth and remove what was there, the forcible extraction of his stomach's contents—this course of proceeding by agents of government to obtain evidence is bound to offend even hardened sensibilities. They are methods too close to the rack and the screw to permit of constitutional differentiation.... It would be a stultification of the responsibility, which the course of constitutional history has cast upon this Court to hold that in order to convict a man the police cannot extract by force what is in his mind but can extract what is in his stomach.

Logically, the police had probable cause to seize the evidence, but the Court disapproved of the circumstances of the police action and the invasiveness of the procedure. Later cases have upheld the seizure of narcotics secreted within the bodily organs of drug smugglers as long as the search and seizure process was conducted in a reasonable and safe manner.

Selective Incorporation of Federal Rights into the Fourteenth Amendment

Of equal or greater importance to the Supreme Court's intervention into state practices that violated fundamental rights in ways that "shocked the conscience" was the Court's intervention into the procedural mechanisms of state criminal justice systems. In the area of criminal procedure, two major questions were presented to the courts. First, should every federal procedural protection listed in the Bill of Rights apply to the states, or only those protections essential to the "fundamental principles of liberty and justice which lie at the base of all our civil and political institutions?"[2] Second, when specific clauses in the Bill of Rights are applied to the states, must the states implement them in exactly the same manner as the federal courts?

The Court considered these questions in *Palko v. Connecticut*, 302 U.S. 319 (1937), a double jeopardy case. The Court considered whether a state could employ a statute regarding the application of double jeopardy that differed from federal procedures. *Palko* involved a murder trial in which the district attorney attempted to offer Mr. Palko's confession as evidence of his guilt. In the confession, Palko described in detail how he had committed the vicious and brutal murder. The trial judge suppressed the confession, and the jury did not hear it. Nevertheless, the jury convicted Palko of second-degree murder and sentenced him to life in prison.

A Connecticut statute allowed prosecutors as well as defendants the right, during the course of a trial, to appeal evidentiary rulings, and on the basis of that statute the district attorney filed an immediate appeal against the judge's ruling that suppressed the confession. Handing down its decision after the trial verdict had been rendered, the appellate court ruled that the confession should have been admitted into evidence, and ordered a new trial. At the second trial, the jury heard the confession, convicted Palko of first-degree murder, and sentenced him to death.

Under federal law, the second trial would not have been possible, but the Supreme Court held that federal intervention into a state case under these circumstances was unnecessary. The Court declined to rule that the states must implement the double jeopardy clause in exactly the same manner as in the federal courts. The Court asked:

> Is that kind of double jeopardy to which the statute has subjected him a hardship so acute and shocking that our polity will not endure it? Does it violate those "fundamental prin-ciples of liberty and justice which lie at the base of all our civil and political institutions?" The answer surely must be "no." What the answer would have to be if the state were permitted after a trial free from error to try the accused over again or to bring another case against him, we have no occasion to consider. We deal with the statute before us and no other. The state is not attempting to wear the accused out by a multitude of cases with accumulated trials. It asks no more than this, that the case against him shall go on until there shall be a trial free from the corrosion of substantial legal error.... The edifice of justice stands, its symmetry, to many, greater than before.

The conviction was allowed to stand, and Palko was executed. Had he been acquitted by the jury rather than convicted, he could not have been tried again.[3] To do so would have violated a "fundamental principle of liberty and justice."

Palko demonstrated, in 1937, the Court's reluctance during that era to interfere with states' rights unless this was necessary to rectify violations of due process that "shocked the conscience." It was not until the term of Chief Justice Earl Warren (1953–1969) that the Court fully abandoned its reluctance to apply exact federal procedural standards to the states. In the area of criminal procedure, the Warren Court is known mostly for its famous decisions in *Mapp v. Ohio* and *Miranda v. Arizona*,[4] but the Court decided many other cases that brought profound changes for defendants and society.

Trial by Jury

In *Duncan v. Louisiana*, 391 U.S. 145 (1968), the Warren Court decided that, in a criminal case, states must afford their citizens the right to a trial by jury that was comparable to the right given in federal courts. The State of Louisiana, with its origins as a French colony, did not have a strong English tradition of trial by jury, and in 1968 did not grant trial by jury for crimes punishable by less than two years' imprisonment. Mr. Duncan was tried and con-victed of a crime for which imprisonment for two years could have been imposed. Although he was sentenced to only three months in jail, he nevertheless appealed the conviction on the grounds that he had been entitled to a jury trial. The Louisiana courts held that because of the petty sentence imposed he was not entitled to a jury trial. The Supreme Court disagreed, holding that it was the potential sentence that mattered. The Court stated:

Because we believe that trial by jury in criminal cases is fundamental to the American scheme of justice, we hold that the Fourteenth Amendment guarantees a right of jury trial in all criminal cases which—were they to be tried in federal court—would come within the Sixth Amendment guarantee.

Duncan demonstrated the progression of the Court's application of federal rights to the states. In 1936, in *Brown v. Mississippi*, 297 U.S. 278, the Court had said, "The State may abolish trial by jury." In 1968, the Court overruled that statement as it pertained to state crimes that carried a substantial prison sentence. Two years later, in *Baldwin v. New York*, 399 U.S. 66 (1970), the Court demonstrated that state procedures must accord with federal procedures in substance but not necessarily in the exact same manner. Because the clauses of the Bill of Rights are applied to the states through the Fourteenth Amendment, some variations in the application of procedural rights are allowable. Although in federal courts a jury trial is required for any crime punishable by a potential sentence of incarceration, the Court drew the line for state jury trials at crimes that carried prison sentences of six months or more.

Unanimous Verdicts

The Court continued examining state trial practices, and addressed the question of whether a criminal court jury verdict had to be unanimous. The Sixth Amendment of the Constitution said only that "the accused shall enjoy the right to a speedy and public trial, by an impartial jury of the State and district wherein the crime shall have been committed..." It did not mandate how many jurors were required or whether the verdict had to be unanimous.

In practice, states had convicted defendants on 10-2 or 11-1 verdicts.

In 2020, the Court decided *Ramos v. Louisiana*, 590 U.S. ... (2020), 140 S.Ct. 1390 (2020), a case in which the defendant, Evangelisto Ramos, had been sent to prison for life without a possibility of parole after a 10-2 jury verdict convicted him of stabbing and murdering someone with whom he had been sexually involved.

In the past, the Supreme Court had upheld non-unanimous verdicts, and to rule in Ramos' favor, the Court had to overturn its own 1972 precedent in *Apodaca v. Oregon*, 406 U.S. 404 (1972). Justice Neil Gorsuch, writing for the majority, observed that the unanimous verdict standard could be traced back to English common law and was the law in Louisiana until that state adopted its constitution of 1898. The Court overturned its precedent and ruled that defendants cannot be convicted of serious crimes unless by unanimous verdict.

The ruling upheld the high standard of American justice that convictions cannot be obtained without stringent standards being met; however, it was not without costs because thousands and thousands of convictions based on non-unanimous verdicts could be vacated. Also, the unanimous-verdict requirement allows one recalcitrant or obstinate juror to prevent a just verdict and cause a mistrial.

Self-incrimination

The Warren Court brought about major changes in the application of the Fifth Amendment's privilege against self-incrimination. Before its 1966 decision in *Miranda v. Arizona*, the Court in two significant cases, *Malloy v. Hogan*, 378 U.S. 1 (1964), and *Griffin v. California*, 380 U.S. 609 (1965), had incorporated this privilege into the Fourteenth Amendment due process clause.[5]

The actual Fifth Amendment language, "...nor be compelled in any criminal case to be a witness against himself," has left much room for interpretation. Courts have attempted to balance the needs of criminal justice against the need to protect citizens from oppressive practices, but the lines between legitimate government inquiry and unlawful compulsion have not always been clear. Torturing a person to obtain a confession for use in a criminal trial has been clearly forbidden. Less clear have been the circumstances under which a person may be compelled to take the witness stand to answer questions that might lead to self-incrimination. Also less clear has been whether a defendant's silence may be held against him.

The words "against himself" allow the government to compel a person to be a witness against others. If subpoenaed, a person may be held in contempt of court for refusing to answer or for evading questions. However, if the questions pertain to criminal activity by the witness, the witness may refuse to answer on the grounds that the answers may be self-incriminating.[6] In that instance, to require the person to testify, the government has to grant immunity from prosecution. The type of immunity generally granted is *use immunity*, which precludes the government from using the compelled testimony and any derivative evidence in a criminal prosecution of the witness. With use immunity, however, the witness could be prosecuted on the basis of other independent evidence.

Some states, such as New York, grant *transactional immunity*, which is broader than use immunity. Transactional immunity precludes the government from prosecuting a compelled witness in connection with the subject matter of the immunized testimony, even when the government has other independent evidence against the witness. This is a far-reaching protection. To ensure that witnesses do not gain immunity for crimes not contemplated by the grant of transactional immunity, only answers that are directly responsive to the questions are covered by the grant.[7]

Right to Remain Silent and Presumption of Innocence

The right to remain silent is a corollary of the privilege against self-incrimination. The privilege would have little value if a defendant's decision to remain silent could be used against him as an indication of his guilt or as a means of overcoming the presumption of innocence. However, it is common sense to expect that an innocent person accused of a crime would speak out in denial. That being the case, courts have attempted to address the contradiction between the right to remain silent and the actual, commonsense expectations of jurors. Courts emphatically instruct jurors not to draw an adverse inference against a defendant for his decision to remain silent, but can jurors truly be expected to disregard a defendant's decision to remain silent when the evidence against the defendant could be counteracted by the defendant's explanation of his actions or whereabouts? Another difficult question is whether jurors should differentiate between a defendant's silence when first accused of a crime by the police and a defendant's silence during his criminal trial.

Problem

Detective Harry Pursuit was investigating a residential burglary at 11 Hill Street in which several expensive furs were stolen. Detective Pursuit found a window that had been pried open, and three fingerprints on the windowsill. On the ground outside the window, he found a handkerchief and a retail store receipt. Crime scene technicians lifted the fingerprints and digitally transmitted copies to the state and FBI criminal identification databases.

No matches were found in the databases. Detective Pursuit checked the retail store receipt, which came from a local hardware store. The hardware store manager looked at the receipt and remembered that the item sold was an extra-large screwdriver. He also remembered the purchaser, a local person known as Billy. He described Billy as a tall, thin young man with long, blondish hair. Pursuit made inquiries in the neighborhood and identified a possible suspect, William "Billy" Klutz. With another detective, he went to Billy's house. Billy, who fit the description given by the store manager, answered the door and allowed the detectives to enter in order to speak to him.

Detective Pursuit, without mentioning the burglary, asked Billy whether he knew the occupants of 11 Hill Street or whether he had ever been at that house.

"Maybe, but I don't know where you're talking about. I could have been anywhere. But I don't know what house you mean," Billy said.

Pursuit asked him whether he knew anyone on Hill Street and whether he ever went up to Hill Street.

Billy hesitated and then said, "I don't know. Maybe. When do you mean?"

"Have you recently bought anything at the hardware store?" Pursuit asked.

Billy turned his back on the detectives, "I don't want to talk anymore."

Pursuit persisted. "Did you buy a large screwdriver at the hardware store?"

"You have to leave," Billy said. "I'm not talking anymore."

"Listen, this is a serious matter," Pursuit said. "The house was burglarized. Burglary is 15 years in prison. But we want to give you the benefit of the doubt. We have fingerprints of the burglar."

"What does that have to do with me?"

"We'd like you to come with us to the station so we can take your fingerprints to clear this up," Pursuit said.

"No way in hell," Billy said.

After the detectives left the house, they conferred with the district attorney, Sue Smart, who issued a grand jury subpoena for Billy to appear at the police station to have his fingerprints taken. Billy complied, and when his fingerprints were checked against the three fingerprints on the windowsill, they matched. Billy was arrested and charged with burglary. At Billy's trial, Detective Pursuit testified regarding his investigation, and he related the details of the conversation he had had with Billy. The hardware store manager identified Billy as the person who purchased the screwdriver that was recorded on the receipt. Billy did not testify in his own defense. During her summation, District Attorney Smart argued to the jury:

> When Detective Pursuit first interviewed the defendant at his house, the defendant refused to offer any explanation as to how his fingerprints got on that windowsill—the windowsill of the house that was broken into. He wouldn't voluntarily consent to having his fingerprints taken, which any innocent person would do in order to clear their name. He wouldn't offer any explanation as to how the receipt from the hardware store got outside that window. Clearly, the person who broke into this house at some point took out his handkerchief, maybe to hold the screwdriver or to wipe away sweat. When he took the handkerchief out of his pocket, the receipt from the hardware store came out with it. And both items fell to the ground. We know the defendant purchased a large screwdriver, and a screwdriver, most probably, was used to make the marks on the window frame. Unfortunately, we don't have that screwdriver that the defendant purchased. If we had it, we could make a comparison, but the defendant hasn't seen fit to produce it. He hasn't

tried to prove it wasn't the one used to pry open the window. The judge will instruct you that the defendant does not have an obligation to present evidence in his own defense, but if he really didn't do it, he could have cooperated with Detective Pursuit. He could have simply gone to the police station to be fingerprinted, instead of having to be subpoenaed and forced to give his prints. He didn't because he knew his prints would match the prints found at the burglary. Only one person knows how his fingerprints and the hardware receipt came to be at that broken window.

After a short deliberation, the jury found Billy guilty.

Questions

1. The Fifth Amendment states that no person "shall be compelled in any criminal case to be a witness against himself." Was the questioning of Billy during the first interview at his house a compulsion to testify against himself?
2. May a jury consider a person's statements and reactions when first confronted and accused of a crime as circumstantial evidence of guilt?
3. May a jury consider flight, evasiveness, failure to offer an explanation, or refusal to cooperate as circumstantial evidence of guilt?[8]
4. Are the words "right to remain silent" or "presumption of innocence" written anywhere in the Constitution?
5. Are the right to remain silent and the presumption of innocence implied by the right not to be compelled to be a witness against oneself?
6. Were Billy's rights to remain silent and not to be compelled to be a witness against himself violated during the prosecutor's summation?
7. When District Attorney Smart, in her summation, recounted Billy's statements and reactions during his first interview with Detective Pursuit, did she violate Billy's right against self-incrimination?
8. Did District Attorney Smart, in her summation, violate Billy's rights by implying that it was his obligation to explain how his fingerprints and the hardware receipt came to be at the burglarized house?
9. Would it "shock the conscience" or violate "the fundamental principles of liberty and justice which lie at the base of all our civil and political institutions" to allow a jury to draw an adverse inference against a defendant who failed to explain what an innocent defendant would try to explain?[9]
10. Should the conviction be vacated and a new trial ordered?

In *Griffin v. California*, 380 U.S. 609 (1965), the Court definitively answered that prosecutors cannot comment on a defendant's silence during trial. The right not to testify implies the right to remain silent without suffering adverse consequences for remaining silent. The Court held that "the imposition of any sanction which makes assertion of the Fifth Amendment 'costly' is constitutionally impermissible."

Griffin, however, did not settle the question of whether a prosecutor may properly comment on a defendant's silence when first confronted or accused by the police. The question has two parts: (1) May a prosecutor, during his direct case, attempt to use a defendant's silence as circumstantial evidence of guilt? (2) May a prosecutor, during cross-examination, attempt to impeach a defendant who takes the stand and for the first time offers an exculpatory explanation of his actions?[10] In deciding these questions, courts have had to decide whether a defendant's silence before receiving *Miranda* warnings should be treated differently from a defendant's silence after receiving *Miranda* warnings.

In *Doyle v. Ohio*, 426 U.S. 610 (1976), the Supreme Court held that the post-*Miranda* silence of a defendant cannot be used by a prosecutor as evidence to prove the crime, and, in *Wainwright v. Greenfield*, 474 U.S. 284 (1986), that post-*Miranda* silence cannot be used to impeach the credibility of a defendant who testifies. On the other hand, in *Fletcher v. Weir*, 455 U.S. 603 (1982), it was held that a defendant's pre-*Miranda* silence when he was confronted with accusations by the police or others may be used to impeach his credibility when he takes the stand to testify.

The Supreme Court has yet to settle whether a prosecutor can use a defendant's pre-*Miranda* silence as evidence during a prosecutor's case-in-chief, rather than only to impeach a defendant's credibility during cross-examination. Lower courts have issued conflicting opinions on the matter, and two Circuit Courts of Appeals have issued conflicting rulings in cases with almost identical fact patterns. In *United States v. Frazier*, 408 F.3d 1102 (8th Cir. 2005), the Eighth Circuit ruled that pre-*Miranda* silence may be used, but in *United States v. Velarde-Gomez*, 269 F.3d 1023 (9th Cir. 2001), the Ninth Circuit ruled that it may not. In both cases, police searched and found illegal drugs in vehicles that the defendants were driving. When the defendants were confronted with the evidence, they both remained silent and displayed little reaction. Their silence and reactions, along with other evidence, were presented to the juries, and both defendants were convicted. Subsequently, on the basis of the right to silence issue, the Eighth Circuit affirmed Frazier's conviction while the Ninth Circuit reversed Velarde-Gomez's conviction. The Supreme Court will eventually have to resolve this conflict between the circuits.

Warren Court Criminal Procedure Decisions

The following are the major criminal procedure decisions of the Warren Court that applied federal constitutional rights directly to the states:

- *Mapp v. Ohio*, 367 U.S. 643 (1961)—Exclusionary rule mandated as a means of enforcing the Fourth Amendment against the states
- *Robinson v. California*, 370 U.S. 660 (1962)—Eighth Amendment ban against criminal punishment for being a drug addict
- *Gideon v. Wainwright*, 372 U.S. 335 (1963)—Right to free legal counsel for indigents
- *Malloy v. Hogan*, 378 U.S. 1 (1964)—Fifth Amendment right against self-incrimination
- *Aguilar v. Texas*, 378 U.S. 108 (1964)—Fourth Amendment probable cause requirement for warrant based on confidential informant
- *Escobedo v. Illinois*, 378 U.S. 478 (1964)—Combined Sixth Amendment right to counsel and Fifth Amendment right against compulsory self-incrimination; later modified by *Moran v. Burbine*, 475 U.S. 412 (1986)
- *Griffin v. California*, 380 U.S. 609 (1965)—Fifth Amendment right to remain silent
- *Pointer v. Texas*, 380 U.S. 400 (1965)—Sixth Amendment right to confront witnesses
- *Miranda v. Arizona*, 384 U.S. 436 (1966)—Fifth Amendment right to remain silent while in custody
- *Parker v. Gladden*, 385 U.S. 363 (1966)—Sixth Amendment right to an impartial jury
- *Washington v. Texas*, 388 U.S. 14 (1967)—Sixth Amendment right to compulsory process for obtaining witnesses
- *Klopfer v. North Carolina*, 386 U.S. 213 (1967)—Sixth Amendment right to speedy trial

- *In re Gault*, 387 U.S. 1 (1967)—Fifth and Sixth Amendment rights for juveniles charged with delinquency that may result in commitment to an institution
- *Duncan v. Louisiana*, 391 U.S. 145 (1968)—Sixth Amendment right to jury trial when possibility of substantial punishment exists
- *Benton v. Maryland*, 395 U.S. 784 (1969)—Fifth Amendment right against double jeopardy
- *Terry v. Ohio*, 392 U.S. 1 (1968)—Fourth Amendment not violated by a stop and frisk of a suspect based on reasonable suspicion of crime and reasonable grounds to believe suspect may be armed with a weapon
- *Spinelli v. United States*, 393 U.S. 410 (1969)—Fourth Amendment probable cause requirement for warrant based on confidential informant
- *Chimel v. California*, 395 U.S. 752 (1969)—Fourth Amendment limitation on extent of search incidental to an arrest

The following is a list of Warren Court decisions issued in federal courts against the United States; the rulings in these decisions must also be followed by the states:

- *Wong Sun v. United States*, 371 U.S. 471 (1963)—Fourth Amendment violation requires suppression of derivative evidence under the fruits-of-the-poisonous-tree doctrine
- *Massiah v. United States*, 377 U.S. 201 (1964)—Right to counsel was violated by using an informer to "question" defendant after indictment
- *Katz v. United States*, 389 U.S. 347 (1967)—Fourth Amendment was violated by infringing on a person's expectation of privacy by eavesdropping without a warrant
- *United States v. Wade*, 388 U.S. 218 (1967)—Fourth Amendment provides for right to counsel at a post-indictment lineup

The above cases constitute, to a large extent, what has been called the defendants' rights revolution. This revolution has been both applauded and criticized. Much of the criticism has been directed at the Warren Court's so-called judicial activism. Irrespective of the criticism, most of what the Court initiated has nonetheless become settled law, and although subsequent courts have modified many of the cases they have not overturned them to any substantial degree. As a result of the Warren Court's decisions, all but two of the Bill of Rights protections for criminal defendants have been incorporated into the due process clause of the Fourteenth Amendment and applied to the states. The two exceptions are the right to grand jury indictment[11] and the right against excessive bail.[12]

Right to Keep and Bear Arms

As often happens in the world of judicial interpretation of the Constitution, precedents won by one political faction advocating a particular legal position turn out to be useful to other political factions fighting to establish different and sometimes contrary legal positions. An example came to pass on June 28, 2010, when the Supreme Court ruled, in *McDonald v. Chicago*, 130 S.Ct. 3020 (2010), that the Second Amendment right to keep and bear arms applies to the states through the Fourteenth Amendment due process clause. The case involved the City of Chicago's ban on the possession of handguns within the city, and the Court struck down the ban as a violation of the Fourteenth Amendment.

The long and successful march to establish that the Fourteenth Amendment meant that the states could not abridge the protections afforded by the Bill of Rights to all persons, including criminal defendants, such as the right against unreasonable searches and seizures and the rights to a jury trial, to counsel, and so on, also established that the states could not unreasonably abridge the right to keep and bear arms for self-defense. Over the years, the tendency has been for the more liberal groups and associations, such as the American Civil Liberties Union, to fight for defendants' rights against the authority of the state, but, on the other hand, to argue in support of the state's authority to regulate and confiscate firearms. More conservative groups and associations, such as the National Rifle Association, have resisted the expansion of defendants' rights while advocating against the state's authority to regulate and confiscate guns. *McDonald* used the well-established Fourteenth Amendment doctrine of incorporation of the other Amendments of the Bill of Rights to also incorporate the Second Amendment.

McDonald was a five-to-four opinion. Justice Samuel Alito wrote the majority opinion, and he included interesting and striking historical material that highlighted the concern that freed slaves should be able to defend themselves. Part of the historical context follows:

> In debating the Fourteenth Amendment, the 39th Congress referred to the right to keep and bear arms as a fundamental right deserving of protection. Senator Samuel Pomeroy described three "indispensable" "safeguards of liberty under our form of Government." One of these, he said, was the right to keep and bear arms:
>
> "Every man... should have the right to bear arms for the defense of himself and family and his homestead. And if the cabin door of the freedman is broken open and the intruder enters for purposes as vile as were known to slavery, then should a well-loaded musket be in the hand of the occupant to send the polluted wretch to another world, where his wretchedness will forever remain complete."
>
> ... Evidence from the period immediately following the ratification of the Fourteenth Amendment only confirms that the right to keep and bear arms was considered fundamental. In an 1868 speech addressing the disarmament of freedmen, Representative Stevens emphasized the necessity of the right:
>
> "Disarm a community and you rob them of the means of defending life. Take away their weapons of defense and you take away the inalienable right of defending liberty.... The Fourteenth Amendment, now so happily adopted, settles the whole question." And in debating the Civil Rights Act of 1871, Congress routinely referred to the right to keep and bear arms and decried the continued disarmament of blacks in the South.... In sum, it is clear that the Framers and ratifiers of the Fourteenth Amendment counted the right to keep and bear arms among those fundamental rights necessary to our system of ordered liberty. [internal citations omitted]

The Court held that the right of self-defense in the traditional American manner of keeping a handgun was "fundamental to our scheme of ordered liberty." Nonetheless, *McDonald*, in similar fashion to *District of Columbia v. Heller*, 554 U.S. 570 (2008), still allows a state or the federal government to impose reasonable regulations on the possession of firearms.

New York for a long time imposed reasonable regulations on the possession of a firearm in one's home or business. An applicant had to be of good moral character, and to establish that the gun would be handled and stored safely. To carry a firearm in public, the regulations were more stringent. An applicant for an unrestricted license to carry a concealed handgun in public had to show "proper cause," which has been defined as "a special need for self-protection distinguishable from that of the general community." In practice, applicants had to prove that they were special because they handled or traveled with large amounts of cash, negotiable bonds, valuables, prescription drugs, or hazardous materials. General self-defense, by itself, was not a proper cause for a concealed carry permit.

After the Supreme Court decisions in *Heller* and *McDonald*, which established that the Second Amendment's right to keep and bear arms was an individual right like the other rights in the Bill of Rights, New York's carry-permit law was ripe for challenge.

In 2022, two members of the NYS Rifle & Pistol Association applied for carry permits, and were denied. Their Association filed an action in the federal court, in *New York State Rifle & Pistol Association v. Bruen*, 597 U.S. ...(2022), 142 S.Ct. 2111 (2022) claiming that the "special needs" requirement violated their civil rights. The lower courts dismissed their action, but the Supreme Court reversed this decision, holding that New York's law was unconstitutional because it failed to establish that "there is any such historical tradition limiting public carry only to those law-abiding citizens who demonstrate a special need for self-defense." The Court stressed that there "is no other constitutional right that an individual may exercise only after demonstrating to government officers some special need."

In addition to New York, the gun-control laws of four other states—Massachusetts, New Jersey, Maryland, and California—are modified by *Bruen*.

The ruling did not eliminate all regulations, and the Court noted, "Nothing in our opinion should be taken to cast doubt on longstanding prohibitions on the possession of firearms by felons and the mentally ill, or laws forbidding the carrying of firearms in sensitive places such as schools and government buildings, or laws imposing conditions and qualifications on the commercial sale of arms."

This trio of Supreme Court decisions, while clarifying the issues, did not end the public debate over gun control. With over 40,000 people killed each year by guns, and with horrific mass shootings repeatedly occurring at schools, nightclubs, and shopping centers, there are powerful arguments for stronger gun control and for limiting the number of guns available, but there are contrary arguments that armed law-abiding citizens deter and prevent crime and violence, saving uncounted lives and injuries each year. These are uncounted because when people display a gun to deter a crime or violence, such incidents often are not reported.

The national divide over gun control continues. Most states have laws that carry permits must be granted when an applicant satisfies threshold requirements, such as good character, physical ability, safe storage, and training, but five states have laws that allow local authorities to deny carry-permit applications to people who, although they satisfy the same threshold requirements, do not establish "proper cause."

New York State required "proper cause," and *Bruen* declared the New York law unconstitutional. In response, New York passed the Firearms Control Act of 2023. The legislature, taking its cue from the Supreme Court, prohibited the carrying of firearms in sensitive locations such as schools, churches, government buildings, subways, and even Times Square. Going beyond sensitive locations, the New York law made it unlawful to bring a firearm into a building unless the owner of the building granted express permission or posted a permission sign. The new regulations make carrying a licensed gun on a regular basis highly impractical, effectively nullifying the permit, and the sensitive-locations ban is likely to be challenged in the courts. Because of the importance of the issue and the conflicting lower court rulings, these challenges are likely to reach the Supreme Court.

Notes

1 In *Gitlow v. New York*, 268 U.S. 652 (1925), the Supreme Court wrote that the First Amendment right to free speech was a substantive Fourteenth Amendment due process right of liberty and could not be unreasonably abridged by the states. This was not a procedural due process case, but it established the Fourteenth Amendment as constitutional authority for federal judicial review of state infringement of individual rights.
2 *Hebert v. Louisiana*, 272 U.S. 312 (1926).
3 *Benton v. Maryland*, 395 U.S. 784 (1969).
4 367 U.S. 643 (1961); 384 U.S. 436 (1966).
5 *Malloy v. Hogan* and *Griffin v. California* overturned the prior precedents that had been established in *Twining v. New Jersey*, 211 U.S. 78 (1908), and *Adamson v. California*, 332 U.S. 46 (1947).
6 *Brown v. United States*, 356 U.S. 148 (1958).
7 New York Criminal Procedure Law, § 190.40(2)(b).
8 See *Jenkins v. Anderson*, 447 U.S. 231 (1980).
9 *Palko v. Connecticut*, 302 U.S. 319 (1937).
10 *United States v. Robinson*, 485 U.S. 25 (1988).
11 In 1884, in *Hurtado v. California*, 110 U.S. 516, the Supreme Court declined to apply to the states the right to be prosecuted by grand jury indictment. The Court rejected the argument that each right in the Bill of Rights was incorporated into the Fourteenth Amendment.
12 *Schilb v. Kuebel*, 404 U.S. 357 (1971); *United States v. Salerno*, 481 U.S. 739 (1987), upheld the federal Bail Reform Act of 1984, which allows preventive detention without bail of dangerous defendants.

References

Adamson v. California, 332 U.S. 46 (1947), overruled by *Griffin*.
Doyle v. Ohio, 426 U.S. 610 (1976).
Fletcher v. Weir, 455 U.S. 603 (1982).
Griffin v. California, 380 U.S. 609 (1965).
Malloy v. Hogan, 378 U.S. 1 (1964).
State (Oregon) v. Marple, 780 P.2d 772 (1989).

Chapter 5

Principles of Criminal Law

The punishment of individuals is justified as a means of social control primarily because crime is a wrong that harms the public welfare, as distinguished from a wrong that merely harms the interests of a private individual. To be sure, when an individual is unlawfully assaulted, it is both a private wrong and a public wrong. The victim of the assault might sue the assailant for compensation while the government might prosecute and incarcerate the assailant for a crime against the order and security of society.

Theories of punishment have been expounded over the centuries. To oversimplify, a debate has persisted between punishment for the purpose of achieving moral justice and punishment to achieve utilitarian aims. As John Rawls summarized:

> There are two justifications of punishment. What we may call the retributive view is that punishment is justified on the grounds that wrongdoing merits punishment. It is morally fitting that a person who does wrong should suffer in proportion to his wrongdoing. That a criminal should be punished follows from his guilt, and the severity of the appropriate punishment depends on the depravity of his act. The state of affairs where a wrongdoer suffers punishment is morally better than the state of affairs where he does not; and it is better irrespective of any of the consequences of punishing him.
>
> What we may call the utilitarian view holds that on the principle of bygones are bygones, and that only future consequences are material to present decisions, punishment is justifiable only by reference to the probable consequences of maintaining it as one of the devices of the social order. Wrongs committed in the past are, as such, not relevant considerations for deciding what to do. If punishment can be shown to promote effectively the interest of society it is justifiable; otherwise it is not.[1]

The retributive view is illustrated best by the nineteenth-century philosopher Immanuel Kant's categorical imperative argument that even if an unpunished criminal were the only person left in a society, he should nonetheless receive his punishment. As Kant speculated:

> Even if a civil society resolved to dissolve itself with the consent of all its members—as might be supposed in the case of a people inhabiting an island resolving to separate and scatter themselves throughout the whole world—the last murderer lying in the prison ought to be executed before the resolution was carried out. This ought to be done in order that every one may realize the desert of his deeds, and that blood-guiltiness may not remain upon the people; for otherwise they might all be regarded as participators in the murder as a public violation of justice.[2]

DOI: 10.4324/9781003415091-7

The utilitarian philosophers Jeremy Bentham and John Stuart Mill did not believe in punishment as an end in itself and would have rejected the punishment of guilty persons if no future benefit to society would have obtained or if more harm to society than good would have resulted. Nonetheless, even under modern utilitarian theories, justification for the infliction of punishment by society presupposes a level of moral guilt or blameworthiness on the part of the person who committed the criminal act. Clearly, a pure utilitarian doctrine that would allow the punishment of an innocent person in order to accomplish a greater societal good is untenable in a society that values inalienable human rights.

Although utilitarianism is a major component of modern criminal justice, the traditional moral principle of fairness remains a fundamental requirement for a person to be held liable for a crime. For criminal liability, as a general rule, two elements must coincide: first, the person must have committed an *actus reus*, or a voluntary act, and, second, the person must have done so with the *mens rea*, or state of mind, associated with criminal culpability.

Actus Reus

The voluntary act might consist of a physical movement, such as striking a blow, pointing a weapon at another person, taking property, driving a car, filing a document, or sending a letter or an e-mail. Also, a voluntary act might consist of a verbal statement, such as an order, a threat, an offer, a solicitation, or an agreement. Verbal statements can constitute crimes; however, a criminal act is not a mere thought or an intention. People can think all the evil thoughts they desire as long as they do not act upon them.

Involuntary physical movements cannot constitute a criminal act; for example, a person who suffers an epileptic seizure or is pushed into another person is not criminally liable for injuries that result. Also, a person's status is not an act. In *Robinson v. California*, 370 U.S. 660 (1962), the U.S. Supreme Court ruled that a state law could not make it a crime for a person to be "addicted to the use of narcotics." Although a person could be guilty of possession of narcotics, it is unconstitutional to make a person a criminal for their health status and without requiring an *actus reus*.

A voluntary act can include the failure to perform a required act, such as a lifeguard who fails to attempt to save a drowning person, parents who neglect to obtain necessary medical assistance for their child, or a citizen who fails to pay income taxes. To be criminally liable for such an omission one must have a legal duty to act and the physical capability to act. The legal duty can arise from the following:

1. Statute
2. Contract
3. Voluntary assumption (Good Samaritan)
4. Creating peril
5. Status, such as:
    a. Parent
    b. Guardian
    c. Trustee
    d. Employer
    e. Landlord
    f. Public servant

A voluntary act can include the actual or constructive possession of an object, even without physically holding the object, such as when the individual exercises dominion and control over property. Examples might occur when a person orders another person to move or secure contraband, electronically transfers money, or keeps property in a safety-deposit box.

Mens Rea

To hold a person responsible for criminal conduct, our traditions, values, and law require proof of the criminal's *mens rea* ("guilty mind"), or culpable mental state. As Supreme Court Justice Robert Jackson wrote in *Morissette v. United States*, 342 U.S. 246 (1952):

> The contention that an injury can amount to a crime only when inflicted by intention is no provincial or transient notion. It is as universal and persistent in mature systems of law as belief in freedom of the human will and a consequent ability and duty of the normal individual to choose between good and evil. A relation between some mental element and punishment for a harmful act is almost as instinctive as the child's familiar exculpatory "But I didn't mean to," and has afforded the rational basis for a tardy and unfinished substitution of deterrence and reformation in place of retaliation and vengeance as the motivation for public prosecution. Unqualified acceptance of this doctrine by English common law in the Eighteenth Century was indicated by Blackstone's sweeping statement that to constitute any crime there must first be a "vicious will."
>
> Crime, as a compound concept, generally constituted only from concurrence of an evil-meaning mind with an evil-doing hand, was congenial to an intense individualism and took deep and early root in American soil.

A person who commits a voluntary act without the requisite culpable mental state cannot be held criminally liable. General categories of *mens rea* include the following:

- *Intentional*—Conscious objective is to cause a particular result or to engage in particular conduct
- *Knowing*—Person is aware that his conduct is of such a nature or that such circumstance exists
- *Reckless*—Person is aware of and consciously disregards a substantial risk
- *Criminally negligent*—Person fails to perceive a substantial and unjustifiable risk that result will occur. The failure to perceive must be a gross deviation from what a reasonable person would observe in the situation.

Criminal charges for the same voluntary act will vary depending on the state of mind of the actor. Intentional and knowing acts are treated more seriously than reckless or criminally negligent acts. If a person throws a baseball at another person who is not looking and the baseball strikes that person on the head, killing him, the thrower could be convicted of murder, manslaughter, or criminal negligent homicide, or could face no charge, depending on his state of mind at the time he threw the baseball.

If the thrower intentionally threw the baseball with the conscious objective of killing the victim, the thrower would be guilty of intentional murder, a crime with a penalty of 25 years to life imprisonment or, in some states, the death penalty.

If the thrower was aware that the victim was not looking and threw the baseball, not with the intent to injure but in order to surprise or frighten the victim, the thrower might be deemed guilty of reckless manslaughter, a felony usually carrying a prison sentence of about 15 years.

If the thrower failed to perceive the danger but unreasonably assumed the victim would see and catch the baseball, the thrower might be deemed guilty of criminally negligent homicide, a felony usually carrying a maximum one- to three-year prison term.

If the thrower reasonably thought the victim would see the baseball coming and would catch it, the incident might be deemed an accident caused by ordinary negligence, which could be the basis for a civil lawsuit for monetary damages but not criminal charges.

The facts and circumstances surrounding an incident generally determine which category of liability will apply. For example, a person driving a car within the speed limit but carelessly through a stop sign, thereby causing a collision, might be liable for negligence in a civil lawsuit. However, if the person had been driving excessively above the speed limit, he would likely be guilty of, at least, criminal negligence. Furthermore, if the person had been intoxicated or had greatly exceeded the speed limit, he might be guilty of recklessness.

Some forms of reckless conduct are so dangerous that they are deemed the equivalent of intentional conduct. If a criminal fires a gun at a crowd of people without the intention of killing any particular person, but he does so under circumstances evincing a depraved indifference to human life, recklessly creating a grave risk of death to another person and thereby causing the death of another person, his conduct carries the same level of culpability as intentional conduct. Setting a building on fire while knowing people are sleeping therein might be another example of depraved indifference reckless murder.

Some intentional crimes require the additional element of a specific intent to cause a certain result. It is not the intent to perform a physical act but the intended result that matters. Larceny is a specific intent crime. It requires more than the intentional carrying away of another person's property; it also requires a specific intent to deprive that person of the property for a substantial amount of time or to keep the property for oneself or a third person. To pick up an unattended umbrella or briefcase in order to take it to the lost-and-found is an intentional physical act but not a specific intent criminal act.

Forgery is a specific intent crime. A person might forge the signature of another on the back of a check, but this must be for the purpose of defrauding, deceiving, or injuring the other. If the person forges the check for convenience only in order to deposit it in the other person's bank account, not to appropriate the money for himself, no crime has occurred.

Bribery is a specific intent crime. A person might give money to a police officer as an after-the-fact reward for doing something good without committing the felony of bribery, which requires that the person give the money with the specific intent to influence the officer's forthcoming action or exercise of discretion. Giving a reward to a police officer might be the lesser crime of giving unlawful gratuities, a misdemeanor, but it is not bribery.

Specific intent crimes require concurrence of the specific intent and the voluntary act. For example, burglary is a specific intent crime that requires the person to knowingly enter or remain unlawfully in a building with the intent to commit a crime therein. The intent must arise at the time of the unlawful entry or at the time the person decides to unlawfully remain. If a person unlawfully enters a building with the intent only to trespass in the building and, while they are there, a subsequent opportunity arises to steal something, the theft will not turn the trespass into a burglary. The person would be guilty of the separate crimes of trespass and larceny.

Concurrence of specific intent with the voluntary act is a requirement in prosecutions for larceny by false promise. A person who borrows money from another, such as by using a credit card, but then does not pay back the money as promised, cannot be guilty of larceny unless he had the specific intent not to repay the debt from its inception. Persons who borrow money with the intention to pay it back but who are unable to do so are not guilty of larceny but of failure to repay a debt. However, a person who does not intend to repay a loan when he takes it out can be guilty of larceny.

The concurrence requirement must be adjusted when the perpetrator of a criminal act causes an injury but not the intended injury. Under the doctrine of transferred intent, a legal fiction is employed to satisfy the concurrence requirement. When a criminal intentionally attempts to injure person A but his action results in an unintended injury to person B, the intent to injure A is transferred to B. For example, if the criminal shoots a firearm at a potential victim but misses, and the bullet strikes an innocent bystander, the criminal will be guilty of the intentional assault of the innocent bystander, even though that was not his intention.

Transferred intent might also apply when a criminal steals property from person A, whom he believes is the owner of the property, but the property, in fact, belongs to person B. Although the criminal intended to deprive A of the property, he will be guilty of depriving B of the property.

The transferred intent doctrine only applies to similar crimes; therefore, if a criminal throws a rock with the intent to cause property damage but instead strikes a person, causing physical injury, the dissimilar intents may not be transferred. In such an instance, the criminal might be guilty of recklessly causing the physical injury, a crime considered less serious than intentional assault.

Causation

Whereas concurrence addresses the link between the *actus reus* and the *mens rea*, causation addresses the link between the defendant's *actus reus* and the harm that results. No argument can stand that people should be guilty for harms they did not cause, and the prosecution has the burden of proving causation beyond a reasonable doubt. In some cases, it is a simple matter. Showing that a defendant struck a victim in the face with a bat and the victim's face immediately swelled is a clear case of direct causation. On the other hand, showing that six months after being hit with the bat the same victim died of a brain hemorrhage is not such a clear case of causation. Other evidence could establish the causation, such as testimony that the victim was continuously hospitalized from the time of the assault to his death. On the other hand, the victim could have died from other causes.

Usually, medical examiners or coroners testify to their opinion about the cause of death. To be sufficient to prove causation, their opinions must be based on facts that establish the causation to a reasonable degree of medical certainty. The opinion may not be based on speculation or conjecture. Merely stating that it was possible that the assault with the bat caused the death would be insufficient.

Legal causation, or what has been termed the *proximate cause*, requires the establishment of a sufficient causal link between an act and a result. The premise that "but for" the defendant's act the harm would not have occurred is insufficient by itself to establish legal causation. The sufficiency of a causal link necessary to find a defendant legally liable is a matter of a degree and judgment. Contrasting examples can illustrate how judgments are made and lines are drawn. If a robber enters a store, takes money from the cash register, and flees without injuring anyone, but the store proprietor then leaves the store to report the robbery and while walking to the police station is struck by a car and killed, the robber cannot be held to have caused the death. The argument that "but for" the robbery the proprietor would not have walked to the police station would be insufficient to establish proximate causation. On the other hand, had the proprietor chased the robber in order to retrieve his property and while running through the streets been struck by a car and killed, the robber could be held accountable because his act was the proximate cause of the death.

Most often, the determining question in whether an act was the proximate cause of an injury is whether the injury was foreseeable. In the above examples, it was foreseeable that the store proprietor might give chase, and the robber assumed that risk; however, it was not foreseeable that the proprietor would be struck by a car while walking to the police station. The latter was too remote from the robbery for a direct causal link to be found. The car that struck the proprietor while he walked to the police station was an unexpected intervening factor that broke the chain of causation.

Not all intervening factors break the chain of causation between the triggering act and the injury. If the intervening factor was a reasonably foreseeable result of the defendant's triggering act, the intervening factor will not relieve the defendant of liability. In a stabbing case in which the victim was taken to a hospital emergency room and while under treatment died because of an error committed during the emergency treatment, the defendant who stabbed the victim could be guilty of murder because the intervening error by the medical personnel was a foreseeable consequence of the stabbing. On the other hand, had the victim been admitted to the hospital and several days later died because a nurse injected the victim with the wrong drug, which had been intended for a different patient, the defendant/stabber would not be liable for the death because the unexpected intervening act of the nurse broke the chain of causation.

An accidental act that is not deemed unlawful cannot be the predicate for criminal liability. The triggering act that puts in motion a chain of causation leading to criminal liability must be an unlawful act, and it also must be the proximate cause of the harm.

Proximate cause was the issue in *People v. Armitage*, 194 Cal. App.3d 405 (1987). Armitage was convicted of operating a boat while intoxicated and causing the death of his friend Peter Maskovich, a passenger in the boat. He admitted that he and Peter had been drinking. He admitted operating the boat at a high speed and zigzagging until the boat capsized. Both men held onto the overturned boat, but Peter abandoned the boat and attempted to swim to shore. He drowned while doing so.

Armitage appealed his conviction on the grounds that his actions were not the proximate cause of Peter's death. He claimed that Peter's decision to swim to shore constituted a break in the natural and continuous sequence of events arising from the unlawful operation of the boat, thereby relieving him of responsibility. However, the court upheld the conviction, stating:

> In criminal law a victim's predictable effort to escape a peril created by the defendant is not considered a superseding cause of the ensuing injury or death.... Here Armitage, through his misconduct, placed the intoxicated victim in the middle of a dangerous river in the early morning hours clinging to an overturned boat. The fact that the panic-stricken victim recklessly abandoned the boat and tried to swim ashore was not a wholly abnormal reaction to the perceived peril of drowning.

Proximate cause was also the issue in *People v. Kibbe*, 35 N.Y.2d 407 (1974). Defendants Barry Kibbe and Roy Krall had been drinking in several Rochester taverns with the victim, George Stafford, who was thoroughly inebriated and flashing $100 bills. Kibbe and Krall gave Stafford a ride in Kibbe's automobile. Krall drove the car while Kibbe demanded Stafford's money. Kibbe slapped Stafford several times, took his money, and compelled him to lower his trousers and to take off his shoes. When the defendants were satisfied that Stafford had no more money on his person, the defendants forced Stafford to exit the vehicle.

About 9:30 PM, as Stafford was thrust from the car, his trousers were still down around his ankles, he was shoeless, and he had been stripped of any outer clothing. His eyeglasses remained in the vehicle. The temperature was near zero; there was snow on both sides of the roadway and no artificial lighting on the rural highway.

About 10:00 PM, a college student driving a pickup truck saw Stafford sitting in the middle of the road with his hands up in the air. The driver did not have time to react before his vehicle struck and killed Stafford.

The defendants were convicted of depraved indifference reckless murder and appealed on the grounds that causation had not been proven.

The New York Court of Appeals disagreed and affirmed the conviction, holding:

> We subscribe to the requirement that the defendants' actions must be a *sufficiently direct cause* of the ensuing death before there can be any imposition of criminal liability, and recognize, of course, that this standard is greater than that required to serve as a basis for tort liability…. [W]e conclude that their activities… were a sufficiently direct cause of the death…. Kibbe and Krall left a helplessly intoxicated man without his eyeglasses in a position from which, because of these attending circumstances, he could not extricate himself and whose condition was such that he could not even protect himself from the elements. The defendants do not dispute the fact that their conduct evinced a depraved indifference to human life which created a grave risk of death, but rather they argue that it was just as likely that Stafford would be miraculously rescued by a Good Samaritan. We cannot accept such an argument. There can be little doubt but that Stafford would have frozen to death in his state of undress had he remained on the shoulder of the road. The only alternative left to him was the highway, which in his condition, for one reason or another, clearly foreboded the probability of his resulting death.

Felony Murder

Under some circumstances, the wrongful causation of a death allows for an adjustment to the *mens rea* for criminal liability. Most states have passed felony-murder statutes that provide that a person who, while committing a particular felony, causes the death of an innocent person is guilty of murder even though the felon had no intention of causing the death. In effect, the intent to commit the underlying felony is transferred to the unintended victim injured as a result of the felony. This type of transferred intent is more expansive than the more common transfer of intent when a perpetrator intending to injure A injures B instead. In felony murder, the underlying intent is not to assault or kill but to commit another crime. The *mens rea* of the underlying felony is imputed to the homicide. This kind of attenuated transferred intent has been deemed appropriate for the utilitarian purpose of deterring dangerous conduct.

Typical crimes designated as predicates for felony murder include the following:

- Burglary
- Arson
- Robbery
- Kidnapping

* Escape
* Rape (forcible)
* Sodomy (forcible)

Felony-murder statutes are not uniform. Forty states have some form of the rule. Some states, rather than using specific felonies, such as robbery, burglary, and so on, use more general designations, such as "inherently dangerous felonies."[3]

In any case, the victim of the felony murder need not be the intended target of the underlying predicate felony; for example, he may be an innocent bystander or a police officer attempting to apprehend the felon. The usual case occurs when the perpetrator causes the death of a nonparticipant in the crime. To wit, a perpetrator of a robbery who points a gun at a victim and thereby causes the victim to suffer a fatal heart attack should be criminally liable for the death. Also, a kidnapper who ties up and gags a victim, thereby causing the victim to suffocate, should be criminally liable for murder.

In some cases, a third party inflicts the fatal injury, but the felon is nevertheless responsible for it. In *People v. Hernandez and Santana*, 82 N.Y.2d 309 (1993), the defendants planned to rob a man by pretending to sell him drugs and luring him into a building stairwell to complete the transaction. They did not know that the intended victim was an undercover state trooper, wearing a transmitter and backed up by fellow officers.

In the building, Hernandez pointed a gun at the undercover trooper's head. A fight ensued in which the trooper fired his gun. Hernandez, still armed, ran into a courtyard where he encountered members of the police backup team. He aimed his gun at one of the troopers, and the troopers began firing. As a result, one trooper was fatally shot in the head by a bullet fired by one of the other troopers.

Hernandez and Santana were convicted of felony murder for the death. They appealed their convictions on the grounds that neither one of them fired the fatal shot. The New York Court of Appeals denied their claim and affirmed their convictions, holding that the trooper's death was a foreseeable result of the robbery:

> It was foreseeable that police would try to thwart crime, and Hernandez was aware that police were on the scene at the point he resisted arrest and remained armed.... It is simply implausible for defendants to claim that defendants could not have foreseen a bullet going astray when Hernandez provoked a gun battle outside a residential building in an urban area.

Accomplice Liability

People v. Hernandez and Santana also illustrates the doctrine of accomplice liability. Although Santana did not resist arrest, surrendered, and was unarmed, he was convicted of the felony murder because he was acting in concert with Hernandez and was equally responsible for the results they caused when they embarked on the robbery. He was responsible even though he had no intention to engage in a gun battle with the police.

An affirmative defense was available to Santana if he could prove by a preponderance of the evidence that: (1) he did not cause the death, (2) he was unarmed, (3) he had no reason to believe that his accomplice was armed, and (4) he had no reason to believe that his accomplice would engage in conduct likely to result in death or serious physical injury. However, he knew Hernandez was armed, and the nature of the robbery itself gave him reason to believe Hernandez would engage in dangerous conduct; therefore, he could not establish the affirmative defense.

Accomplice liability often arises when two criminals, intending to commit a crime, are present at the occurrence; however, an accomplice need not be present at the occurrence of the crime. When one person engages in conduct that constitutes a crime, another person is criminally liable for such conduct when, acting with the mental culpability required for the commission thereof, he solicits, requests, commands, importunes, or intentionally aids such person to engage in such conduct.[4] For example, if the owner of a building, in order to collect on an insurance policy, pays an arsonist to set the building on fire, the owner will be as guilty as the arsonist who actually sets the fire.

Accomplice liability need not involve a monetary benefit for either party; it may arise from other motives, such as a love triangle, a desire for revenge, or a desire to eliminate a spouse. If the planner of a burglary provides a plan to burglars who are to carry it out, and it happens that during the burglary one of the burglars kills an innocent person, the planner will be equally guilty of the murder.

In traditional common law, strict rules differentiated principals and accessories to a crime. Principals actually committed the crime or were present when the crime was committed. Accessories were either accessories before the fact or accessories after the fact. The former helped the principal before the crime; the latter helped the principal after the crime. Because at common law felonies were punishable by death, it was important to separate those persons with lesser culpability. Principals could be hanged; accessories would usually receive a lesser sentence.

Under modern penal statutes, thousands of felonies have been created, and the death penalty is authorized only for the most egregious crimes; therefore, the incentive to distinguish principals from accessories has been significantly reduced. Principals and accessories before the fact have merged. Accessories after the fact are not prosecuted for the principal crime but are charged with separate crimes, such as hindering prosecution, harboring a fugitive, or tampering with evidence.

Death of Accomplice

While most states hold that the person killed must be a nonparticipant in the underlying felony, some states hold that a defendant can be charged with felony murder for causing the death of an accomplice or co-felon.

An unusual case occurred in 2022 in Alabama, when a prison inmate, Corey White, who was serving a life sentence for murder, convinced a prison guard, Vicky White, no relation, to help him escape. They were romantically involved, and after the escape, Vicky stayed with Corey, and they traveled together for ten days trying to avoid capture. They made a suicide pact in which Corey vowed to shoot it out with the police if they were caught. Then, on the tenth day of their escape, U.S. marshals located and attempted to arrest them. The couple fled in their car, and a high-speed chase ensued. When their car crashed and the marshals approached the car, Vicky committed suicide by shooting herself in the head. Corey surrendered without a fight.

Corey was convicted of felony murder because his escape caused the death of Vicky even though she died by her own hand. He was guilty also because in Alabama felony murder applies to the death of co-felons. In most other states the decedent must be a nonparticipant.

Strict Liability Crimes

As modern industrial society has developed, legislatures have passed strict liability statutes without regard to *mens rea*. These statutes include regulatory and public welfare types of offenses that address problems created by industrial activities, hazardous materials, and new technologies. A person in control of hazardous materials will be held responsible if those materials leak from their containers and pollute the environment—no intent, knowledge, recklessness, or negligence is required for liability.

Violations of traffic regulations are strict liability offenses. When a driver goes through a red light it does not matter that they did not notice the light, and when a driver exceeds the speed limit it does not matter that they thought they were driving within it. More serious traffic violations, such as driving while intoxicated, might also be considered strict liability, though that is a debatable proposition.

As a matter of general practice, when people who do not know or believe they are intoxicated drive while intoxicated, they are deemed strictly liable and guilty of drunk driving. On the other hand, intoxicated driving, arguably, is not a strict liability crime. A drunk driver, although not intending to drive while drunk, nonetheless intends to drink and also intends to drive. These intentional acts set in motion the chain of events leading to the unintended intoxicated driving; therefore, driving while intoxicated is not wholly a strict liability crime. Also, it might be argued that a person who drinks before driving acts recklessly by disregarding the risk that the alcohol might cause intoxication. In either case, the defined mental state of a drunk driver is not easily determined. To simplify matters, driving while intoxicated is treated as a strict liability crime, which, in effect, means that the prosecution does not have to prove that the driver intended to get drunk.

Statutory crimes designed for the protection of minors are generally strict liability. For example, a bartender who violates a statute against selling alcohol to minors will be guilty even though the minor presented fraudulent proof of age to the bartender. A person who engages in sexual intercourse with a minor is guilty of statutory rape even though the person believed the minor was an adult. Under statutory rape laws, a minor could have lied about her age, but that would not be a viable defense for the accused person.

Problem

Jim and Ellen agree to kill Ellen's husband, Harry, so they can have a love affair. They go to Harry's office to kill him and to rob the safe to take all the money so they can fly away to Rio de Janeiro. Jim puts a gun to Harry's head to make him open the safe. After Harry opens the safe, Jim intentionally points the gun at him and fires. Harry ducks and the bullet hits Ellen instead, killing her. While Harry stares in disbelief, Jim removes the money from the safe and starts to run down the stairs. At that point, Harry's loyal secretary appears and tries to stop Jim. As Jim runs, he unintentionally bumps into her, and she falls down the stairs, bumps her head, and dies.

Questions

1. May Jim be lawfully convicted of Ellen's murder?
2. If so, on what theory can Jim be lawfully convicted of Ellen's murder?
3. May Jim be lawfully convicted of Ellen's murder even though he did not intend to kill her?
4. May Jim be lawfully convicted of Ellen's murder on the basis of a felony-murder theory?
5. Is it correct to state that Jim may not be lawfully convicted of the secretary's murder because she died as the result of an accident?
6. May Jim be lawfully convicted of the secretary's murder?

7. If so, may Jim be lawfully convicted of the secretary's murder on the legal theory of transferred intent?
8. If so, may Jim be lawfully convicted of the secretary's murder on the legal theory of felony murder?
9. Could Ellen be lawfully convicted of anything?
10. If Ellen had been taken to hospital and resuscitated, could she lawfully be convicted of the secretary's murder?

Notes

1 Rawls, John, Two concepts of rules, *Philosophical Review*, 64(1), 3, 1955.
2 Kant, Immanuel, *The Philosophy of Law: An Exposition of the Fundamental Principles of Jurisprudence as the Science of Right*, translated by W. Hastie, Clark, Edinburgh, 1887.
3 *State v. Stewart*, 663 A.2d 912 (R.I. 1995).
4 New York State Penal Law, § 20.00.

References

People v. Kibbe, 35 N.Y.2d 407 (1974).
People v. Hernandez and Santana, 82 N.Y.2d 309 (1993).
Tennessee v. Garner, 471 U.S. 1 (1985).

Crimes and Punishments

Individually defined crimes have been enacted into statute in order to provide notice and clarity, and the statutes have been codified into cohesive penal law systems to provide an understanding of the applicable principles and purposes of the law. The purposes of a penal law are to:

1. Proscribe conduct that unjustifiably or inexcusably causes or threatens substantial harm to individual or public interests.
2. Give fair warning of the nature of the conduct proscribed and of the sentences authorized upon conviction.
3. Define the act or omission and the accompanying mental state that constitute each offense.
4. Differentiate on reasonable grounds between serious and minor offenses and prescribe proportionate penalties.
5. Provide for appropriate public response to particular offenses, including consideration of consequences for the victim, including the victim's family, and the community.
6. Ensure public safety by preventing the commission of offenses through the deterrent influence of the sentences authorized, the rehabilitation of those convicted, the promotion of their successful and productive reentry and reintegration into society, and their confinement when required in the interests of public protection.

The elements and principles associated with the individually defined crimes selected below are applicable to a wide array of similar and related crimes.

Assault and Self-defense

Simple third-degree assault is a common crime committed when a person with intent to cause physical injury to another person causes such injury to such person or to a third person. It is a misdemeanor, which carries a penalty of up to one year in prison.

It is also committed when a person recklessly causes physical injury to another person, or when a person with criminal negligence causes physical injury to another person by means of a deadly weapon or dangerous instrument.

Deadly weapons are weapons designed primarily to injure, and include loaded firearms, switchblade knives, gravity knives, metal knuckles, daggers, and blackjacks.

A dangerous instrument can be any instrument, article, or substance, including a vehicle, which, under the circumstances in which it is used, is readily capable of causing death or

DOI: 10.4324/9781003415091-8

other serious physical injury. The instrument may have perfectly legitimate functions, but when used as a weapon with a culpable mental state, it is used unlawfully.

A baseball bat, a wrench, or a hammer can be a dangerous instrument when it is used as a weapon. A pen used to stick in a person's eye, the ground used to bang a person's head against, a handkerchief used to gag a kidnap victim, and steel-toed construction boots used to kick a person, are all dangerous instruments.

The use of a deadly weapon or dangerous instrument will raise the degree of the crime.

Assault second-degree occurs when a person with intent to cause physical injury causes such injury by means of a deadly weapon or dangerous instrument.

Assault second-degree occurs when a person intends serious physical injury and causes serious physical injury.

Assault first-degree occurs when the two methods of second-degree are combined, and thus it occurs when a person intends serious physical injury and causes serious physical injury by means of a deadly weapon or dangerous instrument.

Second-degree assault is usually a D felony with a maximum sentence of seven years in prison.

First-degree assault is usually a B felony with a maximum sentence of twenty-five years in prison.

Self-defense

A person may lawfully use physical force to defend himself or a third person from what he reasonably believes to be the use or imminent use of unlawful physical force by another person, unless the first person was the initial aggressor. However, even if the first person was the initial aggressor, he may use physical force if he withdraws from the encounter and communicates his withdrawal but the other person persists in continuing to use or threaten physical force.

Homicide

Homicide is conduct by a person that causes the death of another person; however, homicide is not necessarily a crime. Murder, manslaughter, or criminally negligent homicide is a crime, but negligently causing the death of a person might only constitute the civil tort of wrongful death. Furthermore, some intentional homicides are justifiable, as in cases of self-defense, while others are lawful, as per a warrant to execute a court-ordered death sentence or under military authority.

Murder is the most culpable type of homicide. Under English common law, a conviction for murder required proof of premeditation or malice aforethought. Sir Edward Coke defined murder as follows:

> When a man of sound memory and of the age of discretion unlawfully kills any reasonable creature in being, and under the King's peace, with malice aforethought, either express or implied by law, the death taking place within a year and a day.[1]

Common-law premeditation or malice aforethought required a finding that the defendant engaged in planning and an exercise of unfettered will, such as lying in wait to attack, preparing a weapon, or poisoning. In contrast, modern statutes generally employ such words as *deliberate*, *willful*, *purposeful*, or *intentional*, and most courts have held that such culpable mental states can be formulated within a few seconds.[2]

Modern statutes and courts draw distinctions between levels of murderous culpability. Some states distinguish between first-degree and second-degree murder, with the latter including killings that did not involve premeditation, such as during a spontaneous fight. Other states use manslaughter statutes to define homicides of lesser grades than murder; for example, an intentional murder may be reduced to manslaughter when the defendant unlawfully killed another because of an understandable provocation, or the defendant acted in the heat of passion. The foremost example of the heat of passion defense arises when a husband finds his wife *in flagrante delicto* committing adultery. Even if the husband intentionally kills his wife or her paramour, the murder will be reduced to manslaughter as long as certain conditions are present:

> In order to reduce the crime from murder to manslaughter, it is necessary that it should be shown that the prisoner found the deceased in the very act of adultery with his wife. I do not mean to say that the prisoner must stand by and witness the actual copulative conjunction between the guilty parties. If the prisoner saw the deceased in bed with his wife, or saw him leaving the bed of the wife, or if he found them together in such position as to indicate with reasonable certainty to a rational mind that they had just committed the adulterous act... it will be sufficient to satisfy the requirements of the law in this regard; and if, under such circumstances, he then and there struck the mortal blow, his offense would amount to manslaughter only.[3]

Other requirements for a heat of passion defense include the following:

1. Husband must have been lawfully married to the wife.
2. Husband must find the wife and her paramour *in flagrante delicto* or immediately after adulterous act (learning of past adultery does not satisfy this criterion).
3. Husband must actually experience the heat of passion.
4. No cooling-off period has occurred between the discovery and the killing.

Under several modern penal law statutes, the provocation and heat of passion defenses have been renamed as the *defense of extreme emotional disturbance*, which allows for a defense when the defendant acted under the influence of extreme emotional disturbance for which there was a reasonable explanation or excuse, the reasonableness of which is to be determined from the viewpoint of a person in the defendant's situation under the circumstances as the defendant believed them to be.[4]

Accordingly, the courts have liberalized the requirements to sustain the defense. Some courts have sustained the emotional disturbance defense when the provocations comprised mere words, such as taunts or bragging about adultery, while other courts have allowed a longer time period between the provocation and the homicide.[5]

The distinction between murder and manslaughter is also apparent when considering felony-murder statutes and reckless manslaughter statutes. Felony-murder statutes incorporate the underlying crimes of robbery, rape, burglary, arson, and kidnapping, each of which involve some level of intentionality; in contrast, manslaughter by reckless conduct excludes intentionality because the actor disregards facts and risks.

Despite the law's rational categorization of homicides, it must be kept in mind that juries can look at the circumstances of a provocation or heat of passion defense and decide to acquit the defendant entirely. Such determinations are within the realm of American justice. In earlier American law until the 1960s, some states allowed an honor defense when a husband killed his wife's lover, thereby making the killing justifiable and thus wholly innocent. Texas followed the wholly innocent standard, while other states imposed nominal punishments;[6] for example, Delaware limited punishment for an honor killing to a $1000 fine and one year in prison.[7]

Manslaughter

Manslaughter statutes define homicides of lesser culpability than murder.

Manslaughter in the first degree occurs when a person, not with intent to cause death but with intent to cause serious physical injury to another person, causes the death of such person or of a third person. For example, it is manslaughter in the first degree when a person punches another person and that person falls down, hits his head, and dies.

Manslaughter in the second degree occurs when a person recklessly causes the death of another person. Recklessness occurs when a person commits a voluntary act while he or she is aware of its risk and danger but consciously disregards the risk and danger. For example, it is manslaughter in the second degree if a person driving a car sees a red light but speeds through it, causing a collision and the death of another person.

Criminally negligent homicide occurs when a person commits a voluntary act while failing to perceive a substantial risk or danger, thereby causing the death of another person. The risk must be of such a nature and degree that the failure to perceive it constitutes a gross deviation from the standard of care that a reasonable person would observe in the situation, such as when a person driving a car does not see a red light because he is looking in the backseat, playing with the radio dials, or texting on his cell phone.

A distinction between criminal negligence and civil negligence is that the defendant's action violated a statute and constituted an offense. For example, when a fire occurs in a premises—a restaurant, factory, or movie theatre—and people are injured or killed, the owner may be civilly liable for negligently causing the fire. However, if the owner had violated safety-code statutes, by locking the exit doors or not having exit lights, and such violations contributed to the deaths, the owner might be guilty of criminally negligent homicide.

Justification

Whereas heat of passion, provocation, and extreme emotional disturbance defenses excuse otherwise intentional criminal conduct and result in a lesser degree of responsibility, the justification defenses of self-defense or lawful arrest completely exonerate the actor. Subject to state variations and provisos, a person may use physical force to defend himself or a third party from what he reasonably believes to be the use or imminent use of unlawful physical force. Furthermore, a person, subject to variations and provisos, may intentionally use deadly physical force and thereby cause death or serious physical injury when he reasonably believes such to be necessary to prevent or terminate:

- The use of imminent deadly physical force against himself or a third party
- Robbery
- Burglary
- Arson
- Kidnapping

- Escape
- Rape (forcible)
- Sodomy (forcible)

A person may use physical force to apprehend someone who has committed a crime, and deadly physical force to apprehend someone who is in immediate flight from the commission of:

- Murder
- Manslaughter
- Robbery
- Rape (forcible)
- Sodomy (forcible)

For the person to be justified in the use of such force to arrest a person, the crime must in fact have been committed by the person apprehended.

On the other hand, peace officers have greater powers to use justifiable physical force to apprehend criminals. Peace officers will be justified when they act if they have reasonable cause to believe a suspect committed a crime; therefore, an officer might be justified even when the suspect did not in fact commit the crime. Furthermore, peace officers have much broader arrest powers; they can use deadly physical force to apprehend a suspect who committed a felony involving the imminent use or threat of violence or who is armed with a firearm or deadly weapon. In addition, peace officers can use deadly physical force to apprehend suspects for certain felonies that may not have involved the use of imminent physical force. For example, some states authorize such force for a peace officer to apprehend suspects for the commission of the following crimes:

- Burglary first degree
- Arson
- Kidnapping
- Escape first degree

The justification of the reasonable and necessary use of force to apprehend a suspect does not allow reckless conduct by a peace officer with respect to innocent persons whom the officer is not seeking to arrest or retain in custody.

For all persons, a distinction must be drawn between using deadly physical force in self-defense and using it to apprehend a suspect. For example, if an actor fires a gun in justifiable self-defense but the shot misses its intended target and strikes an innocent bystander, the actor is, nonetheless, exonerated. However, if the actor fires a gun to apprehend a suspect and the shot misses and strikes an innocent bystander, the actor may be guilty of recklessly causing injury to the bystander. Depending on the extent of the injury, the conduct might amount, respectively, to misdemeanor assault for physical injury, felonious assault for serious physical injury, or manslaughter for death.

Citizen's Arrest

Using physical force to apprehend a suspected criminal is a precarious undertaking for both police officers and private citizens. While a police officer may make an arrest and use reasonable force on the basis of probable cause that the suspected criminal committed a crime, a private citizen making a citizen's arrest must meet a higher standard. For the private citizen to be justified, the suspected criminal must have, in fact, committed the crime. If it turns out that the charges against the suspect are dismissed or he is found not guilty after trial, he may sue the citizen who arrested him for false arrest and other damages. Furthermore, if it is determined that the arrest was unlawful, it follows that any physical force used will also be deemed unlawful, which could subject the citizen to criminal charges.

These principles were dramatically illustrated in the case in Georgia against three white men, Gregory McMichael, 65, his son, Travis McMichael, 35, and Roddy Bryan, 51, for the February 2020 murder of Ahmaud Arbery, a 25-year-old African-American man. At the Georgia trial, evidence showed that Gregory and Travis believed Arbery to be a burglar. There had been thefts in the area and Arbery had been seen wandering around a residential construction site. The defendants armed themselves with a Remington shotgun and a .357 Magnum revolver, and attempted to arrest Arbery. He ran, and they chased him with their truck.

The chase passed the home of Roddie Bryan, who got in his truck and joined in, and it went on for four to five minutes until Travis got out of his truck, and pointed a shotgun at Arbery. When Arbery tried to defend himself, Travis shot him in the chest. Although wounded, Arbery grabbed for the gun, and Travis shot him two more times. Arbery died in the street.

The three men were charged with murder under Georgia law.

In their defense, they claimed justification because they were making a lawful citizen's arrest for the felony of burglary, and Arbery had resisted the arrest and violently attacked Travis, who acted in self-defense.

Under Georgia law, persons threatened with deadly force while making a proper citizen's arrest can use deadly force to defend themselves, and since Georgia is a stand-your-ground state, they are allowed to use deadly force against the aggressor without any obligation to retreat from the confrontation.

The defendants' justification and stand-your-ground arguments both rested on the arrest being lawful, and since the arrest was deemed unlawful because it was not proven that Arbery had, in fact, committed a burglary, their justification argument for the use of deadly physical force collapsed.

Travis McMichael was convicted of malicious murder, and all three defendants were convicted of felony murder. Gregory McMichael and Roddy Bryan had not pulled the trigger, but they had acted as accomplices of Travis and were equally guilty. They were all sentenced to life in prison.

After the state trial, the U.S. Justice Department prosecuted the defendants for their actions under 18 U.S.C. § 249 for federal civil rights violations on the basis of evidence that they each harbored a racial animus against black people, and on the theory that, but for Arbery being black, the defendants would not have assumed he was a criminal, chased him down, and shot him.

The defendants were convicted of hate crimes, interfering with civil rights, attempted kidnapping, and use of weapons. The McMichaels were sentenced to life in prison, and Bryan to thirty-five years in prison. Their sentences were to run concurrently with their Georgia state sentences.

Their convictions by two independent, sovereign jurisdictions, Georgia and the United States, further confirm the wisdom that private citizens should not attempt to make arrests unless they are certain that a crime was committed and that the suspect, in fact, committed the crime. Police officers have room for error because they may act under the relatively lenient probable cause standard, but citizens have no room for error because they can only act under the stringent "in fact" standard.

Negative and Affirmative Defenses

The prosecution is required to prove a criminal charge against a defendant by proof beyond a reasonable doubt of each element of the crime. Even when the evidence is sufficient to prove each element of the crime, it is nevertheless possible for a defendant to obtain an acquittal or a conviction for a lesser crime. Negative defenses, if successful, absolve a defendant completely. Affirmative defenses can absolve the defendant completely or partially.

Justification is a negative and complete defense. If justification is proved, it negates an element of the crime (i.e., the mental culpability). If a person is legally justified in committing an act—for example, if he or she is acting in self-defense—he or she has not committed a crime. The defendant says, "Yes, I did it, and any reasonable person in the same situation would do the same thing." For the issue to be submitted to the jury, the defendant must introduce some amount of credible evidence to support the defense of justification. This is called the *burden of production*. Once the issue has been raised, the prosecution has the burden of overcoming the defense and disproving it beyond a reasonable doubt.

Other complete defenses are infancy and alibi. A condition of raising these defenses is that the prosecution must be notified in advance of the trial so that the claim can be investigated. In most states, the prosecution must be notified of a proposed alibi within ten days of the arraignment in order to allow investigation and avoid surprise at the trial.

Affirmative defenses include duress, entrapment, renunciation, and insanity. For these, the defendant has to do more than simply introduce some credible evidence; the defendant must prove the affirmative defense by a preponderance of the evidence, which might be characterized as more than 50% of the evidence. The entrapment defense, for example, requires the defendant to do more than simply claim that he was talked into committing a crime; he must show that his will was overpowered and he otherwise would not have committed the crime.

In *Patterson v. New York*, 432 U.S. 197 (1977), the U.S. Supreme Court ruled that proving an affirmative defense is different from requiring a defendant to negate or disprove the elements of the crime charged; therefore, it is constitutionally permissible to require defendants to prove affirmative defenses as a means of excusing their conduct.

The duress defense requires the defendant to show that he was coerced into committing the act because of the use or threatened use of unlawful physical force upon him or a third person which a person of reasonable firmness in his situation would have been unable to resist. Duress also requires a balancing of benefits and costs. The injury avoided must be more harmful than the injury inflicted; thus, persons cannot commit murder to save themselves from a lesser harm. On the other hand, they might be justified in committing a robbery to save themselves or another from death.

Renunciation is an affirmative defense. When a defendant stops short of completing a crime but an accomplice completes the crime, the defendant may claim renunciation by showing that he voluntarily and completely renounced the criminal purpose and withdrew from participation prior to the commission of the crime and made a substantial effort to prevent the crime.

In affirmative defense cases in which the defendant does not introduce enough evidence to satisfy the preponderance of evidence standard, the issue will not be submitted to the jury for a verdict—the judge will not instruct the jury to consider the affirmative defense. In cases in which the defendant introduces sufficient evidence to meet the preponderance standard, the district attorney has the burden of disproving the affirmative defense beyond a reasonable doubt. The issue of proof will be submitted to the jury for their verdict.

Insanity used to be a negative defense, but since the attempted assassination of President Ronald Reagan and the acquittal of the perpetrator on the grounds of insanity, the trend has been to reclassify insanity as an affirmative defense. In *Clark v. Arizona*, 548 U.S. 735 (2006), the Supreme Court upheld an Arizona statute that narrowed the possibility of proving insanity and required the defendant to prove the insanity by clear and convincing evidence, a more stringent standard than preponderance of the evidence.

Most successfully imposed defenses and affirmative defenses result in acquittals. However, in many states, a successful insanity defense will result in a verdict of not guilty by reason of insanity, and the defendant will be committed to a maximum-security mental hospital until he regains his sanity.

The affirmative defense of acting under extreme emotional disturbance is not equivalent to insanity. It may partially absolve a defendant of murder, but the defendant will be convicted of manslaughter instead.

Mistake of Fact and Factual Impossibility

Mistake of fact is a defense that can negate the mental culpability element of a crime and therefore, if proven, will result in an acquittal. Unlike the common-law maxim that "ignorance of the law is no excuse," which provides no relief for a defendant, mistake of fact is a complete defense. It arises when a person engages in prohibited conduct but does so under a mistaken belief of fact that negates the culpability required for the commission of the offense. To illustrate, if a homeowner mistakes someone climbing in a window for a burglar, but, in fact, the person was not a burglar and was lawfully present on the premises, the homeowner might be charged for the shooting but might raise the defense of a reasonable mistake of fact and be acquitted.

In contrast to mistake of fact, factual impossibility is not a defense or an excuse. For example, when a pickpocket, intending to steal a person's wallet, puts his hand in the person's pocket but there is no wallet, it is impossible for him to steal the supposed wallet. Nevertheless, the pickpocket is guilty of attempted larceny because he intended to commit a crime and he engaged in conduct that tended to effect the commission of such crime.

A classic example is the criminal who shoots an already dead person. If the criminal believed the person to be alive, he is guilty of attempted murder.

An interesting case dealing with factual impossibility was *People v. Dlugash*, 41 N.Y.2d 725 (1977). In that case, in December 1973, Michael Geller, 25, was shot and died in his Brooklyn apartment. The body was found lying faceup on the floor, and an autopsy revealed that the victim had been shot twice in the chest, once in the hand, and five times in the head at close range.

One bullet to the chest passed through the left lung and penetrated the heart chamber. The other bullet entered the left lung and passed through the chest without reaching the heart area. Ballistics tests established that the bullets recovered from the chest were .38 caliber, while the bullets recovered from the head were .25 caliber.

Melvin Dlugash and Joseph Bush, acquaintances of the victim, were arrested for the crime. During questioning, Dlugash told the police that the three men had been drinking and the victim had demanded that Bush pay him $100 that he owed him. Bush drew his .38

caliber pistol and shot Geller three times. After a few minutes, Dlugash drew his .25 caliber pistol and fired five shots into the victim's head.

Dlugash contended that by the time he fired his gun, it looked like Geller was already dead.

Dlugash was indicted and tried for murder in that, acting in concert with another, he intentionally caused the death of Geller. At his trial, there were two critical issues: first, which bullets caused the death, and, second, at what point in time did the victim die?

The medical examiner testified for the prosecution that the bullets in the chest would have killed the victim, but that the victim would have remained alive until the chest cavity filled with blood, which might have taken 5 to 10 minutes, and so Geller could have been alive when Dlugash shot him in the head, depending on when the shots were fired.

The defense medical expert testified that the wounds to the heart and lungs would have been rapidly fatal, and concluded that the victim might have already been dead when Dlugash shot him.

The jury convicted Dlugash of murder, but on appeal, the Appellate Division reversed the conviction and dismissed the indictment, ruling that "the People failed to prove beyond a reasonable doubt that Geller had been alive at the time he was shot by the defendant; the defendant's conviction thus cannot stand" (*People v. Dlugash*, 51 AD2d. 975).

The prosecution appealed the reversal to the Court of Appeals of New York, and that court agreed with one part of the Appellate Division ruling, saying that "all three medical expert witnesses testified that they could not, with any degree of medical certainty, state whether the victim had been alive at the time the latter shots were fired by the defendant. Thus, the People failed to prove beyond a reasonable doubt that the victim had been alive at the time he was shot by the defendant. Whatever else it may be, it is not murder to shoot a dead body. Man dies but once" (*People v. Dlugash*, 41 N.Y.2d 725 (1977)).

However, the Court ruled that even though the defendant could not be guilty of murder, he could, nevertheless, be guilty of attempted murder. The Court said, "there is sufficient evidence in the record from which the jury could conclude that the defendant believed Geller to be alive at the time defendant fired shots into Geller's head... the jury could conclude that the defendant's purpose and intention was to administer the coup de grace."

Problem

On Monday, Artie and Billy decided to rob a local bank where they had once worked. On Tuesday, they obtained a stolen gun and a smoke grenade, and they solicited Clyde the mechanic to supply a get-away car and to drive it when they committed the robbery on Thursday, agreeing to pay him $500 for his trouble. They told Clyde that they were going to rob the bank by using a threatening note.

On Wednesday night, Artie and Billy went to the home of Mr. Monet, the bank manager. When they had worked at the bank, they had learned that Monet had been embezzling funds, and they threatened to inform the police unless Monet gave them the combination to the bank vault.

After Monet divulged the combination, Artie suddenly decided to kill him so that he could not testify against them. He shot Monet in the head, killing him.

On Thursday morning, Artie and Billy, both dressed in suits and ties, entered the bank while Clyde waited outside in the car with the engine running. Artie displayed the gun and announced a hold-up. Billy showed the smoke grenade and said that if anyone moved he would blow up the whole place. A woman customer screamed, scaring Billy. He dropped the smoke grenade, setting it off and filling the bank with smoke. Several customers ran toward the front door, and Artie fired a shot at them but missed and hit Billy instead, killing him.

An off-duty police officer, Johnny Jones, dressed in civilian clothes and wearing a baseball cap turned sideways, had been in the bank as a customer. Officer Jones pulled his gun and began shooting at Artie. A uniformed, on-duty police officer, Ronnie Rookie, heard the commotion. He entered the bank with his gun drawn, mistook Jones for the bank robber, and shot him. Jones died of his wounds.

Questions

Are the following statements true or false?

1. Artie, Billy, and Clyde could be guilty of conspiracy to commit the bank robbery.
2. Clyde could be guilty of the murder of Monet even though he had not agreed and did not know about that aspect of the conspiracy.
3. Because Monet was killed in the course of the crime of larceny by extortion, Billy could be guilty of felony murder for his death.
4. Because Monet was killed in the furtherance of the conspiracy to rob the bank, Billy could be guilty of murder for his death.
5. Artie could be guilty of felony murder for killing Billy.
6. Artie could not be guilty of felony murder for the killing of Officer Johnny Jones because Jones was killed by a police officer who made a mistake.
7. Officer Ronnie Rookie might be guilty of manslaughter for recklessly killing Johnny Jones.
8. If Rookie was charged with manslaughter, he could raise the defense of justification in that he had reasonable cause to believe that Jones was committing a felonious assault and robbery.
9. If Clyde was charged with felony murder for the death of Johnny Jones, he could raise the affirmative defense that he did not cause the death, he was not armed himself, and he did not know that Artie was armed with a gun or that Artie intended to cause a serious physical injury.
10. In order for Rookie's defense and Clyde's affirmative defense to be submitted for the jury's consideration, Rookie would have to raise his defense only by submitting some credible evidence in support of his position, but Clyde would have to prove his affirmative defense by a preponderance of the evidence.

Death Penalty

The criminal law attempts to distinguish the most culpable types of homicide from those that are less culpable in order to determine the appropriate punishment. Within the murder category, further distinctions are drawn to determine whether the appropriate penalty should be long-term incarceration or the death penalty. Under traditional common law, the death penalty was the mandated penalty for murder. To avoid such a blanket approach and to avoid the phenomenon of jurors acquitting guilty defendants because they did not want to impose the death penalty, many American states divided murder into first- and second-degree murder. A benefit of the first- and second-degree scheme was that it allowed jurors to find a defendant guilty of second-degree murder, which did not carry a death sentence. A disadvantage was that jurors had little guidance regarding how to make the choice, and did not have complete information about the defendant's background, character, or previous criminal record. Consequently, the imposition of life or death sentences occurred under total jury discretion and the results quite often seemed inconsistent or discriminatory. Eventually, the Supreme Court, through the Eighth Amendment's cruel and unusual clause and its application to the states through the Fourteenth Amendment, took control of the issue and applied constitutional principles to the application of capital punishment.

The Framers of the Constitution obviously contemplated the use of capital punishment, as the Fifth Amendment states, "No person shall be held to answer for a capital... crime, unless on a presentment or indictment of a Grand Jury." Also, "nor shall any person be subject for the same offence to be twice put in jeopardy of life or limb... nor be deprived of life, liberty, or property... without due process of law." Nevertheless, the Supreme Court has placed substantial restraints on its application. In 1972, in *Furman v. Georgia*, 408 U.S. 238, the Court examined how the death penalty had been applied, and ruled that it had been applied in an unguided, discriminatory, and, therefore, unconstitutional manner.

Consequently, the death penalty was inoperable until Georgia and most other capital punishment states revised their statutes to address the concerns raised by the Court. In *Gregg v. Georgia*, 427 U.S. 153 (1976), the Court ruled that the revised Georgia statute was a constitutional way of implementing the death penalty. The Court determined that the new statute had sufficiently corrected the problems identified in *Furman*. The Georgia statute mandates a bifurcated trial for cases in which the state seeks the death penalty. In the first part of the trial, the jury determines guilt. In the second part, the jury considers aggravating and mitigating factors to determine whether the death sentence should be imposed. To impose death, the jury must find that the homicide incorporated an aggravating factor, such as:

1. The defendant had a prior conviction for a capital felony.
2. The defendant was engaged in another capital felony, aggravated battery, burglary, or arson in the first degree.
3. The defendant was a contract killer (i.e., he killed for money).
4. The victim was a judicial officer or district attorney.
5. The victim was a peace officer, corrections employee, or fireman while engaged in the performance of official duties.
6. The offense was outrageously or wantonly vile, horrible, or inhuman in that it involved torture, depravity of mind, or an aggravated battery to the victim.
7. The defendant had escaped from lawful custody or from confinement.

Other states have additional aggravating factors, such as:

1. The defendant was serving a life sentence.
2. The defendant was a serial killer.
3. The defendant killed more than one person.
4. The defendant killed a potential or actual witness.

Death penalty statutes also require the jury to consider mitigating factors, such as the defendant's age, mental condition, childhood, and background. Currently, 37 states and the federal government authorize capital punishment for first-degree murder and certain other crimes.

Although the constitutionality of the death penalty has been upheld, the Court has placed limits on the persons on whom it may be imposed. The Court has used its "evolving standards of decency" rationale to prohibit the execution of murderers who were mentally handicapped or who were under 18 years old when they committed their crimes.[8] It has also addressed the types of crimes for which the death penalty may be imposed.

Federal law authorizes execution for dozens of federal crimes, including treason, murder of a federal law enforcement officer or official, kidnapping, carjacking, child abuse homicide, bank robbery resulting in death, airplane hijacking, and terrorism.[9] In addition, the Anti-Drug Abuse Act of 1988 allows the death penalty for "drug kingpins" who control "continuing criminal enterprises" whose members commit homicides in furtherance of the enterprise.[10]

The Supreme Court upheld the death penalty sentence and the execution of Timothy McVeigh for his role in the 1995 bombing of the federal office building in Oklahoma City and the murder of federal officials; however, the Court has not yet ruled on many of the other recently enacted federal death penalty statutes. All courts, whether federal or state, that uphold death penalty sentences do so only for the most culpable crimes.

In *Byford v. State*, 994 P.2d 700 (2000), the Nevada Supreme Court upheld a jury's death sentence for a defendant's conviction of murder. In *Byford*, the defendant Robert Byford and two male friends, Smith and Williams, drove Monica Wilkins, an 18-year-old woman, into the desert. The young men were angered at Wilkins for various reasons. They stopped their Jeep at a ravine in the desert.

> Byford handed Williams a handgun and said "he couldn't do it." Williams then shot Wilkins in the back three to five times. She screamed and fell to the ground. Wilkins got up, walked to Williams, and asked him why he had shot her. He told her that he had only shot around her. Wilkins walked up and out of the ravine but then felt the back of her neck, saw that she was bleeding, and again confronted Williams.
>
> Williams told her that he shot her because she was a "bitch." He then walked behind her and shot her again repeatedly. Wilkins screamed and fell to the ground again. Byford then took the gun from Williams, said that he would "make sure the bitch is dead," and fired two shots into her head. Byford then got a can of gasoline from the Jeep and poured it on Wilkins. Byford tried to hand a lighter to Smith and get him to light the gasoline, but Smith refused. Byford called him a "wussie" and lit the body. As it burned, the three drove off. As they returned to Las Vegas, Byford pointed the handgun at Smith and threatened to kill him if he ever told anyone.

Byford and Williams were tried and convicted of the murder. At the penalty phase of the trial, witnesses testified to aggravating and mitigating factors. Byford spoke briefly and said that he was sorry for his part in Wilkins' death. Nevertheless, the jury sentenced both Byford and Williams to death.

Byford appealed on several grounds, including issues pertaining to the proof of premeditation. The Court upheld his conviction, concluding that the evidence was clearly sufficient to establish the deliberation, premeditation, and torture that justified the imposition of the death penalty. The Court summarized:

> Williams and Byford then calmly and dispassionately shot the victim in the absence of any provocation, confrontation, or stressful circumstances of any kind. Williams shot her several times and then, after a passage of some time, shot her several more times. Byford watched this transpire, and when the victim was helpless on the ground, he took the gun from Williams, said that he would make sure she was dead, and shot her in the head twice.

The Court took the opportunity to compose instructions on the *mens rea* required for first-degree murder. These instructions were meant for lower Nevada courts to follow:

> Murder of the first degree is murder which is perpetrated by means of any kind of willful, deliberate, and premeditated killing. All three elements—willfulness, deliberation, and premeditation—must be proven beyond a reasonable doubt before an accused can be convicted of first-degree murder.
>
> Willfulness is the intent to kill. There need be no appreciable space of time between the formation of the intent to kill and the act of killing.
>
> Deliberation is the process of determining upon a course of action to kill as a result of thought, including weighing the reasons for and against the action and considering the consequences of the action.
>
> A deliberate determination may be arrived at in a short period of time. But in all cases the determination must not be formed in passion, or if formed in passion, it must be carried out after there has been time for the passion to subside and deliberation to occur. A mere unconsidered and rash impulse is not deliberate, even though it includes the intent to kill.
>
> Premeditation is a design, a determination to kill, distinctly formed in the mind by the time of the killing.
>
> Premeditation need not be for a day, an hour, or even a minute. It may be as instantaneous as successive thoughts of the mind. For if the jury believes from the evidence that the act constituting the killing has been preceded by and has been the result of premeditation, no matter how rapidly the act follows the premeditation, it is premeditated.
>
> The law does not undertake to measure in units of time the length of the period during which the thought must be pondered before it can ripen into an intent to kill which is truly deliberate and premeditated. The time will vary with different individuals and under varying circumstances.
>
> The true test is not the duration of time, but rather the extent of the reflection. A cold, calculated judgment and decision may be arrived at in a short period of time, but a mere unconsidered and rush impulse, even though it includes an intent to kill, is not deliberation and premeditation as will fix an unlawful killing as murder of the first degree.

Rape

For state crimes other than murder, the Supreme Court addressed the constitutionality of the death penalty in *Coker v. Georgia*, 433 U.S. 584 (1977), holding that the rape of an adult woman could not warrant capital punishment:

> Although rape deserves serious punishment, the death penalty, which is unique in its severity and irrevocability, is an excessive penalty for the rapist, who, as such and as opposed to the murderer, does not take human life.

Because *Coker* referred to "a mere adult woman," the Louisiana state legislature and five other states reacted by amending their statutes to allow the death penalty for the rape of a child. Subsequently, the Louisiana Supreme Court in *State v. Wilson*, 685 So.2d 1063 (1993), upheld a conviction and the statute on the basis of the need for retribution and deterrence, stating:

Self-help is not permitted in our society, so there is a need for retribution in our criminal sanctions. The death penalty for rape of a child less than twelve years old would be a deterrent to the commission of that crime.

Unfortunately, the statute did not deter a Louisiana resident, Patrick Kennedy, from raping his eight-year-old stepdaughter. Louisiana convicted him of the crime and sentenced him to death. In *Kennedy v. Louisiana*, 129 S.Ct. 1 (2008), his appeal reached the Supreme Court, which reversed the death sentence, holding that the Eighth Amendment's cruel and unusual clause prohibited the death penalty even for the rape of a child. The Court reiterated its rationale that, "Evolving standards of decency must embrace and express a respect for the dignity of the person, and the punishment of criminals must conform to that rule.... When the law punishes by death, it risks its own sudden descent into brutality, transgressing the constitutional commitment to decency and restraint."

In *Kennedy*, the Court supported its evolving standards of decency rationale by arguing that a national consensus against the death penalty for the rape of a child was growing and the direction of the nation's opinion was against the death penalty. It pointed out that 37 states and the federal government authorized the death penalty, but that after the *Coker* decision, only six had enacted death penalty statutes for the rape of a child. In a clear exercise of judicial activism, the Court nullified the six recently enacted statutes and reignited the debate about whether the Court should confine itself to the words and understanding of the Framers or whether it should treat the Constitution as a living, breathing document that can be adjusted to meet the needs and values of a changing society.

After the decision was rendered, the Court and the lawyers representing Louisiana were subject to embarrassment when it emerged that in 2006 the U.S. Congress had passed a death penalty punishment for rapists of children in the Uniform Code of Military Justice. Neither the lawyers presenting the arguments in *Kennedy* nor any of the justices had mentioned this recently enacted death-penalty statute. Assuming that the U.S. Congress expresses the consensus of the people, the *Kennedy* majority misrepresented the direction of the nation's opinion.[11]

Whether the issue of the death penalty for the rape of a child ever reaches the Supreme Court again remains to be seen, but issues about the appropriate and lawful punishment of rapists and sexual abusers in all probability will reach the Court. While the Supreme Court has lessened the ultimate penalty for rape, states have been aggressively updating and strengthening their laws against all types of rape. The common-law doctrines that a man could not be guilty of raping his wife, and the requirement that a woman had to show that she put up the "utmost resistance," have been abandoned.[12] Furthermore, in most states, the child's age of consent has been raised to 17 years from 10 years.

Rape is sexual intercourse without consent. Lack of consent can result from forcible compulsion or incapacity to consent. A person is deemed incapable of consent when he or she is:

- Younger than the legal age of consent for sexual intercourse
- Mentally disabled
- Mentally incapacitated
- Physically helpless

In most states, the penalties for rape of a child increase inversely to the age of the child. For example, in New York, a person is guilty of third-degree rape when he or she, being 21 years old or more, engages in sexual intercourse with a person who is less than 17 years old; second-degree rape when he or she, being 18 years old or more, engages in sexual intercourse with a person who is less than 15 years old; and first-degree rape when he or she engages in sexual intercourse with a person who is less than 11 years old.[13] These age-related rapes are called *statutory rape*, and they are strict liability crimes, meaning that the prosecution need not prove that the defendant knew the victim's age, and the defendant cannot raise lack of knowledge of the victim's age as a defense.

First-degree rape, whether forcible rape or the rape of child less than 11 years old, carries penalties from between 25 years in prison to life imprisonment.

Larceny

Property crimes generally carry less severe sentences. The most common property crime is larceny, which is the unlawful stealing of property with the intent to benefit oneself or deprive the owner of its value or use. Larceny can occur by the following methods:

- Common-law wrongful taking
- Trick
- Embezzlement
- False pretenses
- Acquiring lost property
- Issuing a bad check
- False promise
- Extortion

Often, prosecutors prove a person's intent through the presumption that a person intends the natural and probable consequences of his or her acts. Therefore, when a person takes the property of another and walks away, it might be difficult to prove his intent, but the law allows the proof to be based simply on the presumption. To be sure, the presumption can be rebutted by evidence to the contrary.

An exception to the above rule is larceny by false promise, which is a unique crime. It requires that the defendant intended to steal the property at the time of the promise, but such intent cannot be proved by presumption. Many promises given in exchange for remuneration are broken, both business and personal promises. Without initial bad intent, broken promises are not crimes. When a person makes a promise with the intent to fulfill it, but fails to complete the promise because of subsequent circumstances, such as losing their job and not being able repay a loan, no crime has been committed. A civil lawsuit would be the remedy for failure to repay a loan.

Larceny by extortion occurs when an actor compels or induces another person to deliver property to him by means of instilling a fear that the actor will:

- Cause physical injury to some person in the future
- Cause damage to property
- Accuse some person of a crime or cause criminal charges to be instituted against him
- Expose a secret or publicize a fact tending to subject some person to hatred, contempt, or ridicule
- Cause an unlawful strike or boycott
- Use or abuse his position as a public servant so as to affect some person adversely

Threatening to cause physical injury in the future is treated as the most serious kind of extortion, and is usually categorized as grand larceny in the first degree. If the threat is to cause immediate physical injury, the crime is not extortion but robbery. It is interesting that grand larceny by extortion warrants a longer prison term than third-degree robbery. This is so because the legislature contemplated that extortion by threat of physical injury was the kind of conduct engaged in by organized crime operators, and substantial penalties were required to combat such conduct.

Three Strikes

Many states have enacted "three strikes and you're out" laws that authorize life imprisonment for persons convicted of crimes committed on three separate occasions, including property crimes. These laws have been examined by the Supreme Court, which has ruled that the Eighth Amendment's cruel and unusual clause applies not only to the execution and physical treatment of prisoners but also to the duration of prison sentences.

In *Solem v. Helm*, 463 U.S. 277 (1983), the defendant was convicted of larceny by issuing a bad check for $100. He had prior convictions for nonviolent crimes of burglary, obtaining money under false pretenses, grand larceny, and driving while intoxicated. Under the South Dakota habitual-offender statute, he was sentenced to life imprisonment without possibility of parole. The Supreme Court vacated the sentence, stating:

> We find that Helm has received the penultimate sentence for relatively minor criminal conduct. He has been treated more harshly than other criminals in the State who have committed more serious crimes.... We conclude that his sentence is significantly disproportionate to his crime, and is therefore prohibited by the Eighth Amendment.

Solem was a five-to-four decision and another example of the Supreme Court exercising its constitutional power to review and nullify state statutes.

In *Ewing v. California*, 538 U.S. 11 (2003), the makeup of the Court had changed from the *Solem v. Helm* decision, and, in a five-to-four decision, the Court shifted its approach and deferred to state authority. In *Ewing*, the defendant, Gary Ewing, who was on parole, was arrested and convicted for stealing three golf clubs, priced at $399 apiece. Ewing had a long criminal history with convictions for grand theft auto, petit larceny, battery, burglary, possession of drug paraphernalia, unlawful possession of a firearm, and trespassing. Consequently, under California's three-strikes law, he was sentenced to between 25 years and life in prison. He appealed, citing *Solem v. Helm* for the precedent that the sentence violated the Eighth Amendment. However, the Supreme Court upheld the sentence. Because Ewing's sentence was not as onerous as Solem's and a possibility of parole was included in the sentence, it was not grossly disproportionate. The Court reviewed the California legislation and found that it was "justified by the State's public-safety interest in incapacitating and deterring recidivist felons." Justice Sandra Day O'Connor wrote the opinion and stated:

> We do not sit as a "super-legislature" to second-guess these policy choices. It is enough that the State of California has a reasonable basis for believing that dramatically enhanced sentences for habitual felons advances the goals of its criminal justice system in any substantial way.

The one-vote shift of the Court toward a position of more deference to states' rights parallels the Court's shift to its position of placing limits on the authority of the federal government to enact criminal laws under the blanket authority of the interstate commerce clause. Much of the federal government's authority stems from its enumerated power in Article I, Section 8, of the Constitution to regulate interstate commerce.

The interstate commerce power authorizes Congress to regulate: (1) the channels and instrumentalities used in interstate commerce, (2) persons and articles that move in interstate commerce, and (3) any commercial activity that substantially affects interstate commerce, even when the activity occurs entirely within a single state.

Federal Crimes

The enactment of federal criminal laws on the basis of the commerce clause to regulate conduct traditionally regulated by the states has proceeded almost nonstop. Since the 1930s, Congress has created more than seven thousand new federal felonies. From the time of President Franklin Delano Roosevelt's New Deal during the 1930s until 1995, the Supreme Court did not strike down any newly enacted federal statute for being outside the scope of interstate commerce regulatory power.

On the basis of the commerce clause, Congress enacted criminal laws to regulate the use of the mail and telecommunications systems to defraud.[14] It enacted federal criminal laws to prosecute persons who transport stolen goods, unlawful narcotics, or kidnapping victims across state lines.[15] Also, the Mann Act made it a federal crime to transport a minor across state lines for immoral purposes.[16]

In 1946, Congress enacted the Hobbs Act to prosecute persons who interfere with interstate commerce by means of violence, extortion, or bribery:

> Whoever in any way or degree obstructs, delays, or affects commerce or the movement of any article or commodity in commerce, by robbery or extortion or attempts or conspires so to do, or commits or threatens physical violence to any person or property in furtherance of a plan or purpose to do anything in violation of this section shall be fined under this title or imprisoned not more than twenty years, or both.[17]

The Hobbs Act was the primary statute used by the FBI and other government enforcement agencies. It has been augmented by other statutes aimed at organized crime and unlawful drug traffickers.

The Racketeer Influenced and Corrupt Organizations statute (RICO), enacted as part of the 1970 Organized Crime Control Act, made it a crime to belong to, profit from, or operate an organization that engages in a pattern of racketeering and has committed two specified crimes within ten years. The specified crimes include Hobbs Act violations, bribery, counterfeiting, embezzling from a union, loan-sharking, mail or wire fraud, obstruction of state or federal justice, Mann Act violations, bankruptcy scam frauds, drug violations, and promoting obscenity. The authorized criminal punishments for RICO violations are fines or imprisonment for not more than 20 years, or both. In addition, civil forfeiture actions can be enforced for treble damages.[18]

As part of the Comprehensive Drug Abuse Prevention and Control Act of 1970, Congress enacted the Continuing Criminal Enterprise Act, which makes it a crime to belong to an organization of five or more persons for the purpose of committing or conspiring to commit a continuing series of felony drug violations. The authority for the Act was the interstate commerce clause, not taxing authority, which had been the authority used in prior unsuccessful attempts to combat unlawful drugs.[19]

The unimpeded trend of increasing federal power met its first real resistance in 1995 when the Supreme Court put the brakes on the criminalization of almost any wrongful conduct on the basis of the interstate commerce clause. In *United States v. Lopez*, 514 U.S. 549 (1995), the Court ruled that Congress lacked the power to enact the Gun-Free School Zones Act, which had made it a federal crime to possess a firearm near a school. The Court held that the connection between the gun possession and interstate commerce was too attenuated. Then, in *United States v. Morrison*, 529 U.S. 598 (2000), the Court ruled that Congress lacked the power to enact the Violence Against Women Act, which attempted to create a federal remedy for victims of gender-motivated violence. Both *Lopez* and *Morrison* reestablished the requirement of a substantial nexus to interstate commerce.

It remains to be seen whether *Lopez* and *Morrison* were just temporary obstacles on the path to greater federal power to create and enforce new criminal laws. This is an important question because it has ramifications for the relationship between government and citizens.

Double Jeopardy

It goes without saying that the greater the number of federal crimes, the more jeopardy citizens face. Moreover, when the same underlying conduct can be prosecuted under both state and federal law, the protection against double jeopardy is diminished.

Because the double jeopardy prohibition does not prevent separate prosecutions by different sovereign entities when the offense is a crime against the laws of each, a citizen who is accused of a crime and acquitted in a state jurisdiction may then face a second prosecution under federal jurisdiction. Bank robbery is the classic example: it can be prosecuted in the state in which it occurred and, because banks are federally insured, also in the federal courts. As the number of federal crimes has increased, the overlap of federal and state crimes has also increased, and citizens accused of such crimes who wish to defend themselves may have to win not one but two acquittals.

The double jeopardy clause was important to the Framers who cast the Bill of Rights. They feared that a citizen might be subjected to multiple prosecutions until he or she was either convicted or driven into bankruptcy. Knowing both human nature and politics, they knew that government prosecutors could be motivated by political considerations or other malicious intent. However, they did not know the extent to which federal criminal law would develop, and they did not foresee the commensurate danger of dual prosecutions by separate sovereigns. If they had foreseen the expansion of federal criminal power, one might argue that they would have strengthened the double jeopardy clause to protect against dual-sovereignty prosecutions.

Perhaps the most prominent and controversial double jeopardy issue arose in connection with the infamous 1991 Rodney King incident for which four California police officers were charged by the State of California with assaulting King. During the incident:

> California Highway Patrol officers observed King's car traveling at a speed they estimated to be in excess of 100 m.p.h. The officers followed King with red lights and sirens activated and ordered him by loudspeaker to pull over, but he continued to drive.
>
> King left the freeway, and after a chase of about eight miles, stopped at the entrance to a recreation area. The officers ordered King and his two passengers to exit the car and to assume a felony prone position—that is, to lie on their stomachs with legs spread and

arms behind their backs. King's two friends complied. King, too, got out of the car but did not lie down. Petitioner Stacey Koon arrived... and as sergeant, Koon took charge. The officers again ordered King to assume the felony prone position. King got on his hands and knees but did not lie down. Officers... tried to force King down, but King resisted and became combative, so the officers retreated. Koon then fired taser darts (designed to stun a combative suspect) into King.

The events that occurred next were captured on videotape by a bystander. As the videotape begins, it shows that King rose from the ground and charged toward Officer Powell. Powell took a step and used his baton to strike King on the side of the head. King fell to the ground. From the 18th to the 30th second on the videotape, King attempted to rise, but Powell and (Officer) Wind each struck him with their batons to prevent him from doing so.

From the 35th to the 51st second, Powell administered repeated blows to King's lower extremities; one of the blows fractured King's leg. At the 55th second, Powell struck King on the chest, and King rolled over and lay prone. At that point the officers stepped back and observed King for about 10 seconds. Powell began to reach for his handcuffs.

At one-minute, five-seconds (1:05) on the videotape, (Officer) Briseno..."stomped" on King's upper back or neck. King's body writhed in response. At 1:07, Powell and Wind again began to strike King with a series of baton blows, and Wind kicked him in the upper thoracic or cervical area six times until 1:26. At about 1:29, King put his hands behind his back and was handcuffed.[20]

A California jury acquitted the officers of the assault charges. Unfortunately, the case had gained so much notoriety that, in response to the acquittals, riots erupted in many cities across the nation. The riots in Los Angeles were particularly destructive; many people were killed, and property worth millions of dollars was burned and destroyed.

To quell the public outrage over the acquittals, the federal government indicted the four officers for violating King's constitutional rights under color of state law, 18 U.S.C. § 242. After a federal jury trial, two of the four officers were convicted and sentenced to prison terms. They were convicted on the basis of the exact same conduct for which they had been acquitted by the state jury.

Although it is hoped that the King matter was a one-off incident, dual sovereignty and the double set of statute books expose all citizens to the prospect of facing two sets of charges for the same conduct.

In our society, the increase in the number of enforceable crimes from the nine common-law felonies to the thousands of statutory felonies in existence today has turned a wide range of conduct that would have been lawful in prior times into criminal conduct. Undoubtedly, the federal government's growing participation in the enforcement of criminal law has strengthened society's ability to combat organized crime and other ruthless criminals. On the other hand, it has opened more possibilities for government abuse and created greater jeopardy for individuals accused of crimes.

Felon in Possession of Firearm Act

The Federal Government's ability to prosecute individuals has been greatly increased by the Felon in Possession of a Firearm Act (FPF), 18 U.S.C. § 922(g). This law makes it a federal crime for a person convicted of a felony, in either a state or a federal court, to possess a firearm of any kind, or ammunition for a firearm, or a silencer. The penalty is up to ten years in prison and a $250,000 fine.

Like the federal government had done in the Rodney King case when the police officers who had been acquitted of assault in the state court were then tried and convicted in the federal court of civil rights violations, the government began using the FPF to re-prosecute individuals acquitted in state courts.

This was challenged in *Gamble v. United States*, 587 U.S. .... (2019), 139 S.Ct. 1960 (2019). In that case, a motorist, Terance Martez Gamble, was pulled over by an Alabama police officer for driving with a faulty headlight. The officer smelled marijuana, searched the car, found a 9-mm handgun, and arrested Gamble. Because Gamble had a prior conviction for robbery, he was charged under Alabama law with being a felon-in-possession. He pled guilty and was sentenced to one year in prison.

The federal government was not satisfied with the sentence and indicted Gamble under the federal FPF law based on the same facts. Gamble filed a motion to dismiss on the grounds that the successive federal prosecution, based on the same facts as the Alabama prosecution, violated the Fifth Amendment's double jeopardy clause. The District Court denied the motion, and Gamble was convicted and sentenced to four years in federal prison in addition to the Alabama prison sentence.

The Supreme Court affirmed the conviction, invoking the separate sovereigns doctrine, which holds that the double jeopardy clause does not always bar successive prosecutions for the same conduct. Since offenses are defined and proscribed by the laws of separate, independent sovereigns, the same conduct can constitute separate offenses, and a defendant can be tried for the separate offenses in the separate jurisdictions without the double jeopardy clause being violated.

Patterson v. New York

The following case abridgement illustrates the interrelations between such legal concepts as presumption of innocence, due process of law, burden of proof, standards of proof, malice aforethought, heat of passion, and affirmative defenses.

U.S. Supreme Court
Patterson v. New York, 432 U.S. 197 (1977)
MR. JUSTICE WHITE delivered the opinion of the Court.

The question here is the constitutionality under the Fourteenth Amendment Due Process Clause of burdening the defendant in a New York State murder trial with proving the affirmative defense of extreme emotional disturbance as defined by New York law.

I

After a brief and unstable marriage, the appellant, Gordon Patterson, Jr., became estranged from his wife, Roberta. Roberta resumed an association with John Northrup, a neighbor to whom she had been engaged prior to her marriage to appellant. On December 27, 1970, Patterson borrowed a rifle from an acquaintance and went to the residence of his father-in-law. There, he observed his wife through a window in a state of semi-undress in the presence of John Northrup. He entered the house and killed Northrup by shooting him twice in the head.

Patterson was charged with second-degree murder. In New York there are two elements of this crime: (1) "intent to cause the death of another person"; and (2) "causing the death of such person or of a third person." N.Y. Penal Law, Section 125.55. Malice aforethought is not an element of the crime. In addition, the State permits a person accused of murder to raise an affirmative defense that he "acted under the influence of extreme emotional disturbance for which there was a reasonable explanation or excuse."

New York also recognizes the crime of manslaughter. A person is guilty of manslaughter if he intentionally kills another person "under circumstances that do not constitute murder because he acts under the influence of extreme emotional disturbance." Appellant confessed before trial to killing Northrup, but at trial he raised the defense of extreme emotional disturbance.

The jury found appellant guilty of murder. Judgment was entered on the verdict, and the Appellate Division affirmed. While appeal to the New York Court of Appeals was pending, this Court decided *Mullaney v. Wilbur*, 421 U.S. 684 (1975), in which the Court declared Maine's murder statute unconstitutional. Under the Maine statute, a person accused of murder could rebut the statutory presumption that he committed the offense with "malice aforethought" by proving that he acted in the heat of passion on sudden provocation. The Court held that this scheme improperly shifted the burden of persuasion from the prosecutor to the defendant and was therefore a violation of due process. In the Court of Appeals appellant urged that New York's murder statute is functionally equivalent to the one struck down in Mullaney and that therefore his conviction should be reversed.

The Court of Appeals rejected appellant's argument, holding that the New York murder statute is consistent with due process. The Court distinguished Mullaney on the ground that the New York statute involved no shifting of the burden to the defendant to disprove any fact essential to the offense charged since the New York affirmative defense of extreme emotional disturbance bears no direct relationship to any element of murder. This appeal ensued, and we noted probable jurisdiction. We affirm.

II

It goes without saying that preventing and dealing with crime is much more the business of the States than it is of the Federal Government, and that we should not lightly construe the Constitution so as to intrude upon the administration of justice by the individual States. Among other things, it is normally "within the power of the State to regulate procedures under which its laws are carried out, including the burden of producing evidence and the burden of persuasion," and its decision in this regard is not subject to proscription under the Due Process Clause unless "it offends some principle of justice so rooted in the traditions and conscience of our people as to be ranked as fundamental."

In determining whether New York's allocation to the defendant of proving the mitigating circumstances of severe emotional disturbance is consistent with due process, it is therefore relevant to note that this defense is a considerably expanded version of the commonlaw defense of heat of passion on sudden provocation and that at common law the burden of proving the latter, as well as other affirmative defenses—indeed, "all... circumstances of justification, excuse or alleviation"—rested on the defendant.

In 1895, the common-law view was abandoned with respect to the insanity defense in federal prosecutions. *Davis v. United States*, 160 U.S. 469 (1895). This ruling had wide impact on the practice in the federal courts with respect to the burden of proving various affirmative defenses, and the prosecution in a majority of jurisdictions in this country sooner or later came to shoulder the burden of proving the sanity of the accused and of disproving the facts constituting other affirmative defenses, including provocation. Davis was not a constitutional ruling, however, as *Leland v. Oregon* [343 U.S. 790, 798 (1952)] made clear.

At issue in *Leland v. Oregon* was the constitutionality under the Due Process Clause of the Oregon rule that the defense of insanity must be proved by the defendant beyond a reasonable doubt. Noting that Davis "obviously establish[ed] no constitutional doctrine," the Court refused to strike down the Oregon scheme, saying that the burden of proving all elements of the crime beyond reasonable doubt, including the elements of premeditation and deliberation, was placed on the State under Oregon procedures and remained there throughout the trial. To convict, the jury was required to find each element of the crime beyond a reasonable doubt, based on all the evidence, including the evidence going to the issue of insanity. Only then was the jury "to consider separately the issue of legal sanity per se." This practice did not offend the Due Process Clause even though among the 20 States then placing the burden of proving his insanity on the defendant Oregon was alone in requiring him to convince the jury beyond a reasonable doubt.

In 1970, the Court declared that the Due Process Clause "protects the accused against conviction except upon proof beyond a reasonable doubt of every fact necessary to constitute the crime with which he is charged." *In re Winship*, 397 U.S. 358 (1970). Five years later, in *Mullaney v. Wilbur*, 421 U.S. 684 (1975), the Court further announced that under the Maine law of homicide, the burden could not constitutionally be placed on the defendant of proving by a preponderance of the evidence that the killing had occurred in the heat of passion on sudden provocation. THE CHIEF JUSTICE and MR. JUSTICE REHNQUIST, concurring, expressed their understanding that the Mullaney decision did not call into question the ruling in *Leland v. Oregon*, *supra*, with respect to the proof of insanity.

Subsequently, the Court confirmed that it remained constitutional to burden the defendant with proving his insanity defense when it dismissed, as not raising a substantial federal question, a case in which the appellant specifically challenged the continuing validity of *Leland v. Oregon*. This occurred in *Rivera v. Delaware*, 429 U.S. 877 (1976), an appeal from a Delaware conviction which, in reliance on Leland, had been affirmed by the Delaware Supreme Court over the claim that the Delaware statute was unconstitutional because it burdened the defendant with proving his affirmative defense of insanity by a preponderance of the evidence. The claim in this Court was that *Leland* had been overruled by *Winship* and *Mullaney*. We dismissed the appeal as not presenting a substantial federal question.

III

We cannot conclude that Patterson's conviction under the New York law deprived him of due process of law. The crime of murder is defined by the statute, which represents a recent revision of the state criminal code, as causing the death of another person with intent to do so. The death, the intent to kill, and causation are the facts that the State is required to prove beyond a reasonable doubt if a person is to be convicted of murder. No further facts are either presumed or inferred in order to constitute the crime. The statute does provide an affirmative defense—that the defendant acted under the influence of extreme emotional disturbance for which there was a reasonable explanation—which, if proved by a preponderance of the evidence, would reduce the crime to manslaughter, an offense defined in a separate section of the statute. It is plain enough that if the intentional killing is shown, the State intends to deal with the defendant as a murderer unless he demonstrates the mitigating circumstances.

Here, the jury was instructed in accordance with the statute, and the guilty verdict confirms that the State successfully carried its burden of proving the facts of the crime beyond a reasonable doubt. Nothing in the evidence, including any evidence that might have been offered with respect to Patterson's mental state at the time of the crime, raised a reasonable doubt about his guilt as a murderer; and clearly the evidence failed to convince the jury that Patterson's affirmative defense had been made out. It seems to us that the State satisfied the mandate of *Winship* that it prove beyond a reasonable doubt "every fact necessary to constitute the crime with which [Patterson was] charged."

In convicting Patterson under its murder statute, New York did no more than *Leland* and *Rivera* permitted it to do without violating the Due Process Clause. Under those cases, once the facts constituting a crime are established beyond a reasonable doubt, based on all the evidence including the evidence of the defendant's mental state, the State may refuse to sustain the affirmative defense of insanity unless demonstrated by a preponderance of the evidence.

The New York law on extreme emotional disturbance follows this pattern. This affirmative defense, which the Court of Appeals described as permitting "the defendant to show that his actions were caused by a mental infirmity not arising to the level of insanity, and that he is less culpable for having committed them," does not serve to negative any facts of the crime which the State is to prove in order to convict of murder. It constitutes a separate issue on which the defendant is required to carry the burden of persuasion; and unless we are to overturn *Leland* and *Rivera*, New York has not violated the Due Process Clause, and Patterson's conviction must be sustained.

We are unwilling to reconsider *Leland* and *Rivera*. But even if we were to hold that a State must prove sanity to convict once that fact is put in issue, it would not necessarily follow that a State must prove beyond a reasonable doubt every fact, the existence or nonexistence of which it is willing to recognize as an exculpatory or mitigating circumstance affecting the degree of culpability or the severity of the punishment. Here, in revising its criminal code, New York provided the affirmative defense of extreme emotional disturbance, a substantially expanded version of the older heat-of-passion concept, but it was willing to do so only if the facts making out the defense were established by the defendant with sufficient certainty. The State was itself unwilling to undertake to establish the absence of those facts beyond a reasonable doubt, perhaps fearing that proof would be too difficult and that too many persons deserving treatment as murderers would escape that punishment if the evidence need merely raise a reasonable doubt about the defendant's emotional state. It has been said that the new criminal code of New York contains some 25 affirmative defenses which exculpate or mitigate but which must be established by the defendant to be operative. The Due Process Clause, as we see it, does not put New York to the choice of abandoning those defenses or undertaking to disprove their existence in order to convict of a crime which otherwise is within its constitutional powers to sanction by substantial punishment.

The requirement of proof beyond a reasonable doubt in a criminal case is "bottomed on a fundamental value determination of our society that it is far worse to convict an innocent man than to let a guilty man go free." *Winship*, 397 U.S., at 372 (Harlan, J., concurring). The social cost of placing the burden on the prosecution to prove guilt beyond a reasonable doubt is thus an increased risk that the guilty will go free. While it is clear that our society has willingly chosen to bear a substantial burden in order to protect the innocent, it is equally clear that the risk it must bear is not without limits; and Mr. Justice Harlan's aphorism provides little guidance for determining what those limits are. Due process does not require that every conceivable step be taken, at whatever cost, to eliminate the possibility of convicting an innocent person. Punishment of those found guilty by a jury, for example, is not forbidden merely because there is a remote possibility in some instances that an innocent person might go to jail.

It is said that the common-law rule permits a State to punish one as a murderer when it is as likely as not that he acted in the heat of passion or under severe emotional distress and when, if he did, he is guilty only of manslaughter. But this has always been the case in those jurisdictions adhering to the traditional rule. It is also very likely true that fewer convictions of murder would occur if New York were required to negative the affirmative defense at issue here. But in each instance of a murder conviction under the present law, New York will have proved beyond a reasonable doubt that the defendant has intentionally killed another person, an act which it is not disputed the State may constitutionally criminalize and punish. If the State nevertheless chooses to recognize a factor that mitigates the degree of criminality or punishment, we think the State may assure itself that the fact has been established with reasonable certainty. To recognize at all a mitigating circumstance does not require the State to prove its nonexistence in each case in which the fact is put in issue, if in its judgment this would be too cumbersome, too expensive, and too inaccurate.

We thus decline to adopt as a constitutional imperative, operative countrywide, that a State must disprove beyond a reasonable doubt every fact constituting any and all affirmative defenses related to the culpability of an accused. Traditionally, due process has required that only the most basic procedural safeguards be observed; more subtle balancing of society's interests against those of the accused have been left to the legislative branch. We therefore will not disturb the balance struck in previous cases holding that the Due Process Clause requires the prosecution to prove beyond a reasonable doubt all of the elements included in the definition of the offense of which the defendant is charged. Proof of the non-existence of all affirmative defenses has never been constitutionally required, and we perceive no reason to fashion such a rule in this case and apply it to the statutory defense at issue here.

This view may seem to permit state legislatures to reallocate burdens of proof by labeling as affirmative defenses at least some elements of the crimes now defined in their statutes. But there are obviously constitutional limits beyond which the States may not go in this regard. "[I]t is not within the province of a legislature to declare an individual guilty or presumptively guilty of a crime." The legislature cannot "validly command that the finding of an indictment, or mere proof of the identity of the accused, should create a presumption of the existence of all the facts essential to guilt," also makes the point with sufficient clarity.

Long before *Winship*, the universal rule in this country was that the prosecution must prove guilt beyond a reasonable doubt. At the same time, the long-accepted rule was that it was constitutionally permissible to provide that various affirmative defenses were to be proved by the defendant. This did not lead to such abuses or to such widespread redefinition of crime and reduction of the prosecution's burden that a new constitutional rule was required. This was not the problem to which *Winship* was addressed. Nor does the fact that a majority of the States have now assumed the burden of disproving affirmative defenses—for whatever reasons—mean that those States that strike a different balance are in violation of the Constitution.

...

IV

As we have explained, nothing was presumed or implied against Patterson, and his conviction is not invalid under any of our prior cases. The judgment of the New York Court of Appeals is

Affirmed.

Notes

1 4 Blackstone, *Commentaries on the Laws of England* (1765), 4, p. 197.
2 *State v. Snowden*, 313 P.2d 706 (Idaho 1957); *Macias v. State*, 283 P.711 (Ariz. 1929).
3 *Rowland v. State*, 35 So. 826 (1904).
4 New York Penal Law § 125.25.1(a).
5 *People v. Berry*, 18 Cal. 3d 509 (1976).
6 *Reed v. State*, 59 S.W.2d 122 (1933).
7 Del. Code. Ann. Tit. 11, 575(a), (b) (1953).
8 *Atkins v. Virginia*, 536 U.S. 304 (2002); *Roper v. Simmons*, 543 U.S. 551 (2005).
9 Federal Death Penalty Act of 1994.
10 21 U.S.C. § 848(e).
11 Greenhouse, Linda, In court ruling on executions, a factual flaw, *The New York Times,* July 3, 2008.
12 *State in the Interest of M.T.S.*, 609 A.2d 1266 (N.J. 1992).
13 New York Penal Law §§ 130.25, 130.30, 130.35.
14 18 U.S.C. §§ 1341, 1343.
15 18 U.S.C. §§ 2312, 1201.
16 18 U.S.C. § 2423.
17 18 U.S.C. § 1951(a).
18 18 U.S.C. §§ 1961–1968.
19 21 U.S.C. § 848.
20 *Koon v. United States*, 518 U.S. 81 (1996).

Reference

New York State Penal Law, Article 35, § 35:30.

Chapter 7

The Exclusionary Rule and the Fourth Amendment

As government law enforcement agencies were given greater resources and authority during the twentieth century and as the number and types of criminal laws increased exponentially, courts counterbalanced the growing government power by expanding individual rights and by creating new protections for persons accused of crimes. The most comprehensive and generous protection devised for individuals was the exclusionary rule.

The exclusionary rule, contrary to popular belief, is not written in the Bill of Rights: the Framers neither mentioned nor contemplated the imposition of the rule. Moreover, the Framers intended the Bill of Rights as a check on the powers of the newly formed federal government and had no intention of interfering with the states' abilities to enforce local, traditional criminal laws.

For injuries caused by actions of the federal government, a citizen could sue for damages, but the exclusionary rule was not a recognized remedy, and for 123 years, from the ratification of the Bill of Rights in 1791 to 1914, it was essentially nonexistent. It was first applied to enforce the Fourth Amendment in the federal mail-fraud case of *United States v. Weeks*, 232 U.S. 383 (1914). In that case, after the defendant had been arrested, a U.S. marshal entered the defendant's home without a warrant and seized letters and envelopes that were used as evidence to convict the defendant of mail fraud. Before the trial, the defendant brought an action for return of his property on the grounds that it had been seized illegally. His action was denied, and the evidence was used at his trial. He appealed to the U.S. Supreme Court, and the Court ruled that the entry into the home without a warrant was a violation of the Fourth Amendment and that the evidence obtained should have been returned to the defendant and should not have been admitted for use against him at his trial. The Court proclaimed:

> The effect of the Fourth Amendment is to put the courts of the United States and *Federal* officials, in the exercise of their power and authority, under the limitations and restraints as to the exercise of such power and authority, and to forever secure the people, their persons, houses, papers and effects against all unreasonable searches and seizures under the guise of law. This protection reaches all alike, whether accused of a crime or not, and the duty of giving to it force and effect is obligatory upon all entrusted under our Federal system with the enforcement of the laws. [emphasis added]

The above ruling clearly limited the *Weeks* doctrine to agents of the federal government.

DOI: 10.4324/9781003415091-9

Six years later, in *Silverthorne Lumber Co. v. United States*, 251 U.S. 385 (1920), the Supreme Court decided a similar case in which federal agents had seized business records without a warrant. In that case, knowing that the *Weeks* precedent would require the return of the documents, the agents copied the information from the records, returned the records, and subsequently subpoenaed them for use at the defendant's criminal trial. When the defendant refused to comply with the subpoena, he was jailed for contempt of court.

The Supreme Court reversed the lower court's contempt ruling and excluded the use of the subpoenaed records. In addition, it precluded any use of the knowledge gained by the unlawful seizure of the records. In the majority opinion, Justice Oliver Wendell Holmes wrote that the evidence "shall not be used at all."

The *Silverthorne* rule later became known as the fruits-of-the-poisonous-tree doctrine, which holds that evidence derived from inadmissible evidence is likewise inadmissible.[1] Not only is evidence obtained directly as a result of a constitutional violation tainted but secondary evidence derived from the information obtained during the violation is also tainted and may not be used against the person whose rights were violated. For example, if, while unlawfully arresting a suspect for possession of stolen property, the police learn from records in the suspect's possession where additional stolen property is hidden, the additional stolen property, if recovered, cannot be used as evidence against the suspect because it was derived from the initial unlawful arrest.[2]

Both *Weeks* and *Silverthorne* involved personal property and records lawfully possessed by citizens. Neither case involved possession of unlawful contraband, such as narcotics, guns, counterfeit money, or stolen property. Obviously, the Court could not have ordered the return of unlawfully possessed property. Later cases established the procedure that unlawfully possessed contraband would be excluded from evidence but not returned to the person from whom it was seized.[3]

The *Weeks* exclusionary remedy and the *Silverthorne* "poisonous-tree" rule were judge-made rules and were far from universally approved. Neither English common law nor European civil law recognized the exclusionary rule as a necessary legal device.[4]

After *Weeks* and *Silverthorne*, the exclusionary rule was applied in federal courts, but it was not initially applied against state courts where most criminal cases are tried. Debate arose as to whether federal courts should mandate that the rule be applied against the states, and many of the greatest and most respected justices ruled against its imposition on the states. Benjamin Cardozo, while he was the leading judge on the New York Court of Appeals and prior to his appointment to the Supreme Court, ruled against the exclusion of evidence as a remedy for search and seizure violations. He framed the issue for the upcoming debates:

> No doubt the protection of the statute would be greater from the point of view of the individual whose privacy had been invaded if the government were required to ignore what it had learned through the invasion. The question is whether protection for the individual would not be gained at a disproportionate loss of protection for society. On the one side is the social need that crime shall be repressed. On the other, the social need that law shall not be flouted by the insolence of office.[5]

The debate was not about whether the local police or government agents could violate the constitutional rights of citizens with impunity; rather, it was about what the remedy should be when such violations occurred and what should be done to deter such violations. The exclusionary rule debate reached the Supreme Court in 1949 in *Wolf v. Colorado*, 338 U.S. 25.

Wolf v. Colorado

Wolf v. Colorado addressed two issues. First, the Supreme Court applied the Fourth Amendment protections against unreasonable searches and seizures to the states through the Fourteenth Amendment due process clause. Second, the Court declined to mandate that the states apply the exclusionary rule as the remedy for Fourth Amendment violations.

The case involved a police intrusion into a home without a warrant. Justice Felix Frankfurter wrote the majority opinion:

> The knock at the door, whether by day or by night, as a prelude to a search, without authority of law but solely on the authority of the police, did not need the commentary of recent history to be condemned as inconsistent with the conception of human rights enshrined in the history and the basic constitutional documents of English-speaking peoples.
>
> Accordingly, we have no hesitation in saying that were a State affirmatively to sanction such police incursion into privacy it would run counter to the guaranty of the Fourteenth Amendment.

Although the first part of the ruling was another major development in the application of federal due process protections to the states, the second part weakened the effects of the ruling by failing to employ the exclusionary rule as the necessary and severe sanction for Fourth Amendment violations. The majority in *Wolf* accepted as sufficient the other available remedies that states employed to rectify violations. Police who violated citizens' rights could be sued in civil actions for trespass, battery, unlawful imprisonment, or other torts according to the circumstances. Violators who acted with the requisite criminal intent could be prosecuted, and other violators could be subjected to discipline by their agencies, including termination of employment.

The Court noted that, at the time of its decision, 31 states had rejected the *Weeks* doctrine and employed other remedies to address police misconduct. Sixteen states had adopted the *Weeks* doctrine as their remedy, and the Court ruled that fashioning appropriate remedies should be left to the individual states rather than the federal courts. Justice Frankfurter wrote:

> But the ways of enforcing such a basic right raise questions of a different order. How such arbitrary conduct should be checked, what remedies against it should be afforded, the means by which the right should be made effective, are all questions that are not to be so dogmatically answered as to preclude the varying solutions which spring from an allowable range of judgment on issues not susceptible of quantitative solution. ...But the immediate question is whether the basic right to protection against arbitrary intrusion by the police demands the exclusion of logically relevant evidence obtained by an unreasonable search and seizure because, in a federal prosecution for a federal crime, it would be excluded. As a matter of inherent reason, one would suppose this to be an issue as to which men with complete devotion to the protection of the right of privacy might give different answers. When we find that in fact most of the English-speaking world does not regard as vital to such protection the exclusion of evidence thus obtained, we must hesitate to treat this remedy as an essential ingredient of the right.

In an important dissenting opinion in *Wolf*, Justice Frank Murphy argued that suppression of evidence was the only effective means of deterring police from violating constitutional rights. He argued that the remedy of bringing a lawsuit against the police was ineffective because "even if the plaintiff hurdles all these obstacles, and gains a substantial verdict, the individual officer's finances may well make the judgment useless—for the municipality, of course, is not liable without its consent."[6] Justice Murphy also argued that neither criminal prosecution nor administrative sanctioning of police is an effective deterrent, because district attorneys were reluctant to prosecute the officers on whom they depended and police agencies had not proven they could be trusted to engage in self-policing.

Although the remedy part of *Wolf* was overruled 12 years later in *Mapp v. Ohio*, 367 U.S. 643 (1961), *Wolf* is often relied on by those opposed to the exclusionary rule. The question remained what the appropriate remedy for a Fourth Amendment violation should be.

Mapp v. Ohio

In *Mapp v. Ohio*, 367 U.S. 643 (1961), the Court of Chief Justice Earl Warren overruled the second part of *Wolf v. Colorado* and mandated that, for search and seizure violations, the exclusionary rule must be the remedy applied by all the states. The Court adopted Justice Murphy's dissent in *Wolf* and found that the remedies employed by states were "worthless and futile" and, therefore, that the *Weeks* exclusionary rule was the only effective remedy.

In *Mapp*, Cleveland police officers, acting on information that a person they were looking for in connection with a bombing was hiding in Dollree Mapp's residence, attempted to enter the residence. The officers did not have a search warrant, and Ms. Mapp refused to admit them. Approximately three hours later, the officers returned, forcibly opened the door, and entered the residence. Ms. Mapp demanded to see a search warrant. One of the officers held up a piece of paper and claimed it was a warrant. She grabbed the paper out of his hand and placed it in her bosom. A struggle ensued. The officers recovered the piece of paper, which was not a warrant, and handcuffed her. The officers then conducted a widespread search of the residence and found pornographic material. Mapp was arrested and convicted of possession and distribution of pornographic material.

The Supreme Court reversed the conviction, holding that the search without a warrant was unlawful. The Court stated:

> Today we once again examine *Wolf's* constitutional documentation of the right to privacy free from unreasonable state intrusion, and, after its dozen years on our books, are led by it to close the only courtroom door remaining open to evidence secured by official lawlessness in flagrant abuse of that basic right, reserved to all persons as a specific guarantee against that very same unlawful conduct. We hold that all evidence obtained by searches and seizures in violation of the Constitution is, by that same authority, inadmissible in a state court.

Considering that there are approximately 87,000 federal law enforcement agents compared with approximately 800,000 sworn local and state law enforcement officers, *Mapp* was a ninefold expansion of the exclusionary rule. *Mapp* solidified the Court's preference for warrants. A search and seizure pursuant to a warrant carries a presumption of validity, and a defendant who brings a motion to suppress evidence seized pursuant to a warrant has the burden of proof to show that the warrant was issued unlawfully (e.g., without probable cause). On the other hand, when a search and seizure is conducted without a warrant, the prosecution has the burden of proving the existence of a recognized exception to the warrant requirement, such as plain view, consent, or emergency.

Payton v. New York

In 1980, in *Payton v. New York*, 445 U.S. 573, the U.S. Supreme Court extended the Fourth Amendment search warrant requirements imposed by *Weeks*, *Wolf*, and *Mapp* to arrests of a suspect in his or her home. The Court mandated that, for police to arrest a suspect in his home, an arrest warrant was required unless consent to enter the home was obtained or the police acted under emergency or exigent circumstances. Under the prior law in most states, when police or other officials had probable cause to arrest a suspect, they could enter a home without a warrant to make the arrest. This had arguably been true under common law for hundreds of years and was not changed by the ratification of the Constitution.

During the twentieth century, to grant and clarify police authority, many states enacted statutes authorizing warrantless entries to make arrests. In some states, the arrests had to be for felonies; in other states, either felonies or misdemeanors. In 1971, New York State enacted Criminal Procedure Law 140.15 (4), which stated:

> In order to effect such an arrest, a police officer may enter premises in which he reasonably believes such person to be present, under the same circumstances and in the same manner as would be authorized… if he were attempting to make such arrest pursuant to a warrant of arrest.

Payton struck down this statute as it applied to warrantless arrests of defendants inside their homes, but it did not declare the entire statute unconstitutional. The police may still enter without a warrant to effect arrests in "premises," which includes offices, workplaces, and the homes of other persons. Although *Payton* created a new Fourth Amendment protection, it relied on traditional common-law concepts for its justification. The Court noted:

> The weight of authority as it appeared to the Framers was to the effect that a warrant was required, or at the minimum that there were substantial risks in proceeding without one. The commonlaw sources display a sensitivity to privacy interests that could not have been lost on the Framers. The zealous and frequent repetition of the adage that a "man's house is his castle" made it abundantly clear that both in England and in the Colonies "the freedom of one's house" was one of the most vital elements of English liberty.

Violations of *Payton* require the suppression of physical or statement evidence obtained during the arrest in the home.

Motions to suppress evidence take place before a trial. If the defendant succeeds, the challenged evidence will not be admissible at the trial, but, if the defendant fails, the evidence may be admissible. In the latter case, when the defendant is convicted, he or she may appeal the conviction on the grounds that the evidence should have been suppressed.

In some cases, the prosecution will appeal an unfavorable suppression ruling, but such an appeal must be resolved before trial since a defendant's acquittal is final and a ruling by an appellate court that evidence should have been admissible at trial will not allow an acquittal to be reversed. To do so would violate double jeopardy protections.[7]

How Far Does the Exclusionary Rule Go?

Silverthorne Lumber Co. v. United States, 251 U.S. 385 (1920), established that not only evidence obtained directly as a result of a constitutional violation but also evidence obtained indirectly, or one step removed from the constitutional violation, must be suppressed. Does that mean that all evidence obtained against a defendant subsequent to a violation of his rights must be suppressed? The question was addressed in *Wong Sun v. United States*, 371 U.S. 471 (1963), a case that has earned the nickname of the "Chinese puzzle" because of its complications.

In *Wong Sun*, decided before *Miranda* warnings were established in 1966, two defendants (Yee and Wong Sun) were convicted in connection with narcotics trafficking. The circumstances of each arrest were different, and the subsequent court rulings produced differing results. To summarize the facts: Federal narcotics agents, without a warrant, forcibly entered the residence of a man known as Blackie Toy. They handcuffed Toy and searched for narcotics but found none. Nevertheless, Toy told the agents that he knew a person, Johnny Yee, who sold narcotics.

Acting on Toy's information, the agents, without a warrant, entered the residence of Mr. Yee and questioned him. Yee surrendered a tube of heroin to the agents and stated that the heroin had been brought to him by Wong Sun. The agents then entered Wong Sun's residence, also without a warrant. They arrested him and searched for narcotics but found none.

Yee and Wong Sun were arraigned in federal court and released on their own recognizance. Several days later, they voluntarily returned to the police facility for a pretrial interview by a federal agent during which they made incriminating statements regarding their involvement in narcotics dealing. At their trials, four key pieces of evidence were admitted against them:

1. Yee's statements made in his residence at the time of his arrest.
2. The heroin surrendered by Yee.
3. Yee's statement made at the pretrial interview.
4. Wong Sun's statement made at the pretrial interview.

Regarding Yee, the Supreme Court ruled that the statement Yee made in his residence to the agents must be excluded because it was the fruit of the poisonous tree of the unlawful entry into his home, which was made without probable cause and without a warrant. Furthermore, the heroin must also be excluded for use against Yee because it, too, would not have been obtained but for the illegal entry into Yee's residence. Because Yee's conviction was reversed on these grounds, the Court did not have to reach the question of whether his pretrial statement at the police facility was admissible.

Regarding Wong Sun, however, opposite results were obtained. The Supreme Court ruled that the heroin obtained from Yee could be admissible against Wong Sun because the violation of Yee's rights was not transferable to Wong Sun. The entry into Yee's residence did not violate Wong Sun's Fourth Amendment right to privacy; moreover, the unlawful entry into Wong Sun's residence did not require the exclusion of his pretrial statement at the police facility because the statement was given several days after his release. Wong Sun had voluntarily returned to make the statement, and the connection between the arrest and the statement had "become so attenuated as to dissipate the taint."

As *Wong Sun* demonstrates, the suppression of evidence obtained after a constitutional violation is not an absolute rule. The Court explained:

> We need not hold that all evidence is "fruit of the poisonous tree" simply because it would not have come to light but for the illegal actions of the police. Rather, the more apt question in such a case is "whether, granting establishment of the primary illegality,

the evidence to which instant objection is made has been come at by exploitation of that illegality or instead by means sufficiently distinguishable to be purged of the primary taint."

The time and place distances between the unlawful entry into Wong Sun's residence and his statement at the police station were breaks in the causal connection and were key factors in the Court's determination that the statement was not the fruit of the poisonous tree. Had Wong Sun made an incriminating statement in his residence at the time of the unlawful entry and arrest, the statement would have been suppressed as tainted fruit, but his statement was made three days after the unlawful arrest, and the links between the arrest and the statement were attenuated, or too thinly connected. As a policy matter, *Wong Sun* established that an unlawful arrest or search cannot immunize a defendant forever. New evidence developed after an unlawful arrest can provide the basis for a subsequent lawful arrest and prosecution.

Drawing attenuation distinctions between evidence obtained directly from a primary illegality and evidence obtained from a distinguishable secondary source has been a major issue in thousands of wiretap, interrogation, search and seizure, and right to counsel cases. Since *Silverthorne*, the treatment of derivative evidence by federal and state courts has undergone several expansions, contractions, and changes of direction.[8] How courts deal with derivative evidence will be a recurring theme throughout this text.

Independent Source Exception

The costs of the fruits-of-the-poisonous-tree doctrine can sometimes be catastrophic. The exclusion of otherwise reliable, relevant, and vital evidence often results in clearly guilty defendants going free and victims left without justice. To reduce the effects of the poisonous-tree doctrine, courts have adopted exceptions to the doctrine when it is possible to do so without undermining its deterrent value. In *Murray v. United States*, 487 U.S. 533 (1988), federal agents observed the defendants driving trucks into and out of a warehouse. When the trucks left, several agents entered the warehouse and observed numerous burlap-wrapped bales, consistent with marijuana packaging. They did not disturb the bales, and they left to obtain a search warrant. Other agents followed the trucks, lawfully arrested the drivers, and found marijuana in the trucks.

On the basis of the contraband in the trucks, the agents obtained a search warrant for the warehouse. In applying for the warrant, they did not mention the first entry into the warehouse or the observations of the bales. With the warrant in hand, they reentered the warehouse and seized 270 bales of marijuana.

The defendants were subsequently convicted of conspiracy to possess and distribute illegal drugs. They appealed, arguing that the warrant was tainted because the agents had not informed the judge about the prior unlawful warrantless entry and that the warrant was therefore invalid.

The Supreme Court rejected the defendants' argument. The agents' information and belief regarding the presence of marijuana in the warehouse was assuredly acquired at the time of the unlawful entry, but it was also acquired at the time the trucks were lawfully seized. The seizure of the trucks provided a lawful source of information for the warrant application. Had the judge issued the warrant on the basis of information obtained from the unlawful entry, the evidence would have been suppressed, but the judge knew nothing of that circumstance and issued the warrant on the basis of independent information.

Problem

A police department received a 911 call from an anonymous caller who said that a man had a gun in his coat pocket. The caller said that the man was standing at a bus stop, and the caller described the man as about 6 feet tall and 200 pounds, wearing a brown jacket. The caller hung up before giving any further description or information.

Police officers Able and Dunkin were patrolling in the area in their marked patrol car, and they were dispatched to the bus stop to investigate the call. The officers saw a young man, approximately 20 years old and about 6 feet, 3 inches tall, but he appeared to weigh only about 160 pounds. He was wearing a brown military-style jacket.

The officers parked in front of the bus stop and looked at the young man. Officer Dunkin waved to him to come over to the police car, but the young man, later identified as Carl Stooper, began walking away. With that, the officers exited the car and frisked Stooper. In his jacket pocket, they found a loaded automatic pistol.

After arresting Stooper, the officers searched him and found $300, mostly in $20 bills, in the lining of his jacket. Some of the bills had bloodstains on them. The officers sent the pistol to the police ballistics laboratory, where the pistol was test-fired.

The test-fired bullet was compared to bullets in a ballistic evidence computerized data-base, and it was matched to a bullet removed from a murder victim who had been killed during the robbery of a dry-cleaning store several days earlier. There were no witnesses to the dry-cleaning store robbery; however, the detectives who were investigating the case sent the bloodstained bills to a DNA laboratory, where the bloodstains were matched to the murder victim.

On the basis of the forensic evidence, Stooper was indicted for murder, robbery, and unlawful possession of the gun, but his attorney moved to have all the evidence, including the gun and the bloodstained bills, excluded from evidence because they were obtained in violation of Stooper's Fourth Amendment rights when the officers frisked him.

Questions

1. Did the police have probable cause to arrest Stooper on the basis of the anonymous call?
2. Did the police have reasonable suspicion to stop and frisk Stooper on the basis of the anonymous call?
3. Did the additional factor of Stooper walking away from the officers instead of going to the police car give the officers either probable cause or reasonable suspicion to arrest or stop and frisk him?
4. Should the gun that was taken from Stooper's pocket be excluded from evidence at his trial?
5. Should the bloodstained bills taken from Stooper's jacket after he was arrested be excluded from evidence at his trial?
6. Would the independent source exception allow the evidence to be admitted?
7. If a court ruled that the gun and the bloodstained bills had to be suppressed, and barring any other evidence, would all the charges against Stooper have to be dismissed?

Notes

1 *Nardone v. United States*, 308 U.S. 338 (1939).
2 *Wong Sun v. United States*, 371 U.S. 471 (1963); *Brown v. Illinois*, 422 U.S. 590 (1975); *Dunaway v. New York*, 442 U.S. 200 (1979).

3 *United States v. Trupiano*, 334 U.S. 699 (1949); *United States v. Jeffers*, 342 U.S. 48 (1951).
4 *People v. Adams*, 176 N.Y. 351 (1903); *People v. Defore*, 242 N.Y. 13 (1926); *Wolf v. Colorado*, 338 U.S. 25 (1949).
5 *People v. Defore*, *supra*.
6 *Wolf v. Colorado*, 338 U.S. 25 (1949), at 42, dissent. (In 1978, municipalities were deemed potentially liable for the conduct of their employees in *Monell v. Department of Social Services*, 436 U.S. 658.)
7 *Benton v. Maryland*, 395 U.S. 784 (1969).
8 *Brewer v. Williams*, 430 U.S. 387 (1977); *Segura v. United States*, 468 U.S. 796 (1984); *Murray v. United States*, 487 U.S. 533 (1988); *United States v. Patane*, 542 U.S. 630 (2004).

References

Draper v. United States, 358 U.S. 307 (1959).
Florida v. J.L., 529 U.S. 266 (2000).
Illinois v. Gates, 462 U.S. 213 (1983).
Murray v. United States, 487 U.S. 533 (1988).
Segura v. United States, 468 U.S. 796 (1984).
Terry v. Ohio, 392 U.S. 1 (1968).

Section III

Search and Seizure

Chapter 8

Search Warrants

To obtain a search warrant, the applying officer must submit a sworn affidavit to a neutral and detached magistrate detailing sufficient facts and information that will allow the magistrate to make an independent determination of probable cause and the appropriateness of a search warrant. An affidavit is a signed document attesting, under oath or affirmation, to certain facts of which the affiant (the person submitting the affidavit) has knowledge. Magistrates are public officials with limited judicial authority, such as justices of the peace. Judges have greater powers than magistrates, and in some jurisdictions can appoint magistrates to conduct preliminary proceedings in both civil and criminal cases. The affidavit is submitted to a magistrate or judge who may or may not issue a search warrant. In *Johnson v. United States*, 333 U.S. 10 (1948), Supreme Court Justice Robert Jackson provided the rationale for the warrant requirement:

> The point of the Fourth Amendment… is not that it denies law enforcement the support of the usual inferences reasonable men draw from evidence. Its protection consists in requiring that those inferences be drawn by a neutral and detached magistrate instead of being judged by the officer engaged in the often competitive enterprise of ferreting out crime.

Oath or Affirmation

An oath or affirmation is required to ensure that the information provided to the court is trustworthy. Traditionally, an oath required that the attesting person swear to God or on the Bible to tell the truth. Today, an affirmation can be the equivalent of an oath and can be given without a religious reference. An oath or affirmation can take any form as long as it is calculated to awaken the conscience and impress the mind of the person taking it in accordance with his religious or ethical beliefs to tell the truth.[1]

For search warrant affidavits, the affiant attests that the information in the affidavit is true and accurate and does so under penalty of perjury, meaning that the oath or affirmation invokes the possibility of prosecution for perjury if the affiant intentionally provides false material information. To require less would allow individuals to cause the issuance of an unlawful warrant without any meaningful recourse against them.

In cases in which a police officer prepares an affidavit for a warrant on the basis of information obtained from a confidential informant, the officer must swear that the informant exists and provided the proffered information. In addition, the officer must provide some specific facts that tend to corroborate the informant's allegations. An affidavit is insufficient

DOI: 10.4324/9781003415091-11

for the issuance of a search warrant if it is based merely on the affiant's suspicion or belief without stating the facts and circumstances that support probable cause.

An insufficient affidavit cannot be augmented and made sufficient by oral testimony because that would leave too much leeway for after-the-fact revisions.[2] This rule must be distinguished from telephonic search warrant applications.

Some jurisdictions authorize telephonic search warrant applications, by which an officer gives his sworn statement to the magistrate via telephone, video conferencing, or other means of communication. If the magistrate approves the warrant, he prepares an original warrant and the officer prepares a duplicate that he uses during the execution of the warrant. The sufficiency of the warrant must be judged on the content of the written original.[3] Electronically recorded sworn oral testimony has been found no less reliable than a sworn, written affidavit, and the recording satisfies the requirements of an affidavit.[4]

Probable Cause and Particularity

Search warrants must "particularly describe the place to be searched and the persons or things to be seized." They may be issued to recover:

- Evidence of a crime
- Contraband (e.g., unlawful narcotics, weapons)
- Property designed for use, intended for use, or used in committing a crime
- A person to be arrested
- A person who is being unlawfully restrained[5]

The description of the particular place to be searched must be as specific as possible and sufficient enough that the officer with the search warrant can with reasonable effort ascertain the place intended in the warrant.[6] Searches that are too broad or open-ended are not allowed. A search warrant for a multiple-occupancy building will usually be invalid if it fails to describe the particular apartment or other subunit to be searched. On the other hand, if a warrant was obtained for a building that appeared to be a single-occupancy dwelling and upon the execution of the warrant it was discovered that the building contained multiple subunits, the warrant might still be valid if the discovery of the multiple units occurred only after the police had proceeded to a point where withdrawal would jeopardize the search, and they made reasonable efforts to confine the search to the area most likely connected with the suspected criminality.

Although the search warrant must be sufficiently definite so that the officer executing it can identify the property sought with reasonable certainty, the description of the particular things to be seized may often be more general than that for the place to be searched. For example, a search warrant for the premises of a suspected murder scene will allow a search for evidence without specific knowledge of what evidence may remain at the premises. The warrant may specify a search for bloodstains, hair follicles, rug or garment fibers, fingerprints, and so on, but the existence of these items may be quite speculative. Also, search warrants for premises suspected of housing ongoing criminal activities are generally issued not for the seizure of a specifically identified item but for categories of contraband, such as illegal drugs, pornography, or gambling records. Nonetheless, a sufficient degree of particularity is required. The more specific the description of the things to be seized, the more likely that probable cause has been established.

Confidential Informants

Law enforcement agencies throughout the nation have developed standard operating procedures for investigating ongoing criminal activity. Because ongoing criminal enterprises do not operate openly, law enforcement agents need to obtain inside information to successfully prosecute these enterprises, and they necessarily obtain this information through confidential informants. However, because confidential informants are often criminals who have made a deal to help the police in exchange for leniency or money, courts have continually expressed concerns with their reliability and truthfulness. The Warren Court established a two-step criterion for judging the reliability of confidential informants, which became known as the *Aguilar–Spinelli* test and was derived from *Aguilar v. Texas*, 378 U.S. 108 (1964), and *Spinelli v. United States*, 393 U.S. 410 (1969). It required both of the following:

1. The affiant (police officer) to affirm that the informant he or she is relying on has been reliable in the past. This is usually established by recounting past instances in which the informant's information was accurate and productive.
2. The affiant (police officer) to describe the informant's basis of knowledge for the current information he is alleging. This is usually established by recounting the facts that the informant claims to have seen or heard.

This test is most often applied in narcotics trafficking cases in which police are attempting to arrest those criminals who are higher up in the drug-dealing hierarchy. To develop strong cases against such individuals, the police attempt to persuade their accomplices to provide information about them and to assist in locating their illegal drugs. The so-called "little fish to big fish" investigation is the usual method employed. Typically, it commences when an undercover police officer buys a small amount of heroin, cocaine, or amphetamine from a low-level dealer who is an accomplice in the drug organization. The police arrest the low-level dealer and, in exchange for a reduced sentence, enlist him or her as a confidential informant. When the informant cooperates and identifies the supplier, the police might be able to arrest the supplier; however, because the law mandates that a defendant cannot be convicted on the uncorroborated testimony of an accomplice, the police need additional evidence to secure a conviction. The best corroborating evidence would be to arrest the supplier in possession of a large amount of drugs; therefore, the police attempt to find the location or stash house of the drugs and to pinpoint the time when drugs will be at that location. Because most illegal drug supplies are stored in apartments or homes, search warrants are needed, and to obtain such search warrants the police need specific information.

The difficulty that police have with the *Aguilar–Spinelli* test for establishing confidential informant reliability is that both criteria have to be satisfied. An informant may have what seems to be specific and timely information, but if the police have not worked with him in the past they cannot obtain a warrant on the basis of the information, because the informant's reliability has not been established.

The Rehnquist Supreme Court addressed this problem in *Illinois v. Gates*, 462 U.S. 213 (1983). Modifying the *Aguilar–Spinelli* test, the Court established the totality of the circumstances test for evaluating probable cause and rejected the prior hyper-technical two-pronged test. In *Illinois v. Gates*, the police received an anonymous letter that described in detail the operations of an interstate drug smuggling ring. After the police conducted surveillance that confirmed most of the detailed information in the letter, they executed search warrants, recovered illegal narcotics, and made arrests. The defendant appealed his conviction on the grounds that the prior reliability of the anonymous letter writer had not been established.

The Supreme Court rejected the appeal. As it would be impossible to establish the prior reliability of an anonymous person, the Court held that a failing in one part of the two-pronged test could be compensated for by strength in the other part of the test. Here, the confirmed details of the letter established a strong basis of knowledge that compensated for the lack of prior reliability, and under a totality of circumstances analysis the issuance of the search warrant was reasonable.

Nevertheless, in most confidential investigations, the police know the confidential informant, and it is prudent for them to establish the informant's reliability before applying for a search warrant. Below are factors that courts have considered in determining an informant's reliability:

1. The informant has supplied information in the past that led to at least one arrest and conviction; convictions are not necessary if the information led to more than one arrest but involved different criminal incidents.
2. The informant has supplied information in the past that led to the seizure of evidence, contraband, or stolen property.
3. If two or more informants corroborate the information, the informants must not be known to each other and must act independently of each other.
4. The information constitutes a declaration against penal interest that connects the informant to the crime or otherwise incriminates him.
5. The police observe sufficient details that corroborate the information and indicate the informant knew of what he spoke; for example, they are able to corroborate the information with respect to:
   a. The suspect's dress, mannerisms, route, or conveyance used.
   b. The suspect's appearance at the time and place provided by the informant and the suspect's actions being consistent with the informant's details.
   c. Police observation of the suspect in possession of objects or containers matching the quantity, shape, or physical characteristics of the reported contraband.

Information from apparently reputable persons who are willing to identify themselves is presumed to be credible and need not be scrutinized to the same degree as information from confidential informants.[7] Nonetheless, an officer applying for a warrant must make a reasonable assessment and must have reasonable cause to believe the information is true.

A judge may reject or approve a warrant application. It must be kept in mind, however, that an approved warrant is still subject to challenge after it has been executed. For obvious reasons, a defendant cannot challenge the warrant before its execution, but afterwards it may be challenged on the grounds that it was issued without probable cause. The challenge is conducted at a motion to suppress hearing to determine whether the evidence will be admissible at the trial.

If it is subsequently determined that the warrant was invalid, the evidence seized pursuant to the warrant would ordinarily be inadmissible under the exclusionary rule doctrine, although exceptions to this general rule have arisen. For circumstances in which the police acted in reliance on a facially valid warrant that was later determined to be defective, arguments arose that it was hyper-technical and counterproductive to apply the exclusionary rule to the seized evidence. The Supreme Court addressed this issue in *United States v. Leon*, 468 U.S. 897 (1984).

In *Leon*, the Court established the good-faith exception to the warrant requirement. In that case, police officers in Burbank, California, had conducted an extensive investigation into the activities of a drug-dealing ring. The officers obtained a search warrant, and during its execution recovered quantities of unlawful drugs. After the indictments of the ring members, the defendants challenged the validity of the search warrant.

The District Court held an evidentiary hearing and, while recognizing that the case was a close one, concluded that the affidavit for the search warrant was insufficient to establish probable cause. The District Court suppressed part of the evidence.

The prosecution appealed the ruling to the Supreme Court, and the Court reversed the lower court ruling, stating, "Our evaluation of the costs and benefits of suppressing reliable physical evidence seized by officers reasonably relying on a warrant issued by a detached and neutral magistrate leads to the conclusion that such evidence should be admissible in the prosecution's case in chief."[8]

The Court explained that the purpose of the exclusionary rule was to deter the police from committing constitutional violations. In this case, the officers had acted in objective good faith, obtained a search warrant, and acted within its scope: "There is no police illegality and thus nothing to deter." In summary, the Court stated, "We conclude that the marginal or nonexistent benefits produced by suppressing evidence obtained in objectively reasonable reliance on a subsequently invalidated search warrant cannot justify the substantial costs of exclusion."[9]

Leon made it clear that, in cases in which the rule does not have the effect of deterring future police misconduct, imposition of the rule serves no purpose. In cases in which the rule may have a minimal, indirect effect of deterring future police violations, the rule must be weighed against the costs of withholding reliable, physical evidence from the truth-seeking process, and against both the costs to crime-prevention efforts and the costs to the crime victims and their families.

The *Leon* good-faith exception is not applicable when the judge is misled by information in the affidavit that the officer knew or should have known was false. Additionally, the good-faith exception is not applicable when the affidavit is so lacking in sufficient probable cause or particularity regarding the place to be searched and the things to be seized that the officer could not presume the warrant to be valid. For example, a search warrant for a single-family residence at 10 Smith Street would not be valid if the police find that 10 Smith Street is a multi-family building, and the police could not search the entire building simply because the address was the same as on the warrant.

The good-faith exception has also been applied to the after-issuance recordkeeping aspects of a warrant, such as mistakes as to whether a warrant was active or inactive. In *Herring v. United States*, 129 S. Ct. 695 (2009), a police officer arrested the defendant on the basis of a purported outstanding warrant recorded in a police database. Incidental to the arrest, the officer searched the defendant and found illegal amphetamines and a gun. Shortly thereafter, it was determined that the warrant had been rescinded and was no longer in effect. Due to a clerical error, the warrant had not been removed from the active file. When the defendant was indicted, he moved to suppress both the drugs and the gun because no probable cause to arrest him had existed and the search therefore violated his Fourth Amendment rights.

The Supreme Court majority voiced the opinion that the search was not necessarily unreasonable; however, the government in lower court proceedings had conceded that point. Consequently, the only issue preserved for the Court was whether applying the exclusionary rule in these circumstances would have a deterrent effect on future police misconduct. The Court ruled that it would not—the clerical error that prompted the arrest was the result of isolated negligence, and any benefit obtained by suppressing the evidence would be marginal or nonexistent and would not outweigh its social costs. Following its precedents, *Franks v. Delaware*, 438 U.S. 154 (1978), *Illinois v. Gates*, 462 U.S. 213 (1983), *United States v. Leon*, 468 U.S. 897 (1984), *Massachusetts v. Sheppard*, 468 U.S. 981 (1984), *Arizona v. Evans*, 514 U.S. 1 (1995), and *Hudson v. Michigan*, 547 U.S. 586 (2006), the Court stated:

> To trigger the exclusionary rule, police conduct must be sufficiently deliberate that exclusion can meaningfully deter it, and sufficiently culpable that such deterrence is worth the price paid by the justice system. As laid out in our cases, the exclusionary rule serves to deter deliberate, reckless, or grossly negligent conduct, or in some circumstances recurring or systemic negligence. The error in this case does not rise to that level.

Challenging the Truthfulness of a Warrant Application

After a search warrant is executed, a defendant often challenges the facial sufficiency of the warrant by bringing a motion to suppress the seized evidence. The reviewing court must decide whether the assertions in the affidavit were sufficient to support a finding of probable cause. If they were sufficient, the search warrant should be upheld and the recovered evidence should be admitted. Even if the assertions turn out to be false, the search might still be upheld because the officer who applied for the warrant and the judge who issued the warrant had a reasonable belief that the assertions were true. As often happens, a nongovernmental informant may have provided false information on which the police relied; nevertheless, the warrant and search are deemed to have been lawful. It is another matter when the police knew the information was false or they lied about their own efforts to corroborate the information.

For some time, courts were split as to whether a defendant could go beyond challenging the facial sufficiency of a warrant and introduce evidence at a suppression hearing to show that the underlying assertions in the warrant affidavit were false. In *Franks v. Delaware*, 438 U.S. 154 (1978), the Supreme Court resolved the split and ruled that under some conditions a defendant could challenge the underlying truthfulness of the allegations. To do so, the defendant must "point out specifically the portion of the warrant affidavit that is claimed to be false" and "provide a statement of supporting reasons." Upon a sufficient showing, a hearing (which has come to be known as a *Franks* hearing) will be held, at which the defendant has the burden of proving, by a preponderance of the evidence, that the challenged statements are false and that their inclusion in the affidavit amounted to perjury or reckless disregard of the truth. The key question is whether the deliberate falsity or reckless disregard of the truth was provided by a government affiant or a nongovernmental informant. If it was a government officer, the warrant and the evidence will be suppressed; if it was an informant, the warrant likely will be upheld and the evidence admitted.

In *Herring v. United States*, 129 S. Ct. 695 (2009), the Court reiterated the *Franks* principles that police conduct encompassing "deliberate falsehood or reckless disregard of the truth" will require the exclusion of evidence obtained as a result.

Problem

A 25-year-old woman, Grace White, appeared in person at a police station and spoke with Detective Harry Ready. She explained to the detective that she had information about a narcotics trafficking gang and could help the police make a big drug bust, but her identity must remain confidential. Also, she insisted that the police promise not to arrest her boyfriend.

Detective Ready informed her that, without knowing more of the details, he could not guarantee her confidentiality and that he did not have the authority to provide immunity for her boyfriend. He did say, however, that he would do his best to keep her name quiet if he could and would not arrest her boyfriend.

Ms. White related that her boyfriend, Carlos Johnson, worked for a drug dealer. The boyfriend did not sell drugs but was paid to provide security, drive cars, keep lookout, and perform other duties. She was afraid that Carlos would be arrested and sent to prison, and, ultimately, she was afraid that he would get killed. She had heard that the drug dealer had killed a couple of his workers in the past because he thought they might cooperate with the police. She did not want the same thing to happen to Carlos.

"What's the drug dealer's name?" Detective Ready asked. "Cabellero," Ms. White replied.

"What's his first name?"

"I don't know," she said. "They call him Boss to his face. To his back, they call him El Loco."

White explained that Cabellero owned or ran a restaurant named The Café, on Main Street, and that this was the headquarters for his drug trafficking gang. His main drug supplies were delivered to the restaurant along with the regular restaurant supplies. The drugs were then repackaged and distributed to his street dealers when they came into the restaurant.

"How do you know this?" Ready asked.

"Everybody in the neighborhood knows," she said.

"Have you ever seen these drugs?"

"No, but Carlos makes a lot of money for just standing around."

"Has Carlos seen the drugs?"

"He won't tell me anything specific, but he gets paid in cash every Monday after the accounts are settled."

"What accounts?"

"The street dealers get their supply up front. On Mondays they have to bring back the cash."

"Where does this take place?"

"In The Café."

White gave Ready further details about the gang, including a description of Cabellero and the black BMW he drove. She agreed to find out any other information that she could and to call the detective again.

After she left, Detective Ready opened an investigation and began gathering information to corroborate White's story. Two weeks later, he prepared an affidavit to obtain a search warrant for The Café, as follows:

I am a Smith County Police Detective. For the past two weeks I have received information from an informant that John Cabellero has been distributing narcotics—cocaine and heroin—at The Café Restaurant on Main Street in Smith County. The informant states that she has received first-hand information from a person known to her regarding the ongoing narcotics trafficking at The Café. The person known to her, whose identity is known to the undersigned officer, works in the narcotics organization of Mr. Cabellero. He has related to the informant that Cabellero's main drug supplies are delivered to the restaurant along with the regular restaurant supplies. The drugs are repackaged and then distributed to his street dealers when they come into the restaurant. On Mondays, the accounts are settled when the street dealers turn in the money they accumulated during the week selling the narcotics supplied to them by Cabellero.

The undersigned officer has conducted a surveillance of The Café to corroborate the informant's information. Cabellero was observed entering and exiting the location on numerous occasions. He drove a black BMW as described by the informant. During the two weeks of surveillance, numerous males and females were observed entering The Café and leaving after a short period of time. Last Monday, many of the males and females who had visited the location during the week entered the location and remained for periods of between one and two hours.

The undersigned requests a warrant to search The Café for narcotics contraband, records of narcotics transactions, and proceeds of the sale of unlawful narcotics.

Sworn under penalty of perjury,

Dated _____ Detective Harry Ready

Questions

1. Should the magistrate issue a search warrant for The Café?
2. Must the confidential informant (Ms. White) appear in court to testify to the information she provided before the warrant may be issued?
3. If the magistrate issued the search warrant and the detective recovered narcotics and arrested Cabellero, on what grounds could Cabellero challenge the admissibility of the items into evidence?
4. In a state court that adhered to the *Aguilar–Spinelli* criteria for establishing probable cause on the basis of a confidential informant, would the information provided in the affidavit have met the criteria?
5. In a federal court that followed the *Illinois v. Gates* totality of the circumstances criteria for establishing probable cause on the basis of a confidential informant, would the information provided in the affidavit have met the criteria?
6. Were the observations by the police sufficient to confirm the confidential informant's reliability?
7. Were the observations by the police that only confirmed details that did not necessarily suggest criminal activity sufficient to confirm the confidential informant's reliability?
8. At a suppression hearing, should the defense attorneys be entitled to know the informant's identity and basis for the allegations?
9. If the magistrate refused to issue a search warrant on the basis of the detective's affidavit, what other measures could the detective take to obtain more evidence to establish the necessary probable cause to issue a warrant?
10. Was it necessary for the police to make an undercover drug buy from one or more of the alleged street dealers to establish sufficient probable cause for the search warrant?

Anticipatory Warrants and Controlled Deliveries

Today, most search warrants are issued in connection with the "war on drugs," and a substantial number are issued in pornography cases. Courts have recognized the difficult challenges law enforcement officers face in their efforts to combat drug trafficking and pornography, and they have made adjustments to the warrant requirements. Courts have acknowledged the tactics employed by criminals in such cases, and they have recognized the need for law enforcement to employ counter tactics.

One police tactic that courts have approved is the anticipatory warrant, or a warrant contingent upon the occurrence of a future, triggering event. Courts have held that anticipatory warrants are permissible as long as the evidence creates a substantial probability that the property will be on the premises at the time the warrant is executed, rather than the traditional requirement that the property is at the location at the time the warrant is issued.[10]

A typical case occurs when the U.S. Postal Service or a commercial transportation company finds that a package in transport contains unlawful drugs. Depending on the locale, the commercial company will notify federal authorities or the local police. However, because the senders of these packages generally use fictitious names, it is difficult for law enforcement officers to identify and arrest them. To arrest the recipient of the package for possession of the unlawful drugs, proof is required that the recipient knowingly took possession of the drugs.

The most feasible way for law enforcement to proceed is to delay delivery of the package long enough to obtain an anticipatory warrant, allow the package to be delivered, ascertain that the recipient accepted the package (the triggering event), and then execute the search warrant to recover the package.

In *United States v. Grubbs*, 547 U.S. 90 (2006), a pornography case, the Supreme Court upheld the constitutionality of anticipatory search warrants, stating: "An anticipatory warrant is a warrant based upon an affidavit showing probable cause that at some future time (but not presently) certain evidence of crime will be located at a specified place." The defendant in *Grubbs* ordered a videotape containing child pornography from an Internet website run by undercover postal inspectors.

Before allowing delivery of the videotape, the postal inspectors applied for a search warrant for the defendant's home. The affidavit for the warrant stated that the warrant would not be executed until a person received the package and physically took it into the home. When the package was accepted at the home, the postal inspectors executed the warrant, recovered the videotape, and arrested the defendant.

The Supreme Court upheld the conviction and the issuance of the search warrant because the triggering condition (i.e., the successful delivery of the videotape) plainly established probable cause for the search. Had the postal inspectors executed the warrant before the delivery, the warrant would have been invalid.

Procedures and Statutory Rules

In addition to the Fourth Amendment probable cause requirements, law enforcement officers must be aware of the statutory requirements for obtaining and executing warrants. State and federal statutes define the authority and procedures. Generally, the officer to whom a search warrant is addressed must execute it, and the officer must have it in hand during the execution. This differs from an arrest warrant, which may be executed by any police officer and the officer need not have the warrant in hand.

Search warrants contain other important limitations and differences from arrest warrants. Because the information for the search warrant must be current, most jurisdictions require that search warrants be executed within ten days of their issuance.[11] This differs from arrest warrants, which can remain in effect indefinitely or until the subject is apprehended.

Search warrants must generally be executed during the day, defined as between 6:00 A M and 9:00 P M in some jurisdictions and 6:00 A M and 10:00 P M in others,[12] whereas arrest warrants in most states may be executed at any time of day or night. Some states draw a distinction between felony and misdemeanor arrest warrants. Night-time execution is authorized for the former but not for the latter. For search warrants, a judge may specifically include a written night-service endorsement on the basis of sufficient cause, such as concern for safety or destruction of evidence.

In executing either a search warrant or an arrest warrant, the officer must make a reasonable effort to give notice of his authority and purpose to the occupants of the premises before entry. This is called the knock-and-announce rule. In most states, the judge issuing a warrant may dispense with the knock-and-announce rule and instead issue a no-knock warrant when sufficient cause exists. The officer executing a warrant may use as much physical force, other than deadly physical force, as necessary to execute the warrant. An officer may use deadly physical force if he or she reasonably believes such to be necessary to defend him- or herself or another from the use or imminent use of deadly physical force.

The provision for the use of deadly physical force may seem the same as the standard right of self-defense; however, the right of self-defense might not apply were an officer illegally entering a person's residence or illegally using force against a person. The warrant legalizes the officer's actions and enables him to invoke the right to self-defense.

Knock-and-Announce Rules

At common law, it was long accepted that officers must knock and announce their presence and authority before entering private premises to execute a warrant. The purpose of the rule was to:

1. Reduce the potential for violent confrontations.
2. Protect individual privacy.
3. Give the occupant time to voluntarily admit the officers.

An interesting question is whether a violation of the rule invokes the Fourth Amendment and the exclusionary rule. For example, if the police execute a search warrant without properly knocking and announcing their authority and purpose before entering a residence, should any recovered evidence be suppressed?

In *Wilson v. Arkansas*, 514 U.S. 927 (1995), the Supreme Court ruled that the knock-and-announce rule was a constitutional requirement. In *Wilson*, the police obtained a search warrant for the defendant's house. Part of the information for the warrant was that the defendant had waved a semiautomatic pistol in the informant's face and threatened to kill her. When the police executed the warrant, they found the main door to the home open. "While opening an unlocked screen door and entering the residence, they identified themselves as police officers and stated that they had a warrant." Inside, they seized unlawful drugs and arrested the defendant. The defendant claimed that because the officers had not knocked and announced when they were outside the home, the evidence should be suppressed.

The Supreme Court found that, although the common-law knock-and-announce rule is not written in the Fourth Amendment, the Framers considered it a reasonable requirement for search and seizures; however, reasonable exceptions for dangerous circumstances are recognized. In *Wilson* the Court remanded the case to the Arkansas court to determine whether an exception applied to the case.

In *United States v. Banks*, 540 U.S. 31 (2003), the Court indicated that each case had to be decided on the totality of the circumstances. In *Banks*, the police executed a search warrant to seize narcotics at a home. The Supreme Court ruled that the police had acted reasonably when, after knocking and announcing that they had a warrant and after waiting 15 to 20 seconds with no answer, they forced the door open. In this case, reasonableness was determined not by the time it would take a person to answer the door but by the time the person needed to flush the drugs down a drain.

In *Hudson v. Michigan*, 547 U.S. 586 (2006), the Supreme Court ruled that a violation of the knock-and-announce rule did not invoke the exclusionary rule. In *Hudson*:

> Police obtained a warrant authorizing a search for drugs and firearms at the home of petitioner Booker Hudson. They discovered both. Large quantities of drugs were found, including crack cocaine rocks in Hudson's pocket. A loaded gun was lodged between the cushion and armrest of the chair in which he was sitting.... When the police arrived to execute the warrant, they announced their presence, but waited only a short time—perhaps "three to five seconds"—before turning the knob of the unlocked front door and entering Hudson's home. Hudson moved to suppress all the inculpatory evidence, arguing that the police should have waited more than five seconds before entering and the premature entry violated his Fourth Amendment rights.

The Michigan trial court had suppressed the evidence, ruling that the police did not wait long enough after knocking to enter the premises and that a violation of search warrant knock-and-announce requirements mandated the suppression of evidence found during the execution of the warrant.

The Supreme Court reversed the Michigan court decision and ruled that the exclusionary rule was inapplicable to this kind of police action. The Supreme Court pointed out that the purpose of the knock-and-announce rule "is the protection of life and limb, because the unannounced entry may provoke violence in supposed self-defense by the surprised resident." Other purposes are to protect property and individual dignity. The Court stated: "What the knock-and-announce rule has never protected... is one's interest in preventing the government from seeing or taking evidence described in a warrant. Since the interests that were violated in this case have nothing to do with the seizure of the evidence, the exclusionary rule is inapplicable." The Court observed that the social costs of excluding relevant incriminating evidence outweigh any deterrent effect the exclusionary rule might provide, and that civil rights lawsuits and improved internal police discipline now provide sufficient deterrents.

The Court recognized that it could not realistically be expected that police officers investigating serious crimes will make no errors. Before penalizing the police through the application of the exclusionary rule, it should be determined whether suppressing the evidence serves a valid and useful purpose.

Despite the Supreme Court's ruling in *Hudson v. Michigan*, law enforcement officers should not disregard knock-and-announce rules and other statutory requirements and procedures. A state court reviewing police actions may decline to follow Supreme Court cases such as *Hudson*. State courts are required to provide, at least, the minimum protections of the U.S. Constitution, but they may provide greater protections under their own constitutions. For example, many state courts adhere to the *Aguilar–Spinelli* test for determining probable cause from a confidential informant source, rather than the *Gates* totality of the circumstances standard.[13] Moreover, several state courts have been reluctant to apply the *Leon* good-faith exception;[14] therefore, police officers must not only act in accordance with general Fourth Amendment principles but also know and comply with the specific court rulings and statutory law in their particular jurisdictions.

Administrative Warrants

In our highly regulated society, an individual's Fourth Amendment expectation of privacy often conflicts with government efforts to ensure public health and safety. A vast array of government agencies monitor and inspect the activities of their constituents, and under some circumstances these agencies conduct administrative searches of homes or businesses to ensure compliance with various statutes and regulations. Whether a warrant is required to conduct a particular administrative search depends on the nature and purpose of the search.

To lawfully conduct an inspection or search of a home, business, or other premises to enforce fire, health, housing, employment, safety, environmental, and other regulatory schemes, government agents must obtain an administrative warrant.[15] Such a warrant may be issued on the basis of a valid public interest and some evidence of an existing violation. These warrants need not meet the stringent probable cause standard for a search warrant to obtain evidence in connection with a criminal prosecution.[16]

For closely regulated businesses, however, such as pharmacies, nursing homes, meat markets, cigarette dealers, transporters of hazardous materials, licensed firearms dealers, and liquor manufacturers and distributors, the courts have allowed warrantless inspections and searches. The justification for this policy is the government's strong interest in protecting the public in relation to these industries, and also the diminished expectation of privacy of those who conduct business in these industries.

The rationale that the Supreme Court adopted in *United States v. Biswell*, 406 U.S. 311 (1972), a gun dealer case, applies to most closely regulated businesses:

> If inspection is to be effective and serve as a credible deterrent, unannounced, even frequent, inspections are essential. In this context, the prerequisite of a warrant could easily frustrate inspections; and if the necessary flexibility as to time, scope and frequency is to be preserved, the protections afforded by a warrant would be negligible.
>
> It is also plain that inspections for compliance with the Gun Control Act pose only limited threats to the dealer's justifiable expectations of privacy. When a dealer chooses to engage in this pervasively regulated business and to accept a federal license, he does so with the knowledge that his business records, firearms, and ammunition will be subject to effective inspection.

For an administrative search to be lawful, the purpose of the search must be to ensure compliance with a regulatory scheme, not to obtain evidence for a criminal prosecution. If the purpose is to obtain evidence of a crime, a search warrant should be obtained.

Drawing lines between administrative searches that require warrants and those that do not can be difficult. Determining when a regulatory administrative search becomes a search to advance a criminal prosecution is also difficult. In one situation, the search of an automobile junkyard business, or what is commonly referred to as a "chop shop," was held unconstitutional by the New York Court of Appeals, but constitutional by the U.S. Supreme Court.

In *People v. Burger*, 67 N.Y.2d 338 (1986), the New York court held that a statute that allowed unannounced inspections and searches of automobile dismantling businesses and searches pursuant to the statute were unconstitutional. The court ruled that the evidence obtained during the search should have been excluded from the defendant's criminal trial because the statute did not serve a purely administrative purpose and was designed to uncover evidence of criminality.

The Supreme Court granted a writ of certiorari to review the case and in *New York v. Burger*, 481 U.S. 691 (1987), reversed the New York decision. The Court held that the extensive registration and recordkeeping aspects of the statute made the New York junkyard industry a closely regulated business and, therefore, subject to warrantless inspections and searches. Holding that the evidence was admissible, the Court outlined three criteria that the statutory scheme satisfied. First, the state has a substantial interest in regulating the vehicle dismantling industry because this industry is closely associated with the significant problem of motor vehicle theft. Second, surprise inspection is necessary if stolen vehicles and parts are to be detected. Third, the statute provides a constitutionally "adequate substitute for a warrant" by informing junkyard operators to expect inspections on a regular basis during business hours. By implication, searches conducted after regular business hours require a search warrant.

The Supreme Court remanded the case back to New York, but for technical reasons New York did not issue a further ruling pertaining to *Burger*. However, the New York Court of Appeals addressed the issue again in *People v. Keta*, 79 N.Y.2d 474 (1992), and ruled that the chop-shop inspections statute violated the New York Constitution. This is another example of state law differing from federal law.

In situations when an administrative search changes into a search to uncover evidence for a criminal prosecution, a search warrant that meets Fourth Amendment probable cause and particularity standards will be required. In *Michigan v. Tyler*, 436 U.S. 499 (1978), a furniture store had burned down during the night. The fire department fought the blaze and, after the fire was reduced to embers, the fire chief, while investigating the cause of the fire, discovered two plastic containers of flammable liquid. He summoned a detective, and more evidence of arson was found and seized. A month later, an arson investigator visited the fire scene without a warrant and obtained additional evidence that was used at the defendant's trial.

The Court held that the investigative activity on the date of the fire was legal but the entry into the premises a month later was not:

> We hold that an entry to fight a fire requires no warrant, and that once in the building officials may remain there for a reasonable time to investigate the cause of the blaze. Thereafter, additional entries to investigate the cause of the fire must be made pursuant to the warrant procedures governing administrative searches.... Evidence of arson discovered in the course of such investigations is admissible at trial, but if the investigating officials find probable cause to believe that arson has occurred and require further access to gather evidence for a possible prosecution, they may obtain a warrant only upon a traditional showing of probable cause applicable to searches for evidence of crime.

Evidence observed in connection with emergency entries into premises by fire, police, or other government agents will generally be admissible, but after the initial emergency has passed a continued search for evidence requires a search warrant.

Special Needs Searches

Similar to the closely regulated industry doctrine that allows inspections and searches of premises without warrants, the special needs doctrine, under specified circumstances, allows warrantless inspections and searches of persons and their property. The special needs doctrine is invoked for border and airport security; for prisoner, parolee, and probationer supervision; and for public school student safety. Although a special needs status does not invalidate an individual's Fourth Amendment rights, the status is relevant in determining the reasonableness of a search by balancing the state interest against the individual's expectation of privacy.

Border and Airport Searches

The government has a compelling interest to secure the borders and control persons and property entering the country, and persons entering the country know they may be stopped and detained merely because they are crossing the border. By their voluntary action they give implied consent to a search, and they forfeit some of their expectation of privacy as they pass through the customs inspection stations at the geographical border or at an interior airport.

An airport is the functional equivalent of a border when it receives passengers from international arrival flights. At borders and on the arrival of international arrival flights, U.S. customs agents can conduct searches to determine whether merchandise is being illegally imported, either because of nonpayment of a required duty tax or because it is contraband. The agents may search a person's luggage and other belongings without a warrant and without probable cause; however, the search of clothing worn by the person, or the person's body, entails some limitations. Such searches may be divided into three levels of intrusion.

First, a pat-down search can be justified by a minimal level of suspicion, but the suspicion must be based on legitimate factors such as excessive nervousness, unusual conduct, inadequate luggage, evasiveness, or contradictory answers. One court upheld an airport pat-down of a passenger who was traveling alone without any checked baggage, who disembarked from a flight originating in a country known to be a source of drugs, and who had made a prior trip from that country within a relatively short period of time.[17] Second, a strip search, which entails a substantial intrusion into personal privacy, must be justified by a substantial level of suspicion that the individual is concealing contraband. Third, a body cavity search can only be conducted when justified by a clear indication of smuggling.[18]

Passengers on domestic flights have an expectation of privacy and Fourth Amendment protections. Courts have held, however, that they are subject to reasonable screening such as by the use of a magnetometer to detect the presence of metal upon a person. Because the potential danger inherent in airplane traffic is so evident and the government's interest is so critical, the minimal intrusion of magnetometer screening is reasonable and constitutionally permissible.[19] Under the same theory, x-rays can be used to scan the luggage of boarding passengers.

Prison, Parole, and Probation Supervision

Fourth Amendment rights are not abrogated when a person becomes a prisoner, a parolee, or a probationer. Their rights, however, are modified in accordance with their status, and their status is relevant in determining the reasonableness of a search.

Prisoners lose the most rights. "With the closing of the prison doors behind him an inmate loses or must endure substantial limitations on many rights.... Nevertheless, a prisoner does not lose all rights during incarceration but rather retains those rights that are not inconsistent with his status as an inmate."[20]

A prisoner's rights must be balanced against the security needs of the prison. Cells may be searched without a warrant, strip searches may be conducted to maintain the safety and security of the institution, and letters sent by prisoners may be inspected by prison officials before the letter is sealed. Objectively reasonable searches, conducted for safety and security purposes, are permissible. Unreasonable searches conducted for illegitimate purposes violate the Fourth Amendment.

Parolees are permitted, and agree, to serve their sentences outside a correctional institution under strict supervision. They have a diminished expectation of privacy and are subject to searches that would be unlawful if conducted in the case of an ordinary citizen; however, they do not lose all rights by virtue of their status as parolees, and they cannot be arbitrarily searched for purposes unrelated to their parole supervision. The test of the reasonableness of a search is whether the search was rationally and substantially related to the parole officer's duty. Unannounced visits to a parolee's residence are allowed, and plain-view observations may result in the seizure of contraband or evidence. When parole officers have information and reasonable suspicion that the parolee possesses a weapon or contraband, they may conduct a search without a warrant, but parole officers cannot act as agents of the police to conduct a visit or a search unrelated to the parole supervision that would be unlawful if conducted by a police officer. A parolee's status should not be exploited to allow a search solely to collect evidence for an independent criminal prosecution.

Probationers, in one sense, have greater rights than parolees, yet in another sense they have lesser rights. In most states, when a probation officer has reasonable cause to believe that a probationer has violated the conditions of the probation, the officer cannot automatically conduct a search but must apply for a search order from a court to search the probationer, any premises in which he resides, and any real or personal property that he owns or possesses. In contrast, a parole officer with reasonable cause or reasonable suspicion may search without a warrant.

Consent agreements between a probationer and the state may allow a greater intrusiveness into a probationer's privacy than would be allowed under parolee conditions. The probationer, in exchange for not being sent to prison, consents to a list of conditions individually designed for his or her circumstances. Most often, in cases in which the probationer is concurrently engaged in drug rehabilitation, he or she will consent to a blanket authority for unannounced visits, searches, and drug screening. In *United States v. Knights*, 534 U.S. 112 (2001), the Supreme Court found such search agreements permissible, as they further the goals of rehabilitation and the protection of society from future criminal violations.

Schools and Students

In *New Jersey v. T.L.O.*, 469 U.S. 325 (1985), the Supreme Court addressed the issue of searches by public school officials. In this case, a high school teacher discovered a 14-year-old student smoking in the bathroom. She took her to the vice principal's office, and the vice principal searched the student's purse. In addition to cigarettes, he saw rolling paper commonly used for marijuana cigarettes. He then proceeded to search the purse thoroughly, and he found marijuana, a pipe, a substantial amount of money, an index card containing a list of students who owed the student money, and two letters implicating the student in marijuana dealing. The student was charged with juvenile delinquency, and she filed a motion to suppress the evidence seized from her purse. The Court made three important rulings.

First, the Fourth Amendment applies to searches conducted by public school officials, and school officials are not exempt from the Amendment's dictates by virtue of the special nature of their authority over schoolchildren. In carrying out their disciplinary functions, school officials act as representatives of the state, not merely as surrogates of the parents.

Second, schoolchildren have legitimate expectations of privacy. They carry with them a variety of non-contraband items, and they do not necessarily waive all rights to privacy in such items by bringing them into school. However, striking a balance between their expectations of privacy and the school's need to maintain an orderly and safe school environment requires some easing of the search and seizure restrictions. Thus, school officials need not obtain a warrant before searching a student who is under their authority. Moreover, school officials need not be subject to the otherwise strict requirements of probable cause; rather, the legality of the search of a student should depend simply on the reasonableness of the search under its special circumstances.

Third, in this case, the initial search for the cigarettes was reasonable. The report that the student had been smoking warranted a reasonable suspicion that she had cigarettes in her purse, and the discovery of the rolling paper gave rise to a reasonable suspicion that the student was carrying marijuana. This suspicion justified the further search that discovered the additional evidence of drug-related activities.

In summary, public school officials may search a student's personal possessions, including purses, backpacks, or other containers, and student lockers without a warrant or probable cause when the officials have reasonable suspicion that contraband is present. This policy is justified to maintain a safe environment for students and teachers. On the other hand, when law enforcement conducts an investigation into criminal activities by school students, they should not rely on the authority of the school officials but should obtain probable cause search warrants when necessary.

Private schools are not part of the government, and private school officials are not constrained by the Fourth Amendment. The privacy policies in nongovernmental institutions are determined by consensual agreements.

Notes

1 Federal Rules of Evidence, Rule 602; New York Civil Practice Law & Rules, Section 2309(b).
2 *Whiteley v. Warden*, 401 U.S. 560 (1971).
3 Federal Rules of Criminal Procedure, Rule 41(d)(3).
4 *State v. Yoder*, 534 P.2d 771 (Idaho, 1975).
5 Federal Rules of Criminal Procedure, Rule 41(c).
6 *Steele v. United States*, 267 U.S. 498 (1925).
7 *Draper v. United States*, 358 U.S. 207 (1959); *Jaben v. United States*, 381 U.S. 214 (1965).
8 *United States v. Leon*, 468 U.S. 897 (1984).
9 *United States v. Leon*, 468 U.S. 897 (1984) at 922.
10 *People v. Glen*, 30 N.Y.2d 252 (1972); Adams, James, Anticipatory Search Warrants, *Kentucky Law Journal*, 79, 681, 1991.
11 Federal Rules of Criminal Procedure, Rule 41(c), (1-4).
12 New York Criminal Procedure Law, Article 690; Federal Rules of Criminal Procedure, Rule 41(c), (1-4).

13 *People v. Griminger*, 71 N.Y.2d 635 (1988).
14 *People v. Bigelow,* 66 N.Y.2d 417 (1985).
15 *Camara v. Municipal Court,* 387 U.S. 523 (1967).
16 *Marshall v. Barlow's, Inc.,* 436 U.S. 307 (1978).
17 *People v. Robinson,* 163 AD2d 428, 558 N.Y.S.2d 143 (1990).
18 *People v. Materon,* 107 AD2d 408, 487 N.Y.S.2d 334 (1985).
19 *People v. Kuhn,* 33 N.Y.2d 203 (1973).
20 *Rivera v. Smith* 63 N.Y.2d 501 (1984).

References

Aguilar v. Texas, 378 U.S. 108 (1964).
Draper v. United States, 358 U.S. 307 (1959).
Illinois v. Gates, 462 U.S. 213 (1983).
People v. DiFalco, 80 N.Y.2d 693 (1993).
People v. Elwell, 50 N.Y.2d 231 (1980).
Roviaro v. United States, 353 U.S. 53 (1957).
Spinelli v. United States, 393 U.S. 410 (1969).

Chapter 9

The Law of Arrest

An arrest is the taking into custody of a person for the purpose of detaining and holding him to answer a criminal charge. In modern society, built on the rule of law, an arrest is authorized only when it is made in accordance with recognized and accepted standards.

When certain criteria are met, private citizens as well as law enforcement officers can make an arrest without a warrant. In earlier times, citizens and officers had equal arrest authority, but with the advent of modern criminal justice systems and professional police departments, sworn police officers have been given greater arrest powers than private citizens—although the term *greater powers* more properly might be described as *more room for error*.

Under common law, police officers could arrest a person for a misdemeanor committed in their presence and for a felony whether committed in their presence or not. Under modern statutory law, most states have increased the authority of the police, allowing officers to make arrests for misdemeanors not committed in their presence; for example, New York law, which is representative, contains the following statement:

> A police officer may arrest a person for: (a) Any offense (including minor violations) when he has reasonable cause to believe that such person has committed such offense in his presence; and (b) A crime (misdemeanors or felonies) when he has reasonable cause to believe that such person has committed such crime, whether in his presence or otherwise.[1]

For a private citizen, authority to arrest is more limited, and the standard to be met for an arrest by a private citizen is extremely high. Most states have mandates such as the following (emphasis added):

> Any person may arrest another person for a felony when the latter has *in fact* committed such felony, and for any offense when the latter has *in fact* committed such offense in his presence.[2]

The *in fact* standard for private citizens subjects them to civil liability when it is determined that the arrested person did not in fact commit the crime. The private citizen might be sued for false arrest, unlawful imprisonment, or malicious prosecution. Furthermore, were the private citizen to use physical force to make the arrest and were the charges related to the arrest dismissed, the private citizen might be liable for the civil tort of assault and battery, or he might be charged with criminal assault. A police officer, on the other hand, might make a similar arrest on the basis of the same information and circumstances as the foregoing

DOI: 10.4324/9781003415091-12

private citizen, yet the officer might avoid liability even though the charges are subsequently proved to be false. Society authorizes police officers to make arrests on less than certainty.

Probable Cause

Under constitutional law, an arrest by a law enforcement agent is authorized when it is made on the basis of probable cause, which has been defined as facts and circumstances that would lead a person of ordinary intelligence and common sense to conclude that a crime had been, was being, or would be committed by a particular person.

Some statutes use terms such as *reasonable cause to believe* interchangeably with the term *probable cause*. In the context of arrests, New York statutory law defines reasonable cause to believe, which is its version of probable cause, as follows:

> Reasonable cause to believe a person has committed an offense exists when evidence or information which appears reliable discloses facts or circumstances which are collectively of such weight and persuasiveness as to convince a person of ordinary intelligence, judgment and experience that it is reasonably likely that such offense was committed and that such person committed it. Except as otherwise provided in this chapter, such apparently reliable evidence may include or consist of hearsay.[3]

Police officers are not required to believe a suspect is guilty beyond a reasonable doubt before they can take action. Often police officers must act on the word of another person. If a citizen chasing a suspect yells, "Stop thief," a police officer's duty is to chase and apprehend the suspect, and the officer is authorized to arrest the person on the basis of reasonable cause to believe or probable cause. If, due to circumstances, the officer uses force to apprehend the suspect, such force may be authorized on the basis of the officer's reasonable cause to believe the force was necessary.

The *reasonable cause to believe* or *probable cause* standard is, in effect, a *room for error* standard, and it is an enormous grant of authority and power. Even when an officer arrests the wrong person or uses force against an innocent person, he will not be subject to liability as long as he acted on the basis of probable cause to arrest, had reasonable cause to believe that force was necessary, and used only a reasonable amount of force.

The relatively lenient probable cause standard allows police to prevent the escape of suspected criminals, prevent potential violence, and secure evidence. Arrests provide prosecutors with the time to weigh the evidence for its sufficiency, accuracy, and admissibility and to decide whether to charge a suspect with a crime.

In those cases, however, in which a police officer makes an arrest without the requisite probable cause, the court may suppress the evidence seized or obtained as a result of the unlawful arrest, including physical objects, contraband, confessions, identifications, and derivative evidence. Also, an unlawful arrest will void a defendant's consent to search his or her property.

Suppression of evidence may prevent the possibility of further prosecution, unless the government can establish that the evidence to be used at trial came from an independent source and was not a result of the unlawful arrest. In some cases, a defendant who was released before trial due to a lack of probable cause or the suppression of evidence might be re-arrested and prosecuted if new evidence is developed.

Probable cause not only makes an arrest lawful but also cures other illegalities. The U.S. Supreme Court has ruled that an illegal arrest resulting from a seizure of the person outside the proper jurisdiction of the court, even by kidnapping from a foreign jurisdiction, may proceed on the merits as long as probable cause exists. Once a defendant is before the proper court, the court has jurisdiction no matter how the defendant's appearance was secured.[4]

As the Supreme Court noted in *Frisbee v. Collins*, 342 U.S. 519 (1952):

> This Court has never departed from the rule announced in *Ker* that the power of a court to try a person for a crime is not impaired by the fact that he had been brought within the court's jurisdiction by reason of forcible compulsion.... There is nothing in the Constitution that requires a court to permit a guilty person rightfully convicted to escape justice because he was brought to trial against his will.

Instances of defendants being kidnapped by police are rare. For the average unlawful arrest case, the most common repercussion for law enforcement is the suppression of evidence. The purpose of most appeals filed on the grounds of unlawful arrest is to invoke the exclusionary rule and suppress evidence. Therefore, for law enforcement officers, establishing probable cause is the essential foundation of their authority and effectiveness. It legalizes their actions and insulates them from civil lawsuits for false arrest and related charges.[5]

Arrest Warrants

An arrest warrant is a written order by a judge or magistrate authorizing a police officer to arrest a named person and to bring that person before the court to answer a criminal charge. The police officer may delegate other officers to execute the warrant.

Warrants are most often issued after grand juries have indicted suspects or when the police have been unable to summarily arrest a suspect. They are issued to make it possible for any police officer to arrest the suspect, and because it is often uncertain when the police will be able to apprehend the suspect, arrests warrants may be executed on any day of the week and at any hour of the day or night.

A lawful arrest warrant must be based on a written complaint that alleges sufficient facts to establish probable cause that the named person committed the criminal offense. Many judges tend to require a strong case establishing probable cause before they issue an arrest warrant, and they may require more evidence for an arrest warrant than they would for a search warrant. They reason that a search, no doubt, is a significant governmental intrusion into privacy, but in most cases is less intrusive than an arrest. As Justice Lewis Powell wrote in *United States v. Watson*, 423 U.S. 411 (1976), "A search may cause only an annoyance and temporary inconvenience to the law-abiding citizen, assuming more serious dimension only when it turns up evidence of criminality... [whereas an arrest] is a serious personal intrusion regardless of whether the person seized is guilty or innocent."

As intrusive as an arrest may be, an arrest inside a person's home is the ultimate intrusion. Out of concern for the rights of privacy and the traditional respect for a person's home, the Supreme Court ruled in *Payton v. New York*, 445 U.S. 573 (1980), that arrest warrants are required to arrest suspects in their homes (see discussion in Chapter 7). This prohibition in most cases does not hinder law enforcement. Police may arrest suspects outside their homes without warrants, and in emergency or other exigent circumstances they may enter a home to make an arrest without a warrant.

When the police obtain an arrest warrant, they must remember that probable cause for an arrest warrant does not automatically allow a search of the entire location where the arrest occurs. Conversely, probable cause for a search warrant does not automatically allow the arrest of the occupants of the location searched. In some circumstances, to clarify what a court has ordered, an arrest warrant and a search warrant will be issued simultaneously.

An important difference between a search warrant and an arrest warrant is that the former may be executed when the premises to be searched are unoccupied. This makes sense because the search is for physical evidence, not for a person. On the other hand, an arrest warrant may be executed only when the officer has reasonable grounds to believe that the person to be arrested is present within the premises. This makes sense because an arrest warrant does not authorize the police, at their unfettered discretion, to repeatedly enter premises looking for a suspect. Otherwise, an arrest warrant would effectively become a general search warrant and would grant police the authority to enter and search any place at any time they wished.

To arrest a suspect inside another person's residence, a search warrant is recommended because the search warrant provides protection for the other person's right to privacy. If the police enter a third party's residence to arrest a suspect without an arrest warrant, the arrest of the suspect will be lawful as long as the officers had probable cause for the arrest. However, if the police enter the third party's residence without a search warrant, any evidence or contraband that they seize will not be admissible against the third party because they violated the third party's constitutional right to privacy.

Elements of an Arrest

How much restraint upon a person's freedom to go on his or her way constitutes an arrest? When the police handcuff someone, bring him to the police station, and book him, undoubtedly an arrest has occurred. On the other hand, when the police stop someone in order to question or even frisk him, an arrest may not have occurred. Police regularly engage with citizens to investigate crime, protect the public safety, or ensure the orderly flow of pedestrian and vehicular traffic. Police give orders to disperse, to move out of the way, to pull a car over; they use physical restraint to break up disputes or fights; they restrain people while asking them questions or obtaining their consent to search personal property or premises. Often it is a matter of degree whether such actions by the police constitute an arrest.

The traditional elements of an arrest are (1) authority, (2) intention, and (3) submission or physical restraint. When an officer announces his intention to arrest and the person submits to the arrest, an arrest has occurred even though physical restraint has not been employed. An arrest has also occurred when the officer with intent to arrest physically seizes and restrains the person for a substantial period of time. An arrest has not occurred when the person refuses to submit and the officer is unable to physically bring the person into custody.[6]

In some situations, police do not subjectively intend to arrest, but their actions are so restraining or obstructive that courts will apply an objective test to determine that an arrest has occurred. This is crucially important when there is a lack of probable cause.

In *Florida v. Royer*, 460 U.S. 491 (1983), the Supreme Court outlined several principles pertaining to the relationships between arrests, consents to search, and searches. In the case, airport police stopped the defendant, who they suspected of transporting narcotics. They asked him to accompany them to a storage room where they searched his luggage and found marijuana. The following are excerpts from the opinion.

Florida v. Royer

U.S. Supreme Court
Florida v. Royer
460 U.S. 491; 103 S. Ct. 1319; 75 L.Ed.2d 229;
1983 U.S. LEXIS 151; 51
October 12, 1982, argued
March 23, 1983, decided
OPINION

We are required in this case to determine whether the Court of Appeal of Florida, Third District, properly applied the precepts of the Fourth Amendment in holding that respondent Royer was being illegally detained at the time of his purported consent to a search of his luggage.

I

On January 3, 1978, Royer was observed at Miami International Airport by two plain-clothes detectives of the Dade County, Fla., Public Safety Department assigned to the county's Organized Crime Bureau, Narcotics Investigation Section. Detectives Johnson and Magdalena believed that Royer's appearance, mannerisms, luggage, and actions fit the so-called "drug courier profile." Royer, apparently unaware of the attention he had attracted, purchased a one-way ticket to New York City and checked his two suitcases, placing on each suitcase an identification tag bearing the name "Holt" and the destination "La Guardia." As Royer made his way to the concourse which led to the airline boarding area, the two detectives approached him, identified themselves as policemen working out of the sheriff's office, and asked if Royer had a "moment" to speak with them; Royer said "Yes."

Upon request, but without oral consent, Royer produced for the detectives his airline ticket and his driver's license. The airline ticket, like the baggage identification tags, bore the name "Holt," while the driver's license carried respondent's correct name, "Royer." When the detectives asked about the discrepancy, Royer explained that a friend had made the reservation in the name of "Holt." Royer became noticeably more nervous during this conversation, whereupon the detectives informed Royer that they were in fact narcotics investigators and that they had reason to suspect him of transporting narcotics.

The detectives did not return his airline ticket and identification but asked Royer to accompany them to a room, approximately 40 feet away, adjacent to the concourse. Royer said nothing in response but went with the officers as he had been asked to do. The room was later described by Detective Johnson as a "large storage closet," located in the stewardesses' lounge and containing a small desk and two chairs. Without Royer's consent or agreement, Detective Johnson, using Royer's baggage check stubs, retrieved the "Holt" luggage from the airline and brought it to the room where respondent and Detective Magdalena were waiting. Royer was asked if he would consent to a search of the suitcases. Without orally responding to this request, Royer produced a key and unlocked one of the suitcases, which one detective then opened without seeking further assent from Royer. Marihuana was found in that suitcase. According to Detective Johnson, Royer stated that he did not know the combination to the lock on the second suitcase. When asked if he objected to the detective opening the second suitcase, Royer said "[no], go ahead" and did not object when the detective explained that the suitcase might have to be broken open. The suitcase was pried open by the officers and more marihuana was found. Royer was then told that he was under arrest. Approximately 15 minutes had elapsed from the time the detectives initially approached the respondent until his arrest upon the discovery of the contraband.

Prior to his trial for felony possession of marihuana, Royer made a motion to suppress the evidence obtained in the search of the suitcases. The trial court found that Royer's consent to the search was "freely and voluntarily given," and that, regardless of the consent, the warrantless search was reasonable because "the officer doesn't have the time to run out and get a search warrant because the plane is going to take off."...Royer was convicted.

II

Some preliminary observations are in order. First, it is unquestioned that without a warrant to search Royer's luggage and in the absence of probable cause and exigent circumstances, the validity of the search depended on Royer's purported consent. Neither is it disputed that where the validity of a search rests on consent, the State has the burden of proving that the necessary consent was obtained and that it was freely and voluntarily given, a burden that is not satisfied by showing a mere submission to a claim of lawful authority.

Second, law enforcement officers do not violate the Fourth Amendment by merely approaching an individual on the street or in another public place, by asking him if he is willing to answer some questions, by putting questions to him if the person is willing to listen, or by offering in evidence in a criminal prosecution his voluntary answers to such questions. Nor would the fact that the officer identifies himself as a police officer, without more, convert the encounter into a seizure requiring some level of objective justification. The person approached, however, need not answer any question put to him; indeed, he may decline to listen to the questions at all and may go on his way. He may not be detained even momentarily without reasonable, objective grounds for doing so, and his refusal to listen or answer does not, without more, furnish those grounds. If there is no detention—no seizure within the meaning of the Fourth Amendment—then no constitutional rights have been infringed.

Third, it is also clear that not all seizures of the person must be justified by probable cause to arrest for a crime. Prior to *Terry v. Ohio* any restraint on the person amounting to a seizure for the purposes of the Fourth Amendment was invalid unless justified by probable cause. *Terry* created a limited exception to this general rule: Certain seizures are justifiable under the Fourth Amendment if there is articulable suspicion that a person has committed or is about to commit a crime....

Fourth, *Terry* and its progeny nevertheless created only limited exceptions to the general rule that seizures of the person require probable cause to arrest. Detentions may be "investigative" yet violative of the Fourth Amendment absent probable cause. In the name of investigating a person who is no more than suspected of criminal activity, the police may not carry out a full search of the person or of his automobile or other effects. Nor may the police seek to verify their suspicions by means that approach the conditions of arrest....

Fifth, statements given during a period of illegal detention are inadmissible even though voluntarily given if they are the product of the illegal detention and not the result of an independent act of free will.

Sixth, if the events in this case amounted to no more than a permissible police encounter in a public place or a justifiable *Terry*-type detention, Royer's consent, if voluntary, would have been effective to legalize the search of his two suitcases. The Florida District Court of Appeal in the case before us, however, concluded not only that Royer had been seized when he gave his consent to search his luggage but also that the bounds of an investigative stop had been exceeded. In its view the "confinement" in this case went beyond the limited restraint of a Terry investigative stop, and Royer's consent was thus tainted by the illegality, a conclusion that required reversal in the absence of probable cause to arrest. The question before us is whether the record warrants that conclusion. We think that it does.

III

...We also think that the officers' conduct was more intrusive than necessary to effectuate an investigative detention otherwise authorized by the *Terry* line of cases. First, by returning his ticket and driver's license, and informing him that he was free to go if he so desired, the officers might have obviated any claim that the encounter was anything but a consensual matter from start to finish....

IV

The State's third and final argument is that Royer was not being illegally held when he gave his consent because there was probable cause to arrest him at that time. Detective Johnson testified at the suppression hearing and the Florida District Court of Appeal held that there was no probable cause to arrest until Royer's bags were opened, but the fact that the officers did not believe there was probable cause and proceeded on a consensual or *Terry*-stop rationale would not foreclose the State from justifying Royer's custody by proving probable cause and hence removing any barrier to relying on Royer's consent to search. We agree with the Florida District Court of Appeal, however, that probable cause to arrest Royer did not exist at the time he consented to the search of his luggage. The facts are that a nervous young man with two American Tourister bags paid cash for an airline ticket to a "target city." These facts led to inquiry, which in turn revealed that the ticket had been bought under an assumed name. The proffered explanation did not satisfy the officers. We cannot agree with the State, if this is its position, that every nervous young man paying cash for a ticket to New York City under an assumed name and carrying two heavy American Tourister bags may be arrested and held to answer for a serious felony charge.

V

Because we affirm the Florida District Court of Appeal's conclusion that Royer was being illegally detained when he consented to the search of his luggage, we agree that the consent was tainted by the illegality and was ineffective to justify the search.

Questions Raised by *Florida v. Royer*

1. Had the detectives handed back the airline ticket and driver's license to Royer before bringing him to the storage room, would the encounter have been a consensual non-arrest detention?
2. Had the detectives asked Royer's permission to search the luggage before bringing him to the storage room and had he voluntarily consented, would the search have been lawful?

3. Were the detectives required to inform Royer that he could decline to give permission for the search?
4. Was it reasonable for the detectives to retrieve Royer's luggage from the airline?
5. Had Royer refused to accompany the detectives to the storage room, what should the detectives have done?
6. Had Royer refused to consent to the search of his luggage, what should the detectives have done?
7. In light of today's heightened terror concerns at airports, would the Court's decision be different today?
8. Does an alert on the basis of a drug-courier profile provide less or more probable cause to believe drug trafficking is occurring than a hearsay tip from a confidential informant?

Good Judgment and Discretion

Although the standard of probable cause is far less stringent than the standard of proof beyond a reasonable doubt that is required for a criminal conviction, police officers must always use reasonable discretion before making arrests, especially non-emergency arrests. As a practical matter, a sliding scale exists regarding the amount of probable cause required in a particular situation. In an emergency situation or when an unidentified suspect is fleeing from a crime scene, police officers may have to act on incomplete and sparse information. In a non-emergency investigation of past crimes in which a suspect is identified and not at risk of fleeing the jurisdiction, investigators should develop as much pertinent information as reasonably possible and should carefully weigh the evidence before arresting the suspect.

Having a certain amount of evidence pointing to probable cause is not sufficient when it is outweighed by countervailing evidence. Probable cause determinations regarding a particular suspect must take into account exculpatory evidence. Police officers who know of evidence that would exonerate the defendant but, nevertheless, proceed to make an arrest violate their oath and the law.

Courts have sanctioned law enforcement officers by suppressing evidence when arrests are made without the requisite probable cause. Not only has physical evidence or contraband been suppressed but also evidence obtained from the defendant's statements.[7]

In *Dunaway v. New York*, 442 U.S. 200 (1979), police detectives took the defendant to a station house to question him about a robbery and homicide. After they gave him *Miranda* warnings, the defendant confessed to the crime, and he was convicted. The Supreme Court reversed the conviction, ruling that even though the defendant had been advised of his rights and had voluntarily confessed, taking the defendant to the station house was an arrest without probable cause and, consequently, the confession had to be suppressed.

In *Davis v. Mississippi*, 394 U.S. 721 (1969), an 86-year-old woman was raped in her home. The police found fingerprints on the window through which the assailant had apparently entered the home. The police picked up a dozen young men from the area, including the defendant, Davis, and took them to the police station for questioning and fingerprinting. The defendant's fingerprints matched the fingerprints on the window, and he was arrested and convicted of the rape. The Warren Court reversed the conviction, holding that the police conduct of taking the defendant to the police station without probable cause to arrest was illegal and required suppression of the fingerprint evidence.

Dunaway, *Davis*, and many similar cases demonstrate the gravity with which courts view the probable cause requirement. Courts suppress perfectly reliable and necessary evidence as a means of enforcing the constitutional right to be free of unreasonable searches or seizures, and law enforcement officers must take heed. While performing their duties, law enforcement officers must work within strict guidelines. They must take all reasonable steps to ensure that probable cause has been established before the all-important, pivotal moment of arrest. In our criminal justice system, an unlawful arrest can be catastrophic to the prosecution—evidence is suppressed, guilty defendants are not brought to justice, convictions are reversed, and the crime victim does not receive justice.

Hearsay

An officer who observes a crime, whether by sight, hearing, touch, or smell, obtains direct evidence for probable cause to make an arrest; however, in cases not occurring in an officer's presence, the officer does not obtain evidence directly but often learns of facts and information from third persons. Such information from witnesses, other police officers, or confidential informants is generally referred to as *hearsay*, a term loosely used outside its proper context in a courtroom.

Reliable hearsay evidence that police receive from third persons during the investigation of a criminal case can constitute sufficient proof to establish probable cause to arrest. This statement may seem counterintuitive, as hearsay is generally excluded from trials due to its inherent unreliability. Nonetheless, the police constantly rely and act on hearsay information. They are not limited to making arrests only for crimes they observe first-hand. In fact, most arrests by police, in whole or in part, are the result of indirect, hearsay information received from third persons.

Hearsay at a trial is testimony to a statement that was made out of court and that is offered in court for the truth of the fact asserted in the statement. Unless a recognized exception applies, hearsay evidence should not be admitted for the purpose of establishing a defendant's guilt or innocence. Consequently, at a defendant's trial for an armed robbery, a police officer may not testify that the victim told him the defendant pointed a gun at him and took his wallet. The victim should come into court and testify directly against the defendant. On the other hand, at a preliminary hearing for the purpose of establishing probable cause to arrest the defendant (not to prove the defendant's guilt or innocence), the police officer may testify that the victim told him the defendant committed the robbery and that because the victim appeared reliable the officer arrested the defendant.

Courts have consistently held that information received from an apparently reliable eyewitness provides probable cause to arrest.[8] In *Chambers v. Maroney*, 399 U.S. 42 (1970), the Supreme Court upheld an arrest for the robbery of a service station. Two teenage eyewitnesses told the police investigating the crime that a blue compact station wagon containing four men, one with a green sweater, had been circling in the vicinity of the gas station and later sped away. The service station attendant verified that one of the two men who robbed him had been wearing a green sweater and that the other had been wearing a trench coat. On the basis of the attendant's statement, the Court ruled that "the police had ample cause to stop (within two miles of the station) a light blue compact station wagon carrying four men and to arrest the occupants, one of whom was wearing a green sweater and one of whom had a trench coat with him in the car." The officers did not have direct knowledge that the men had committed the robbery, but arrested them on the basis of hearsay information from third parties. Law enforcement officers must be cognizant that mistakes are possible in every situation. In order to avoid wrongful arrests, law enforcement officers should endeavor to corroborate hearsay information. In *Chambers v. Maroney*, the teenagers' description of the men in the compact car that had been circling the gas station was corroborated by the gas station attendant's description of the suspect.

Problems arise when information, whether in narrative or descriptive form, is transmitted from one person to another. Information tends to change when it is repeated, and the more people to whom it is repeated, the more likely the information will become altered and inaccurate. When police transmit a "be on the look out" (BOLO) bulletin for a suspect, officers who take action on the basis of the BOLO bulletin do so without personally corroborating the reliability of the information. An officer who takes action on the basis of a secondhand account of the information in the BOLO increases the likelihood of error.

When an arrest is made on the basis of a BOLO, the court examines the reasonableness of the arresting officer's determination that the suspect matched the description provided in the BOLO bulletin, and then the court examines the underlying probable cause for the bulletin. If the bulletin was not based on probable cause, an arrest founded on it is improper, regardless of how well the suspect matched the transmitted description.[9]

Confidential Informants

Hearsay information from confidential informants, who are often turncoat criminals or persons paid for their information, must be given greater scrutiny than information from the average "untainted" citizen. Although confidential informant issues usually arise in connection with warrant cases, they also arise in summary arrest situations when it is not possible for the police to obtain a warrant because of lack of time or other circumstances.

In *Draper v. United States*, 358 U.S. 307 (1959), the Supreme Court distinguished between information given by apparently reliable, law-abiding citizens and information given by confidential informants. In *Draper*, a confidential informant, who in the past had supplied accurate information, told the police that the defendant had gone to Chicago to pick up a supply of illegal drugs. The informant said that the defendant would be returning on a train, carrying a tan bag containing the drugs, and would "walk real fast."

The police staked out the train station and observed the defendant carrying a tan bag and walking very quickly. They arrested him without a warrant, searched him, and found illegal drugs. After the defendant's conviction, he appealed on the grounds that the police did not have probable cause to arrest because the information from the confidential informant was hearsay and would be inadmissible at trial.

The Supreme Court disagreed with the defendant and upheld the conviction, stating that the informant's tip, combined with the officers' corroborating observations, sufficed to establish the probable cause to arrest. Hearsay may be relied on to establish probable cause.

Despite the Court's approval of the arrest in *Draper*, law enforcement officers would be prudent whenever possible to obtain an arrest warrant or a search warrant before taking action on the word of a confidential informant. Moreover, the use of information from confidential informants has limitations. The identity of a confidential informant need not be revealed in open court during a probable cause hearing; however, at a defendant's trial, the confidential informant could be required to testify.[10] If the confidential informant offers testimony based not on personal knowledge but only on hearsay, the testimony may be inadmissible or worthless. If the confidential informant's character can be impugned (which is often the case), the jury may disregard his or her testimony. To proceed to trial against a defendant, where the standard for conviction is proof beyond a reasonable doubt, the prosecution should have additional, independent evidence.

Use of Force to Arrest

The common law and statutes allowed police to use all necessary force, including deadly force, to make an arrest for a felony or to prevent escape from such an arrest. Excessive force, however, was not allowed, and police who used excessive force might be criminally liable for their intentional or reckless criminal conduct, and they might be subject to civil lawsuits for such criminal conduct. Traditionally, actions to remedy excessive force by state officers were taken in state forums; however, in states that authorized a police officer to use deadly physical force when necessary to arrest a felon, the officer was effectively immune from criminal prosecution, and, as a consequence, any fleeing felon, under any circumstances, might be lawfully subject to deadly physical force.

In the landmark decision of *Tennessee v. Garner*, 471 U.S. 1 (1985), the Supreme Court addressed this issue and ruled that the Fourth Amendment prohibition against unreasonable seizures was applicable to state statutes and actions. At the time of *Garner*, several states, including Tennessee, still had laws on their books authorizing police officers to shoot fleeing felons. In the *Garner* case, two officers had responded to a prowler call. At the scene, a witness told them she had heard glass breaking in the house next door. One of the officers saw a suspect running into the backyard of the house and chased the suspect, Garner, an unarmed 15-year-old male, to a fence in the backyard.

With the aid of a flashlight, the officer was able to see Garner's face and hands. He saw no sign of a weapon and, although not certain, was "reasonably sure" and "figured" that Garner was unarmed. While Garner was crouched at the base of the fence, the officer called out "Police, halt" and took a few steps toward him. When Garner began to climb the 6-foot chain-link fence to escape, the officer shot him in the back of the head, killing him.

Although Tennessee law authorized the police to use deadly force to arrest fleeing felons, Garner's family brought suit in federal court alleging the officer had violated Garner's constitutional rights. The Supreme Court ruled that the shooting of Garner was an unreasonable seizure in violation of the Fourth and Fourteenth Amendments of the Constitution. It was not constitutionally permissible for states to allow police officers to shoot and kill unarmed suspects fleeing the scene of minor property crimes.

The Court stated:

> The use of deadly force to prevent the escape of all felony suspects, whatever the circumstances, is constitutionally unreasonable. It is not better that all felony suspects die than that they escape. Where the suspect poses no immediate threat to the officer and no threat to others, the harm resulting from failing to apprehend him does not justify the use of deadly force to do so. It is no doubt unfortunate when a suspect who is in sight escapes, but the fact that the police arrive a little late or are a little slower afoot does not always justify killing the suspect. A police officer may not seize an unarmed, non-dangerous suspect by shooting him dead. The Tennessee statute is unconstitutional insofar as it authorizes the use of deadly force against such fleeing suspect.

Garner distinguished property crimes from violent crimes. The Court said, "If the suspect threatens the officer with a weapon or there is probable cause to believe that he has committed a crime involving the infliction or threatened infliction of serious physical harm, deadly force may be used if necessary to prevent escape."[11]

Problem

Detective Tom Tracer was investigating narcotics dealing in and around a public housing development. He had a confidential informant who told him that at 9:00 PM a large amount of crack cocaine was going to be delivered to a youth nicknamed "Shorty." The informant said that the drugs would be delivered by a man he knew only as Buster, who was a drug supplier in the area. Buster usually dressed in a suit, and the drugs would be in a blue shoulder bag. Shorty would be dressed in a t-shirt, baggy pants, and sneakers.

Detective Tracer and other officers set up surveillance in and around the project buildings with the intention of arresting Buster and Shorty when the drugs were delivered. At 9:00 PM, Buster arrived and sat on a bench in the common area. A minute later, Shorty exited a building, sat next to him, took the shoulder bag, and immediately began walking back toward the building entrance. The police who had been hiding nearby rushed toward both men. Buster surrendered, but Shorty ran. He raced into a nearby building and eluded the police by hiding in a first-floor apartment and then escaping through a window while the police were looking for him elsewhere.

Shorty almost got away unseen, but Detective Tracer had not followed the other officers, and he saw Shorty turning the corner of a building. Tracer ran after him, and a chase ensued during which Tracer dropped his walkie-talkie and was unable to radio for assistance. After about five blocks of running, Tracer became exhausted, and Shorty began to get farther away. Shorty came to a fence next to a railroad yard and began climbing it. Tracer decided that if Shorty got over the fence, he would get away. Tracer shouted, "Stop or I'll shoot," but Shorty continued to climb, and Tracer fired one bullet at him, striking him in the back of the head and killing him.

Questions

1. Should the Fourth Amendment prohibition of unreasonable searches and seizures apply to the amount of force used to seize a suspect?
2. If a fleeing felon is going to escape, is it reasonable in all cases for a police officer to use deadly physical force to prevent the escape?
3. For police use of force, should all felonies be treated the same?
4. Should the use of deadly physical force to apprehend a fleeing felon be allowable only for capital crimes?
5. If a state does not have a death penalty, should a police officer be able to use deadly physical force?
6. Does the use of deadly physical force to apprehend a felon implicate the Eighth Amendment?
7. Was it reasonable to shoot Shorty to prevent his escape?
8. Had Shorty committed a violent crime instead of a drug crime would it have been reasonable to shoot him?
9. Could the unlawful distribution of dangerous drugs be considered a violent crime?
10. Assuming it was determined that Detective Tracer used unreasonable force to seize Shorty, should he be subject to criminal prosecution in state court?
11. Assuming it was determined that Detective Tracer used unreasonable force to seize Shorty, should he be subject to criminal prosecution in federal court for a violation of civil rights?
12. Assuming it was determined that Detective Tracer used unreasonable force to seize Shorty, should he be subject to a civil lawsuit in federal court for a violation of civil rights?

Prosecution

After the police make an arrest, the defendant undergoes processing at a police station, usually known as *booking*. The defendant will be photographed and fingerprinted. In some cases, he or she will be placed in a lineup. The police bring the case to the district attorney who will decide whether there is sufficient evidence to prepare charges. If so, a written accusation or accusatory instrument will be filed with the court of jurisdiction.

The court will arraign the defendant and, depending on the circumstances, set bail, release the defendant without the need for bail, or remand the defendant to jail. When the defendant remains in jail, the next court date will usually be within a week. When the defendant is released, the case may be adjourned for a longer time.

The next stage of the proceedings is to determine whether sufficient evidence to proceed to trial exists. Although a police officer may have made a lawful arrest on the basis of hearsay information, the charges may not be sufficient to proceed to trial. The district attorney must prepare charges that contain not only an accusatory part but also a factual part in which the complaining witness alleges facts of an evidentiary character supporting or tending to support the charges. In order for a case to proceed to trial, the offense charged and the defendant's commission thereof must be supported by non-hearsay allegations in the charging documents or in sworn supporting affidavits. Furthermore, the non-hearsay allegations must support every element of the offense charged sufficiently to establish a *prima facie* case. If they do not, the charges will be dismissed.[12]

A typical example occurs when a woman calls the police and complains that her husband assaulted her. If she appears credible and evidence of physical abuse is present, the police will be required to arrest the husband although they were not present when the alleged assault occurred. The police and the district attorney will prepare a complaint for presentation to the court. If the complaint spells out probable cause, even though it is only based on the officer's hearsay account, the arrest is lawful. As often happens, sometime between the arrest and the next court appearance, the woman changes her mind about pressing charges against her husband. If she does not sign a sworn affidavit that outlines the non-hearsay allegations within a specified time, it is likely that the charges will be dismissed. Even when a sworn affidavit is signed, the case may be dismissed if the non-hearsay allegations do not spell out a crime or show that the defendant committed the crime.

Assuming the charges spell out sufficient evidence to proceed, the district attorney and the defense attorney usually engage in negotiations. In most cases, rather than proceeding to trial, the case will be resolved through plea bargaining. Approximately 90% of all convictions are the result of plea-bargained guilty pleas. Plea bargaining involves negotiating an agreement whereby the defendant pleads guilty in exchange for one or more of the following:

1. Reducing the charge to a less serious offense.
2. Dropping other charges pending against the defendant.
3. Agreeing on a specified sentence.

In some instances, the district attorney will not offer a plea bargain because of the seriousness of the offense or the past record of the defendant. Such cases usually proceed to trial unless the defendant pleads guilty as charged.

Notes

1 New York Criminal Procedure, Article 140.10 (1).
2 New York Criminal Procedure, Article 140.30(1).
3 New York Criminal Procedure, Article 70.10(2).
4 *Ker v. Illinois*, 119 U.S. 436 (1886); *Frisbee v. Collins*, 342 U.S. 519 (1952); *United States v. Verdugo-Urquidez*, 494 U.S. 259 (1990); *United States v. Alvarez-Machain*, 504 U.S. 655 (1992).
5 *Gerstein v. Pugh*, 420 U.S. 103 (1975).
6 *California v. Hodari D.*, 499 U.S. 621 (1991).
7 *Sibron v. New York*, 392 U.S. 40 (1968); *Delaware v. Prouse*, 440 U.S. 648 (1979); *Florida v. Royer*, 460 U.S. 491 (1983).
8 *Jaben v. United States*, 381 U.S. 214 (1965).
9 *United States v. Ventresca*, 380 U.S. 102 (1965); *Whiteley v. Warden*, 401 U.S. 560 (1971); *United States v. Hensley*, 469 U.S. 221 (1985).
10 *McCray v. Illinois*, 386 U.S. 300 (1967).
11 *Tennessee v. Garner*, 471 U.S. 1 (1985).
12 *People v. Alejandro*, 70 N.Y.2d 133 (1987).

References

Graham v. Connor, 490 U.S. 386 (1989).
Ohio v. Robinette, 519 U.S. 33 (1996).
Reid v. Georgia, 448 U.S. 438 (1980).
Schneckloth v. Bustamonte, 412 U.S. 218 (1973).
Tennessee v. Garner, 471 U.S. 1 (1985).
Terry v. Ohio, 392 U.S. 1 (1968).
United States v. Drayton, 536 U.S. 194 (2002).
United States v. Mendenhall, 446 U.S. 544 (1980).
United States v. Place, 462 U.S. 696 (1983).

Chapter 10

Searches without Warrants

Americans place a high value on their rights of personal liberty and privacy. The Fourth Amendment was enacted to protect "the right of the people to be secure in their persons, houses, papers and effects, against unreasonable searches and seizures," and the warrant and probable cause requirements are the instruments to enforce that protection. Nevertheless, in many circumstances, law enforcement officers must act without warrants and often on the basis of limited information. In fact, searches conducted without warrants far outnumber searches with warrants. Because most police incidents require a prompt response, obtaining a warrant is usually not feasible. Courts, while balancing law enforcement needs against individual rights, have recognized reasonable exceptions to the warrant requirement, and they have also recognized circumstances in which the Fourth Amendment probable cause requirements are not applicable.

Plain View

A search occurs when government agents invade a person's expectation of privacy for the purpose of obtaining contraband or evidence. It does not occur when a person voluntarily waives his or her expectation of privacy. In a public place, a police officer does not need a search warrant to seize items of contraband or evidence that are open to public view, because a search does not occur when items of property are voluntarily exposed to the public. Public places include streets and highways, those parts of commercial premises open to the public, and lobbies and hallways of residential apartment buildings. However, items concealed by containers, packaging, or wrapping are not exposed to the public view and are protected by the Fourth Amendment. If an officer, while stopping the driver of a vehicle for a traffic violation on a public street, observed a clear plastic bag containing marijuana in plain view on the seat of the vehicle, the officer could lawfully seize the bag. If, on the other hand, the officer observed an opaque container and merely suspected that it contained marijuana, the officer could not seize the container without more evidence.

Residences receive a higher degree of privacy protection than automobiles or other premises.[1] If a police officer were to peer through the window of a house to look for incriminating evidence, he would violate the occupant's expectation of privacy and, unless there were some hazardous or exigent circumstances, any evidence seized as a result of the violation would be excludable.

Inside private premises, a police officer may seize items of contraband or evidence that are in plain view; however, the officer must have been lawfully in the position from which he made the observation. For example, an officer who is invited into the living room of a home to take a report regarding a past crime is lawfully in place and may seize contraband

DOI: 10.4324/9781003415091-13

in his plain view, but he cannot open the door to a bedroom and look in without lawful justification.

The plain-view doctrine often operates concurrently with other exceptions to the search warrant requirement. It operates in private premises when the police enter those premises lawfully either pursuant to a warrant or without a warrant but pursuant to an emergency, hot pursuit, exigent circumstances, or consent. While lawfully in the private premises, an officer who observes contraband or evidence in plain view may seize the items. To seize items under the plain-view doctrine, it must be immediately apparent that the items are within the following categories of contraband or evidence:

1. Fruits of a crime, such as stolen money or goods, or proceeds of crime (e.g., large amounts of unexplained money found in connection with an investigation into narcotics sales might be seized as proceeds of an illegal enterprise and as evidence).
2. Instrumentalities used to commit crime, such as weapons to commit assaults or tools to commit burglaries.
3. Contraband, which is anything that it is a crime to possess, such as unlicensed handguns or unlawfully possessed drugs.
4. Evidence, which may be any item that connects or associates a suspect with a crime or a crime scene, such as bloodstained clothing of a suspect in a violent assault, a mask or other clothing similar to that worn by a suspect during the commission of a robbery, or receipts and documents linking a suspect to a larceny by fraud.

Immediately apparent does not mean *absolutely certain*. A probable cause standard for concluding that an item falls within one of the above categories is sufficient to justify a seizure. A detective who seizes a suspect's bloodstained clothing will not know for sure that the bloodstains are related to the crime until a laboratory analysis is completed, but the detective may seize the clothing without being certain.

A lawful police entry into private premises does not authorize a blanket, unlimited search of the premises. In *Arizona v. Hicks*, 480 U.S. 321 (1987), the Supreme Court made it clear that police do not have unfettered authority to search premises merely because they had authority to lawfully enter. In *Hicks*, the tenant of an apartment was struck and injured by a bullet that came through the ceiling of his apartment. The police arrived and entered the apartment from where the bullet had come, to look for the shooter, other victims, or weapons. They found three weapons, including a sawed-off rifle, and a stocking-cap mask. One of the police officers "noticed two sets of expensive stereo components, which seemed out of place in the squalid... apartment. Suspecting that they were stolen, he read and recorded their serial numbers—moving some of the components.... On being advised that the turntable had been taken in an armed robbery, he seized it immediately."

The turntable was used as evidence to convict the defendant of the robbery, but the Supreme Court affirmed a reversal of the conviction, holding that the turntable should have been excluded from the trial because "moving some of the components" was a search without probable cause and unrelated to the authority to enter the apartment.

Searches Incidental to a Lawful Arrest: *Chimel v. California*

Until 1969, it was standard police practice when arresting a suspect to search for evidence in areas under the suspect's control. For example, if the police arrested a suspect in his office in connection with a fraudulent check-writing scheme, the police would search for evidence in the office files, desk drawers, closets, and anywhere else in the premises they thought evidence might be found.[2] In *Chimel v. California*, 395 U.S. 752 (1969), the Supreme Court restrained such overreaching conduct and limited the search to the area within the suspect's immediate control. The police, armed with an arrest warrant, had entered Mr. Chimel's residence and arrested him in connection with the burglary of a coin shop. They asked Chimel for permission to search the house for evidence, but he refused. Nevertheless, the police searched the entire house including the attic and garage. They seized coins, medals, and tokens, which were used as evidence to convict Chimel.

He appealed, and the Supreme Court reversed his conviction. The Court held that a search incidental to an arrest must be limited to the immediate or reachable area around the suspect. The Court explained:

> When an arrest is made, it is reasonable for the arresting officer to search the person arrested in order to remove any weapons that the latter might seek to use in order to resist arrest or effect his escape. Otherwise, the officer's safety might well be endangered, and the arrest itself frustrated.
>
> In addition, it is entirely reasonable for the arresting officer to search for and seize any evidence on the arrestee's person in order to prevent its concealment or destruction. And the area into which an arrestee might reach in order to grab a weapon or evidentiary items must, of course, be governed by a like rule. A gun on a table or in a drawer in front of one who is arrested can be as dangerous to the arresting officer as one concealed in the clothing of the person arrested. There is ample justification, therefore, for a search of the arrestee's person and the area "within his immediate control"—construing that phrase to mean the area from within which he might gain possession of a weapon or destructible evidence.

A search of the remainder of the house or areas outside the reach of the suspect would require a search warrant.

The principles outlined in *Chimel v. California* regarding searches incidental to a defendant's arrest inside his or her home also apply to arrests at other locations. Because the person has already been seized, a concurrent search of the person is considered incidental to and part of the same process. Unless an arrest is determined to have been unlawful, evidence or weapons recovered on the person or within his reach may be admissible. Such searches have been called *reachable-area searches*. For example, when the police arrest a person seated in the driver's seat of a typical vehicle, they can search the passenger compartment of the vehicle, but they cannot search the trunk without a separate and distinct justification.

For incidental to arrest searches to be lawful:

1. Probable cause must have existed prior to the arrest and search.
2. The search must occur contemporaneously with or immediately after the arrest.
3. Only the defendant can be searched, not his or her companions.
4. Only the reachable area around the defendant can be searched.

A search incidental to an arrest might be the first of several searches to which a defendant is subjected. In addition to an initial on-the-scene arrest search, a defendant is searched at the police station during the booking process. Furthermore, when a defendant is placed in a detention facility to await a court arraignment, he or she is searched again.

Telephone and Computer Files

Chimel confirmed that, incidental to an arrest, it was reasonable for the arresting officer to search the defendant, and the reachable area surrounding the defendant, not only for weapons, but also for evidence of the crime. Certainly, an officer could seize an arrestee's cell phone, but could the officer open the phone and read the information stored on it?

The Supreme Court addressed the question in *Riley v. California*, 573 U.S. 373 (2014). In 2009, in San Diego, California, David Leon Riley was arrested for driving with a suspended license. He had been a suspect in a gang-related murder that had taken place a few weeks previously. His car was impounded, and the inventory search discovered two loaded handguns under the hood of the vehicle. Later ballistic tests confirmed that the handguns had been used in the gang-related murder.

When the police arrested Riley, they searched his cell phone without a warrant. The cell phone search contained evidence identifying Riley as a member of the Lincoln Park gang. The evidence included photos, phone contacts, text messages, and video clips. It also included a photo of a car that Riley owned and that had been involved in the gang shooting.

Riley was charged with the shooting, and at his criminal trial, he moved to suppress the evidence taken from the phone. The trial judge denied the motion, and Riley was convicted.

His appeals reached the Supreme Court, which ruled that a warrant is required to search the contents of a mobile phone, stating:

> Digital data stored on a cell phone cannot itself be used as a weapon to harm an arresting officer or to effectuate the arrestee's escape. Law enforcement officers remain free to examine the physical aspects of a phone to ensure that it will not be used as a weapon— say, to determine whether there is a razor blade hidden between the phone and its case. Once an officer has secured a phone and eliminated any potential physical threats, however, data on the phone can endanger no one.

The Court indicated that the primary reason for the warrant requirement was the issue of privacy:

> Modern cell phones are not just another technological convenience. With all they contain and all they may reveal, they hold for many Americans "the privacies of life." The fact that technology now allows an individual to carry such information in his hand does not make the information any less worthy of protection for which the Founders fought.

The Emergency Exception

An emergency is an event that requires prompt action to prevent loss of life, injury, or substantial property damage. The types and varieties of emergencies that obviate the need for a warrant are countless. Clearly, firefighters or police officers rushing into a burning building to save people do not need a search warrant. When a child is reported suddenly missing without explanation, the police will conduct an immediate search of any area where the child could possibly be found. Depending on the circumstances, the police might search automobiles, premises, and even residences without obtaining warrants. When a violent crime has been committed and the armed suspect is hiding at a known location, threatening to injure other persons, or attempting to escape, the police might enter private premises to seize the suspect in the interests of public safety.

The police may enter premises to aid individuals in distress, to assist victims of an ongoing or recent crime, or to investigate signs of impending danger. The police should have some reasonable basis to take such actions, although the reasonable basis need not be commensurate with the requirements of probable cause.

In each of the above situations, when officers responding to the emergency find unlawful contraband or evidence of a crime in plain view, they may seize those items without a search warrant. Once the emergency has passed, however, any searching should cease and, if an additional search is necessary, the officers should apply for a warrant.

Hot Pursuits

Acting in accordance with common-law precepts and statutory authority, state police and federal agents may arrest suspects in a public place without a warrant.[3] It has long been established that when a suspect flees from an arrest, the police in continuous "hot pursuit" may chase the suspect into private premises to complete the arrest.[4] For serious crimes, suspects cannot be allowed to thwart an otherwise proper arrest in a public place by retreating into a private house or other premises.

The question of the extent to which the police can search private premises while in hot pursuit of a suspect was addressed in *Warden v. Hayden*, 387 U.S. 297 (1967). In *Hayden*, taxi drivers summoned the police and reported that their taxi company had just been robbed by a suspect with a gun and that they had followed the suspect to a house. The police entered the house and, in the course of searching for the suspect, they found, in a washing machine and under a mattress, clothing that matched the description of the clothing worn by the suspect. They also found a shotgun and a pistol in a bathroom. The clothing and weapons were later used as evidence against the suspect.

The Supreme Court pointed out that the seizure of the items did not fit within the search incidental to arrest exception because the items were seized before the police apprehended the suspect and while they were on a different floor from the suspect. Nevertheless, the entry without a warrant and the subsequent search within the premise were reasonable because the "exigencies of the situation made that course imperative." The Court stated, "The Fourth Amendment does not require police officers to delay in the course of an investigation if to do so would gravely endanger their lives or the lives of others.... Speed here was essential, and only a thorough search of the house for persons and weapons could have insured that Hayden was the only man present and that the police had control of all weapons which could be used against them or to effect an escape."

Hayden does not stand for the proposition that the police could conduct a search of the house without a warrant after the defendant was apprehended and secured. After the defendant was secured, the exigency had passed, and the police would have had to obtain a search warrant to continue searching.

Hot pursuit must commence during or immediately following an attempted arrest, and it must be for a serious crime. Police may not pursue a suspect into their home for a minor offense, such as a traffic violation. In *Welsh v. Wisconsin*, 466 U.S. 740 (1984), the police found a car abandoned in a ditch. A bystander told them that the driver had appeared to be drunk when he exited the vehicle and left the scene. After obtaining Mr. Welsh's address through the car registration, the police entered his home without a warrant to arrest him and to obtain a measurement of his blood-alcohol level before it dissipated. The Supreme Court ruled that this entry, search, and seizure could not be justified under the hot pursuit exception because the State of Wisconsin classified Welsh's offense merely as a non-criminal, civil forfeiture offense for which no imprisonment was possible.

Since *Welsh* was decided in 1984, public sentiment has raised the problem of drunk driving to a level of the utmost seriousness, and most state legislatures have increased the criminal penalties for drunk driving and increased the penalties to felony levels for repeat offenders. Were a similar case decided today, it is likely that the Court would overrule *Welsh* and rule that a drunk driving offense was serious enough to warrant hot pursuit.

Exigent Circumstances

The exigent circumstances exception is generally applied when the police have the necessary probable cause to obtain an arrest or search warrant but do not have the time to do so. It is reasonable for the police to take action without a warrant when a suspect is about to flee or a dangerous condition exists. Once the exigency has been alleviated, the police should cease their search. If a further search is necessary, they should apply for a warrant.

Courts have been reluctant to concede exigent circumstances when police claim that they had to enter private premises merely to prevent the destruction of evidence. While recognizing the need to secure evidence, courts have generally advised police that they should secure the premises and then obtain a search warrant. If necessary, they may prevent persons from entering the premises while the search warrant is being obtained.[5]

When a serious crime or a suspicious death is reported, the police generally conduct a crime scene search for evidence. If the crime scene is located in private premises, the consent of the occupant is generally forthcoming; however, if the occupant is a suspect or does not give consent to the search, the police should obtain a search warrant as soon as possible to continue the crime scene search. In a homicide case, *Mincey v. Arizona*, 437 U.S. 385 (1978), a Tucson, Arizona, undercover police officer was shot and killed in defendant Mincey's apartment. The shooting occurred as the undercover officer, with other narcotics agents, attempted to arrest the defendant for the sale of narcotics. After the shooting, the narcotics agents, thinking that other persons in the apartment might have been injured, looked about quickly for other victims. They found a young woman wounded in the bedroom closet and Mincey apparently unconscious in the bedroom, as well as Mincey's three acquaintances (one of whom had been wounded in the head) in the living room. The agents refrained from further investigation, pursuant to a Tucson Police Department directive that police officers should not investigate incidents in which they were involved. They neither searched further nor seized any evidence; they merely guarded the suspects and the premises.

Within ten minutes, homicide detectives who had heard a radio report of the shooting arrived and took charge of the investigation. "They supervised the removal of the officer and the suspects, trying to make sure that the scene was disturbed as little as possible, and then proceeded to gather evidence. Their search lasted four days, during which period the entire apartment was searched, photographed, and diagrammed. The officers opened drawers, closets, and cupboards and inspected their contents; they emptied clothing pockets; they dug bullet fragments out of the walls and floors; they pulled up sections of the carpet and removed them for examination. Every item in the apartment was closely examined and inventoried, and 200 to 300 objects were seized. In short, the defendant's apartment was subjected to an exhaustive and intrusive search. No warrant was ever obtained."

The defendant was indicted for murder, assault, and three counts of narcotics offenses. He was tried at a single trial and convicted on all the charges. Subsequently, the Arizona courts reversed the murder and assault convictions but upheld the narcotics convictions. The defendant then appealed the narcotics convictions to the Supreme Court, contending that evidence used against him had been unlawfully seized from his apartment without a warrant. The prosecution contended that the search was lawful under the exigent circumstances exception.

The Supreme Court ruled that the search of the crime scene over the four-day period required a search warrant, and the Court suppressed the evidence that was collected during the search because the exigent circumstances exception was inapplicable to this matter. The Court stated: "It simply cannot be contended that this search was justified by any emergency threatening life or limb. All the persons in Mincey's apartment had been located before the investigating homicide officers arrived there and began their search. And a four-day search that included opening dresser drawers and ripping up carpets can hardly be rationalized in terms of the legitimate concerns that justify an emergency search."

Mincey was a controlled situation that did not require urgent actions. Courts approve exigent circumstances exceptions when the police must act during unpredictable, uncertain, and fluid situations that do not allow time for delay. The police must often act while armed with incomplete information or inconclusive observations, and courts assess the reasonableness of such police actions on a case-by-case basis. In *Cupp v. Murphy*, 412 U.S. 291 (1973), the defendant voluntarily came to the police station with his attorney to be questioned about the death by strangulation of his wife. Soon after the defendant's arrival, a detective noticed what appeared to be a bloodstain under the defendant's fingernail and asked him if they could take a sample of scrapings from under his fingernails. The defendant refused and began rubbing his hands behind his back, placing them in his pockets, and rubbing them against keys in his pocket. At this point, the police forcibly held him and scraped the matter from under his fingernails. The substance under the fingernail proved to include the blood of the victim, and it was used as evidence to convict the defendant of his wife's murder. The Supreme Court upheld the seizure on the basis of a combination of plain view and exigency rationales. The Court stated that although the search incidental to arrest doctrine did not apply since the defendant was not yet under arrest, the police had probable cause to believe that "highly evanescent evidence" was being destroyed, and they acted reasonably to prevent the destruction of the critical evidence.

Cupp v. Murphy has received overwhelming support as an obvious and appropriate decision, particularly since the search occurred in a public setting; however, when the police enter private premises, more problematic issues arise regarding the balance between exigent circumstances and privacy. In 2006, in *Brigham City, Utah v. Stuart*, the Supreme Court addressed the question of whether the exigent circumstances justified entering private premises without a warrant.

Brigham City, Utah v. Stuart

U.S. Supreme Court
Brigham City, Utah v. Charles W. Stuart et al.
on writ of certiorari to the Supreme Court of Utah
May 22, 2006

(Abridged: internal citations omitted)
CHIEF JUSTICE ROBERTS delivered the opinion of the Court.

In this case we consider whether police may enter a home without a warrant when they have an objectively reasonable basis for believing that an occupant is seriously injured or imminently threatened with such injury. We conclude that they may.

I

This case arises out of a melee that occurred in a Brigham City, Utah, home in the early morning hours of July 23, 2000. At about 3 a.m., four police officers responded to a call regarding a loud party at a residence. Upon arriving at the house, they heard shouting from inside and proceeded down the driveway to investigate. There, they observed two juveniles drinking beer in the backyard. They entered the backyard, and saw—through a screen door and windows—an altercation taking place in the kitchen of the home. According to the testimony of one of the officers, four adults were attempting, with some difficulty, to restrain a juvenile. The juvenile eventually "broke free, swung a fist, and struck one of the adults in the face." The officer testified that he observed the victim of the blow spitting blood into a nearby sink. The other adults continued to try to restrain the juvenile, pressing him up against a refrigerator with such force that the refrigerator began moving across the floor. At this point, an officer opened the screen door and announced the officers' presence. Amid the tumult, nobody noticed. The officer entered the kitchen and again cried out, and as the occupants slowly became aware that the police were on the scene, the altercation ceased.

The officers subsequently arrested respondents and charged them with contributing to the delinquency of a minor, disorderly conduct, and intoxication. In the trial court, respondents filed a motion to suppress all evidence obtained after the officers entered the home, arguing that the warrantless entry violated the Fourth Amendment. The court granted the motion, and the Utah Court of Appeals affirmed.

Before the Supreme Court of Utah, Brigham City argued that although the officers lacked a warrant, their entry was nevertheless reasonable on either of two grounds. The court rejected both contentions and, over two dissenters, affirmed. First, the court held that the injury caused by the juvenile's punch was insufficient to trigger the so-called "emergency aid doctrine" because it did not give rise to an "objectively reasonable belief that an unconscious, semi-conscious, or missing person feared injured or dead [was] in the home." Furthermore, the court suggested that the doctrine was inapplicable because the officers had not sought to assist the injured adult, but instead had acted "exclusively in their law enforcement capacity."

The court also held that the entry did not fall within the exigent circumstances exception to the warrant requirement. This exception applies, the court explained, where police have probable cause and where "a reasonable person [would] believe that the entry was necessary to prevent physical harm to the officers or other persons." Under this standard, the court stated, the potential harm need not be as serious as that required to invoke the emergency aid exception. Although it found the case "a close and difficult call," the court nevertheless concluded that the officers' entry was not justified by exigent circumstances.

We granted certiorari, in light of differences among state courts and the Courts of Appeals concerning the appropriate Fourth Amendment standard governing warrantless entry by law enforcement in an emergency situation.

II

It is a "basic principle of Fourth Amendment law that searches and seizures inside a home without a warrant are presumptively unreasonable." Nevertheless, because the ultimate touchstone of the Fourth Amendment is "reasonableness," the warrant requirement is subject to certain exceptions. We have held, for example, that law enforcement officers may make a warrantless entry onto private property to fight a fire and investigate its cause, to prevent the imminent destruction of evidence, or to engage in "hot pursuit" of a fleeing suspect....

One exigency obviating the requirement of a warrant is the need to assist persons who are seriously injured or threatened with such injury. "The need to protect or preserve life or avoid serious injury is justification for what would be otherwise illegal absent an exigency or emergency." Accordingly, law enforcement officers may enter a home without a warrant to render emergency assistance to an injured occupant or to protect an occupant from imminent injury....

Respondents do not take issue with these principles, but instead advance two reasons why the officers' entry here was unreasonable. First, they argue that the officers were more interested in making arrests than quelling violence. They urge us to consider, in assessing the reasonableness of the entry, whether the officers were "indeed motivated primarily by a desire to save lives and property." Brief for Respondents 3; see also Brief for National Association of Criminal Defense Lawyers as *Amicus Curiae* 6 (entry to render emergency assistance justifies a search "only when the searching officer is acting outside his traditional law-enforcement capacity"). The Utah Supreme Court also considered the officers' subjective motivations relevant.

Our cases have repeatedly rejected this approach. An action is "reasonable" under the Fourth Amendment, regardless of the individual officer's state of mind, "as long as the circumstances, viewed *objectively*, justify [the] action." The officer's subjective motivation is irrelevant. ("The parties properly agree that the subjective intent of the law enforcement officer is irrelevant in determining whether that officer's actions violate the Fourth Amendment... the issue is not his state of mind, but the objective effect of his actions"); ("[O]ur prior cases make clear" that "the subjective motivations of the individual officers... ha[ve] no bearing on whether a particular seizure is 'unreasonable' under the Fourth Amendment"). It therefore does not matter here—even if their subjective motives could be so neatly unraveled—whether the officers entered the kitchen to arrest respondents and gather evidence against them or to assist the injured and prevent further violence....

Respondents further contend that their conduct was not serious enough to justify the officers' intrusion into the home. They rely on *Welsh* v. *Wisconsin*, 466 U.S. 740, 753, 104 S. Ct. 2091, 80 L.Ed.2d 732 (1984), in which we held that "an important factor to be considered when determining whether any exigency exists is the gravity of the underlying offense for which the arrest is being made." This contention, too, is misplaced. *Welsh* involved a warrantless entry by officers to arrest a suspect for driving while intoxicated. There, the "only potential emergency" confronting the officers was the need to preserve evidence (i.e., the suspect's blood-alcohol level)—an exigency that we held insufficient under the circumstances to justify entry into the suspect's home. Here, the officers were confronted with *ongoing* violence occurring *within* the home. *Welsh* did not address such a situation.

We think the officers' entry here was plainly reasonable under the circumstances. The officers were responding, at 3 o'clock in the morning, to complaints about a loud party. As they approached the house, they could hear from within "an altercation occurring, some kind of a fight.... It was loud and it was tumultuous." The officers heard "thumping and crashing" and people yelling "stop, stop" and "get off me." As the trial court found, "it was obvious that... knocking on the front door" would have been futile. The noise seemed to be coming from the back of the house; after looking in the front window and seeing nothing, the officers proceeded around back to investigate further. They found two juveniles drinking beer in the backyard. From there, they could see that a fracas was taking place inside the kitchen. A juvenile, fists clenched, was being held back by several adults. As the officers watch, he breaks free and strikes one of the adults in the face, sending the adult to the sink spitting blood.

In these circumstances, the officers had an objectively reasonable basis for believing both that the injured adult might need help and that the violence in the kitchen was just beginning. Nothing in the Fourth Amendment required them to wait until another blow rendered someone "unconscious" or "semiconscious" or worse before entering. The role of a peace officer includes preventing violence and restoring order, not simply rendering first aid to casualties; an officer is not like a boxing (or hockey) referee, poised to stop a bout only if it becomes too one-sided.

The manner of the officers' entry was also reasonable. After witnessing the punch, one of the officers opened the screen door and "yelled in police." When nobody heard him, he stepped into the kitchen and announced himself again. Only then did the tumult subside. The officer's announcement of his presence was at least equivalent to a knock on the screen door. Indeed, it was probably the only option that had even a chance of rising above the din. Under these circumstances, there was no violation of the Fourth Amendment's knock- and-announce rule. Furthermore, once the announcement was made, the officers were free to enter; it would serve no purpose to require them to stand dumbly at the door awaiting a response while those within brawled on, oblivious to their presence.

Accordingly, we reverse the judgment of the Supreme Court of Utah, and remand the case for further proceedings not inconsistent with this opinion.

Justice Stevens, concurring.

This is an odd flyspeck of a case. The charges that have been pending against respondents for the past six years are minor offenses—intoxication, contributing to the delinquency of a minor, and disorderly conduct—two of which could have been proved by evidence that was gathered by the responding officers before they entered the home. The maximum punishment for these crimes ranges between 90 days and 6 months in jail. And the Court's unanimous opinion restating well-settled rules of federal law is so clearly persuasive that it is hard to imagine the outcome was ever in doubt....

Questions Raised by *Brigham City, Utah v. Stuart*

In *Brigham City, Utah v. Stuart*, the Supreme Court reversed a Utah state court decision to dismiss the case against the defendant. The Utah court had ruled that the evidence obtained by the officers when they entered the defendant's house was obtained illegally because the officers should not have entered the house without a warrant.

1. What evidence did the Utah court believe was obtained illegally?
2. Were the officers' observations of the defendant's conduct deemed inadmissible?
3. If a trial is allegedly a truth-finding process, is it logical to exclude a police officer's testimony as to what he observed?
4. Do the same exclusionary rule principles that apply to tangible objects apply to observations of conduct?
5. Although the Supreme Court reversed and remanded the case back to the Utah court for further proceedings, ruling that the officers' entry into the premises under the circumstances was reasonable and did not violate the U.S. Constitution, could the Utah court suppress the officer's testimony on the basis of the Utah state constitution?

Protective Sweeps

Another case involving a combination of exigency and plain view is *Maryland v. Buie*, 494 U.S. 325 (1990), which demonstrates that hard and fast rules, such as the search limitations announced in *Chimel v. California*, 395 U.S. 752 (1969), always have exceptions, especially when the circumstances raise safety concerns.

In *Buie*, two men had committed an armed bank robbery. One of the men was described as wearing a red running suit. The same day, the police obtained arrest warrants for the two suspects, and they executed the warrant for Buie at his home. After successfully arresting Buie, one of the officers entered the basement of the house to search for the other suspect and to check for other occupants. As the officer moved through the basement, he saw in plain view a red running suit similar to the one described as having been worn by the robber. He seized the running suit as evidence.

The Supreme Court upheld the seizure of the evidence and the conviction, holding that in such danger-laden circumstances as the apprehension of armed robbers, the police could conduct a protective sweep of the premises:

> To assure themselves that the house in which a suspect is being or has just been arrested is not harboring other persons who are dangerous and who could unexpectedly launch an attack. The risk of danger in the context of an arrest in the home is as great as, if not greater than it is in an on-the-street or roadside investigatory encounter... as an incident to the arrest the officers could, as a precautionary matter and without probable cause or reasonable suspicion, look in closets and other spaces immediately adjoining the place of arrest from which an attack could be immediately launched.

Buie is distinguishable from the hot pursuit doctrine approved in *Warden v. Hayden*, 387 U.S. 297 (1967). In *Hayden*, the officers found the evidence before they apprehended the defendant. In *Buie*, on the contrary, the defendant had already been apprehended when the officers found the evidence; however, in *Buie*, there were two robbery suspects, not one, and the accomplice had not yet been apprehended. With the high probability that the accomplice was present in the house, the Court applied the protective sweep doctrine as a logical extension of the exigent circumstances doctrine.

In addition to a protective sweep, the reasonable movements of an officer at an arrest location are not prohibited. For example, an officer who takes a suspect from one room to another for the suspect to get clothes to wear does not commit a Fourth Amendment violation.[6] When, during the course of performing such reasonable and practical functions, an officer observes objects in plain view that are immediately recognizable as contraband or evidence, the officer may seize the objects. However, the officer cannot use such lawful entries into a room as an excuse to rummage through the contents of the room.

Problem

Federal drug enforcement agents, without a warrant, break into a house and seize five kilos of unlawful cocaine. They arrest "Fat Cat" Payton, the owner of the house, and Johnny "The Rake" Rakas, a visitor. The agents question Payton without *Miranda* warnings, and he tells them Rakas' car is outside. The agents search Rakas' car and find ten more kilos of cocaine in the trunk. Rakas, watching this, blurts out to Fat Cat, "You rat, I'm gonna kill you when I get out."

While this is going on, Harvey Harris knocks on the front door and the agents take him into custody. Harvey starts to cry, and in response to questioning, without *Miranda* warnings, about his identity, blurts out that he was only there to buy a small amount of marijuana. Five minutes later, Danny Dunaway approaches the house, sees the agents, turns quickly, and walks away. Because he looks suspicious, the agents take him into custody and try to question him, but he refuses to answer questions and remains silent.

Then the agents take all four suspects to a detention facility and give them all *Miranda* warnings before questioning them. Payton gives a statement that Rakas was the drug dealer, not him. Rakas gives a statement that Payton is the drug dealer, not him, and that Payton had borrowed his car and must have put the ten kilos into his car.

Harris says he knew that Payton, Rakas, and Dunaway sold cocaine, but again says that he was there only to buy marijuana. Dunaway confesses that he was the supplier of the cocaine, and based on his confession the agents recover records of cocaine transactions indicating that he was making about $10 million per year.

All the suspects are arrested and charged with possession of unlawful cocaine. They are tried separately, and their attorneys file pretrial motions to exclude evidence.

Questions

Are the following statements true or false?

1. In the case against Payton, the five kilos from his house will be excluded from evidence because they were seized without a warrant in violation of his Fourth Amendment rights.
2. In the case against Payton, the ten kilos from Rakas' car will be excluded from evidence against him because it was the fruit of the poisonous tree of the search and seizure violation at his home and the statement taken without *Miranda* warnings.
3. At Payton's trial, an agent could testify to Rakas' out-of-court statement at the police station and it could be used against Payton.
4. In the case against Rakas, he can move to have the cocaine from the house excluded from evidence because it was seized without a warrant.
5. At Rakas' trial, an agent could testify to Payton's out-of-court statement at the police station and it could be used against Rakas.
6. The cocaine from the car will not be admitted into evidence against Rakas because it was seized without probable cause.
7. In Harris' trial, he cannot move to exclude either the cocaine from Payton's house or the cocaine from Rakas' car because he does not have standing to do so.
8. Harris' statement at Payton's house will be excluded because he was not given *Miranda* warnings.
9. Harris' confession at the detention facility may be admitted into evidence because he was arrested with probable cause and was given *Miranda* warnings.
10. Dunaway's confession at the detention facility will be excluded because he was arrested without probable cause and questioned while in custody.
11. Payton will get off. No drugs from the house will be admitted against him. No drugs from the car will be admitted against him. His statements will be excluded. Rakas' out-of-court statement will not be admitted against him. Harris' confession will not be admitted against him. Dunaway's confession will not be admitted against him.

12. Rakas will be convicted. Drugs from the house and the car will be admitted against him. His spontaneous statement, "You rat. I'm gonna kill you when I get out," will be admitted against him as circumstantial evidence of consciousness of guilt.

13. If Harris is unable to rebut the evidence offered against him, he will be convicted. Drugs from the house and car will be admitted against him. His spontaneous statement at the house and his admission at the detention facility that he knew the others sold cocaine will be used against him.

14. Dunaway will get off. He never entered the house, no connection to the car was established, and no spontaneous statements were made. His confession will be excluded because he was arrested without probable cause. The records of drug transactions will be excluded as fruits of the poisonous tree of the unlawful arrest and questioning.

Open Fields

When objects of contraband or evidence situated on private property can be observed from a public place, the police may seize the objects. By placing objects where the public might readily see them, the owners of the objects forgo their expectation of privacy. Fencing and "No Trespassing" signs do not prohibit viewing from a public place. Viewing and photographing objects from an airplane are from a public place and are permissible.[7] For example, marijuana plants growing within a fenced field may not readily be seen from outside the fence but may be readily seen from an airplane flying over the field. In such a circumstance, law enforcement officers could apply for a search warrant to seize the marijuana on the basis of the plain view observations from the airplane.

When an observation discloses imminently dangerous objects or activity, law enforcement officers, under the emergency or exigency doctrines, might lawfully enter the private property without a warrant to seize the dangerous objects or terminate the dangerous activity.

Open fields do not include the curtilage around a house. The curtilage is the enclosed space of ground immediately surrounding a dwelling. It is the space necessarily and habitually used by the occupants of the house, and it has Fourth Amendment protection.

The following is a list of certain circumstances under which searches or seizures may be conducted without warrants:

- Incidental to a lawful arrest
- Emergency
- Exigent circumstances
- Hot pursuit
- Protective sweep
- Open fields
- Stop and frisk (Chapter 12)
- Plain feel (Chapter 12)
- Consent (Chapter 13)
- Abandoned property (Chapter 13)
- Automobiles (Chapter 14)
- Plain hearing (Chapter 21)

Notes

1 *Payton v. New York*, 445 U.S. 573 (1980).
2 *United States v. Rabinowitz*, 339 U.S. 56 (1950).

3 *United States v. Watson*, 423 U.S. 411 (1976).
4 *United States v. Santana*, 427 U.S. 38 (1976).
5 *Illinois v. McArthur*, 531 U.S. 326 (2001).
6 *United States v. Titus*, 445 F.2d 577 (2d Cir. 1971).
7 *Oliver v. United States*, 466 U.S. 170 (1984).

References

Bruton v. United States, 391 U.S. 123 (1968).
Dunaway v. New York, 442 U.S. 200 (1979).
Mapp v. Ohio, 367 U.S. 643 (1961).
Minnesota v. Carter, 525 U.S. 83 (1998).
Miranda v. Arizona, 384 U.S. 436 (1966).
New York v. Harris, 495 U.S. 14 (1990).
Payton v. New York, 445 U.S. 573 (1980).
Rakas v. Illinois, 439 U.S. 128 (1978).

Chapter 11

A Not So Uncommon Police/Citizen Encounter

The following problem scenario is a composite of the kinds of police/citizen encounters that occur daily across the United States. In our society, with unlawful drugs so prevalent, it is not difficult to imagine that an innocent person might find him- or herself enmeshed in a situation similar to that described below. The problem highlights the difficulties that citizens face when confronted by investigating police officers, and the difficulties that police officers face as they attempt to investigate crime while respecting individual rights. The practical and legal issues raised by this scenario are relevant for all crime-related police/citizen encounters, whether or not the encounters involve unlawful drugs or other crimes.

Problem

Johnny Rodriquez and his fiancée, Joanne Taylor, went to a dance club to celebrate Johnny's graduation from college. After an hour at the club, they met another couple, Artie Straw and Linda Rivera. Johnny and Artie had gone to college together before Artie dropped out.

"Do you mind if we join you?" Artie asked.

"Sure. Sit down," Johnny said.

The couples shared the table and had two drinks each. The women drank margaritas; the men drank bourbon and sodas. Their conversation was mostly about their college days and stories about the oddball professors they had. Each story seemed funnier than the one before. At 3:00 AM, when the club lights flickered to indicate closing time, the waitress brought a bill to the table.

"Let's just split the bill," Artie said.

"No. We had more than you," Johnny said.

"That's okay. I'll put it on my credit card. It's a tax write-off, and I can use the cash."

"Are you sure?" Johnny handed Artie $80 for his half of the bill, plus a tip.

"No problem," Artie said, "but maybe you can give us a lift uptown. I don't have my wheels."

"Okay. We'll get the car and meet you out front."

As Johnny and Joanne went to get the car, Artie gave the waitress a credit card.

Linda shook her head. "Are you sure you're not going to get in trouble?"

"No way, that card's clean for another week."

After signing the credit card receipt, Artie walked toward the bathrooms and met with a young man wearing two large gold earrings. Artie gave the man the cash Johnny had given him, and in return the man gave Artie two tinfoil packets of cocaine.

In the meantime, Johnny and Joanne were waiting outside in a black four-door BMW sedan that Johnny's older brother had let him use for the night as part of his graduation gift.

DOI: 10.4324/9781003415091-14

"I like your wheels," Artie said, as he and Linda climbed into the backseat.

"It's my brother's car."

"Since we're riding in style, I know some great after-hours clubs."

"No thanks," Johnny said. "We've got to get home."

After they drove a few blocks on a northbound avenue, Artie asked Johnny to pull the car over. "I don't want you hit any bumps or I might spill this," Artie said.

"Spill what?" Johnny said as he looked back and saw Artie opening a tinfoil packet. He could see the white crystalline powder. "Are you crazy? What do you think you're doing?"

Johnny had taken his eyes off the road, and the car swerved out of his traffic lane. "Look out," Joanne yelled.

Johnny immediately straightened the car, narrowly missing a collision with another vehicle.

"Take it easy," Artie said. "It's no big deal."

"It is a big deal. We don't mess with that stuff. I don't need that kind of trouble."

"You're not getting any trouble. I got a tin for you guys, too, but not if you don't want to."

"Get out," Johnny said.

"You can't drop us here." Artie said. "There're no cabs this time of night."

As the BMW drove north on the avenue, Police Officers Jack Canton and Jennifer Hounder were stopped in their patrol car at a red light on a cross-street. They saw the BMW swerve out of its lane and almost strike the other vehicle.

"Looks like the BMW had too many drinks," Officer Canton said.

"Let's check it out," Officer Hounder said.

The officers turned onto the avenue and within two blocks caught up to the BMW. They pulled behind and turned on their flashing turret lights, but the BMW did not immediately stop.

In the BMW, Johnny and Artie were arguing and no one noticed the police car behind them until Linda saw the flashing lights.

"Oh, no," she said, "the cops."

Everyone in the BMW looked back at the police car.

Artie closed the tinfoil and pushed it toward Linda. "Put it in your bra."

"No way," she said.

"Do it!" he said.

Linda took the tin, but instead of putting it in her bra, she rolled down her window and threw it out toward the sidewalk.

Johnny drove about ten more yards and pulled the car over to the curb. Through the rearview mirror, he saw the two police officers get out of their patrol car and slowly come toward his car.

As the police officers approached, Artie tried to give the second tinfoil to Linda. She would not take it, and without anyone else seeing, he tossed it under the driver's seat.

Officer Canton approached the BMW on the driver's side, while Officer Hounder approached on the passenger's side.

"Can I see your license and registration?" Canton said.

"Yes, officer," Johnny replied, as he looked through his wallet for his license. "Here's my license, but it's my brother's car. The registration might be in the glove compartment."

"Take a look," Canton said.

While the officers shined their flashlights into the car, Johnny and Joanne each took a turn fumbling through the papers in the glove compartment, but they could not find the registration.

"I can't seem to find it," Johnny said. He began to perspire and his hands began to tremble.

"Have you been drinking?" Canton asked.

"No. Not really, officer. We were celebrating my graduation, but I only had a couple. I'm not drunk."

"What kind of drinks did you have?"

"Uh... beers. Two beers."

The officer leaned over with his head slightly into the car window. "You don't smell like beer to me. Step out of the car."

"Officer, he's not a drinker," Joanne pleaded from her passenger seat. "There's no need to do this. He's a careful driver."

"Sir, I'm going to ask you again. Step out of the car."

The ominous tone of the officer's command convinced Johnny to get out.

Once he did, the officer made him place his hands on the top of the car, and the officer frisked him. The officer then walked Johnny to the front of the patrol car.

"I'm going to give you a little test to see whether you're drunk or not. Okay?"

"Okay."

The officer administered the standard sobriety tests. He had Johnny perform the straight-line walking test, which required him to take nine steps on a straight line, placing one foot in front of another, heel to toe, with the heel touching the toe of the other foot. At the completion of the ninth step, he had to pivot around and take nine more steps back in the same manner.

The officer had Johnny perform the one-legged stand test, which required him to stand on one leg and hold the other leg straight and forward for 30 seconds while keeping his hands at his sides.

He had Johnny perform the finger-to-nose test, which required him to tilt his head back, close his eyes, put his arms straight out to the side, then touch his nose with his left index finger, then with his right index finger.

Johnny passed all the tests except the straight-line test. The ground was a little uneven and Johnny lost his balance slightly and stepped off the line.

"Sir, I'm going to have to give you a field alcohol test." The officer held up a plastic device. "Blow into this. It's an alcohol meter. It's to see if you've been drinking."

"Do I have to do this?"

"If you don't, I'll have no choice but to arrest you."

"I need my license. I'm starting a new job, and I need to be able to drive."

"Then I suggest you take the test."

Artie, who had been listening through the passenger window, opened his door and began to get out of the car. "I don't think you should take the test. If you don't take it, they just suspend your license. If you fail it, you get locked up."

The officer pointed at Artie. "Stay in the car."

Artie got out of the car. "You know, he has rights. You can't force him to blow into that stupid thing. How do we know it's not rigged?"

"Listen, pal, if you don't get back into the car right now, I'm going to lock the both of you up."

"You can't lock us up. He just passed all your tests. And this is a free country. I have a right of free speech. Did you ever hear of the First Amendment?"

"I'm not going to argue with you. I can arrest him right now. I can smell the booze on his breath. He admitted he had drinks. He swerved in the middle of the road, almost hit a car, and he couldn't walk a straight line. His only chance is to pass this breath test. So, if you don't mind, get back in the car."

Linda reached out of the car and pulled Artie's arm. "Get in the car."

"Okay. I'll get in, but I don't have to if I don't want to," Artie said as he got back into the car.

In the backseat, Linda said, "What's the matter with you, you moron? You're going to get us all busted."

Officer Hounder heard what Linda said, and she again used her flashlight to inspect the interior of the car. As she did this, the three occupants sat unnaturally still. Hounder did not see any illegal contraband or other evidence of a crime in plain view.

When a backup patrol car arrived with two male officers, Canton again asked Johnny to blow into the alcohol meter.

Johnny blew into the device.

Canton looked at the reading. "It's low."

"What does that mean?"

"You passed."

"Thank God." Johnny ran over to the car window to tell Joanne. "I passed."

"Hold on there, pal." Canton took Johnny's arm and walked him back to the police car. "It doesn't mean you can't be arrested. Sometimes people get intoxicated by other ways than alcohol, if you know what I mean."

"I know what you mean. But I don't do drugs. I never did. We're going to get married. I just graduated college. Got a new job. I'm not a wise guy."

"You seem to hang out with wise guys."

"I just met him in the club and he asked me for a ride uptown."

Joanne stuck her head out of the driver's window and asked, "Officer, can I talk to you?"

"Just stay in the car," he said.

The officer walked Johnny back to the car. "I'm giving you the benefit of the doubt. Sit in your car. If the computer check comes back okay, you'll get a summons for unsafe lane change. Okay?"

"Thank you, officer," Johnny got into the driver's seat. He turned to Joanne. "I'm just getting a summons then we can go."

"I think we should go without them," Joanne said, nodding to the back seat.

Artie leaned forward and whispered, "Just be cool. There's no problem. We'll be on our way in a few minutes. They've got nothing."

Joanne stared at Artie. "I'd just love to tell them what you got in your pocket."

"Don't be stupid, you..."

Johnny pointed at Artie. "Watch it!"

While Officer Canton was seated in the patrol car writing the ticket, Officer Hounder was standing on the curb and could hear the whispering in the BMW. Although she could not hear exactly what was being said, it made her suspicious of the occupants. She asked the backup officers to keep an eye on them. On a hunch, she walked along the route they had driven, using her flashlight to survey the street and the sidewalk. About ten yards back along the curb, her light illuminated the silver tinfoil packet. She picked the packet up, spread the tinfoil a bit, and saw the white powder. On the basis of her training in the police academy and her experience as an officer, she believed the white powder was cocaine.

Hounder came back to the patrol car and showed the tinfoil packet to Canton.

"But we don't know it came from them," he said.

"We have enough probable cause to make an arrest," she said.

"I don't think so, and which one would we arrest?"

"All of them. It came out of the car. And you know there's a presumption that drugs found in a car means possession by all the occupants."

"You don't know it came from the car. You didn't see it. Right?"

"But it's too much of a coincidence," she said. "The tinfoil was right where we stopped them—right after they turned around and saw us. Remember they all turned around. You think it's just by chance that the tinfoil shows up right at that spot?"

"It doesn't matter what I think. It's what we can prove. I don't want to lock anybody up, and then get sued for false arrest."

"You don't have to know for sure. You only need probable cause. And that guy in the back seat, I think he was trying to distract us. I think it was all an act."

"That's not evidence. I can't go to the Lieutenant and tell him the guy in the back seat was a wise guy, so I locked everybody up. And I already told this guy I was letting him go."

"We should take them to the station house for questioning," she said.

"That's the same as an arrest; we need probable cause," he said.

"I think there's plenty of probable cause to search the car. There could be more drugs in it, and I'm not letting them drive away until I find out, one way or the other."

"Take it easy," Canton said. "Let me see if I can get the driver to consent to a search of the car."

Canton approached the car and asked Johnny to step out. "Listen, there's a little problem," he said. "We have reason to believe there's some drugs involved here, and we need to search the car."

"I don't see why," Johnny said.

"Well, you know that I could still arrest you for intoxicated driving, possibly under the influence of drugs."

"That's crazy, I don't do drugs. Not even marijuana. I'm being honest with you. Once or twice maybe, a long time ago when I was a kid, but I don't do drugs."

"I kind of believe you, but I have to do my job. If I search the car and don't find anything, then maybe we can end this. So I need your consent to search the car."

Artie shouted from his window. "No way, he has no right to search the car."

"Just shut up," Johnny said to Artie.

Johnny said to the officer, "Listen, it's my brother's car. He wouldn't want me to let anyone search it. I appreciate that you gave me a break, but I have to stand up for my rights. It's a matter of principle. There's nothing in the car. The only thing I did was to swerve, and I didn't hit anything. That's no crime. Give me the ticket, and let me go. It's getting real late, and we have to go home."

"Wait here. Let me talk to my partner."

The officers conferred. "He won't consent," Canton said.

"We've got probable cause to search the car," Hounder said. "You haven't given him the ticket yet, so you can search him and the car either incidental to the arrest or for a safety check."

"You know better than that. He's not under arrest. A summons is not an arrest. And to search the car, we need probable cause."

"The drugs thrown out the window and all the arguing inside the car is enough for me."

"Without seeing the drugs come out of the window, it won't stand up in court," he said. "You're not going to say you saw it fly out the window. Right?"

"Of course not."

"Then you don't have enough evidence."

"In that case, I'll talk to them and get some evidence," she said.

Back at the BMW, Hounder shined her flashlight on each of the occupants. "You," she said to Artie. "Get out of the car."

Hounder walked Artie back to the spot where she had found the tinfoil packet.

"You know what I found here?"

"No. What?"

"This." She showed him the packet.

"What's that?" Artie said.

"Don't be a wise guy. One of you threw it out of the car when we pulled you over."

"I don't know what you're talking about."

"I saw it come out of the window. That means everyone in the car is under arrest. Unless, of course, someone owns up and says that it was his. So I suggest you guys get together and decide who's going to admit that is was theirs. Now, get back in the car and discuss it with your friends."

"I'm not talking to anybody about anything. If you're going to keep hassling me, I want a lawyer."

"Okay. We'll see that you get a lawyer." Hounder took Artie's arm and walked him to the front of the BMW, where she handcuffed and searched him.

Hounder removed Artie's wallet from his back pocket and some papers from his front pockets.

"Hey, you don't have any right to take my wallet."

Hounder looked through the contents of the wallet and found a license with Artie's picture. "Is this you, Arthur Straw?"

"That's me."

"Then, what's this?" Hounder held up three credit cards. "You've got three credit cards with three different names. Where'd you get them?"

"I told you, I've got nothing to say. I want a lawyer."

Hounder looked through the papers she had taken from his pockets and found a copy of the credit card receipt from the club. The receipt matched the number on one of the credit cards. She smiled. "You're under arrest."

"What for?"

"In addition to the drugs, stolen credit cards, grand larceny, identity theft, and anything else I can think of."

One of the backup officers placed Artie in his patrol car while Hounder took Linda out of the BMW and showed her the tinfoil. Linda denied knowing anything about it. Hounder handcuffed her, searched her purse, and placed her in the back of her patrol car.

Inside the BMW, Johnny and Joanne sat stunned. "Are they going to arrest us?" she asked.

"I don't see how," he said. "Maybe they're only going to arrest them."

"Should we tell them what happened?"

"I think we should get a lawyer," Johnny said. "We shouldn't say anything."

"But I don't want to be arrested."

"You think I do?"

"That officer let you go," she said. "He seems reasonable. If we tell him what happened, maybe he won't arrest us."

"Then we'll have to testify against them."

"If that's what we have to do, then that's what we have to do."

"There's no guarantee that they won't arrest us anyway. We have a right to remain silent. That's what we should do. We'll fight it in court."

Hounder shined her flashlight on Joanne. "Come out."

"No!" Johnny shouted as he got out of the car. "Take me. Arrest me. Just leave her alone."

"Do you want to tell me the drugs were yours?" Hounder said.

"I have nothing to say," Johnny said.

"Then turn around and put your hands behind your back."

With Canton's help, Hounder handcuffed Johnny.

"Don't I get my *Miranda* rights?"

"If we're not asking you any questions, we don't have to give you *Miranda* warnings," Canton said.

From the car window, Joanne said, "I want to talk to you."

"Okay. Come out. You'll get the warnings."

From an index card, Canton read the *Miranda* warnings to Joanne:

"You have the right to remain silent. Anything you say can be used against you in a court of law. You have the right to talk to a lawyer before we ask you any questions, and you have the right to have a lawyer with you during questioning. If you cannot afford a lawyer, one will be appointed for you before any questioning if you wish. Do you understand?"

"Yes. I understand."

Canton asked one of the backup officers to watch Johnny while he and Hounder took Joanne a distance away to talk to her.

Joanne told them exactly what had happened in the club and in the car.

"So you didn't know beforehand that Artie had this tinfoil of cocaine," Canton said.

"No. And I don't know what it is. I don't know whether it's cocaine or something else. All I know is I didn't like it. And neither did Johnny. That's why he almost got in the accident. He was so surprised. Johnny told Artie that we're not into drugs."

"Then what happened?"

"The next thing we knew, you were behind us, with the flashing light. We didn't know what to do. I guess I should have told you right away. I should have told you that she threw it out the window."

"You should have," Hounder said, "because now you've put us in a bad position."

Joanne pressed her hand to her mouth trying to prevent herself from crying. "Please, don't arrest my fiancé. He didn't do anything wrong."

"How much was the bill at the dance club?" Hounder asked. "And who paid it?"

"I think it was almost a hundred dollars a couple. Johnny gave Artie cash. Then we went out to get the car. Artie paid it."

"Did you see him pay it?"

"No. We were outside."

The officers told Johnny that Joanne had told them what had happened and that she was going to cooperate. Johnny agreed to do the same, and he related essentially the same version of events.

The officers conferred again. Canton suggested that if Joanne and Johnny would give them written statements, they would let them go and only arrest the two in the backseat.

Hounder was not sure they had the authority to do that. "The presumption is that everyone in the car was in possession of the drugs," she said.

"That doesn't mean we have to arrest them. If there's reasonable evidence that rebuts the presumption, we don't have to arrest anybody. And, besides that, we didn't find the drugs in the car. You didn't see the drugs fly out the window," Canton said.

The officers told Johnny and Joanne that they would have to come with them to the station house and give their signed statements, and then they would be released.

Johnny asked whether he could park his car at the curb.

"Wait a minute," Hounder said. "I have to search the car."

Canton stared at her.

"Two of them are under arrest." She directed her comment to Canton. "Part of the arrest is searching them and anywhere they could have reached. And that means the inside of the car."

In less than a minute, Hounder found the second tinfoil packet of cocaine that Artie had tossed under the front seat. She held it up, showing it to Canton. "Looks like this changes everything."

Questions

1. Was it lawful for the officers to stop Johnny's car?
2. Was it lawful for Officer Canton to question Johnny about drinking alcohol?
3. Was it lawful for Officer Canton to order Johnny to get out of the car?
4. Did the officer need probable cause to believe that Johnny was intoxicated to lawfully order him out of the car?
5. Was Officer Canton acting lawfully when he frisked Johnny before administering the sobriety test?
6. Was it lawful for the officer to ask Johnny to perform the sobriety tests?
7. Do sobriety tests violate a defendant's Fifth Amendment right against compelled self-incrimination?
8. Does requiring a defendant to exhale into an alcohol meter violate the defendant's right against compelled self-incrimination?
9. Was Artie correct when he said that his First Amendment rights of free speech allowed him to interject into the conversation between Officer Canton and Johnny?
10. Was Canton acting lawfully when he ordered Artie to stay in the car?
11. Had Artie not complied, would the officer have been authorized to arrest him?
12. When Officer Hounder used her flashlight to look into the car, was she conducting a search? If so, was the search a violation of the Fourth Amendment privacy rights of the occupants?
13. Was Officer Hounder correct to contend that she had probable cause to arrest all the occupants of the vehicle on the basis of the tinfoil of cocaine she found at the curb?
14. Did the conduct of the occupants inside the vehicle lend support to Hounder's contention that probable cause existed?
15. Was it absolutely necessary for Officer Hounder to have seen the tinfoil of cocaine fly out of the window for her to arrest the occupants of the car for possession of that tinfoil?
16. Assuming that finding the tinfoil at the curb was not a sufficient basis to arrest the occupants of the car, was it sufficient probable cause to search the car?
17. Under the circumstances, was it lawful for the police to request that Johnny give consent to the search of the vehicle?
18. Although the initial request for consent to search the car would most likely have been lawful, was the consent made unlawful by Officer Canton's implicit threat that he would arrest Johnny for driving while under the influence of drugs if he did not consent?

19. Because the car belonged to Johnny's brother, did Johnny have the right to give or refuse permission to search it?
20. Was Officer Hounder correct to state that, on the basis of the traffic ticket they were going to issue to Johnny, they could search the car?
21. When Officer Hounder arrested Artie, was it lawful for her to search his wallet?

The lines between police questioning a person during a preliminary investigation and questioning a person in custody, which would require *Miranda* warnings, are sometimes difficult to identify. The actions of the police in this case raise several questions regarding *Miranda* warnings, the right against self-incrimination, and the right to counsel.

22. When Officer Hounder took Artie out of the car, showed him the packet of cocaine, and questioned him, should she have read him the *Miranda* rights?
23. If Artie had confessed his guilt at that point, would his confession have been admissible in court?
24. At the point at which both Artie and Linda had been arrested, could the police have lawfully interrogated Artie without his lawyer present?
25. Could they have interrogated Linda without her lawyer present?
26. When the officers first handcuffed Johnny, was it necessary for them to give him *Miranda* warnings?
27. If Joanne was prosecuted for possession of the drugs, would her statement about the packet of cocaine have been admissible against her in court?
28. If Johnny was prosecuted for possession of the drugs, would his statement about the packet of cocaine have been admissible against him in court?
29. Under these circumstances, do the police have discretion to arrest some of the occupants of the car and not others?
30. Should the fact that Officer Hounder found the second tinfoil of cocaine under the driver's seat change the decision not to arrest Johnny and Joanne?

Discussion

A review of the decisions and actions of the participants in the above problem is instructive for practical purposes as well as for legal training. Clearly, the police have statutory authority to enforce traffic regulations, and motorists who are stopped by the police should cooperate with reasonable requests and directions. Not so clear is whether Joanne or Johnny should have immediately told the police about how Artie, without their permission or agreement, had shown them the cocaine. Were they required to report this crime? If they had reported the crime, would they have been exempted from arrest or would they have been subsequently exonerated in court? If they had not reported the crime, did they become complicit? In retrospect, it may have been prudent to have told the police; however, in real life things happen quickly, and people often do not think fast enough or shrewdly enough. Because they initially chose not to tell the officers what happened, the encounter proceeded as it did.

Regarding the decisions and actions of the police officers, stopping the BMW after they observed it swerve and almost cause an accident certainly was proper police procedure. Also, the sobriety tests were justified on the basis of the unsafe driving, the late hour, the alcohol on Johnny's breath, and his admission that he had had "two beers."

A more difficult question is whether the detention and questioning of the vehicle occupants was justified on the basis of the tinfoil packet found on the street. Legal determinations such as whether the officers had reasonable suspicion or probable cause often rest on factual circumstances, probabilities, and commonsense judgments, and a change of one part of a fact pattern may change the outcome of the legal determination.

For example, had the item thrown from the car been a gun instead of a tinfoil packet, the reasonableness of the detention and questioning of the occupants would have been greater. A tinfoil could lie in the gutter for some time without being noticed or picked up by a bystander; the probability that a gun would lie undisturbed for even a short time is very low. Therefore, the probable connection between the vehicle and a gun would have been stronger, and the officers' actions more reasonable.

Other questions pertain to police discretion. When the same evidence might be applied to a group of people, may the police lawfully arrest some in the group but not others? Do the police have authority, on their own, to decline to arrest someone in return for that person's agreement to testify against others? Or must the police obtain permission from the district attorney to do so?

The answers to such questions depend on the particular facts of the case and the application of legal principles to those facts. Often, the answers in a particular case depend on the reasonableness of the actions taken by police officers responsible for enforcing the laws and protecting individual rights.

Cases and materials throughout this text relate to the questions raised by the above scenario. The reader is encouraged to return to the questions in this chapter when they find new cases and materials that apply.

References

Arizona v. Johnson, 129 S.Ct. 781 (2009).
Delaware v. Prouse, 440 U.S. 648 (1979).
Maryland v. Wilson, 519 U.S. 408 (1997).
New York v. Belton, 453 U.S. 454 (1981).
Pennsylvania v. Mimms, 434 U.S. 106 (1977).
Schmerber v. California, 384 U.S. 757 (1966).
Schneckloth v. Bustamonte, 412 U.S. 218 (1973).
Terry v. Ohio, 392 U.S. 1 (1968).
United States v. Robinson, 414 U.S. 218 (1973).
Virginia v. Moore, 128 S.Ct. 1598 (2008).
Whren v. United States, 517 U.S. 806 (1996).

Chapter 12

Stop, Question, and Frisk

When the U.S. Supreme Court mandated, in *Mapp v. Ohio*, 367 U.S. 643 (1961), that states apply the exclusionary rule as the remedy for Fourth Amendment violations, the police found themselves in untenable circumstances. Courts quickly extended the *Mapp* rule regarding searches of residences to searches of individuals in public places. Although the police were required to deter and detect crime, they could no longer rely on the customary practices of stopping, questioning, and searching people at will. New and extraordinary restrictions were placed on their abilities to conduct investigations and to employ crime-prevention tactics. At the same time as these restrictions were being imposed, crime was increasing drastically, especially in large cities where much of the population was transient. Often, in crowded urban areas, the police did not know the identities of most of the people they encountered unless they stopped and questioned them, yet the courts held that to stop individuals and restrain their movements long enough to question them constituted an arrest. To arrest or even detain, the police needed probable cause:

> The basic principles were relatively simple and straightforward. The term "arrest" was synonymous with those seizures governed by the Fourth Amendment. While warrants were not required in all circumstances, the requirement of probable cause, as elaborated in numerous precedents, was treated as absolute.[1]

Were the police to seize and detain a person without probable cause for even a short period of time, the exclusionary rule would apply. Many police/citizen encounters begin as routine inquiries but evolve into more significant encounters; asking questions of witnesses or possible suspects, making inquiries regarding possible dangerous situations, or taking precautions against potential violence can all quickly turn into stop, frisk, or arrest situations. Without probable cause for the initial approach to the suspect, any evidence obtained, whether a physical object or a verbal statement, would often be suppressed and would often result in dismissal of the charges.

In 1968, to remedy this problem, the Supreme Court, in the landmark decision of *Terry v. Ohio*, 392 U.S. 1, carved out the stop and frisk exception to the Fourth Amendment probable cause requirement. Stop and frisk was an intermediary procedure between a common-law inquiry and an arrest that provided the police with a practical tool for crime fighting and performing their routine functions.

In *Terry*, Martin McFadden, a Cleveland police detective with 39 years of experience, noticed Mr. Terry and a companion standing on a street corner. As McFadden put it, "They didn't look right to me at that time." McFadden observed the men take turns walking by

DOI: 10.4324/9781003415091-15

and looking in a store window. They repeated this activity between five and six times each. A third man joined the first two men and conferred with them.

McFadden approached the three men, identified himself as a police officer, and asked for their names. When the men "mumbled something" in response to his inquiries, Officer McFadden grabbed petitioner Terry, spun him around so that they were facing the other two, with Terry between McFadden and the others, and patted down the outside of his clothing. In the left breast pocket of Terry's overcoat, Officer McFadden felt a pistol. He reached inside the overcoat pocket, but was unable to remove the gun. At this point, keeping Terry between himself and the others, the officer ordered all three men to enter the store. As they went in, he removed Terry's overcoat completely, removed a .38 caliber revolver from the pocket, and ordered all three men to face the wall with their hands raised. Officer McFadden proceeded to pat down the outer clothing of the other two men and discovered another revolver.

The Supreme Court upheld the officer's actions and upheld Terry's conviction for possession of an unlawful weapon. Chief Justice Earl Warren wrote the opinion for the court and stated:

> We merely hold that where a police officer observes unusual conduct which leads him reasonably to conclude in light of his experience that criminal activity may be afoot and that the persons with whom he is dealing may be armed and presently dangerous, where in the course of investigating this behavior he identifies himself as a policeman and makes reasonable inquiries, and where nothing in the initial stages of the encounter serves to dispel his reasonable fear for his own or others' safety, he is entitled for the protection of himself and others in the area to conduct a carefully limited search of the outer clothing of such persons in an attempt to discover weapons which might be used to assault him. Such a search is a reasonable search under the Fourth Amendment, and any weapons seized may properly be introduced in evidence against the person from whom they were taken.

Although Detective McFadden did not have probable cause to arrest the men when he first approached them, his conduct was reasonable and therefore not a violation of the Fourth Amendment. After the stop and frisk, the guns that were discovered provided sufficient probable cause to arrest the suspects.

The Court declined to suppress the guns. In his majority opinion, Chief Justice Earl Warren recognized the difficulties of second-guessing the police in street encounters. He wrote:

> A rigid and unthinking application of the exclusionary rule, in futile protest against practices which it can never be used effectively to control, may exact a high toll on human injury and frustration of efforts to prevent crime. No judicial opinion can comprehend the protean variety of the street encounter.[2]

Reasonable Suspicion

Terry does not mean that police officers can stop and frisk anyone who appears suspicious to them. They must have reasonable suspicion, which has been defined as specific facts and circumstances that would lead an officer to reasonably believe that "criminal activity is afoot."[3] The officer need not know of a particular crime and the particular person who committed the crime, but he must reasonably believe that criminal activity has occurred, is occurring, or will occur.

An important purpose of stop, question, and frisk is to prevent crime. Reasonable suspicion that a crime will occur justifies police intervention short of an arrest. When the police stop and identify a person whom they suspect is preparing to commit a crime, the police action often does not result in an arrest but dissuades the person from committing the crime.

Most stops are made when the police suspect that a crime is either in progress or is about to be committed. They are also conducted during the investigation of completed crimes. For example, were the police called to the scene of a shooting at which several persons were present, but at which no one came forward to identify who had fired the shots, the police could not arrest all the persons who were present. However, on the basis of a reasonable suspicion that criminal activity had occurred, they could detain all the persons who were present for a reasonable time.

Time and Place

The duration of the allowable period of detention depends on the circumstances, and courts have been reluctant to set a maximum time. For the investigation of a serious crime involving several persons, the time allowed will certainly be longer than for the investigation of a minor crime involving a single suspect. As a federal Circuit Court of Appeals stated, "The graver the crime, the more latitude the police must be allowed."[4] When suspects are uncooperative, the time allowed will generally be greater than when suspects are cooperative. Two states, Arkansas and Nevada, have passed statutes defining a maximum period after which the police must either release or arrest a detained person. Arkansas allows 15 minutes; Nevada allows 60 minutes (Ark. Code Ann. Section 16-18-204(b); Nev. Rev. St. Section 171.123-4). At the other end of the spectrum, the Supreme Court upheld a 16-hour detention in *United States v. Montoya de Hernandez*, 473 U.S. 531 (1985), an airport drug-smuggling case in which a detainee was suspected of swallowing balloons filled with cocaine, and was held until the balloons passed.

Terry does not mean that police can move a suspect from the location where he was stopped to a police station. *Davis v. Mississippi*, 394 U.S. 721 (1969), *Brown v. Illinois*, 422 U.S. 590 (1975), *Dunaway v. New York*, 442 U.S. 200 (1979), and *Hayes v. Florida*, 470 U.S. 811 (1985), all held that the *Terry* reasonable suspicion standard was insufficient justification for transporting a suspect involuntarily to a station house for fingerprinting, questioning, or other purposes.

The Frisk

The frisk authorized by *Terry* is not a full-blown search. It is generally a pat-down search of a suspect's outer clothing to determine whether the suspect is armed with a weapon. Its purpose is officer and public protection; it is not the uncovering of other evidence or contraband.

Moreover, the authority to stop a person for questioning does not necessarily carry with it the authority to frisk the person. To frisk, in addition to having the grounds for making the stop, an officer must reasonably fear a danger of physical injury. In such case:

He may search the person for a deadly weapon or any instrument, article, or substance readily capable of causing serious physical injury and of a sort not ordinarily carried in public places by law-abiding persons. If he finds such a weapon or instrument, or any other property, possession of which he reasonably believes may constitute the commission of a crime, he may take it and keep it until the completion of the questioning, at which time he shall either return it, if lawfully possessed, or arrest such person.[5]

An officer's reasonable fear for his or her safety may be grounded in the type of crime suspected. A suspected robber, burglar, or drug trafficker would more likely be armed than a bookie, a drunk suspected of sounding a false fire alarm, or teenagers committing mischief.

Most courts have condoned a search of the area immediately surrounding the suspect, including containers such as shoulder bags from which a suspect may obtain a weapon.[6] A search of such containers is limited to an inspection for weapons; it is not designed to search for other non-dangerous items. Nevertheless, if, while conducting a lawful search for weapons, an officer sees in plain view items of unlawful contraband, he may seize the contraband.

A more problematic issue arises when an officer, while frisking for weapons, feels an item of unlawful contraband but not a weapon. In *Minnesota v. Dickerson*, 508 U.S. 366 (1993), the Supreme Court discussed the "plain feel" doctrine. In that case, an officer stopped a person who had come out of a "crack house" and immediately frisked him. Although the officer did not find any weapons, he felt an object in the suspect's pocket. After manipulating the object with his fingers and judging that it was crack cocaine in a cellophane packet, he removed the packet and arrested the suspect for possession of drugs.

The Court stated that an officer conducting a valid frisk might seize any evidence he "feels" and immediately recognizes as contraband, just as he may seize any evidence he sees in plain view. In this case, however, the seizure of the packet was unlawful since the officer did not immediately recognize the object as contraband and his manipulation of the packet went beyond the scope of a valid weapons frisk.

Use of Force

A recurring problem for police is the citizen who refuses to stop when requested, who continues to walk away, or who refuses to provide identification. Citizens believe, correctly in many cases, that they have the right not to comply with a police order to stop or identify themselves. This is true when the police are just making an inquiry of citizens who apparently are not involved in a criminal activity; people can go about their business free of police interference. However, when the police have reasonable suspicion that criminal activity is afoot and that a particular person is involved in the activity, they can detain the person and use physical force, if necessary, to conduct a stop and frisk.

A problem for citizens who are directed by the police to stop is the decision whether or not to comply. Citizens may know that they have not been involved in a crime and they may believe that they should be able to freely continue on their way, but they do not know what information the police have. Even when police officers stop the wrong person, they have the authority to do so if they are acting reasonably on the basis of apparently credible information. The citizen who refuses to comply might risk his refusal adding to the police officers' suspicion and might induce the police to use force, which might escalate the dangers inherent in the situation. No doubt, the most prudent course in most cases is for the citizen to comply with reasonable directions.

By statute, the police may use necessary force to conduct a stop, but it must be only the minimal amount of force necessary to complete the task. An officer can use his arms, legs, and body to hold the suspect, but he should not use a weapon such as a nightstick, pepper spray, or electric stun gun. Of course, if the suspect flees, assaults, or threatens the officer, the officer could employ such force as authorized by his arrest and self-defense powers.

Problem

Police Officer Smart and Police Officer Swift were on patrol at 2:00 A M on a rainy Sunday night in a factory and warehouse district. The area was deserted because most of the buildings were closed for the weekend. As the officers slowly drove around a corner, they saw a solitary car, a four-door green Buick sedan, parked by the sidewalk in front of a warehouse. It was unusual for passenger cars to be parked in the area at that time, and the officers decided to investigate. A man of about 40 years old was seated in the driver's seat, and the car engine was off.

Officer Swift approached the passenger side of the vehicle, while Officer Smart approached the driver's window. "Anything the matter?" Smart said.

"No, officer," the man replied.

"May I ask what you're doing here?"

"Just resting."

"May I see your license and registration?"

"I wasn't driving."

"You didn't drive here?"

"No. Uh. Yes."

"Which is it?"

"Yes, I drove here."

The man produced a license and registration, which the officers checked through the computer in their patrol car. The documents were valid and issued to Ray Raymond, 250 Dock Street, date of birth March 1, 1967.

Officer Smart held up the driver's license, looked at the photograph, and then looked at the driver. "What is your date of birth, sir?"

"March 1, 1967."

"May I ask where you were coming from?"

"What's the difference?" Raymond said. "I told you, I just pulled over to rest. I was tired. Now can I have my license back?"

"It's unusual for people to park here at this time of night," the officer said. "Where were you coming from?"

"My girlfriend's."

"And where's that?"

"I really don't see why you need to know that."

"Well, let's try this. Where were you going?"

"Home."

"Home?"

"Yes. Home."

"If I'm not mistaken, your address, 250 Dock Street, is back that way, east. Why were you driving west, in the opposite direction?"

Raymond did not respond to the question, and he turned his face away from the officer as though to indicate that he was not going to answer any more questions.

Officers Smart and Swift moved back to the patrol car to confer. They decided that, although they had suspicions, they did not have enough reason to detain the suspect any longer. Then, as Smart began to return the license and registration, a man wearing a black windbreaker turned the corner at the end of the block. When the man saw the officers, he abruptly turned and hurried back around the corner. Officer Swift, without saying a word, immediately ran toward the corner.

Officer Smart hesitated. He wanted to follow his partner with the patrol car, but he was not sure he should leave Raymond. A second later, when Raymond started his car engine, Smart ran to the Buick, opened the driver's door, and told Raymond he had to come with him.

"What for?" Raymond said.

"Just get out of the car."

Raymond complied, and Smart spun him around, handcuffed him, and placed him in the backseat of the patrol car.

While Raymond protested, Officer Smart made a U-turn with the patrol car and raced after his partner. After three blocks, he caught up and saw Officer Swift frisking the man wearing the windbreaker.

Swift turned the man's pockets inside out and made him take off his windbreaker so that he could thoroughly search through the lining. Inside the lining, he found a screwdriver.

"He's got a screwdriver, but that's it," Swift said.

Swift handcuffed the man, who said his name was John Jones. As Swift began to place Jones in the patrol car, Smart interceded and took Jones down the street to question him out of earshot of Raymond.

"So your boss makes you get out in the rain and do the heavy lifting," Smart said.

"He's not my boss," Jones said. "I just got out to take a leak."

"Why'd you have to go all the way around the corner?"

"I wanted to find someplace private."

"There's nobody around, come on. Your boss, as soon as he saw us, was leaving. If you weren't doing anything wrong, why would he take off?"

"I don't know, and I told you, Ray is not my boss."

"He says he is."

"He's full of... and I don't want to say anything else."

"In that case, I'm going to have to lock you up."

"For what?"

"The screwdriver—possession of burglar's tools," Smart said.

"I had a screwdriver just because I was nervous about getting out of the car," Jones said. "I wasn't doing no burglary."

"Where were you and Ray coming from?" Smart said.

"We had a few drinks earlier. Then we stopped for some coffee."

"Where?"

"I don't know. On Main Street somewhere."

"Where were you going?"

"He was driving me home."

"Where's that?"

"I want a lawyer."

"Okay, you'll get one."

The officers switched places, and Smart sat in the patrol car with Raymond. "Your friend says you're his boss," Smart said.

"I never saw that guy in my life," Raymond said. "And save your breath. I want a lawyer."

When a sergeant and backup patrol cars arrived, several officers surveyed the area looking for broken windows, gates, or doors in any of the buildings in the area. No signs of a recent crime were found.

Officers Smart and Swift asked the sergeant whether they could arrest Raymond and Jones for possession of burglar's tools or Jones for resisting arrest because he ran. The sergeant did not think they had grounds to arrest them at that time, but he directed the officers to take the suspects to the station house and to hold them until the morning.

He thought that when the area businesses opened, someone might report a break-in or an attempted break-in. If so, they could try to match up any tool marks with Jones' screwdriver.

Questions

1. When the police officers observed Raymond seated in the parked car, did they have the lawful authority to ask for his license and registration?
2. Did they have the lawful authority to question him about his presence and his movements?
3. Prior to the appearance and sudden flight of the second man, Jones, did the police have probable cause to arrest Raymond on the basis of his evasive and inconsistent answers?
4. Could they have lawfully detained him and taken him to the police station for further questioning?
5. After the appearance and flight of Jones, did the police have the lawful authority to detain Raymond?
6. When Officer Smart handcuffed and placed Raymond in the patrol car for the purpose of not allowing him to leave, was that action a detention or an arrest?
7. Is it lawful for the police to arrest a person without knowing whether a crime had been committed?
8. Is it lawful for the police to detain a person without knowing whether a crime had been committed?
9. Was Officer Swift justified in chasing and frisking Jones?
10. Was he justified in searching inside the lining of the windbreaker?
11. Was he justified in seizing the screwdriver?
12. Does handcuffing a person transform a detention into an arrest?
13. Did the contradictory answers of Raymond and Jones regarding their relationship provide the officers with enough evidence to arrest them?
14. Could either Raymond or Jones be arrested for possession of a burglar's tool when the officers were unaware whether a burglary had occurred?
15. Was the sergeant correct to think that no grounds existed to arrest either Jones or Raymond?
16. Was it lawful for the sergeant to direct the officers to take the suspects to the station house and hold them until the morning?

Anonymous Tips

The police frequently receive anonymous tips regarding criminal activity. Standing alone, an anonymous tip does not provide the basis for a lawful *Terry* stop. If it did, anyone could simply call 911, provide a description of a supposed criminal, and induce the police to stop and frisk that person.

An anonymous tip must be corroborated before police may act upon it. The corroboration may come from additional factors indicating criminal activity or from verifying the predictive information contained within the tip itself, such as occurred in *Alabama v. White*, 496 U.S. 325 (1990).

In *White*, an anonymous caller stated that a woman named White would leave an apartment building in a particular vehicle at a certain time. That person would proceed to a motel and would be in possession of cocaine. The police observed White leave the building, get into the vehicle at the designated time, and drive toward the motel. The police stopped her and, after discovering drugs in the car, arrested her. The Supreme Court upheld the stop, search, and arrest of White, explaining that although the tip itself did not amount to reasonable suspicion, once police observations had shown that the caller had accurately predicted White's movements it became reasonable to conclude that the caller had inside knowledge that was reliable.

The Court applied the same totality of the circumstances standard that it had applied in *Illinois v. Gates*, 462 U.S. 213 (1983), when ruling that verification of the predictive information in an anonymous letter provided sufficient probable cause to arrest. Clearly, an argument might be made that predicting a person's movements does not amount to proof that a crime is taking place. For that reason, some state courts have required additional information of how the caller knew the suspect possessed a weapon or was engaged in criminality.

The Supreme Court, in *Florida v. J.L.*, 529 U.S. 266 (2000), drew a clear distinction between anonymous information that included verifiable predictive behavior, as in *White v. Alabama*, and anonymous information that merely provided a description and location of a suspect. The Court ruled that verification of details relating merely to a description and location are insufficient to corroborate the reliability of an anonymous tip. In *Florida v. J.L.*, the juvenile defendant was arrested when the police received a call that a young man, wearing a plaid shirt and standing at a bus stop, was carrying a concealed gun. The police immediately drove to the bus stop where they saw three young men, including J.L., who was wearing a plaid shirt. They frisked him and found a gun.

The Court ruled that the gun must be suppressed, stating:

> The anonymous call concerning J.L. provided no predictive information and therefore left the police without means to test the informant's knowledge or credibility. That the allegation about the gun turned out to be correct does not suggest that the officers, prior to the frisks, had a reasonable basis for suspecting J.L. of engaging in unlawful conduct. The reasonableness of official suspicion must be measured by what the officers knew before they conducted their search. All the police had to go on in this case was the bare report of an unknown, unaccountable informant who neither explained how he knew about the gun nor supplied any basis for believing he had inside information about J.L.

On the basis of an anonymous tip, such as in *Florida v. J.L.*, the police may conduct a common-law inquiry as long as they do not restrain the person. If during the inquiry they learn of additional incriminating information or observe additional suspicious conduct, such as flight, furtive movements, or evasion, they may then possess sufficient reasonable suspicion to conduct a lawful stop and frisk.

Inquiries on Less than Reasonable Suspicion

Police officers are not limited to approaching and questioning people only on the basis of reasonable suspicion of criminal activity. They may approach and question a person as a matter of routine inquiry.

If, while lawfully interacting with the person, they observe evidence of a crime, the inquiry may be expanded to a stop or even an arrest. As long as the police do not first conduct a seizure, it is lawful to approach, question, and observe the person.

A seizure within the meaning of the Fourth Amendment occurs when a person is deprived of freedom of movement and brought under a police officer's control, either through submission to a show of legal authority or by actual physical restraint.[7] Whether a particular contact between the police and a citizen is deemed a seizure or merely an inquiry often determines the admissibility of evidence obtained as a result of the police contact.

The following are instances of police/citizen contact that a court might determine not to be a seizure:

1. Police responding to a building after a 911 call about possible prowlers ask people standing in front of the building whether they called the police.
2. A police officer approaches a group of men who have been standing on a street corner for several hours. He asks, "What are you doing here?"
3. Police respond to a crime scene and ask persons at the location to identify themselves. When one person refuses to do so and begins to walk away, an officer walks with him for a short distance while attempting to persuade him to cooperate.

The following are instances of police/citizen contact that a court might determine to be a seizure:

1. Police responding to a building after a 911 call about possible prowlers see a man coming from the building. An officer stands in front of the man, raises his hand as if signaling traffic to stop, and shouts, "Stop right there. We need to talk to you."
2. A police officer approaches a person, takes out his gun, and says to the person, "Where are you coming from?"
3. Police respond to a crime scene and ask persons at the location to identify themselves. When one person refuses to do so and begins to walk away, a police officer grabs him by the arm and tells him that he cannot leave until he identifies himself.

The line between encounters that are mere inquiries and those that are seizures is not always easy to discern. Some encounters can change from an inquiry to a seizure within a split second—a slight hand movement or a few steps might be determinative.

People v. DeBour, 40 N.Y.2d 210 (1976), is a case often used by New York courts for divining the differences between inquiries and seizures. In *DeBour*, at 12:15 AM on the morning of October 15, 1972, while police officer Kenneth Steck was "walking his beat on a street illuminated by ordinary street lamps and devoid of pedestrian traffic... he and his partner noticed someone walking on the same side of the street in their direction. When the solitary figure of the defendant, Louis DeBour, was within 30 or 40 feet of the uniformed officers, he crossed the street. The two policemen followed suit and when DeBour reached them Officer Steck inquired as to what he was doing in the neighborhood."

DeBour, clearly but nervously, answered that he had just parked his car and was going to a friend's house.

The officer then asked DeBour for identification. As he was answering that he had none, Officer Steck noticed a slight waist-high bulge in the defendant's jacket. At this point, the policeman asked DeBour to unzipper his coat. When DeBour complied with this request Officer Steck observed a revolver protruding from his waistband. The loaded weapon was removed from behind his waistband, and he was arrested for possession of the gun.

In *DeBour*, the gun was not suppressed, and the conviction was upheld. The Court ruled that because DeBour had "conspicuously crossed the street to avoid walking past the uniformed officers," the officers were authorized to make the brief limited inquiry that they did. When the officer noticed the slight bulge in the defendant's jacket, he was authorized to conduct a further stop and frisk.

People v. Moore, 74 N.Y.2d 224 (2006), produced an opposite result from *DeBour*, and it illustrates how nuances can determine whether evidence will be admissible or not. The police actions reviewed in *Moore* occurred on November 12, 1997. Two police officers on routine patrol in their marked police car received a radio call about a dispute involving a black male with a gun, described as approximately 18 years of age, wearing a gray jacket and red hat. The information came from an anonymous phone call. The officers arrived on the scene within a minute of receiving the call. No dispute was taking place, but the officers observed an African-American male, the defendant, Moore, who was wearing a gray jacket and red hat.

The officers approached Moore, who began to walk away. The officers drew their weapons and yelled, "Police, don't move." Moore walked a short distance before stopping. When the officers told Moore to put up his hands, he made a movement toward his waistband as he raised his arms. One of the officers patted down Moore and recovered a gun from the defendant's left jacket pocket.

The New York Court of Appeals ruled that the gun must be suppressed, stating:

Although we agree with the Appellate Division that the anonymous tip authorized only an inquiry, the police here failed to simply exercise their common-law right to inquire. Instead—in ordering him at gunpoint to remain where he was—the police forcibly stopped defendant as soon as they arrived on the scene. Because the officers did not possess reasonable suspicion until after defendant reached for his waistband, however—by which time defendant had already been unlawfully stopped—the gun should have been suppressed. Defendant's later conduct cannot validate an encounter that was not justified at its inception.[8]

The *Moore* decision is of the kind that raises protests from the police community about hyper-technicalities and second-guessing police actions taken during fast-moving street situations. To some observers, the New York court appears to have mandated that in these "gun-run" situations, police officers must wait for the suspect to draw his weapon before the officers can draw theirs.

Other observers might say that the seizure of the gun proved that the officers were correct in their assessment of the situation. This familiar fact pattern has led other courts to conclude that a combination of a 911 gun-run call and a suspect's avoidance or evasion of the police supports a finding of reasonable suspicion.

Justice Robert Smith, in his dissent in *Moore*, viewed the record in that matter. He pointed out that the majority had expanded the exclusionary rule by combining two former predicates for the rule. Previously, the court had ruled that an anonymous tip alone was an insufficient ground for the police to stop a person, and the court separately had ruled that a person's avoidance of contact with the police was an insufficient ground for a stop. In *Moore*, the majority held that even the combination of an anonymous tip and the avoidance of contact would be insufficient. Of course, the police officers, when they stopped Moore on November 12, 1997, did not know that the court would change the rules on February 21, 2006.

From a suspect's point of view, setting *DeBour* and *Moore* side by side, it might seem that in New York the lesson for criminals carrying guns is that they should walk away when the police approach them. DeBour did not walk away and was convicted. Moore walked away and was not convicted. Students might wonder whether *Moore* would have been decided differently had Moore run away from the police rather than merely walking away. In New York, Illinois, and other states, the precedents indicate that flight alone is not sufficient grounds for reasonable suspicion; therefore, in those states, had Moore run the police would not have had the authority to stop him.[9]

The Supreme Court holds a different view. In *Illinois v. Wardlow*, 528 U.S. 119 (2000), the Court attempted to clarify the flight issue. In *Wardlow*, Chicago uniformed police officers investigating drug dealing were driving in the last car of a four-car caravan that converged on an area known for heavy narcotics trafficking. An officer observed the defendant, Wardlow, "standing next to the building holding an opaque bag… [he] looked in the direction of the officers and fled." The officers pursued, cornered, and stopped Wardlow. The officer conducted a protective frisk and discovered a .38 caliber handgun with five rounds of live ammunition. The Illinois courts suppressed the handgun, stating, "Flight may simply be an exercise of this right to 'go on one's way,' and, thus, could not constitute reasonable suspicion justifying a *Terry* stop."[10] The Supreme Court reversed the decision and allowed the admission of the evidence, stating:

> It was not merely respondent's presence in an area of heavy narcotics trafficking that aroused the officers' suspicion but his unprovoked flight upon noticing the police. Our cases have also recognized that nervous, evasive behavior is a pertinent factor in determining reasonable suspicion.… Headlong flight—wherever it occurs—is the consummate act of evasion: It is not necessarily indicative of wrongdoing, but it is certainly suggestive of such.… Unprovoked flight is simply not a mere refusal to cooperate. Flight, by its very nature, is not "going about one's business"; it is just the opposite.[11]

The Supreme Court addressed the contention often raised that flight is not necessarily indicative of ongoing criminal activity. Although conduct such as flight may be susceptible to an innocent interpretation, the conduct may also raise a reasonable suspicion of criminal activity. Under such circumstances, the police can detain a person to resolve the ambiguity. *Wardlow* reiterated the police powers enunciated in *Terry v. Ohio* in 1968, which allowed the police to stop, question, and, if necessary, frisk a suspect, even when the suspect's conduct could turn out to be innocent.[12]

Although *Wardlow* is a clear and definitive decision, state and local police officers must be aware that their state courts may reject or circumvent a Supreme Court precedent by grounding their decision on their state constitutions. States must provide their citizens with at least the minimum civil rights mandated by the U.S. Constitution, but they may provide greater rights according to their own constitutional authority. Consequently, police action that the Supreme Court would uphold as reasonable may be deemed unreasonable by a state court and in violation of state law. The differing interpretations may be a matter of degree or tradition. Some courts have strict limitations, such as not authorizing a stop and frisk on the basis of a 911 call from an anonymous caller; other courts avoid specific rules and employ more flexibility.

The Supreme Court, in *United States v. Cortez*, 449 U.S. 411 (1981), applied a "totality of the circumstances" approach to the review of reasonable suspicion to stop and frisk, similar to its subsequent ruling in *Illinois v. Gates*, 462 U.S. 213 (1983), in which it applied the "totality of the circumstances" test to the review of probable cause for warrants issued on the basis of information provided by an anonymous source. In *Cortez*, the Court stated:

> The totality of the circumstances—the whole picture—must be taken into account. Based upon that whole picture the detaining officers must have a particularized and objective basis for suspecting the particular persons stopped.... The process does not deal with hard certainties, but with probabilities. Long before the law of probabilities was articulated as such, practical people formulated certain common-sense conclusions about human behavior; jurors as fact-finders are permitted to do the same—and so are law enforcement officers.

Summary

Stop, question, and frisk law endeavors to maintain a balance between the interests of individuals in being protected from unreasonable intrusion into their privacy and the interests of crime prevention and detection. Because the probable cause standard for arrests and searches would restrict the ability of law enforcement officers to prevent and detect crime, the less stringent standard of reasonable suspicion that criminal activity is afoot has been adopted; however, reasonable suspicion is more than mere suspicion.

When police have less than reasonable suspicion, they may approach a person and make inquiries, but they may not restrict the person's free movement and may not use force. When police have such reasonable suspicion, they may stop and question the person suspected at the location for a relatively short period of time and, if necessary, employ the minimum amount of force necessary to detain the person.

During a stop, if an officer reasonably believes that the suspect may be armed and dangerous, the officer may conduct a frisk. Factors to assess the need for a frisk may include the type of criminal activity involved, the suspect's reputation for violence, visual clues indicating the presence of a weapon, and furtive or suggestive movements by the suspect.

The purpose of a frisk is to detect weapons; therefore, it is generally limited to a pat-down of the outer clothing. When, by plain feel, an apparent weapon or obvious contraband is detected, the officer may reach inside the clothing to seize the object.

Notes

1 *Dunaway v. New York*, 442 U.S. 200 (1979).
2 *Terry v. Ohio*, 392 U.S. 1 (1968).
3 *Ibid*.
4 *Llaguna v. Mingey*, 763 F.2d 1560 (7th Cir. 1985).
5 New York State Criminal Procedure Law, Article 140.50(3).
6 *Michigan v. Long*, 463 U.S. 1032 (1983).
7 *California v. Hodari D.*, 499 U.S. 621 (1991).
8 *People v. Moore*, 74 N.Y.2d 224 (2006).
9 *People v. Howard*, 50 N.Y.2d 583 (1980); *People v. Holmes*, 80 N.Y.2d 444 (1992).
10 *Illinois v. Wardlow*, 183 Ill.2d, at 312.
11 *Illinois v. Wardlow*, 528 U.S. 119 (2000).
12 *Terry v. Ohio*, 392 U.S. 1 (1968).

References

Bell v. United States, 254 F.2d 81 (1958).
Brinegar v. United States, 338 U.S. 160 (1949).
Davis v. Mississippi, 394 U.S. 721 (1969).
Illinois v. Wardlow, 528 U.S. 119 (2000).
Minnesota v. Dickerson, 508 U.S. 366 (1993).
Terry v. Ohio, 392 U.S. 1 (1968).

Chapter 13

Consent Searches

Voluntary Consent

When people consent to a search of their property, no violation of the Fourth Amendment occurs; however, the consent must be voluntary. It cannot be the result of coercion or duress, either express or implied. Whether consent to search was given voluntarily is a question of fact to be determined from the totality of the circumstances. Often the facts underlying a determination as to whether a person had been seized by the police also determine whether the person voluntarily consented to a search. In *United States v. Drayton*, 536 U.S. 194 (2002), a police officer, engaged in a routine drug and weapons interdiction effort, boarded a bus and approached the defendant, Drayton, who was seated on the bus. The officer asked Drayton, "Mind if I check you?" Drayton responded by lifting his hands for the officer to search him, and the officer patted down his jacket and pockets, including his waist area, sides, and upper thighs. The officer detected two hard packages similar to drug packages detected on other occasions. The officer arrested Drayton, and a further search revealed that the packages contained 295 grams of cocaine. The Supreme Court ruled that the search was lawful, stating:

> Law enforcement officers do not violate the Fourth Amendment's prohibition of unreasonable seizures merely by approaching individuals on the street or in other public places and putting questions to them if they are willing to listen. Even when law enforcement officers have no basis for suspecting a particular individual, they may pose questions, ask for identification, and request consent to search luggage—provided they do not induce cooperation by coercive means. If a reasonable person would feel free to terminate the encounter, then he or she has not been seized.

Had Drayton refused to be searched, the officer would have had to rely on some other justification to frisk, search, or arrest him. Because Drayton consented to the search, the question of whether other lawful justifications existed was not reached by the Court.

In *Schneckloth v. Bustamonte*, 412 U.S. 218 (1973), the Supreme Court addressed the question of whether a person must know that they have a right to refuse a search for their consent to be truly voluntary. The Court held that a person's knowledge of their right to refuse is a factor to be considered regarding voluntary consent, but that such knowledge was not an absolute requirement. Judges should examine all the surrounding circumstances pertaining to an alleged consent. They should examine statements made by the police to the person giving consent and any acts of intimidation. Furthermore, they should assess the state of mind, vulnerability, and motivation of the person who gave the consent.

DOI: 10.4324/9781003415091-16

Police officers who conduct searches in reliance on a person's voluntary consent must be prepared to demonstrate that the consent was, in fact, voluntary. Although not a legal requirement, many police agencies have developed consent forms for the consenting person's signature. Alternatively, having a person sign a statement in an officer's memo book could be satisfactory proof. When time or other considerations preclude the obtaining of a signature, police officers should make notes of the facts surrounding the consent as soon as possible following the incident. Contemporaneous notes often provide valuable evidence as to whether or not voluntary consent was obtained.

Problem

Two police officers on routine patrol observed a young man, Billy Botts, wearing a baseball cap sideways. Botts was driving a four-door, gray Crown Victoria sedan, a car generally driven by older people. The car had Florida plates. The officers joked between themselves that Botts did not look like a Florida snowbird. They decided to stop and question him. Using their turret lights and siren, they directed him to pull over. When the officers asked for a license and registration, Botts produced the documents and told the officers that the car belonged to his uncle. One of the officers noticed what appeared to be a bullet pouch on the front seat and instructed Botts to get out of the car. The officer then searched the passenger compartment. The bullet pouch was empty, but under the front seat the officer found several bullets.

The officers questioned Botts, who stated that the bullets belonged to a gun he had found. After further questioning, he told the officers the gun was in his apartment, and he voluntarily agreed to surrender it to them. The officers took him to his apartment where he gave them the gun.

The officers asked Botts whether they could look around. He said yes. One officer looked in a closet and found a mask. The officer asked Botts why he had a mask, but he would not answer the question. The officers took the mask. At this point, they gave him *Miranda* warnings and arrested him for possession of both the gun and the bullets. A subsequent investigation found that the car, in fact, belonged to Botts' uncle, who had given Botts permission to drive it.

In court, Botts' attorney moved to suppress the use of the bullets at the trial because the stop was based solely on Botts' appearance and the search of the car was unlawful. Additionally, the attorney moved to suppress the use of the gun at trial and the incriminating statements made by Botts because they were derivative evidence from the unlawful stop and search. He argued that under the fruits-of-the-poisonous-tree doctrine, the items and statements must be excluded from evidence.

The district attorney opposed the defense motion on the grounds that the stop and search was lawful because it was based on reasonable suspicion and the plain view of the bullet pouch. Furthermore, Botts had voluntarily consented to surrender the gun as well as to the officers' entry into his apartment and for them to look around.

While awaiting the court's decision regarding the suppression motion, the police conducted a ballistics comparison examination of the gun. The examination disclosed that the bullets test-fired from the gun matched those that had been recovered from the body of a murder victim who had been killed during a robbery several months earlier. In that robbery, the perpetrator wore a mask similar to the one taken from Botts' apartment.

Botts was indicted for the murder and robbery. His attorney made a new motion to suppress the use of the gun, the bullets, the ballistics comparison report, and the mask from the murder and robbery trial.

Questions

1. Was the stop of Botts' car lawful or unlawful?
2. Was the search of the car lawful or unlawful?
3. Should Botts' incriminating statements that the bullets belonged to the gun be admissible against him?
4. Assuming that the stop of the vehicle was unlawful, does that determination nullify any of the subsequent voluntary consents given by Botts?

For the following questions, assume that the stop and search of the vehicle was lawful.

5. Did Botts voluntarily consent to surrender the gun?
6. Did Botts waive his Fourth Amendment rights when he gave the gun to the officers?
7. Did Botts voluntarily consent to the entry and search of his apartment?
8. Should the bullets be excluded from evidence?
9. Should the gun be excluded from evidence?
10. Should the bullet comparison report be excluded from evidence?
11. Should the mask be excluded from evidence?
12. Assuming that Botts was given separate trials—one for possession of the gun and bullets and one for the murder and robbery—would the rulings on the admissibility of the evidence be different in each trial?

Third-party Consent

Who may give consent is often a difficult problem for police officers to determine. Generally, the person in possession of the premises or property can give consent because ownership or title to the premises or property is not the controlling factor. Tenants, including hotel room occupants, have the right of possession. Owners or superintendents of premises cannot give consent to search an area occupied by a tenant. The tenant is the one protected by the Fourth Amendment and, therefore, is the one who must give the consent.

When two or more co-occupants are in mutual possession of premises, one occupant may give consent to search the entire premises, and the consent will be effective against all occupants.[1] However, when part of the premises, such as a private room, closet, or desk, is exclusively used by one of the occupants, that part of the premises cannot be searched without a warrant or the consent of the occupant who has the exclusive use.[2] The police must use reasonable discretion; for example, they cannot rely on a male co-occupant's consent to search his female roommate's purse, even when the purse in located in an area of the premises equally shared by both.[3]

Police often encounter situations in which one occupant who is present consents to a search while another co-occupant is not present. Courts have regularly upheld these searches on the theory that the absent co-occupant has assumed the risk that the present occupant may invite third parties, including the police, into the premises.

A more difficult situation occurs when one occupant consents to a search while a second co-occupant who is present objects to the search. In 2006, the Supreme Court addressed this issue in *Georgia v. Randolph*, 547 U.S. 103 (2006).

Georgia v. Randolph

U.S. Supreme Court
Georgia v. Randolph
on writ of certiorari to the Supreme Court of Georgia
March 22, 2006, decided
278 Ga. 614, 604 S.E.2d 835 (2004), affirmed

(Abridged: internal citations omitted)
JUSTICE SOUTER delivered the opinion of the Court.

The Fourth Amendment recognizes a valid warrantless entry and search of premises when police obtain the voluntary consent of an occupant who shares, or is reasonably believed to share, authority over the area in common with a co-occupant who later objects to the use of evidence so obtained. *Illinois* v. *Rodriguez,* 497 U.S. 177 (1990); *United States* v. *Matlock,* 415 U.S. 164 (1974). The question here is whether such an evidentiary seizure is likewise lawful with the permission of one occupant when the other, who later seeks to suppress the evidence, is present at the scene and expressly refuses to consent. We hold that, in the circumstances here at issue, a physically present co-occupant's stated refusal to permit entry prevails, rendering the warrantless search unreasonable and invalid as to him.

I

Respondent Scott Randolph and his wife, Janet, separated in late May 2001, when she left the marital residence in Americus, Georgia, and went to stay with her parents in Canada, taking their son and some belongings. In July, she returned to the Americus house with the child, though the record does not reveal whether her object was reconciliation or retrieval of remaining possessions.

On the morning of July 6, she complained to the police that after a domestic dispute her husband took their son away, and when officers reached the house she told them that her husband was a cocaine user whose habit had caused financial troubles. She mentioned the marital problems and said that she and their son had only recently returned after a stay of several weeks with her parents. Shortly after the police arrived, Scott Randolph returned and explained that he had removed the child to a neighbor's house out of concern that his wife might take the boy out of the country again; he denied cocaine use and countered that it was in fact his wife who abused drugs and alcohol.

One of the officers, Sergeant Murray, went with Janet Randolph to reclaim the child, and when they returned she not only renewed her complaints about her husband's drug use but also volunteered that there were "items of drug evidence" in the house. Sergeant Murray asked Scott Randolph for permission to search the house, which he unequivocally refused.

The sergeant turned to Janet Randolph for consent to search, which she readily gave. She led the officer upstairs to a bedroom that she identified as Scott's, where the sergeant noticed a section of a drinking straw with a powdery residue he suspected was cocaine. He then left the house to get an evidence bag from his car and to call the district attorney's office, which instructed him to stop the search and apply for a warrant. When Sergeant Murray returned to the house, Janet Randolph withdrew her consent. The police took the straw to the police station, along with the Randolphs. After getting a search warrant, they returned to the house and seized further evidence of drug use, on the basis of which Scott Randolph was indicted for possession of cocaine.

He moved to suppress the evidence, as products of a warrantless search of his house unauthorized by his wife's consent over his express refusal. The trial court denied the motion, ruling that Janet Randolph had common authority to consent to the search.

The Court of Appeals of Georgia reversed, and was itself sustained by the State Supreme Court, principally on the ground that "the consent to conduct a warrantless search of a residence given by one occupant is not valid in the face of the refusal of another occupant who is physically present at the scene to permit a warrantless search." The Supreme Court of Georgia acknowledged this Court's holding in *Matlock*, that "the consent of one who possesses common authority over premises or effects is valid as against the absent, nonconsenting person with whom that authority is shared," and found *Matlock* distinguishable just because Scott Randolph was not "absent" from the colloquy on which the police relied for consent to make the search. The State Supreme Court stressed that the officers in *Matlock* had not been "faced with the physical presence of joint occupants, with one consenting to the search and the other objecting."

We granted certiorari to resolve a split of authority on whether one occupant may give law enforcement effective consent to search shared premises, as against a co-tenant who is present and states a refusal to permit the search. We now affirm.

II

To the Fourth Amendment rule ordinarily prohibiting the warrantless entry of a person's house as unreasonable *per se*, one "jealously and carefully drawn" exception recognizes the validity of searches with the voluntary consent of an individual possessing authority. That person might be the householder against whom evidence is sought, or a fellow occupant who shares common authority over property, when the suspect is absent, and the exception for consent extends even to entries and searches with the permission of a co-occupant whom the police reasonably, but erroneously, believe to possess shared authority as an occupant. None of our co-occupant consent-to-search cases, however, has presented the further fact of a second occupant physically present and refusing permission to search, and later moving to suppress evidence so obtained. The significance of such a refusal turns on the underpinnings of the co-occupant consent rule, as recognized since *Matlock*.

A

The defendant in that case was arrested in the yard of a house where he lived with a Mrs. Graff and several of her relatives, and was detained in a squad car parked nearby. When the police went to the door, Mrs. Graff admitted them and consented to a search of the house. In resolving the defendant's objection to use of the evidence taken in the warrantless search, we said that "the consent of one who possesses common authority over premises or effects is valid as against the absent, nonconsenting person with whom that authority is shared." Consistent with our prior understanding that Fourth Amendment rights are not limited by the law of property, we explained that the third party's "common authority" is not synonymous with a technical property interest:

"The authority which justified the third-party consent does not rest upon the law of property, with its attendant historical and legal refinement, but rests rather on mutual use of the property by persons generally having joint access or control for most purposes, so that it is reasonable to recognize that any of the co-inhabitants has the right to permit the inspection in his own right and that the others have assumed the risk that one of their number might permit the common area to be searched."

...

B

Matlock's example of common understanding is readily apparent. When someone comes to the door of a domestic dwelling with a baby at her hip, as Mrs. Graff did, she shows that she belongs there, and that fact standing alone is enough to tell a law enforcement officer or any other visitor that if she occupies the place along with others, she probably lives there subject to the assumption tenants usually make about their common authority when they share quarters. They understand that any one of them may admit visitors, with the consequence that a guest obnoxious to one may nevertheless be admitted in his absence by another. As *Matlock* put it, shared tenancy is understood to include an "assumption of risk," on which police officers are entitled to rely, and although some group living together might make an exceptional arrangement that no one could admit a guest without the agreement of all, the chance of such an eccentric scheme is too remote to expect visitors to investigate a particular household's rules before accepting an invitation to come in. So, *Matlock* relied on what was usual and placed no burden on the police to eliminate the possibility of atypical arrangements, in the absence of reason to doubt that the regular scheme was in place.

It is also easy to imagine different facts on which, if known, no common authority could sensibly be suspected. A person on the scene who identifies himself, say, as a landlord or a hotel manager calls up no customary understanding of authority to admit guests without the consent of the current occupant. A tenant in the ordinary course does not take rented premises subject to any formal or informal agreement that the landlord may let visitors into the dwelling, and a hotel guest customarily has no reason to expect the manager to allow anyone but his own employees into his room. In these circumstances, neither state-law property rights, nor common contractual arrangements, nor any other source points to a common understanding of authority to admit third parties generally without the consent of a person occupying the premises. And when it comes to searching through bureau drawers, there will be instances in which even a person clearly belonging on premises as an occupant may lack any perceived authority to consent; "a child of eight might well be considered to have the power to consent to the police crossing the threshold into that part of the house where any caller, such as a pollster or salesman, might well be admitted," but no one would reasonably expect such a child to be in a position to authorize anyone to rummage through his parents' bedroom.

C

...To begin with, it is fair to say that a caller standing at the door of shared premises would have no confidence that one occupant's invitation was a sufficiently good reason to enter when a fellow tenant stood there saying, "stay out." Without some very good reason, no sensible person would go inside under those conditions. Fear for the safety of the occupant issuing the invitation, or of someone else inside, would be thought to justify entry, but the justification then would be the personal risk, the threats to life or limb, not the disputed invitation....

D

...Disputed permission is thus no match for this central value of the Fourth Amendment, and the State's other countervailing claims do not add up to outweigh it. Yes, we recognize the consenting tenant's interest as a citizen in bringing criminal activity to light ("[I]t is no part of the policy underlying the Fourth... Amendment to discourage citizens from aiding to the utmost of their ability in the apprehension of criminals"). And we understand a co-tenant's legitimate self-interest in siding with the police to deflect suspicion raised by sharing quarters with a criminal ("The risk of being convicted of possession of drugs one knows are present and has tried to get the other occupant to remove is by no means insignificant").

But society can often have the benefit of these interests without relying on a theory of consent that ignores an inhabitant's refusal to allow a warrantless search. The co-tenant acting on his own initiative may be able to deliver evidence to the police, and can tell the police what he knows, for use before a magistrate in getting a warrant. The reliance on a co-tenant's information instead of disputed consent accords with the law's general partiality toward "police action taken under a warrant [as against] searches and seizures without one"; "the informed and deliberate determinations of magistrates empowered to issue warrants as to what searches and seizures are permissible under the Constitution are to be preferred over the hurried action of officers."

[Footnote] Sometimes, of course, the very exchange of information like this in front of the objecting inhabitant may render consent irrelevant by creating an exigency that justifies immediate action on the police's part; if the objecting tenant cannot be incapacitated from destroying easily disposable evidence during the time required to get a warrant, a fairly perceived need to act on the spot to preserve evidence may justify entry and search under the exigent circumstances exception to the warrant requirement.

Nor should this established policy of Fourth Amendment law be undermined by the principal dissent's claim that it shields spousal abusers and other violent co-tenants who will refuse to allow the police to enter a dwelling when their victims ask the police for help. It is not that the dissent exaggerates violence in the home; we recognize that domestic abuse is a serious problem in the United States.

But this case has no bearing on the capacity of the police to protect domestic victims. The dissent's argument rests on the failure to distinguish two different issues: when the police may enter without committing a trespass, and when the police may enter to search for evidence. No question has been raised, or reasonably could be, about the authority of the police to enter a dwelling to protect a resident from domestic violence; so long as they have good reason to believe such a threat exists, it would be silly to suggest that the police would commit a tort by entering, say, to give a complaining tenant the opportunity to collect belongings and get out safely, or to determine whether violence (or threat of violence) has just occurred or is about to (or soon will) occur, however much a spouse or other co-tenant objected. (And since the police would then be lawfully in the premises, there is no question that they could seize any evidence in plain view or take further action supported by any consequent probable cause). Thus, the question whether the police might lawfully enter over objection in order to provide any protection that might be reasonable is easily answered yes ("[E]ven when... two persons quite clearly have equal rights in the place, as where two individuals are sharing an apartment on an equal basis, there may nonetheless sometimes exist a basis for giving greater recognition to the interests of one over the other...[W]here the defendant has victimized the third party, the emergency nature of the situation is such that the third-party consent should validate a warrantless search despite defendant's objections"). The undoubted right of the police to enter in order to protect a victim, however, has nothing to do with the question in this case, whether a search with the consent of one co-tenant is good against another, standing at the door and expressly refusing consent.

None of the cases cited by the dissent supports its improbable view that recognizing limits on merely evidentiary searches would compromise the capacity to protect a fearful occupant. In the circumstances of those cases, there is no danger that the fearful occupant will be kept behind the closed door of the house simply because the abusive tenant refuses to consent to a search.

The dissent's red herring aside, we know, of course, that alternatives to disputed consent will not always open the door to search for evidence that the police suspect is inside. The consenting tenant may simply not disclose enough information, or information factual enough, to add up to a showing of probable cause, and there may be no exigency to justify fast action. But nothing in social custom or its reflection in private law argues for placing a higher value on delving into private premises to search for evidence in the face of disputed consent, than on requiring clear justification before the government searches private living quarters over a resident's objection. We therefore hold that a warrantless search of a shared dwelling for evidence over the express refusal of consent by a physically present resident cannot be justified as reasonable as to him on the basis of consent given to the police by another resident.

E

...The second loose end is the significance of *Matlock* and *Rodriguez* after today's decision. Although the *Matlock* defendant was not present with the opportunity to object, he was in a squad car not far away; the *Rodriguez* defendant was actually asleep in the apartment, and the police might have roused him with a knock on the door before they entered with only the consent of an apparent co-tenant. If those cases are not to be undercut by today's holding, we have to admit that we are drawing a fine line; if a potential defendant with self-interest in objecting is in fact at the door and objects, the co-tenant's permission does not suffice for a reasonable search, whereas the potential objector, nearby but not invited to take part in the threshold colloquy, loses out.

This is the line we draw, and we think the formalism is justified. So long as there is no evidence that the police have removed the potentially objecting tenant from the entrance for the sake of avoiding a possible objection, there is practical value in the simple clarity of complementary rules, one recognizing the co-tenant's permission when there is no fellow occupant on hand, the other according dispositive weight to the fellow occupant's contrary indication when he expresses it. For the very reason that *Rodriguez* held it would be unjustifiably impractical to require the police to take affirmative steps to confirm the actual authority of a consenting individual whose authority was apparent, we think it would needlessly limit the capacity of the police to respond to ostensibly legitimate opportunities in the field if we were to hold that reasonableness required the police to take affirmative steps to find a potentially objecting co-tenant before acting on the permission they had already received. There is no ready reason to believe that efforts to invite a refusal would make a difference in many cases, whereas every co-tenant consent case would turn into a test about the adequacy of the police's efforts to consult with a potential objector. Better to accept the formalism of distinguishing *Matlock* from this case than to impose a requirement, time-consuming in the field and in the courtroom, with no apparent systemic justification. The pragmatic decision to accept the simplicity of this line is, moreover, supported by the substantial number of instances in which suspects who are asked for permission to search actually consent, albeit imprudently, a fact that undercuts any argument that the police should try to locate a suspected inhabitant because his denial of consent would be a foregone conclusion.

III

This case invites a straightforward application of the rule that a physically present inhabitant's express refusal of consent to a police search is dispositive as to him, regardless of the consent of a fellow occupant. Scott Randolph's refusal is clear, and nothing in the record justifies the search on grounds independent of Janet Randolph's consent. The State does not argue that she gave any indication to the police of a need for protection inside the house that might have justified entry into the portion of the premises where the police found the powdery straw (which, if lawfully seized, could have been used when attempting to establish probable cause for the warrant issued later). Nor does the State claim that the entry and search should be upheld under the rubric of exigent circumstances, owing to some apprehension by the police officers that Scott Randolph would destroy evidence of drug use before any warrant could be obtained.

The judgment of the Supreme Court of Georgia is therefore affirmed.

Questions Raised by *Georgia v. Randolph*

1. Even though the police eventually obtained a search warrant and obtained the evidence against the defendant pursuant to that warrant, why did the court suppress the evidence?
2. In the *Matlock* case cited by the Court, were the police required to ask the defendant, who was in a squad car outside the searched premises, whether he consented to the search?
3. Could the occupant who called the police and consented to the search be prosecuted for the possession of the unlawful items?
4. Had the wife, Janet Randolph, told the police that an illegal gun was on the premises, rather than cocaine, would the Court have ruled that the initial entry by the police into the premises was lawful?
5. Should there be a search warrant exception for guns?
6. Should there be an exception for bombs or poisonous substances?

Good-faith Mistakes

When the police find contraband after being granted permission to search by an apparent occupant of a private premises, and it later turns out that the supposed occupant did not, in fact, have authority to grant the permission, should the contraband be excluded from evidence? The Supreme Court addressed this question in *Illinois v. Rodriguez*, 497 U.S. 177 (1990), in which the defendant was arrested in his apartment and charged with possession of unlawful drugs. The police had entered the apartment without a warrant after a woman, Gail Fisher, complained that the defendant had beaten her. The police drove her to the defendant's apartment, and during the drive she referred to the apartment as "our" place. She let the police in with a key, and when they entered, they saw the drugs in plain view.

The officers did not have any reason to believe that Fisher did not live in the apartment. They did not know that she had moved out a month earlier, had removed her clothing, did not contribute to the rent, and did not have her name on the lease.

The Court ruled that the officers made a reasonable mistake, and a reasonable mistake in a consent case does not violate a defendant's Fourth Amendment rights. Therefore, applying the same reasoning for the good-faith exception to the warrant requirement applied in *United States v. Leon*, 468 U.S. 897 (1984), the evidence need not be suppressed.

Abandoned Property

When people abandon their property, they give up ownership and give implied permission to other people to examine, take, and keep the property. They forfeit their expectation of privacy in the property. It follows that anyone, including police without a warrant, may search and seize the property; however, this broad and seemingly clear abandonment rule is, of course, subject to interpretation and questions.

What constitutes abandonment? Must abandonment occur in a public place? What constitutes a public place? When persons put their trash in a covered garbage can for pickup by the sanitation department, do they abandon the trash? When the garbage container is within the curtilage of the property, is it in a public place? When the garbage can has been placed on the sidewalk for pickup, is it in a public place? If the police look into the garbage can and find items of contraband or evidence, can they immediately seize them? After the trash is dumped into the sanitation truck, is it in a public place?

California v. Greenwood, 486 U.S. 35 (1988), is the authoritative case regarding trash. The case raises questions that are far beyond what at first might appear to be a mundane problem; it raises important issues that are pertinent to other areas of individual privacy and government intrusions.

California v. Greenwood

U.S. Supreme Court
California v. Greenwood
486 U.S. 35 (1988)
January 11, 1988, argued
May 16, 1988, decided
182 Cal. App. 3d 729, 227 Cal. Rptr. 539, reversed and remanded

JUSTICE WHITE delivered the opinion of the Court.

The issue here is whether the Fourth Amendment prohibits the warrantless search and seizure of garbage left for collection outside the curtilage of a home. We conclude, in accordance with the vast majority of lower courts that have addressed the issue, that it does not.

I

In early 1984, Investigator Jenny Stracner of the Laguna Beach Police Department received information indicating that respondent Greenwood might be engaged in narcotics trafficking. Stracner learned that a criminal suspect had informed a federal drug enforcement agent in February 1984 that a truck filled with illegal drugs was en route to the Laguna Beach address at which Greenwood resided. In addition, a neighbor complained of heavy vehicular traffic late at night in front of Greenwood's single-family home. The neighbor reported that the vehicles remained at Greenwood's house for only a few minutes.

Stracner sought to investigate this information by conducting a surveillance of Greenwood's home. She observed several vehicles make brief stops at the house during the late-night and early-morning hours, and she followed a truck from the house to a residence that had previously been under investigation as a narcotics-trafficking location.

On April 6, 1984, Stracner asked the neighborhood's regular trash collector to pick up the plastic garbage bags that Greenwood had left on the curb in front of his house and to turn the bags over to her without mixing their contents with garbage from other houses. The trash collector cleaned his truck bin of other refuse, collected the garbage bags from the street in front of Greenwood's house, and turned the bags over to Stracner. The officer searched through the rubbish and found items indicative of narcotics use. She recited the information that she had gleaned from the trash search in an affidavit in support of a warrant to search Greenwood's home.

Police officers encountered both respondents at the house later that day when they arrived to execute the warrant. The police discovered quantities of cocaine and hashish during their search of the house. Respondents were arrested on felony narcotics charges. They subsequently posted bail.

The police continued to receive reports of many late-night visitors to the Greenwood house. On May 4, Investigator Robert Rahaeuser obtained Greenwood's garbage from the regular trash collector in the same manner as had Stracner. The garbage again contained evidence of narcotics use.

Rahaeuser secured another search warrant for Greenwood's home based on the information from the second trash search. The police found more narcotics and evidence of narcotics trafficking when they executed the warrant. Greenwood was again arrested.

The Superior Court dismissed the charges against respondents.... The court found that the police would not have had probable cause to search the Greenwood home without the evidence obtained from the trash searches...

...We granted certiorari, 483 U.S. 1019, and now reverse.

II

The warrantless search and seizure of the garbage bags left at the curb outside the Greenwood house would violate the Fourth Amendment only if respondents manifested a subjective expectation of privacy in their garbage that society accepts as objectively reasonable. Respondents do not disagree with this standard.

They assert, however, that they had, and exhibited, an expectation of privacy with respect to the trash that was searched by the police: The trash, which was placed on the street for collection at a fixed time, was contained in opaque plastic bags, which the garbage collector was expected to pick up, mingle with the trash of others, and deposit at the garbage dump. The trash was only temporarily on the street, and there was little likelihood that it would be inspected by anyone.

It may well be that respondents did not expect that the contents of their garbage bags would become known to the police or other members of the public. An expectation of privacy does not give rise to Fourth Amendment protection, however, unless society is prepared to accept that expectation as objectively reasonable.

Here, we conclude that respondents exposed their garbage to the public sufficiently to defeat their claim to Fourth Amendment protection. It is common knowledge that plastic garbage bags left on or at the side of a public street are readily accessible to animals, children, scavengers, snoops, and other members of the public. Moreover, respondents placed their refuse at the curb for the express purpose of conveying it to a third party, the trash collector, who might himself have sorted through respondents' trash or permitted others, such as the police, to do so. Accordingly, having deposited their garbage "in an area particularly suited for public inspection and, in a manner of speaking, public consumption, for the express purpose of having strangers take it," respondents could have had no reasonable expectation of privacy in the inculpatory items that they discarded.

Furthermore, as we have held, the police cannot reasonably be expected to avert their eyes from evidence of criminal activity that could have been observed by any member of the public. Hence, "what a person knowingly exposes to the public, even in his own home or office, is not a subject of Fourth Amendment protection."...

Our conclusion that society would not accept as reasonable respondents' claim to an expectation of privacy in trash left for collection in an area accessible to the public is reinforced by the unanimous rejection of similar claims by the Federal Courts of Appeals.... In addition, of those state appellate courts that have considered the issue, the vast majority have held that the police may conduct warrantless searches and seizures of garbage discarded in public areas.

V

The judgment of the California Court of Appeal is therefore reversed, and this case is remanded for further proceedings not inconsistent with this opinion.

Questions Raised by *California v. Greenwood*

1. Almost every human activity generates waste products, and a person's trash can reveal his or her confidential habits, thoughts, reading, romantic interests, and political affiliations. How can people keep personal matters confidential when their trash can be examined at will?

2. Does an opaque, sealed trash bag remove the contents of the bag from public view or, if placed in the trash, are the bag and its contents considered abandoned?

3. Is it not an accepted norm of society that people are rightfully incensed when a meddler, reporter, or detective rifles through their garbage? Therefore, should there be redress against people who rummage through other people's trash, such as a lawsuit for invasion of privacy?

4. Is the examination of a defendant's trash any more intrusive than other police methods of investigation?

5. When police use undercover agents to infiltrate the confidence of suspects, are they violating a societal norm?

6. Should the type of item found in the trash make a difference as to whether a person's privacy is violated?

7. Should personal letters be treated with more privacy protection than unlawful contraband, such as narcotics paraphernalia?

8. Assuming a hypothetical expectation of privacy in a person's trash, should a violation of that privacy be redressed by a civil lawsuit or by the exclusionary rule?

9. Might the Court's doctrine of abandonment be applied to computer files sent to the recycle bin of a computer?
10. Might deleted e-mails be considered abandoned?

Induced Abandonment

California courts, in the case of *In re Hodari D.*, 216 Cal. App. 3d 745 (1989), examined the question as to whether the discarding of an object as a result of police-initiated contact or show of authority constitutes voluntary abandonment. In 1988, as two plainclothes police officers in an unmarked car rounded a corner, "They saw four or five youths huddled around a small red car parked at the curb. When the youths saw the officers' car approaching they apparently panicked, and took flight." Officer Pertoso chased the defendant, Hodari. "Looking behind as he ran, he [Hodari] did not turn and see Pertoso until the officer was almost upon him, whereupon he tossed away what appeared to be a small rock." The officer tackled and handcuffed Hodari. The rock that Hodari had discarded was found to be crack cocaine.

In a pretrial motion, Hodari moved to suppress the crack cocaine on the grounds that when the officer chased him, the officer had unreasonably seized him without probable cause or reasonable suspicion. The trial court denied the motion, but on appeal the California Court of Appeals held that the "seizure was unreasonable under the Fourth Amendment, and that the evidence of cocaine had to be suppressed as the fruit of that illegal seizure."[4]

The prosecution appealed to the Supreme Court. Although the prosecution conceded that the officer did not have reasonable suspicion to justify stopping Hodari, they contended that the cocaine had been abandoned and was thus admissible evidence. In *California v. Hodari D.*, 499 U.S. 621 (1991), the Supreme Court agreed, reversed the decision of the California Court of Appeals, and ruled the crack cocaine admissible because it had been abandoned before any seizure had occurred. In its decision, the Court reasoned that a Fourth Amendment seizure does not take place without touching or holding by the police or by a suspect's submission to police authority. The Court held the following:

The narrow question before us is whether, with respect to a show of authority as with respect to application of physical force, a seizure occurs even though the subject does not yield. We hold that it does not.

The Court drew an analogy to naval warfare: "A ship still fleeing, even though under attack, would not be considered to have been seized as a war prize." A police officer chasing a suspect and shouting "Stop, in the name of the law!" has not seized the suspect, and property discarded by the suspect in response to such actions has not been seized but has been abandoned.

Notes

1 *United States v. Matlock*, 415 U.S. 164 (1974).
2 *United States v. Davis*, 332 F.3d 1163 (9th Cir. 2003); *United States v. Jimenez*, 419 F.3d 34 (1st. Cir. 2005).
3 *Krise v. State*, 746 N.E.2d 957 (Ind. 2001).
4 *In re Hodari D.*, 216 Cal. App. 3d 745 (1989).

References

Beck v. Ohio, 379 U.S. 89 (1964).
Delaware v. Prouse, 440 U.S. 648 (1979).
Florida v. Bostick, 501 U.S. 429 (1991).
Payton v. New York, 445 U.S. 573 (1980).
People v. Breazil, 15 Misc.3d 493, 829 N.Y.S.2d 894 (2007).
People v. Morales, 198 A.D.2d 129, 609 N.Y.S.2d 319 (1993).
People v. Rogers, 52 N.Y.2d 527 (1981).
Schneckloth v. Bustamonte, 412 U.S. 218 (1973).
United States v. Drayton, 536 U.S. 194 (2002).
United States v. Frazier, 408 F.3d 1102 (8th Cir. 2005).
United States v. Velarde-Gomez, 269 F.3d 1023 (9th Cir. 2001).

Chapter 14

Search and Seizure of Vehicles and Occupants

The Bill of Rights expounds general principles that can be adapted to changing circumstances. The coming of the automobile age and the building of the national highway system were changes to which the Constitution, and particularly the Fourth Amendment, had to adapt. In 1925, the U.S. Supreme Court, in *Carroll v. United States*, 267 U.S. 132, recognized the need to create an exception to the warrant requirement when officers had probable cause to believe that evidence of a crime was contained in an automobile.

Mobility and the Automobile Exception

Carroll v. United States occurred during Prohibition. Federal agents stopped a person who was driving what appeared to be a heavily laden car on a highway. They knew the person had previously engaged in the transport of bootleg whiskey, and they searched the car without obtaining a warrant. After cutting open upholstery in the rumble seat of the car, they found 68 bottles of illicit liquor.

The Court upheld the legality of the search because the mobility of the vehicle presented practical problems that are not present when evidence is located in a stationary structure. Officers with probable cause to search a vehicle would lose the evidence if they allowed the suspect to go on his way while they sought a warrant. The Court stated the following:

> On reason and authority, the true rule is that if the search and seizure without a warrant are made upon probable cause, that is upon a belief, reasonably arising out of circumstances known to the seizing officer, that an automobile or other vehicle contains that which by law is subject to seizure and destruction, the search and seizure are valid.[1]

Were the courts to mandate that the officers hold both the vehicle and its occupants while a warrant is obtained, little or no benefit would accrue. To do so would subject the occupants to substantial periods of detention, in some cases for many hours. Warrants would invariably be issued and, except in rare cases, the search would take place.

To allow the search to occur immediately benefits those suspects who are not guilty of transporting or possessing contraband or evidence. It saves time and personnel for the police and frees them to continue their duties. In cases in which the occupants of a vehicle are suspected of having committed a recent crime, a search of the vehicle that clears the occupants allows the police to continue looking for other suspects.

The mobility of vehicles is problematic for our court system because the authority to issue and execute search warrants has geographical limitations. State court systems are structured into jurisdictional hierarchies. The superior courts of most states may issue search warrants

DOI: 10.4324/9781003415091-17

that are executable anywhere within that particular state. The lower courts of most states, such as city, town, and village courts, may issue search warrants executable only in the county in which they are located or in an adjoining county. Consequently, were the police to allow a vehicle to proceed while they applied for a search warrant from a superior court, the occupants of the vehicle would only have to cross state lines to avoid the search altogether. Were the police to apply to a lower court, the occupants of the vehicle would only have to leave the county and the adjoining county to avoid a search.

The *Carroll* decision left open the idea that the automobile's mobility was a subset of the exigent circumstances exception to the warrant requirement, which might lead to a conclusion that when a suspect vehicle is unoccupied no need for the exception exists. However, in *Husty v. United States*, 282 U.S. 694 (1931), the Court made it clear that probable cause was sufficient to authorize the search of an automobile without exigent circumstances. In *Husty*, acting on a tip, the police searched Husty's unoccupied car, found illicit whiskey, and arrested Husty. The Court upheld the search. It dismissed the contention that the police had time to obtain a search warrant, and reasoned that the police did not know when someone would return to the car and drive away.

In *Chambers v. Maroney*, 399 U.S. 42 (1970), the Court repudiated any notion that exigent circumstances were part of the automobile exception.[2] In *Chambers*, the police seized a blue station wagon in connection with a gas station robbery. They transported the vehicle to the police station before searching it and finding evidence. The Court upheld the search even though the vehicle had been safely secured at the police station, stating:

> Arguably, because of the preference for a magistrate's judgment, only the immobilization of the car should be permitted until a search warrant is obtained; arguably, only the "lesser" intrusion is permissible until the magistrate authorizes the "greater." But which is the "greater" and which the "lesser" intrusion is itself a debatable question and the answer may depend on a variety of circumstances. For constitutional purposes, we see no difference between on the one hand seizing and holding a car before presenting the probable cause issue to a magistrate and on the other hand carrying out an immediate search without a warrant. Given probable cause to search either course is reasonable under the Fourth Amendment.
>
> On the facts before us, the blue station wagon could have been searched on the spot when it was stopped since there was probable cause to search and it was a fleeting target for a search. The probable cause factor still obtained at the station house and so did the mobility of the car unless the Fourth Amendment permits a warrantless seizure of the car and the denial of its use to anyone until a warrant is secured. In that event there is little to choose in terms of practical consequences between an immediate search without a warrant and the car's immobilization until a warrant is obtained.[3]

Whether a mobile home is a vehicle or a stationary structure was addressed in *California v. Carney*, 471 U.S. 386 (1985). The place searched was a "mini" mobile home that was parked in a parking lot with access to the roadway. Although the vehicle had "many of the attributes of a home," the Court ruled that it was more like a car than a house; therefore, the search without a warrant was lawful. However, mobile homes that are not readily moveable, such as those without wheels, blocked into a mobile home community, or elevated off the ground, would be considered stationary structures and, therefore, warrants would generally be required for them to be searched.

Lesser Expectation of Privacy

In addition to mobility, courts have considered the lesser expectation of privacy that people have in their vehicles. The privilege to drive on the public highways brings with it the obligation to comply with state registration, licensing, inspection, and safe driving regulations.[4] Drivers know that police will stop them for violating the regulations. They know that their cars may be impounded when necessary for public safety reasons. Courts, recognizing the lesser expectation of privacy for vehicles, have granted law enforcement much greater leeway to search vehicles than to search premises or personal property.

Closed Containers

The automobile exception allows the seizure of contraband or evidence seen in plain view in the vehicle. However, whether closed containers inside a vehicle may be searched without a warrant has been the subject of numerous conflicting and tortured court opinions.[5] In *California v. Acevedo*, 500 U.S. 565 (1991), the Court brought closure to the issue by overturning prior decisions and ruling that when the police have probable cause to search an automobile, they may search the entire vehicle as well as containers in the vehicle.

Rejecting attempts to limit police searches to only some containers in a vehicle but not others depending on the probable cause related to each container, the Court reiterated what had been stated in *United States v. Ross*, 456 U.S. 798 (1982):

> When a legitimate search is under way, and when its purpose and its limits have been precisely defined, nice distinctions between closets, drawers, and containers, in the case of a home, or between glove compartments, upholstered seats, trunks, and wrapped packages, in the case of a vehicle, must give way to the interest of the prompt and efficient completion of the task at hand.

Occupants

Searching a vehicle in accordance with the automobile exception does not necessarily imply the existence of probable cause to search the occupants. It does not authorize a physical search of the occupants' clothes and bodies. To conduct a full search of the occupants of a vehicle, the occupants must be lawfully under arrest; however, in *Wyoming v. Houghton*, 526 U.S. 295 (1999), the Court allowed the search of containers possessed by occupants of a vehicle, stating:

> Effective law enforcement would be appreciably impaired without the ability to search a passenger's personal belongings when there is reason to believe contraband or evidence of criminal wrongdoing is hidden in the car. As in all car-search cases, the "ready mobility" of an automobile creates a risk that the evidence or contraband will be permanently lost while a warrant is obtained. In addition, a car passenger... will often be engaged in a common enterprise with the driver, and have the same interest in concealing the fruits or the evidence of their wrongdoing. A criminal might be able to hide contraband in a passenger's belongings as readily as in other containers in the car, perhaps surreptitiously, without the passenger's knowledge or permission.[6]

Searches Incidental to Arrest

Searching a vehicle in accordance with the automobile exception must be distinguished from conducting a search incidental to the arrest of an occupant of the vehicle. When the police arrest the occupant of a vehicle for offenses unrelated to the contents of the vehicle, they may search the occupant, but, unless probable cause exists to believe evidence may be in the vehicle, they cannot search the entire vehicle under the automobile exception.

In connection with the arrest, they may search the defendant as authorized in *United States v. Robinson*, 414 U.S. 218 (1973), and they may conduct a more limited search of the defendant's reachable area as outlined in *Chimel v. California*, 395 U.S. 752 (1969), and in *New York v. Belton*, 453 U.S. 454 (1981).

In *Belton*, the Supreme Court ruled that incidental to the arrest of a driver or a passenger the police may search the passenger compartment of the vehicle, including closed containers. The search is permissible even when the car's occupants have been removed from the vehicle, as long as the occupants have been lawfully arrested and the searches are contemporaneous with the arrest. The Court stated the following:

> Our reading of the cases suggests the generalization that articles inside the relatively narrow compass of the passenger compartment of an automobile are in fact generally, even if not inevitably, within "the area into which an arrestee might reach in order to gain a weapon or evidentiary item."... Accordingly, we hold that when a policeman has made a lawful custodial arrest of the occupant of an automobile, he may, as a contemporaneous incident of that arrest, search the passenger compartment of that automobile.
>
> It follows from this conclusion that the police may also examine the contents of any containers found within the passenger compartment, for if the passenger compartment is within the reach of the arrestee, so also will containers in it be within his reach.

The *Belton* search is not the automobile exception search. The trunk and other areas of the car that are relatively inaccessible to the occupants cannot be searched incidental to an arrest of the occupants. Only when probable cause exists that contraband or evidence is within the car can the trunk and other inaccessible areas be searched.

In *Arizona v. Gant*, 129 S.Ct. 1710 (2009), the Court made it clear that to justify searching the car incidental to an arrest the defendant must have been in the car when arrested. In *Gant*, Tucson police officers, acting on an anonymous tip that a residence was being used to sell drugs, knocked on the front door of the residence and asked to speak to the owner. Gant answered the door and, after identifying himself, stated that the owner would return later. The officers left the residence and conducted a records check, which revealed that Gant's driver's license had been suspended and an outstanding warrant for his arrest existed.

When the officers returned to the residence that evening, they observed Gant driving his car. They saw him park the car at the end of the driveway, get out, and shut the door. The officers met Gant ten to twelve feet from the car and arrested him on the warrant and for driving with a suspended license. They handcuffed Gant and locked him in the back seat of their patrol vehicle. When they searched his car, they found a gun and a bag of cocaine in the pocket of a jacket on the back seat.

Gant was convicted of the gun and drug crimes. The Supreme Court, however, reversed the conviction and ruled that the evidence obtained from the car should have been suppressed. The Court distinguished *New York v. Belton*. Because Gant had been secured away from the car and the officer-safety rationale of *Belton* was to protect against a defendant reaching into the vehicle to obtain a weapon or destroy evidence, the Court determined that *Belton* did not apply.

Stop and Frisk In and Around Automobiles

The stop and frisk principles that were established in *Terry v. Ohio*, 392 U.S. 1 (1968),[7] addressed frisking a suspect for concealed weapons. When a suspect is in or near an automobile, added danger exists that the suspect might obtain an easily accessible weapon from within the automobile. With this in mind, courts have extended the scope of the stop and frisk principles.

In *Michigan v. Long*, 463 U.S. 1032 (1983), the Supreme Court applied the *Terry* stop and frisk principles to a roadside encounter, ruling that a police officer was justified in searching the passenger compartment of a vehicle as a safety precaution during a lawful investigation. In *Long*, two officers on night patrol had observed a car being driven erratically and then swerving into a ditch. The driver, who appeared intoxicated, met the officers at the rear of the car, then turned and began to walk toward the open door of the car. The officers saw a hunting knife on the floorboard of the car. They frisked the suspect, and one officer shined his flashlight into the car, saw something under the armrest, and, upon lifting the armrest, observed an open leather pouch that contained marijuana.

The Court ruled that a "search of the passenger compartment of an automobile, limited to those areas in which a weapon may be placed or hidden, is permissible if the police officer possesses a reasonable belief based on 'specific and articulable facts which, taken together with the rational inferences from those facts, reasonably warrant' the officer in believing that the suspect is dangerous and the suspect may gain immediate control of weapons."

The "frisk" of the automobile is allowed for the limited purpose of securing weapons that may be a danger to the officer or the public, not for a full-scale search of the automobile for contraband or other evidence. The *Long* safety rationale is separate and distinct from the automobile and incidental to arrest exceptions.

Traffic Stops

The police cannot stop and question a motorist merely to conduct a license or registration check. They cannot stop a vehicle on the basis of mere suspicion. To stop a vehicle, they need a lawful justification, such as an observed traffic violation or reasonable suspicion concerning criminal activity. A vehicle stop made without lawful justification is a violation of the Fourth Amendment and will result in the suppression of evidence obtained as a result of the unlawful stop. In *Delaware v. Prouse*, 440 U.S. 648 (1979), the Supreme Court held that marijuana found on the floor of a car that a police officer had stopped in order to check the driver's license and registration was inadmissible because the officer had violated the driver's Fourth Amendment right against unreasonable search and seizure. The officer did not testify to observing a traffic violation, an equipment deficiency, or any suspicious conduct by the car's occupants; therefore, the officer's notion to stop the defendant's vehicle and effectively seize the driver and the occupants was unreasonable.

When the police observe a traffic infraction, such as a motorist going through a red light, failing to signal, or driving with defective headlights, they may lawfully stop the vehicle, question the driver, and check the driver's license and registration. Evidence obtained during the stop may be admissible, barring some other constitutional violation.

A traffic stop is not the same as a full-blown arrest. Simple traffic infractions are not crimes. Motorists who are stopped by the police for committing such infractions generally receive a citation directing them to appear in court on a later date; they are not arrested and are not subject to search.[8] However, if a motorist does not have identification and cannot be satisfactorily identified, he or she may be arrested because the issuance of a citation would be precluded. In that case, as with any arrest, the defendant may be searched.[9]

When motorists commit more serious violations of the law, such as driving with a suspended license or driving while under the influence of alcohol or drugs, they may be arrested and searched. Another question arises when motorists who would normally receive a citation for a minor offense are arrested instead. Should these motorists be subject to search?

On April 23, 2008, the Supreme Court addressed the question in *Virginia v. Moore*, 553 U.S. 164, 128 S.Ct. 1598, 170 L.Ed.2d 539 (2008), in which a police officer, rather than issuing a citation as required by Virginia law, arrested the defendant Moore for the misdemeanor of driving with a suspended license. A search incidental to the arrest yielded crack cocaine, and Moore was tried and convicted of drug charges.

Virginia statutory law mandated that driving with a suspended license does not allow a custodial arrest except with respect to those who fail or refuse to discontinue the violation, those reasonably believed likely to disregard a citation, or those likely to harm themselves or others.[10] The Virginia high court ruled that the arrest was unauthorized under Virginia law and therefore that the search and seizure were unreasonable and violated the Fourth Amendment; consequently, they suppressed the evidence and reversed Moore's conviction. The Supreme Court, however, reversed the Virginia court, holding that as long as the police had probable cause to arrest the defendant the Fourth Amendment was not violated and the exclusionary rule need not be invoked. The Supreme Court explained that linking Fourth Amendment protections to state law would cause the protections to vary between time and place, and incorporating the nuances of state arrest laws into the Constitution would produce a vague and unpredictable regime. "The constitutional standard would be only as easy to apply as the underlying state law, and state law can be complicated indeed."

Adhering to the bright-line probable cause rule, the Court reiterated the holding of *United States v. Robinson*, 414 U.S. 218 (1973): "A custodial arrest of a suspect based on probable cause is a reasonable intrusion under the Fourth Amendment; that intrusion being lawful, a search incident to the arrest requires no additional justification." Moreover, no matter whether the charges are serious or minor, the officers face the same uncertainties and risks that provide "an adequate basis for treating all custodial arrests alike for purposes of search justification."

The Court ruled that Virginia is free to employ an exclusionary rule under the authority of its own constitution, but it has chosen not to do so. The remedies that Virginia has adopted for violations of the citation-only instruction are administrative discipline and/or a tort suit against the officer. It would be illogical for the Supreme Court to invoke its exclusionary rule to enforce an unusual state statute that the state does not see fit to enforce by employing its own prerogative to invoke a state-based exclusionary rule.

Problem

The police stop a vehicle, occupied by three individuals, for going through a red light. Although the car is properly registered to the driver, he has a suspended license and the police arrest him. Outside of the vehicle, they handcuff and search the driver, and they find a plastic baggy filled with marijuana in his jacket pocket.

The passengers in the car, a male and a female, are friends of the driver. The police order them to exit the car, and then frisk each of them. During the frisk, they find a vial of crack cocaine in the male's front pocket and a glassine envelope of heroin in the female's bra. One officer searches the passenger compartment of the car and in the glove compartment finds a glass jar filled with illegal amphetamines.

Although to convict each occupant the state must prove the occupants knowingly possessed the drugs, all three are charged with possession of unlawful controlled substances. Each occupant is charged with separate counts for possession of marijuana, possession of cocaine, possession of heroin, and possession of amphetamines.

To prove their knowledgeable possession of the controlled substances, the state relies on its statutory law that states the following:

The presence in an automobile of an unlawfully possessed controlled substance is presumptive evidence of the knowing possession of the controlled substance by each and every person in the automobile at the time the controlled substance was found. No presumption applies... when the controlled substance is concealed upon the person of one of the occupants.

The defendants intend to present evidence to rebut the above presumption as it applies to them individually; however, before proceeding to the trial, they challenge the constitutionality of the searches conducted by the police.

Questions

1. Was the stop of the vehicle lawful?
2. Was the custodial arrest of the driver a constitutional violation because he should have been issued with a citation?

Assume for the remaining questions that the arrest of the driver was lawful.

3. Was the search of the driver's jacket lawful?
4. Was the stop of the vehicle lawful?
5. Was the order to the passengers to exit the vehicle when they were not yet under arrest an unlawful seizure of the occupants?
6. At the point at which they were ordered to exit the car, could the passengers have been lawfully arrested on the basis of the statutory presumption of knowing possession of the marijuana?
7. Did the police have reasonable suspicion and reasonable fear of danger to their safety that warranted frisking the passengers?
8. Was the search and seizure of the cocaine in the male passenger's pocket lawful?
9. Was the search and seizure of the heroin in the female passenger's bra lawful?
10. Was the search of the passenger compartment after all the occupants were outside of the car lawful?
11. Was the search of the glove compartment lawful?
12. Was the search of the glove compartment justified as a search incidental to an arrest?
13. Was the search of the glove compartment justified under the automobile exception?
14. Are the amphetamines from the glove compartment admissible against all the defendants?
15. Is the marijuana admissible against all the defendants?

16. Is the cocaine admissible against all the defendants?
17. Is the heroin admissible against all the defendants?
18. Assume the judge admits all of the evidence. Based on the statutory presumption, may all of the defendants be presumed to have had knowing possession of the amphetamines in the glove compartment?
19. Assume the judge admits all of the evidence. Based on the statutory presumption, may all of the defendants be presumed to have had knowing possession of the drugs that were concealed on the persons of the other defendants?
20. Must a jury convict the defendants on the basis of the knowledge presumptions only?
21. May the defendants rebut the presumptions of knowing possession?

Detention of Drivers and Passengers

In most traffic stops in which the police issue a citation to the driver, they will tell the driver to stay in the car. On some occasions, when the circumstances raise issues of officer safety, the police will order the driver to step out of the car. In *Pennsylvania v. Mimms*, 434 U.S. 106 (1977), the Court found this procedure to be reasonable and pointed out that, once a car has been lawfully stopped for a violation of law, the added intrusion of requesting the driver to step out of the car is minor.

It should be recognized that a citation is issued in lieu of arrest. Before issuing a citation, the officer must determine whether the driver is properly identified, licensed, and able to operate the vehicle safely. It is not unreasonable to have the driver step out of the car during the investigation process, and the Court left that decision to the discretion of the officer.

Whether passengers can be ordered to step out of the car while the police are investigating or issuing a citation to the driver was addressed in *Maryland v. Wilson*, 519 U.S. 408 (1997). The Court held that the *Mimms* rule applied to passengers as well as to drivers, reasoning that "an officer making a traffic stop may order passengers to get out of the car pending completion of the stop" because of the high degree of risk associated with car stops.

Even though in a typical car stop there is no basis to stop or detain passengers, as the passengers are already detained while waiting for the police to issue the citation to the driver, the order to exit the car merely changes their location. The Court balanced this minimal intrusion against the possibility that the passengers inside the car might have greater access to weapons than they would while standing outside the car.

Furthermore, *Mimms* and *Wilson*, taken together, held that once outside the stopped vehicle the driver and passengers may be patted down for weapons if the officer reasonably concludes that they might be armed and dangerous. These holdings were reiterated in *Arizona v. (Lemon Montrea) Johnson*, 129 S.Ct. 781, decided January 26, 2009. In *Johnson*, police officers serving in the Arizona gang task force and patrolling near a Tucson neighborhood associated with the Crips gang stopped an automobile after learning that its registration had been suspended. The car had three occupants. One officer directed the driver to step out of the car; another officer stayed with the front-seat passenger, who remained in the vehicle throughout the stop; and Officer Maria Treviso questioned Johnson, who was seated in the back seat. Treviso had noticed that as the police approached, Johnson looked back and kept his eyes on the officers. Treviso observed that Johnson was wearing clothing and a bandana consistent with Crips membership, and she also noticed a police scanner in Johnson's jacket pocket.

Treviso testified that she wanted to question Johnson away from the front-seat passenger to gain intelligence about gang activity. She asked him to step out of the car, and he complied. Suspecting that he might have a weapon on him, she patted him down for officer safety and found a gun near his waist. Johnson was convicted of possession of a weapon by a prohibited possessor and appealed on the grounds that the gun should have been suppressed. Essentially, he claimed that the officer had no right to pat him down because the traffic stop had evolved into a consensual conversation about his gang affiliation, which was unrelated to the traffic stop. Therefore, the authority for the frisk had ended, unless additional authority stemmed from a reasonable suspicion that Johnson had engaged, or was about to engage, in criminal activity. The Supreme Court disagreed and upheld the frisk:

> A lawful roadside stop begins when a vehicle is pulled over for investigation of a traffic violation. The temporary seizure of driver and passengers ordinarily continues, and remains reasonable, for the duration of the stop. Normally, the stop ends when the police have no further need to control the scene, and inform the driver and passengers they are free to leave. See *Brendlin*, 551 U.S., at 258. An officer's inquiries into matters unrelated to the justification for the traffic stop, this Court has made plain, do not convert the encounter into something other than a lawful seizure, so long as those inquiries do not measurably extend the duration of the stop. See *Muehler v. Mena*, 544 U.S. 93, 100-1001 (2005).

Johnson continues the line of cases from *Terry v. Ohio*, 392 U.S. 1 (1968) and *Michigan v. Long*, 463 U.S. 1032 (1983), in which the Court has sided with the interest of officer safety rather than individual privacy. Significantly, the majority decision was written by Justice Ruth Bader Ginsburg, long noted for her support of defendants' rights and privacy protections. Justice Ginsburg's positioning here, in favor of a law enforcement interest, may mark a shift in the jurisprudential balance of the Court.

Traffic Violations as a Pretext to Stop, Frisk, or Search

Most drivers will, on occasion, commit a minor traffic violation. They may roll through a stop sign, fail to signal as they change lanes or make a turn, or double park. Sometimes, when police stop and question drivers for traffic violations, the interaction leads to frisks or searches, and evidence is discovered that can be used against the driver. Defense attorneys have challenged the admissibility of such evidence under the claim that the traffic violation was a pretext to a frisk or search. This issue of pretext reached the Supreme Court in *Whren v. United States*, 517 U.S. 806 (1996).

In *Whren*, plainclothes police officers driving an unmarked car in a high drug-crime area saw a truck stopped at an intersection for an unusual amount of time. When the officers made a U-turn to head back toward the truck, the truck suddenly turned right without signaling and sped off at an excessive speed. The officers stopped the truck for traffic infractions and subsequently observed drugs in Whren's hands. Whren challenged the seizure of the drugs, claiming that the traffic stop was merely a pretext to search, as plainclothes officers generally do not enforce traffic laws. The Court rejected this argument, holding that a car stop does not violate the Fourth Amendment as long as the police have probable cause to believe that a traffic infraction occurred. In line with other decisions, the Court chose to apply an objective reasonableness standard to police actions, stating "subjective intentions play no role in ordinary, probable cause Fourth Amendment analysis."

Were the Court to condone inquiries into the subjective intentions of police officers in such routine cases, it would increase litigation exponentially. Nevertheless, the Court indicated that an exception to the objective reasonableness standard would apply to claims of intentional racial discrimination, such as racial profiling, that might invoke the Fourteenth Amendment equal protection clause.

Roadblocks and Safety Checks

Our freedom of movement, freedom to travel, and freedom to cross state lines are often taken for granted. Just as citizens are free to walk on their way unencumbered by government intrusion, they are free to drive on the public highways as long as they comply with reasonable regulations. The police cannot stop and question a motorist without a lawful justification, such as an observed traffic violation or reasonable suspicion concerning criminal activity. See *Delaware v. Prouse*, 440 U.S. 648 (1979).

On the other hand, safety checks conducted in a systematic manner that do not unjustifiably single out an individual have been held to be reasonable. In *Michigan Department of State Police v. Sitz*, 496 U.S. 444 (1990), the Court authorized a roadblock that briefly stops every driver to ascertain whether he is intoxicated. The Court justified such stops because of the "magnitude of the drunk driving crisis" combined with the minimal inconvenience of causing a motorist to stop briefly for a quick check.

Inventory Searches

Police agencies are charged with the responsibility for protecting public safety and safeguarding property, and accordingly, for a wide variety of reasons, they are required to impound vehicles and other property. As stated in *South Dakota v. Opperman*, 428 U.S. 364 (1976), "The authority of police to seize and remove from the streets vehicles impeding traffic or threatening public safety and convenience is beyond challenge."

Vehicles are impounded when a driver is arrested, injured, or ill and the vehicle cannot be safeguarded on the street or highway. Vehicles are impounded when they are needed as evidence in a criminal case or a serious accident investigation or when subject to state or federal forfeiture laws. Recovered stolen vehicles are taken to police facilities for safeguarding. Impounded vehicles and their contents must be inventoried to protect the owner's property while in police custody; to protect the police against claims or disputes over lost, stolen, or vandalized property; and to protect the police from potential danger. Searching vehicles to inventory their contents does not violate the Fourth Amendment, and contraband or evidence found during the search may be admissible in court. However, an inventory search is unlawful when it is shown that the search was not in accordance with standard departmental procedures and was conducted for investigation purposes or in bad faith to harass a person. In such cases, any evidence found during the inventory search is inadmissible.

Standing to Challenge Searches

For defendants to challenge the admissibility of evidence found as a result of the search of an automobile, they must have standing to contest the constitutionality of the search. Standing belongs only to those individuals whose expectation of privacy is violated by the governmental action. Mere presence at the location of a search does not confer standing to challenge the search, and merely being a passenger in an automobile that is searched does not automatically confer standing. To challenge a search, a passenger must have had an expectation of privacy in the area searched; for example, were the police to search a vehicle in which a defendant was a mere passenger and were the police to find an illegal gun in the glove compartment or trunk, the defendant would not have standing to challenge the search because he did not have an expectation of privacy in those areas.

The driver of the car would more likely have standing to challenge the search, which raises the possibility of the anomalous result that the driver of the vehicle is acquitted while the passenger is convicted. The Supreme Court in *Rakas v. Illinois*, 439 U.S. 128 (1978), held that a passenger does not have an expectation of privacy in the glove compartment, the area under the seat, or the trunk of a vehicle. The *Rakas* rule applies only when the police lawfully stop a car. On the other hand, when they stop a car without sufficient justification, all occupants of the vehicle stopped (seized) can challenge the seizure. When the initial seizure is found to have been unlawful, any evidence found during a related search may be deemed fruits of the poisonous tree and excluded.

The Supreme Court clarified this issue in *Brendlin v. California*, 127 S.Ct. 2400, 168 L.Ed.2d 132 (2007). In *Brendlin*, a deputy sheriff pulled over a vehicle to verify that its displayed permit matched the vehicle. The deputy sheriff admitted later that there was nothing unusual about the permit or the way it was affixed. As the deputy sheriff spoke to the driver, he recognized a passenger, Brendlin, as a parole violator for whom an arrest warrant had been issued. Additional police arrived to arrest Brendlin, and when they searched him and the car they found illegal drug paraphernalia.

Brendlin was charged with the possession and manufacture of methamphetamine, and he moved to suppress the evidence as the fruits of an unconstitutional search, arguing that the deputy sheriff lacked probable cause or reasonable suspicion to make the traffic stop. The prosecution conceded that the deputy sheriff did not have adequate justification to pull over the car, but they argued that the passenger was not seized by the traffic stop because the driver was its exclusive target.

The Court ruled in favor of Brendlin, stating:

> Although we have not, until today, squarely answered the question whether a passenger is also seized, we have said over and over in dicta that during a traffic stop an officer seizes everyone in the vehicle, not just the driver.

The seizure need not be accomplished by actual physical restraint; it may occur by acquiescence to a show of police authority. The test for a seizure by acquiescence, rather than by physical restraint, is whether "in view of all the circumstances surrounding an incident, a reasonable person would have believed that he was not free to leave."[11] In this case, because it is reasonable for passengers to expect that police offices at the scene of a crime, arrest, or investigation will not let people move around in ways that could jeopardize the officers' safety, a reasonable passenger, here in the guise of Brendlin, would have felt compelled to remain in the car. Consequently, the drug paraphernalia should have been suppressed because Brendlin had been unconstitutionally seized, and the evidence was the fruit of that poisonous tree.

Summary

1. *Automobile exception*
   a. Police may search a mobile vehicle without a warrant when there is probable cause to believe the vehicle contains contraband or evidence of a crime.

    b. The vehicle may be searched immediately or at some time later, even at another location where it is secured.

    c. Closed containers in the vehicle may be searched.

    d. Probable cause to search the vehicle does not necessarily imply authority to search the occupants of the vehicle.

    e. When probable cause exists to search a vehicle, containers possessed by occupants in the vehicle may be searched.

2. *Arrests of drivers or passengers*

    a. The arrest of a driver or passenger in a vehicle does not authorize a search of the entire vehicle. A search of the entire vehicle requires probable cause to believe the car contains contraband or evidence.

    b. However, the arrest of a driver or passenger authorizes a search of the reachable area of the passenger compartment. This search would not include the trunk or other parts of the car not readily accessible.

    c. When the police arrest and secure a driver outside of his vehicle, they cannot search the vehicle incident to the arrest. To search the vehicle, probable cause that it contains contraband or evidence is required.

3. *Detention of drivers or passengers*

    a. The police may stop and detain the occupants of a vehicle in order to issue a traffic citation to the driver. While doing so, they may order the driver and any passengers to step out of the car.

    b. When the police have reasonable suspicion of criminal activity, they may question and/or frisk occupants in accordance with the principles of *Terry v. Ohio*.

    c. When a frisk of an occupant is authorized, the reachable area of the passenger compartment may also be searched as part of the frisk.

4. *Justification for vehicle stop*

    a. The police may not arbitrarily stop a particular vehicle without cause. They may stop a vehicle for a traffic violation, reasonable suspicion of criminal activity, probable cause to arrest an occupant, or probable cause to believe the vehicle contains evidence.

    b. Ulterior motives for conducting a vehicle stop on the basis of a traffic violation are irrelevant as long as the police believe that they have in fact observed a violation of law.

    c. As part of a systematic program of vehicle and driver safety checks conducted according to standardized procedures, police may stop vehicles briefly to conduct a safety check.

5. *Inventory searches*

    a. Vehicles impounded in accordance with standard operating procedures may be searched in order to inventory the contents. Evidence found during an inventory search may be admissible in court.

6. *Standing*

    a. Only parties whose privacy rights are violated by a search may challenge the constitutionality of the search. Evidence obtained in violation of one party's Fourth Amendment rights may be used against another party whose rights were not violated during the search.

    b. A passenger in a car may challenge the constitutionality of the car stop. If the car stop is found to have been unlawful, any evidence seized as a result may be suppressed.

c. When a car stop is lawful, passengers may not challenge the constitutionality of searches of parts of the car in which they had no expectation of privacy, such as the glove compartment or trunk. They may challenge searches of their person.

Notes

1 *Carroll v. United States*, 267 U.S. 132, at 149.
2 See also *Texas v. White*, 423 U.S. 67 (1975); *Michigan v. Thomas*, 458 U.S. 259 (1982); *Pennsylvania v. Labron*, 518 U.S. 928 (1996).
3 *Chambers v. Maroney*, 399 U.S. 42, at 51–52.
4 *New York v. Class*, 475 U.S. 106 (1986).
5 *United States v. Chadwick*, 433 U.S. 1 (1977); *Arkansas v. Sanders*, 442 U.S. 753 (1979); *Robbins v. California*, 453 U.S. 420 (1981); *United States v. Ross*, 456 U.S. 798 (1982).
6 *Wyoming v. Houghton*, 526 U.S. 295, at 304–305.
7 *Terry v. Ohio*, 392 U.S. 1 (1968): "Where a police officer observes unusual conduct which leads him to reasonably conclude in light of his experience that criminal activity may be afoot and that the persons with whom he is dealing may be armed and presently dangerous, where in the course of investigating this behavior he identifies himself as a policeman and makes reasonable inquiries, and where nothing in the initial stages of the encounter serves to dispel his reasonable fear for his own or others' safety, he is entitled for the protection of himself and others in the area to conduct a carefully limited search of the outer clothing of such persons in an attempt to discover weapons which might be used to assault him."
8 *Knowles v. Iowa*, 525 U.S. 113 (1998).
9 *United States v. Robinson*, 414 U.S. 218 (1973).
10 Virginia Code Ann. § 19.2-74.
11 *United States v. Mendenhall*, 446 U.S. 544, 554 (1980).

References

Brendlin v. California, 127 S.Ct. 2400, 168 L.Ed.2d 132 (2007).
Maryland v. Wilson, 519 U.S. 408 (1997).
New York v. Belton, 453 U.S. 454 (1981).
Rakas v. Illinois, 429 U.S. 128 (1978).
Sandstrom v. Montana, 442 U.S. 510 (1979).
United States v. Robinson, 414 U.S. 218 (1973).
Virginia v. Moore, 128 S.Ct. 1598, 170 L.Ed.2d 539 (2008).
Whren v. United States, 517 U.S. 806 (1996).

The Individual as the Subject of Government Investigation

The Privilege against Compelled Self-incrimination and *Miranda v. Arizona*

"No person... shall be compelled in any criminal case to be a witness against himself."

When the above clause from the Fifth Amendment was written, it addressed several issues pertaining to compulsion to incriminate oneself. The Framers of the Bill of Rights knew that torture had been used throughout history to obtain confessions and information, and they were determined to outlaw such practices. Torture by burning, drowning, or the rack (a wheel-and-pulley device for stretching a victim's body and causing excruciating pain) were not from the remote past but had been used within the memory of living persons.[1] The Framers knew of the brutal practices employed by the English Star Chamber and the continental European inquisitions.

In England, the use of torture had been common, although in later centuries it was eventually curtailed. A time came when an accused could not be tortured to obtain an initial confession, but once he was convicted on the basis of independent evidence, he could then be tortured to reveal the identity of his accomplices.[2] In 1689, the English Bill of Rights purportedly ended all such practices of torture, though torture evidently persisted into later periods.

The Framers also knew that during colonial times accused persons had been compelled to incriminate themselves, not by outright physical torture but by duress, threats, and coercion. The Framers worried that the new American government at some point in the future might revive such practices;[3] however, notwithstanding the Framers' desire to provide greater protections for American citizens than had been provided for them as British subjects, the practice continued of questioning suspects against their will.

Into the nineteenth century, apprehended suspects could be questioned, and their answers, evasions, lies, or silence could be considered to determine their guilt or innocence.[4] At an arraignment, for example, a magistrate might question the defendant for purposes of determining probable cause and setting bail.[5] Then, at the defendant's trial, although the defendant could not be compelled to give answers, the magistrate could testify to the defendant's responses or non-responses at the arraignment. In effect, the privilege against self-incrimination applied only to testimony under oath at a trial. Contrary to today's law according to which the privilege applies once a defendant is taken into custody, the privilege then did not apply to the pretrial evidence of a criminal investigation, the actual apprehension, or the arraignment of the suspect.

Throughout history, apprehending and questioning suspects as soon as possible after the commission of a crime represented the most efficient means of solving a crime. To do so, communities employed the "hue and cry" and the *posse comitatus*. In both, a citizen sounded an alarm, and fellow citizens came to his aid. As a group, they chased or captured a

DOI: 10.4324/9781003415091-19

suspected offender. If they captured the suspect, they searched him for evidence of the crime, questioned him, gave him a chance to offer an explanation, and decided whether to bring him before a magistrate or other authority.

In America, questioning by magistrates at arraignments gradually diminished as professional police departments came into existence. Boston (in 1837), New York (in 1844), and Philadelphia (in 1854) established the first American metropolitan police departments. Throughout the nineteenth century, other police departments were formed across the nation, and most eventually instituted detective divisions.[6] Over time, the responsibility for investigating crimes and questioning suspects was ceded from magistrates to detectives, and detectives and other police often used harsh methods of interrogation. As society grew to expect that government should provide civil and humane treatment to all, the methods of interrogation by detectives evolved from extreme forms of physical coercion or duress to more subtle techniques of psychological manipulation.

Confessions

Before advancements in forensic and scientific evidence, interrogations were the primary means used to investigate serious crime and to prove guilt. Under Anglo-American common law, convictions require proof beyond reasonable doubt, so confessions in many cases have been the only viable means of meeting that high standard. As Lord Patrick Devlin noted:

> The least criticism of police methods of interrogation deserves to be most carefully weighed because the evidence which such interrogation produces is often decisive; the high degree of proof which the English law requires—proof beyond a reasonable doubt—often could not be achieved by the prosecution without the assistance of the accused's own statement.[7]

Although abusive practices have occurred while interrogating suspects, many suspects confess almost willingly—they simply respond to the pressure of being accused and confronted with evidence. Some are "glad to get it off their chests." Other suspects resist, but through the art of interrogation detectives ultimately persuade many of them to confess. Sometimes, they confess as the result of a rational decision that admitting their crime will be in their best interests; more often, they confess because of emotional stress.

In law, confessions have long been recognized as important evidence:

> Confessions constitute the highest and most satisfactory species of evidence. This is for the reason that no innocent man, in full possession of his faculties, can be supposed ordinarily to be willing to risk his life, liberty, or property voluntarily by a false confession.[8]

In *Miranda v. Arizona*, 384 U.S. 436 (1966), the case that has done so much to discourage confessions, the Warren Court recognized their value:

> Confessions remain a proper element in law enforcement. Any statement given freely and voluntarily without any compelling influence is, of course, admissible in evidence.... There is no requirement that the police stop a person who enters a police station and states that he wishes to confess to a crime, or a person who calls the police to offer a confession or any other statement he desires to make. Volunteered statements of any kind are not barred by the Fifth Amendment and their admissibility is not affected by our holding today.[9]

There is a need to confess that springs from the moral, religious, and psychological founda-tions of human experience. For the individual involved in a serious criminal matter, con-fession can be a healthy release from overbearing layers of psychological constraint or an attempt to set matters right. A confession not only provides direct evidence of the guilt of the accused person but also provides leads to additional evidence against others who may have been involved in the crime.

Although courts have excluded many confessions on the grounds that the confessions were involuntary, unreliable, or unfair, they have not ruled that custodial police interroga-tions are *per se* unlawful, and they have distinctly recognized that police interrogation is a necessary crime-fighting tactic. In *Culombe v. Connecticut*, 367 U.S. 568 (1961), Justice Felix Frankfurter described their necessity:

> Despite modern advances in the technology of crime detection, offenses frequently occur about which things cannot be made to speak. And where there cannot be found innocent human witnesses to such offenses, nothing remains—if police investigation is not to be balked before it has fairly begun—but to seek out possibly guilty witnesses and ask them questions, witnesses, that is, who are suspected of knowing something about the offense precisely because they are suspected of implication in it.
>
> The questions which these suspected witnesses are asked may serve to clear them. They may serve, directly or indirectly, to lead the police to other suspects than the per-sons questioned. Or they may become the means by which the persons questioned are themselves made to furnish proofs which will eventually send them to prison or death. In any event, whatever its outcome, such questioning is often indispensable to crime detec-tion. Its compelling necessity has been judicially recognized as its sufficient justification, even in a society which, like ours, stands strongly and constitutionally committed to the principle that persons accused of crime cannot be made to convict themselves out of their own mouths.

A voluntary, truthful confession solidifies the case against a defendant, and it also reduces the chances of an innocent persons being convicted on the basis of misapplied circumstan-tial evidence. Obtaining a truthful confession reduces the need to rely on informants to testify against a defendant in exchange for lesser charges or a reduced sentence. A defend-ant's confession obviates the need to rely on eyewitness testimony, which has been shown to be substantially unreliable and which has led to many wrongful convictions.

Experience has shown that confessions and admissions obtained from suspects soon after the crime are of high evidentiary value, as the suspects often impart information not already in the possession of the police. Verifying the information after the suspect offers it or finding evidence where a suspect directs the police to find it lends a high degree of reliability to the truthfulness of the suspect's statements. Such confessions are viewed as more trustworthy than confessions obtained after the police have collected other evidence and developed a theory of the case.

Cases built solely on circumstantial evidence usually contain some level of doubt, and to prevent injustices in such cases courts have employed the "inconsistent with innocence" standard for circumstantial evidence convictions:

> Unless there be a confession or direct testimony by observers of the act, dependence must be upon circumstances attending the event and then the question, in a capital case, which is presented to us for our consideration is whether the guilt of the accused has been

established to a moral certainty by circumstances which not only point to the guilt of the accused but are inconsistent with his innocence.[10]

Direct evidence cases are generally presumed to be stronger than purely circumstantial evidence cases. Of course, such a presumption depends on the reliability of the defendant's confession. Determining the reliability of a confession is problematic. Its reliability has a direct correlation to its voluntary nature; however, for police and courts, the line between voluntary and involuntary is often difficult to discern.

False Confessions

Although confessions are indispensable to fully effective law enforcement, members of the criminal justice system must be on constant guard against false confessions. Over the years, instances of police employing improper force, duress, and other forms of coercion to obtain confessions have come to light, and such practices have led to false confessions. The public often countenanced the improper police behavior because the confessions ratified the guilt of the defendants, and false confessions by innocent defendants were considered a rarity. Many people believed that a moderate use of force to persuade an accused to tell the truth was acceptable. They underestimated the power of coercion to cause an accused to give a false confession, and false confessions were undoubtedly not as rare as people thought. Such confessions have been an age-old problem, as noted in 1831 in *King v. Parratt*, 4 Car. & P. 570:

> A free and voluntary confession is deserving of the highest credit, because it is presumed to flow from the strongest sense of guilt... but a confession forced from the mind by flattery of hope, or by the torture of fear, comes in so questionable a shape... that no credit ought to be given to it; and therefore it is rejected.

Even today, false confessions may not be as rare as most people think. False confessions arise from a defendant's hope of mitigating his punishment, or gaining the favor of the police, or for no reasonable motive whatsoever.[11] They arise through the power of suggestion, through confusion, and through intimidation. Worse yet, in many instances, courts have been unable to unearth the falsity of confessions, and wrongful convictions have resulted. As Justice Joseph Story observed:

> It is not even certain that criminals, who, in capital cases, plead guilty, and, by confession of their guilt in open court, submit to the sentence of the law, are always guilty of the offense. Cases have occurred in which men have been accused and tried, and convicted of murder, upon their own solemn confession in a court of justice; where it has been afterwards ascertained that the party could not have been guilty; for the person supposed to be murdered was found to be still living, or lost his life at another place, and at a different period.[12]

False confessions in open court are unusual; false confessions in police stations are not so unusual. In either case, it is clear that deficiencies exist in our system of obtaining confessions and verifying their truthfulness. Under traditional common-law rules, judges hear evidence to determine whether a confession was given freely and voluntarily by a competent person and under circumstances indicating reliability. After a judge decides to admit a confession into evidence, the jury then assesses the reliability and truthfulness of the confession.

Although false confessions in most cases are involuntary, it does not follow that all involuntary confessions are false. Some are truthful. However, because courts have had great difficulty discerning which are truthful and which are false, they have adopted a strict bright line between voluntary and involuntary as the criterion for admitting or excluding a confession. Justice Frankfurter summarized the rule in *Culombe v. Connecticut*, 367 U.S. 568 (1961):

> The ultimate test remains that which has been the only clearly established test in Anglo-American courts for two hundred years: the test of voluntariness. Is the confession the product of an essentially free and unconstrained choice by its maker? If it is, if he has willed to confess, it may be used against him. If it is not, if his will has been overborne and his capacity for self-determination critically impaired, the use of his confession offends due process. The line of distinction is that at which governing self-direction is lost and compulsion, of whatever nature or however infused, propels or helps to propel the confession.

In practice, determining the voluntary or involuntary nature of a confession is often as difficult as determining its truth or falsity. The circumstances of each case, including the duration and conditions of a suspect's detention and his physical and mental state, must be considered. How much pressure, stress, manipulation, or badgering by the police during an interrogation turns a voluntary confession into an involuntary confession is a subjective judgment.

Supervision of Police Interrogation Practices

Until 1966, the U.S. Supreme Court addressed the propriety of police interrogations on a case-by-case basis. The due process clauses of the Fifth and Fourteenth Amendments made an involuntary confession inadmissible, and the use of physical force rendered a confession involuntary.[13] Whether the third degree, which might not involve actual physical force but might involve duress, psychological pressure, or long hours of continuous questioning, made a confession involuntary was addressed by the Court in *Ashcraft v. Tennessee*, 322 U.S. 143 (1944).

In *Ashcraft*, the police did not beat the defendant, but they questioned him in relays for 36 hours until he confessed to murdering his wife. The Court held that, even without the use of physical force, the long, continuous questioning was sufficient compulsion to deem the defendant's confession to be involuntary.

Threats and psychological pressures that cause a defendant to confess can amount to unlawful coercion and a determination that the confession was involuntary.[14] Some judges have leaned toward the position that any interrogation without the presence of the defendant's attorney is inherently coercive, and, consequently, any statements made would be involuntary and inadmissible.[15] No doubt imposing such a rule would virtually mean the end of confessions. As has been said, no attorney worth his salt would allow a guilty client to talk with the police.

Problem

Sheriff Stringer arrested three young men on suspicion of murdering an elderly woman in her bed. The woman had lived by herself in a rural area, and on the day of the murder the young men had been seen walking on the road in the vicinity of the woman's house. The suspects, Danny Smalls, Tommy King, and Buster Johnson, were each 18 years old. They were taken to police headquarters and placed in separate interrogation rooms. Their clothing was taken from them for laboratory analysis, and they were given hospital robes and slippers to wear. They were read their *Miranda* rights, and each signed a waiver indicating that they agreed to answer questions.

For five hours, they were interrogated by teams of detectives. King and Johnson each adamantly denied they were involved in the killing in any manner. Their families contacted lawyers, and the lawyers called the police and advised them to stop questioning their clients. The police complied and moved King and Johnson out of the interrogation rooms.

No one called on behalf of Smalls, and his interrogation continued. After another hour, Sheriff Stringer took control of the interrogation. He told Smalls that there was a ton of evidence against him. King and Johnson had implicated him in the murder and said it had been Smalls' idea to burglarize the house. When they entered through a back window, they were surprised by the woman. One thing led to another and they assaulted and raped her.

"They said that they didn't know she died," the Sheriff said, "but they also said that you stayed in the house after they left."

"That's a lie," Smalls said. "This is crazy. I don't know anything about no rape."

"Maybe so," the Sheriff said, "but you're in a heap of trouble. Your friends are trying to put the blame on you."

"Sheriff, please believe me. I didn't do anything."

"There is one thing going for you."

"What's that?"

"We didn't find your fingerprints inside, only outside on the windowsill. But we found your friends' fingerprints in the woman's bedroom."

"If they went in, I don't know anything about it."

"Well, Danny. You're putting me in a bad position. Those two are admitting they did it, but you aren't. And those two are putting you as the last person who saw her alive. So that gives me no choice but to charge you with the rape and the murder."

"This ain't right."

"I'm trying to help you. If you tell the truth, if you cooperate, maybe things won't go so bad on you."

"What do you mean?"

"I'll put it to you this way. If you don't cooperate and tell us what we want to know, you're going to get the electric chair. And you know what happens when they turn the juice on?"

"What?"

"Your head goes on fire."

"Come on."

"I saw it plenty of times. You don't want that. But if you cooperate, I'll see that it doesn't happen."

"How can I cooperate when I wasn't there?"

"But you were walking on that road, right?"

"Yes."

"Near the woman's house, right?"

"Yes."

"With King and Johnson, right?"

"Yes."

"So will you tell me that?"

"Yes. I'll say that."

"Good. That's a start. And you saw them climb in the back window?"

"Do I have to say that?"

"Listen. They're saying you went in. That it was your idea. That you killed her. You better defend yourself. You better tell me what they did. They climbed in the window, right?"

"Yes."

"You saw them climb in the window?"

"Yes."

"And you went in after them?"

"Well, I didn't..."

"Danny, you can't do this half way. You have to tell me it all or you're not cooperating. That's our agreement. You went in after them?"

"Okay, I went in after them."

"And you saw them grab the woman?"

"Okay."

"Well, did you or did you not see them grab the woman?"

"Yes."

"And they attacked her in the bedroom?"

"Yes."

"And you were there?"

"Yes."

"You saw it?"

"Yes."

"Okay, now tell it to me again."

"I saw them climb in the window. I went in. I saw them grab her in the bedroom."

"And you were there?"

"Yes."

"And you saw them rape her?"

"No, that's it. I'm not saying anything else. I should have a lawyer."

"If you don't cooperate, we don't have a deal."

"I can't say something I didn't see."

"Okay, fine."

Danny was charged with murder. His confession as related by the sheriff and two other detectives was admitted into evidence, and he was convicted on the basis of the confession and being seen in the vicinity of the house on the day of the murder. King and Johnson were not charged and did not testify.

Questions

1. Was Smalls' confession truthful?
2. Was Smalls' confession voluntary?
3. Does signing a waiver of *Miranda* rights render a subsequent confession voluntary?
4. Does five hours or more of intensive interrogation render a confession inadmissible?
5. Does lying to a suspect that his associates are implicating him render a confession inadmissible?
6. Does lying to a suspect about having physical evidence implicating him render a confession inadmissible?
7. Does a promise of leniency in exchange for a confession render the confession inadmissible?

Miranda v. Arizona

The Warren Court believed that deciding each confession case on the basis of a subjective assessment of the voluntary nature of the confession left the law in an unsettled state and left too much leeway for the police to intimidate suspects. Consequently, in 1966, the Court shifted from a case-by-case due process approach to a statutory-like rule for custodial interrogations.

In *Miranda v. Arizona*, 384 U.S. 436 (1966), the Court imposed a complex set of ground rules for law enforcement to follow during interviews and interrogations of suspects and defendants. The Court extended the Fifth Amendment right against self-incrimination from the post-arraignment or post-indictment stage of a criminal prosecution to the arrest stage and even the pre-arrest stage. When a suspect is in police custody, whether formally charged with a crime or not, he must be read his rights before any questioning related to the crime occurs.

The Court ruled that questioning in a police station is inherently coercive, and "the prosecution may not use statements, whether exculpatory or inculpatory, stemming from custodial interrogation of the defendant unless it demonstrates the use of procedural safeguards effective to secure the privilege against self-incrimination."

In addition to suppressing Miranda's confession to rape, the Court went far beyond the requirements of the case. It imposed a nationwide requirement on all law enforcement agencies that before custodial interrogation a suspect must be given the following warnings:

1. You have the right to remain silent.
2. Anything you say can be used against you in court.
3. You have the right to have an attorney present and to consult with an attorney.
4. If you cannot afford an attorney, one will be appointed for you prior to any questioning if you so desire.

The Court summarized its extensive ruling:

> To summarize, we hold that when an individual is taken into custody or otherwise deprived of his freedom by the authorities in any significant way and is subjected to questioning, the privilege against self-incrimination is jeopardized. Procedural safeguards must be employed to protect the privilege, and unless other fully effective means are adopted to notify the person of his right of silence and to assure that the exercise of the right will be scrupulously honored, the following measures are required. He must be warned prior to any questioning that he has the right to remain silent, that anything he says can be used against him in a court of law, that he has the right to the presence of an attorney, and that if he cannot afford an attorney, one will be appointed for him prior to any questioning if he so desires. Opportunity to exercise these rights must be afforded to him throughout the interrogation. After such warnings have been given, and such opportunity afforded him, the individual may knowingly and intelligently waive these rights and agree to answer questions or make a statement. But unless and until such warnings and waiver are demonstrated by the prosecution at trial, no evidence obtained as a result of interrogation can be used against him.

Without the warnings, a voluntary confession by a defendant in custody would be deemed the equivalent of an involuntary confession and, therefore, a violation of the defendant's rights. *Miranda* emphasized concerns about incommunicado, backroom police tactics, not only physical but also psychological tactics:

> "...this Court has recognized that coercion can be mental as well as physical and that the blood of the accused is not the only hallmark of an unconstitutional inquisition." Interrogation still takes place in privacy. Privacy results in secrecy and this in turn results in a gap in our knowledge as to what in fact goes on in the interrogation rooms.[16]

The Court found police stations to be inherently coercive and found that the police used tactics that could often induce a suspect to make a statement that he would not otherwise make. The Court pointed to police textbooks that outlined such tactics as the good-guy/bad-guy routine, assuming the suspect's guilt, providing the suspect with excuses for his actions, and casting blame on the victim or society. To counteract such police practices, the warnings were instituted, and the Fifth Amendment privilege against compelled statements was extended to custodial interrogations.

Miranda was a five-to-four decision and contained a strong dissent from the four dissenting justices, who argued that the Constitution prohibited only compelled judicial interrogation. The dissent voted against extending the privilege to out-of-court confessions and voted against abandoning the traditional voluntary test for the competency of confessions.[17]

The majority in *Miranda* disagreed. Furthermore, in addition to the institution of the prophylactic warnings that were designed to aid a suspect during custodial interrogation, the Court ruled that when a suspect asks to consult a lawyer, all questioning must stop until a lawyer is present. By these rulings, the Court took on an active legislative role, usually the province of Congress. Critics argued that instead of deciding whether Miranda's confession was voluntary or involuntary, or deciding the case on the basis of its facts and a just result for the particular case, the Court preemptively decided future confession cases without yet knowing the facts of those cases, and without knowing whether the confessions in those cases were voluntary or not.

Although the *Miranda* decision focused on custodial interrogations in police stations, subsequent court decisions extended the custody question to any location. An important factor for determining whether custody occurred is not where the custody occurred but whether the suspect believed he was free to leave. It is not the intention of the police officer in contact with a suspect that controls, but what a reasonable person in the suspect's position would have understood his situation to be.[18]

Courts consider the following factors to determine whether a suspect was in custody:

- Length of the interrogation
- Isolated surroundings
- Threats
- Threatening presence of police officers
- Blocking doorways
- Displayed weapons
- Physical touching
- Physical restraint
- Intimidating tone of voice or language
- Orders not to move

The above factors are not absolute or all-inclusive. Courts will consider them in a case-by-case context.[19]

Miranda has contributed greatly to the reform of police practices. Although debate continues over its costs and benefits, it has provided rules and guidance that have contributed to the development of professionalism in the law-enforcement community.

Understanding all the complexities of *Miranda* jurisprudence may be difficult; however, the basic principles are simple, and law enforcement officers should endeavor to apply them in good faith. Officers, while interrogating suspects or possible suspects, should always keep in mind their responsibility not to misuse their power. They must be mindful of the inherent dangers in interrogations and the possibility that too much pressure on a suspect may lead to an involuntary and potentially false confession. They must also be mindful that when occasions arise that require actions to prevent serious crime and to protect life, they are required to take appropriate action, and the law recognizes this. As the cases demonstrate, the Constitution honors reasonableness, and courts will inevitably find a balance between protections for individuals and the obligations of law enforcement.

The difficulties of maintaining the balance between conducting a proper investigation to obtain evidence, admissions, or confessions, and, at the same time, protecting a suspect's rights and guarding against involuntary or false confessions, were sensationally demonstrated in the infamous Central Park jogger case.

The case began at 9:00 PM, on April 19, 1989, in New York City's Central Park when a group of about thirty teenagers entered the park, and, doing what was later termed "wilding," began attacking people who were walking, biking, or jogging near the north end of the park. The teenagers threw rocks, knocked people off their bikes, and stole items from them. They robbed a pedestrian, Antonio Diaz, who was 52 years old, of his food and beer, assaulted him, and left him unconscious.

The teenagers continued roaming south and attacking people, including John Loughlin, a 40-year-old schoolteacher, who was severely beaten and robbed between 9:40 and 9:50 PM. He was hit in the head with a pipe and a stick, and knocked unconscious.

Calls were made to the police, who responded and apprehended about twenty teenagers. By midnight, it seemed that the worst of the wilding attacks were over, and the police would process the teenagers they had caught. But, at 1:30 AM, a female jogger was found lying unconscious in the North Woods area of the park. She had been pulled off the walking path into the brush, brutally beaten almost to death, and raped. She had suffered major blood loss, skull fractures, brain damage, and internal bleeding, and was in a coma that lasted twelve days.

Recognizing that she might die, the police intensified their investigation, and assigned scores of detectives to identify suspects in the attacks on the pedestrians and bicyclists, assuming that one or more of them might have assaulted the female jogger or might know who had. During the next two days, they took another fourteen teenagers into custody and questioned them, some with their parents, some without.

Because so many crimes had been committed, and so many people had been involved as suspects, victims, or witnesses, it was not easy to keep all the facts and narratives organized, but, ultimately, four teenagers were indicted for riot, assault, and robberies of the pedestrians and bicyclists. Six other teenagers were indicted for attempted murder, assault, and rape of the female jogger.

In January 1991, one of the six indicted for attempted murder pled guilty to lesser charges and received a reduced sentence. The five remaining defendants pled not guilty and were tried for assault and rape, primarily on the basis of the admissions and confessions they had made during their police interrogations.

Two trials were held, with three defendants in the first, and two defendants in the second.

The first group were acquitted of attempted murder, but were convicted of the assault and rape of the female jogger. They were also convicted of the assault and robbery of John Loughlin, the bicyclist.

In the second trial, one defendant was convicted of the attempted murder of the jogger and also the robbery of Mr. Loughlin. The other defendant was acquitted of attempted murder and rape, but convicted of sexual assault, sodomy, and riot.

It is noteworthy that jurors interviewed after the verdicts said that they were not convinced by the youths' confessions, but were impressed by the physical evidence introduced by the prosecutors: semen, grass, dirt, and two hairs consistent with the victim's hair that were recovered from a defendant's underwear.

The defendants received sentences of five to fifteen years, and during the ensuing years, in appeals and at parole board hearings, they acknowledged witnessing or participating in other wrongdoing against the pedestrians and bicyclists, but each maintained their innocence in the attack on the jogger.

Then, thirteen years later, in 2002, an inmate, Matias Reyes, who was serving a life sentence in prison for murder and several rapes, met one of the defendants, Korey Wise, in an upstate prison. Shortly after conversing with Wise, Reyes told a correction guard that he had raped the Central Park jogger.

An investigation was commenced, and it was found that Reyes' DNA matched the semen found in and on the jogger.

With this new evidence, the district attorney's office filed a motion to vacate the defendants' convictions, stating:

> A comparison of the [defendants'] statements reveals troubling discrepancies... The accounts given by the five defendants differed from one another on the specific details of virtually every major aspect of the crime—who initiated the attack, who knocked the victim down, who undressed her, who struck her, who held her, what weapons were used in the course of the assault, and when in the sequence of events the attack took place.

The Court vacated the defendants' convictions as they pertained to the jogger and, surprisingly, also the convictions for the crimes against the other victims. The defendants were released from prison.

In 2003, the defendants sued the City of New York for false arrest and unlawful imprisonment, and a settlement was reached for $40,000,000.

For thirty years, the Central Park jogger case has stirred controversy. Criticism of the police, the prosecutors, the trials, and the settlement has come from all sides. What we can learn from the case is that achieving criminal justice and accurately reconstructing past crimes is not an easy undertaking, and is often the subject of vehement criticism.

Just as the convictions of the defendants spurred criticism from many quarters, the vacation of their convictions and the $40,000,000 settlement spurred criticism by the police and many others who believed the police had acted properly and correctly. The latter pointed out that if, in fact, Reyes participated in the rape, this did not necessarily mean that the defendants had not.

The supporters of the police also pointed out that Reyes came forward only after he met and spoke to Korey Wise in prison. It is conceivable that Wise told Reyes to say that he acted alone in the attack, and told him the details of the crime so that Reyes could relate them to the investigators. Furthermore, Reyes only came forward after the statute of limitations had expired. He faced no jeopardy and could not be prosecuted for the crime.

Ironically, the district attorney's office chose to believe Reyes despite his lack of character and credibility. They chose to believe his claim that he acted alone even though there was evidence of multiple attackers, particularly the victim's hair on the underwear of one of the defendants.

Moreover, those who supported the police pointed out that the defendants were guilty of the other serious crimes and did not deserve to be rewarded.

In any event, we do not know the exact truth of what happened because our ability to reconstruct and assess the perceptions, memories, and motivations of people are not perfect. What we know is that the participants in the criminal justice system must adhere to the highest professional standards of impartiality and objectivity.

This extraordinary case spurred calls for reform of police interrogation practices, and, in response, New York State passed a statute requiring videos of all custodial interrogations for non-drug A-1 felonies such as homicides and sex assaults.[20] Failure to video an interrogation could result in a confession being inadmissible as evidence, and the majority of states have adopted similar requirements to video-record interrogations.

Notes

1 Lowell, A. Lawrence, The judicial use of torture, *Harvard Law Review*, 11(4), 220, 1897.
2 *Ibid.*
3 Alschuler, Albert, A peculiar privilege in historical perspective: the right to remain silent, *Michigan Law Review*, 94, 2625, 1996.
4 Langbein, John H., The historical origins of the privilege against self-incrimination at common law, *Michigan Law Review*, 92, 1047, 1994.
5 Penney, Steven, Theories of confession admissibility: a historical view, *American Journal of Criminal Law*, 25, 309, 1998.
6 Roberg, Roy R., *Police and Society*, 3rd ed., Roxbury, Los Angeles, 2005.
7 Devlin, Patrick, *The Criminal Prosecution in England*, Yale University Press, New Haven, CT, 1958, p. 58.
8 Prince, Jerome, *Richardson on Evidence*, 10th ed., Brooklyn Law School, 1973, Section 556; *People v. Bennett*, 37 N.Y. 117 (1867); *People v. Joyce*, 233 N.Y. 61 (1922).
9 *Miranda v. Arizona*, 384 U.S. 436 (1966).
10 *People v. Feldman*, 299 N.Y. 153 (1949).
11 *People v. Buffom*, 214 N.Y. 53 (1915).
12 *United States v. Gilbert*, 2 Sumner 19, 26 (1st Cir. 1834).
13 *Bram v. United States*, 168 U.S. 532 (1897); *Brown v. Mississippi*, 297 U.S. 278 (1936).
14 *Payne v. Arkansas*, 356 U.S. 560 (1958); *Spano v. New York*, 360 U.S. 315 (1959); *Culombe v. Connecticut*, 367 U.S. 568 (1961); *Lynumn v. Illinois*, 372 U.S. 528 (1963); *Davis v. North Carolina*, 384 U.S. 737 (1966); *Beecher v. Alabama*, 389 U.S. 35 (1967); *Greenwald v. Wisconsin*, 390 U.S. 519 (1968).
15 *Escobedo v. Illinois*, 378 U.S. 478 (1964).
16 *Miranda v. Arizona*, 384 U.S. 436 (1996).
17 *Miranda v. Arizona*, 384 U.S. 436 (1996), dissent.
18 *Stansbury v. California*, 511 U.S. 318 (1994).
19 *Orozco v. Texas*, 394 U.S. 324 (1969); *Oregon v. Mathiason*, 429 U.S. 492 (1977).
20 NYS Criminal Procedure Law, Section 60:45, 3a, 3b.

Chapter 16

Refining *Miranda*

Questions Raised by *Miranda*

Immediately after *Miranda v. Arizona*, 384 U.S. 436 (1966), a firestorm of criticism arose from legal scholars, police officials, and conservative politicians. Legal scholars argued that the Court had usurped the legislative function and had made law instead of interpreting law. The police complained about the restraint on their ability to investigate crime. Conservative politicians railed against what they deemed to be handcuffing of the police and coddling of criminals.

In 1969, Warren Burger, who later became Chief Justice of the U.S. Supreme Court, predicted that *Miranda* would create an incomprehensible and contradictory set of rules that it would be impossible to follow:

> The seeming anxiety of judges to protect every accused person from every consequence of his voluntary utterances is giving rise to myriad rules, sub-rules, variations and exceptions which even the most alert and sophisticated lawyers and judges are taxed to follow. Each time judges add nuances to these "rules" we make it less likely that any police officer will be able to follow the guidelines we lay down. We are approaching the predicament of the centipede on the flypaper—each time one leg is placed to give support for relief of a leg already "stuck," another becomes captive and soon all are securely immobilized. Like the hapless centipede on the flypaper, our efforts to extricate ourselves from this self-imposed dilemma will, if we keep it up, soon have all of us immobilized. We are well on our way to forbidding any utterance of an accused to be used against him unless it is made in open court. Guilt or innocence becomes irrelevant in the criminal trial as we founder in a morass of artificial rules poorly conceived and often impossible of application.[1]

Sometimes predictions are proved correct. After *Miranda*, courts had to deal with a long list of recurring questions and arguments. The Supreme Court had to resolve more than 90 critical *Miranda*-related questions, including: What constitutes custody, questioning, or a valid waiver of rights? Must the exercise of the privilege be unequivocally expressed? Once a privilege is exercised, may the police question the subject at a later time or regarding other matters? Under what circumstances can a suspect rescind an earlier invocation of the privilege? Does an earlier un-Mirandized confession void a subsequent Mirandized confession? Must the police administer the full and exact wording of the *Miranda* warnings for them to be effective?

DOI: 10.4324/9781003415091-20

Over several decades, the Court dealt with all of the above questions and more. In 1974, the Supreme Court addressed the "full and exact" wording question in *Michigan v. Tucker*, 417 U.S. 433. In this case, the defendant confessed to the rape and beating of a 43-year-old woman. Before questioning the defendant, the police had asked him whether he wanted an attorney and whether he knew his constitutional rights. The defendant replied that he did not want an attorney and he understood his rights. The police then advised him further that any statements he might make could be used against him in court; however, they did not advise him that he could be assigned an attorney if he could not afford one.

At the defendant's trial, his confession was suppressed, and the Supreme Court affirmed the suppression because the warnings given by the police did not completely meet the requirements of *Miranda*. The Court ruled that, even though the defendant had stated that he did not want an attorney, the police nevertheless should have completed the warnings and advised him of his right to have an attorney appointed for him if he could not afford one.

In *Michigan v. Mosely*, 423 U.S. 96 (1975), the Court dealt with the reach of a suspect's invocation of the right to remain silent. The defendant, Mosely, while in custody for a series of robberies and after receiving *Miranda* warnings, indicated that he did not want to answer questions about the robberies. Two hours later, other detectives questioned him about an unrelated homicide. They gave him fresh *Miranda* warnings, and he made incriminating statements pertaining to the homicide. The Supreme Court allowed the statements into evidence, holding that the exercise of the right to remain silent in one case does not forever prevent the police from questioning the defendant regarding other cases. As long as the suspect is given fresh *Miranda* warnings and he waives his right to remain silent, he may be questioned.

Edwards v. Arizona, 451 U.S. 477 (1981), dealt with another aspect of the waiver of rights. Defendant Edwards was arrested for robbery. At the police station, detectives advised the defendant of his rights, and questioned him. During the course of the questioning, he stated, "I want an attorney before making a deal." This statement invoked the right to counsel before any further questioning, as opposed to the defendant in *Mosely*, who invoked only the right to remain silent without asking for an attorney.

Edwards asked for an attorney, and the detectives ceased questioning him. The following night, however, two other detectives visited the defendant in jail and initiated questioning again without his counsel present. They gave him *Miranda* warnings, and he said he was willing to talk, but he first wanted to hear a taped statement of an accomplice who had implicated him in the crime. He then confessed to the crime. The Supreme Court suppressed the confession, holding:

> Although we have held that after initially being advised of his Miranda rights, the accused may himself validly waive his rights and respond to interrogation... the Court has strongly indicated that additional safeguards are necessary when the accused asks for counsel; and we now hold that when an accused has invoked his right to have counsel present during custodial interrogation, a valid waiver of that right cannot be established by showing only that he responded to further police-initiated custodial interrogation even if he has been advised of his rights. We further hold that an accused, such as Edwards, having expressed his desire to deal with the police only through counsel, is not subject to further interrogation by the authorities until counsel has been made available to him, unless the accused himself initiates further communication, exchanges, or conversations with the police.

The Court's declaration that an accused can waive the presence of an attorney when "the accused himself initiates further communications, exchanges, or conversations with the police" was surely made in contemplation of a situation in which a defendant, after thinking about his or her situation, voluntarily decides to cooperate or make a deal with the police.[2]

More than 50 years later, courts are still grappling with problems and questions created by *Miranda*. On February 24, 2010, in *Maryland v. Shatzer*, 559 U.S. 98 (2010), 129 S.Ct. 1043, the Supreme Court examined the issue of whether a break in custody allowed the police to re-interview a suspect who had invoked the right to remain silent and the right to have counsel present during questioning. Shatzer was convicted of sexually abusing his three-year-old son. During the initial investigation of the case, he had been incarcerated regarding an unrelated child abuse case when he was questioned about a report that he had abused his own son.

Shatzer invoked his *Miranda* rights and refused to be questioned without his attorney present. Without enough evidence to prosecute, the police closed the case. However, two years and seven months later, the police interviewed the child, who was now six years old and able to provide more details about the crime. They reopened the case and re-interviewed Shatzer. This time he made incriminating statements, such as "I didn't force him," that corroborated the occurrence of the crime.

Shatzer was tried and convicted, but he appealed on the grounds that his incriminating statements should have been suppressed because they were taken in violation of the rule of *Edwards v. Arizona*, 451 U.S. 477 (1981), which held that once a defendant requests an attorney during custodial interrogation the police cannot initiate any further attempts at interrogation unless the accused's attorney is present. The Maryland Court of Appeals agreed and reversed the conviction.[3]

The attorney general's office of Maryland appealed to the U.S. Supreme Court, which distinguished Shatzer's circumstances from Edwards' and reasoned that Shatzer, although incarcerated, was not subject to uninterrupted isolation in police-dominated pretrial custody. The Court concluded that Shatzer's "return to the general prison population qualified as a break in custody" that adequately eliminated the risks of coercion so long as he was once again advised of his *Miranda* rights.

Consequently, the incriminating statement should have been admissible, and his conviction should have been affirmed.

For future cases, the Court set a bright-line rule that after a fourteen-day break from custody, the police could attempt to re-question a suspect. The bright-line rule allows the police to know in advance when they can attempt to re-question a suspect after the suspect has asserted the right to counsel.

If there is no break in custody, the police cannot try to re-question the suspect unless his or her attorney is present.

On June 1, 2010, the Supreme Court addressed another *Miranda* issue in *Berghuis, Warden v. Thompkins*, 560 U.S. 370 (2010), 130 S.Ct. 2250 (2010), No. 08-1470. Detective Helgert attempted to interview defendant Thompkins about a shooting in which one victim died and another was seriously injured. Helgert read Thompkins the *Miranda* rights and asked him to sign a form acknowledging that he understood the rights. Thompkins declined to sign the form. Nevertheless, the detectives questioned him for about three hours. During the questioning, Thompkins was mostly silent, although he did give a few limited verbal responses, such as "yeah," "no," or "I don't know." On occasion, he communicated by nodding his head. He also said that he "didn't want a peppermint" and the chair he was "sitting on was hard."

About two hours and forty-five minutes into the interrogation, Helgert asked Thompkins, "Do you believe in God?" The defendant answered "Yes." Helgert asked, "Do you pray to God?" The defendant answered "Yes." Helgert asked, "Do you pray to God to forgive you for shooting that boy down?" Thompkins answered "Yes" and looked away.

The incriminating statement and other evidence was used against him, and he was convicted of first-degree murder. He appealed on the grounds that he had invoked his privilege to remain silent by not saying anything for such an extended period that the interrogation should have ceased before he made the incriminating statement. The Supreme Court ruled against Thompkins. Relying on their prior ruling in *Davis v. United States*, 512 U.S. 452 (1994), the Court held that an assertion exercising the right to remain silent must be made unambiguously. If an accused makes an ambiguous or equivocal statement or makes no statement, the police are not required to end the interrogation. *Davis* was decided in the context of the right to counsel, but the same principle applies to the right to remain silent.

Problem

In 2005, David Scrum was arrested for molesting a six-year-old child and attempting to molest a ten-year-old child. Detectives from the sex-crimes division attempted to interrogate Scrum. They gave him *Miranda* warnings, but he said he did not want to talk to them, and the detectives ended the interview.

Because the six-year-old child had difficulty communicating exactly what had happened and the police did not have corroborating evidence, those charges were dropped. In the other case, however, Scrum was convicted for molesting the ten-year-old, and Scrum was sentenced to prison. He was housed with the general prison population. For several years, the six-year-old underwent psychological therapy, and in 2010 the child was able to remember and explain what had occurred in 2005. The detectives were notified, and they reopened the case. As part of their investigation, they interviewed Scrum in the prison visiting room. After they gave him *Miranda* warnings, he agreed to talk with the detectives without an attorney present, and he made an incriminating statement to the effect that he did not force the six-year-old child and the child consented to the physical contact. On the basis of his incriminating statement that corroborated the child's account, Scrum was indicted.

In a pretrial motion, his attorney moved to suppress the incriminating statements on the grounds that the detectives violated his right to counsel and to remain silent, which he had invoked in 2005.

Questions

1. Did the fact that Scrum was in prison mean that he was in police custody?
2. Was the transfer of Scrum into the general prison population a break in custody from the initial custodial interrogation?
3. Was it necessary for the detectives to give *Miranda* warnings to Scrum before questioning him the second time?
4. Would the administration of the *Miranda* warnings support a finding that his statement was voluntary?
5. Should Scrum's invocation of his right to remain silent in 2005 have precluded the detectives from questioning him in 2010 without his counsel present?
6. Absent the presence of his attorney, was the 2010 waiver of his right to counsel valid?
7. If it is determined that Scrum was not in police custody, should the rule of *Michigan v. Mosely*, 423 U.S. 96 (1975), have precluded the 2010 interrogation?

8. If it is determined that Scrum was not in police custody, should the rule of *Edwards v. Arizona*, 451 U.S. 477 (1981), have precluded the 2010 interrogation?

Suppressing Confessions to Enforce the Fourth Amendment

Dunaway v. New York, 442 U.S. 200 (1979), held that an arrest without sufficient probable cause tainted a subsequently obtained confession even when *Miranda* warnings had been given prior to the confession and the confession was voluntary. In *Dunaway*, police were investigating an attempted robbery that resulted in a murder. Without probable cause to arrest, they picked up Dunaway in his neighborhood.

The defendant was transported to the police station, placed in an interrogation room, given *Miranda* warnings, and questioned. Although he was not told he was under arrest, he would have been restrained had he attempted to leave. He eventually made statements and drew sketches of the crime scene, incriminating himself. After his conviction, he appealed on the grounds that his statements and sketches should have been suppressed.

The Court discussed the possibility that a confession might be admitted when the causal connection between an illegal arrest and a confession is significantly attenuated by time, *Miranda* warnings, or other factors that purge the primary taint of the illegal arrest; however, the facts in *Dunaway* were insufficient to break the causal connection, and the confession should have been suppressed as the fruits of the poisonous tree. Therefore, the Court reversed Dunaway's conviction.

The suppression of confessions to serious violent crimes in *Tucker*, *Edwards*, *Dunaway*, and many other cases raised calls for the elimination or modification of *Miranda* and the exclusionary rule. Many critics blamed legal technicalities and soft judges for the rising national crime rate. The Supreme Court began to respond to its critics by carving out exceptions to *Miranda* and the exclusionary rule.

Exceptions to *Miranda*

Public Safety

In *New York v. Quarles*, 467 U.S. 649 (1984), the Court applied the public safety exception to the *Miranda* warning requirement. In *Quarles*, police officers arrested the defendant for a rape while armed with a gun. When the police apprehended Quarles inside a supermarket, he did not have the gun in his possession. They asked the defendant where he had hidden the gun, and he told them where it was hidden in the supermarket.

New York courts suppressed the defendant's statement and the gun because the police had not given him *Miranda* warnings before asking him where he had hidden the gun and because the gun was the fruit of the poisonous tree of the *Miranda* violation.

The Supreme Court reversed the New York court, ruling, "The need for answers to questions in a situation posing a threat to the public safety outweighs the need for the prophylactic rule protecting the Fifth Amendment's privilege against self-incrimination."[4]

Traffic Enforcement

In *Berkemer v. McCarty*, 468 U.S. 420 (1984), the Court addressed the issue of whether motorists stopped for misdemeanor traffic offenses are in custody and thus entitled to *Miranda* warnings before police questioning. The facts were that an Ohio State Highway Patrol Trooper observed McCarty's car weaving in and out of a lane on an interstate highway. After following the car for two miles, the trooper forced McCarty to stop, and asked him to step out of the vehicle. McCarty complied but had difficulty standing. At that point, the trooper concluded that McCarty would be charged with drunk driving, but he did not tell him that he would be taken into custody. The trooper asked McCarty to perform a field sobriety test, which McCarty was unable to perform without falling.

When the trooper asked McCarty whether he had been drinking, McCarty replied that he had consumed two beers and had smoked several joints of marijuana. McCarty was placed under arrest. At no time was he given *Miranda* warnings. Convicted of driving while intoxicated, McCarty appealed to the Supreme Court on the grounds that his statements should have been deemed inadmissible. The Court upheld the conviction and the admissibility of the statement. Acknowledging that a traffic stop significantly curtails a driver's freedom of action, the Court nevertheless held that the vast majority of roadside detentions are brief and the motorist's reasonable expectation is that they will spend only a short time answering questions and waiting while the officer conducts a license and registration check. At worst, the motorist might be given a citation, but in the end they will be allowed to continue on their way.

The Court distinguished the atmosphere surrounding an ordinary traffic stop from the traditional police-dominated custodial interrogation, and found that the initial stop of McCarty's car did not constitute a custodial situation. Although the trooper had decided from the outset that McCarty would be arrested, he never communicated his intention. The essence of the situation was that a single police officer asked McCarty a modest number of questions and requested him to perform a simple balancing test at a location visible to passing motorists. Under the circumstances, the Court said this situation could not fairly be characterized as the functional equivalent of a formal arrest, and thus that *Miranda* warnings were not required.

Attenuation

In 1985, in *Oregon v. Elstad*, 470 U.S. 298, the Court decided whether a preliminary exchange about a crime between the police and a suspect voided the suspect's subsequent Mirandized confession. In *Elstad*, the police, armed with an arrest warrant for burglary, entered Elstad's home and during the arrest, a detective, without giving *Miranda* warnings, asked him whether he knew about the burglary. Elstad answered, "Yes. I was there."

At the police station, after the defendant was given *Miranda* warnings, he voluntarily signed a full, written confession. The Oregon Court of Appeals excluded the confession because the defendant's admission at his house "let the cat out of the bag" and "tainted" the voluntary nature of the written confession.

The Supreme Court disagreed with the Oregon state court, reversed their judgment, and held that the connection between the initial admission and the later confession was too remote to require suppression of the confession: "We hold today that a suspect who has once responded to unwarned yet uncoercive questioning is not thereby disabled from waiving his rights and confessing after he has been given the requisite *Miranda* warnings."[5]

Waiver

In another statement case, *Colorado v. Spring*, 479 U.S. 564 (1987), the Court ruled that a suspect's voluntary waiver of the right to remain silent does not require the police to advise the suspect of all the areas about which they intend to question him. In *Colorado v. Spring*, agents of the Bureau of Alcohol, Tobacco, and Firearms (ATF) had been enlisted to investigate the defendant in connection with a murder. They arrested the defendant for selling stolen firearms to an undercover agent. After being advised of his *Miranda* rights, the defendant signed a statement that he understood and waived his rights and was willing to answer questions. The agents then questioned him about the firearms transactions that led to his arrest. They also asked him whether he had ever shot anyone. He answered that he "shot another guy once."

Subsequently, Spring was tried for murder, and his statement that he had shot a guy once was admitted as evidence against him. He was convicted, and appealed on the grounds that his waiver of his *Miranda* rights was invalid because he had not been told that he would be questioned about the murder. The Supreme Court held that a suspect's awareness of all the crimes about which he may be questioned is not relevant to determining the validity of his decision to waive his Fifth Amendment privilege; therefore, the incriminating statement was admissible and the conviction valid.

With such decisions and others, the Supreme Court has attempted to modify the *Miranda* rules and mitigate their most egregious results. On a case-by-case basis, the Court has attempted to apply commonsense standards to the practicalities of police procedures and to balance the mission to prevent and detect crime against the duty to protect individual rights.

Diluting the Poisonous-Tree Doctrine

In 1979 and 1980, two powerful Supreme Court cases strengthened and expanded the exclusionary rule. *Dunaway v. New York*, 442 U.S. 200 (1979), clearly established that the fruits-of-the-poisonous-tree doctrine required courts to suppress station house confessions obtained after arrests made without probable cause in violation of the Fourth Amendment. *Payton v. New York*, 445 U.S. 573 (1980), ruled that a Fourth Amendment violation of the right against unreasonable search and seizure presumptively occurs when the police arrest a person in his or her home without a warrant. The decision upheld the long-standing maxim that "a man's home is his castle." *Payton* violations required the suppression of any physical evidence obtained during the arrest in the home, even evidence recovered from a suspect's person or within his or her reach.

Reading *Dunaway* and *Payton* together could lead to the logical contention that the poisonous-tree doctrine should be extended to require the suppression of station house confessions obtained after an arrest made without a warrant in a defendant's home in violation of the Fourth Amendment. The Supreme Court addressed the contentions raised by the conjectured *Dunaway–Payton* combination in *New York v. Harris*, 495 U.S. 14 (1990), an especially controversial decision with far-reaching implications that brought the Supreme Court into collision with the New York Court of Appeals.

In *Harris*, the police found the nearly decapitated body of Thelma Staton in her apartment. They developed information that her ex-boyfriend, Bernard Harris, had committed the crime. As a result, three detectives went to Harris' apartment. They did not have an arrest warrant.

Inside the apartment, the detectives advised Harris of his *Miranda* rights. After sipping some wine, he told them, "I am glad you came for me." He confessed to cutting Ms. Staton's throat, saying he did it because "she was a bad mother."

Harris was arrested and taken to the station house. After being advised of his *Miranda* rights again, he confessed a second time. A detective took down the confession, and Harris signed it. Later, an assistant district attorney arrived to take a videotaped confession. The district attorney asked Harris whether he wanted to speak about Thelma Staton's death.

Harris answered, "Well, I really don't know what to say right now. I have said all I can say." Nevertheless, he gave a third videotaped confession.

During the state trial proceedings, the first confession was suppressed because the police had entered Harris' apartment without an arrest warrant as required by *Payton v. New York*, 445 U.S. 573 (1980). The third confession was also suppressed because Harris' statement, "I have said all I can say," indicated he wanted to stop. Therefore, any further questioning violated his right to remain silent.

The second confession became the issue of extensive litigation. It was admitted into evidence at Harris' trial, and he was convicted of the murder. Harris appealed to the New York Appellate Division, which affirmed his conviction. In their decision, four of the five Appellate judges agreed with the trial judge that the second confession was admissible.[6]

Harris then appealed to the New York Court of Appeals, and in *People v. Harris*, 72 N.Y.2d 614 (1988), that court reversed the Appellate Division, overturned the murder conviction, and ordered a new trial. The court ruled that the second confession should have been suppressed because it violated the Supreme Court's ruling in *Payton v. New York*, and there was insufficient attenuation (breaking the chain of causation) between the *Payton* violation and the interrogation at the station house.[7]

The New York District Attorney appealed the New York decision to the Supreme Court, arguing that Payton did not require suppression of the confession that had been taken outside of the home. The Supreme Court, in *New York v. Harris*, 495 U.S. 14 (1990), agreed with the district attorney, reversed and remanded the New York decision, and ruled that, despite the *Payton* violation, the obtaining of the confession did not violate the U.S. Constitution. Justice Byron White wrote the majority opinion:

> We decline to apply the exclusionary rule in this context because the rule in *Payton* was designed to protect the physical integrity of the home; it was not intended to grant criminal suspects, like Harris, protection for statements made outside their premises where the police have probable cause to arrest the suspect for committing a crime…. To put the matter another way, suppressing the statement taken outside the house would not serve the purpose of the rule that made Harris' in-house arrest illegal… We hold that where the police have probable cause to arrest a suspect, the exclusionary rule does not bar the State's use of a statement made by the defendant outside of his home, even though the statement is taken after an arrest made in the home in violation of *Payton*.[8]

New York did not concede, and declined to follow the Supreme Court ruling. New York relied on the theory of "state constitutionalism," which propounds that, although a state must grant its citizens at least the minimum rights guaranteed by the U.S. Constitution, a state may grant greater rights and protections to its citizens.[9]

In February 1991, after the Supreme Court decision and seven years after Thelma Staton's murder, the New York Court of Appeals, in *People v. Harris*, 77 N.Y.2d 434, again suppressed the second confession. The New York court held:

> The Supreme Court's rule does not adequately protect the search and seizure rights of citizens of New York. Accordingly, we hold that our State Constitution requires that statements obtained from an accused following a *Payton* violation must be suppressed unless the taint from the violation has been attenuated.[10]

Harris points out the need for law enforcement officers to know not only U.S. constitutional law as interpreted by the Supreme Court but also how their own states interpret and apply criminal procedure rights.

Congressional Attempt to Overrule *Miranda*

The exceptions to *Miranda* applied only to narrow and specific circumstances, and thus courts were still required to suppress thousands of voluntary confessions. Moreover, police have been unable to solve many serious criminal cases because *Miranda* warnings have deterred many guilty suspects from giving statements or confessions. Critics of *Miranda*, including professor of law Paul G. Cassell,[11] have for many years advocated its elimination or restriction and have tried to activate 18 U.S.C. § 3501 of the Omnibus Crime Control and Safe Streets Act of 1968, a statute that Congress had passed two years after the Supreme Court ruling.

The statute's purpose was to maintain and reinforce the traditional common-law rule that voluntary confessions should be admissible. The statute was not designed to allow law enforcement leeway to obtain involuntary confessions. Such confessions have traditionally been inadmissible under the common law and the due process clause because of their inherent unreliability.

The statute declared that the totality of circumstances should be used to determine whether a confession was voluntary or involuntary. Rejecting the *Miranda* rationale that a confession without the warnings is presumptively involuntary and the result of coercion, Congress said that giving a defendant *Miranda* warnings or their equivalent should be only one factor in the totality of circumstances used to determine the voluntary or involuntary nature of a confession. The statute stated:

(a) In any criminal prosecution brought by the United States or by the District of Columbia, a confession, as defined in subsection (e) hereof, shall be admissible in evidence if it is voluntarily given. Before such confession is received in evidence, the trial judge shall, out of the presence of the jury, determine any issue as to voluntariness. If the trial judge determines that the confession was voluntarily made, it shall be admitted in evidence and the trial judge shall permit the jury to hear relevant evidence on the issue of voluntariness and shall instruct the jury to give such weight to the confession as the jury feels it deserves under all the circumstances.

(b) The trial judge in determining the issue of voluntariness shall take into consideration all the circumstances surrounding the giving of the confession, including
    (1) the time elapsing between arrest and arraignment of the defendant making the confession, if it was made after arrest and before arraignment,
    (2) whether such defendant knew the nature of the offense with which he was charged or of which he was suspected at the time of making the confession,
    (3) whether or not such defendant was advised or knew that he was not required to make any statement and that any such statement could be used against him,
    (4) whether or not such defendant had been advised prior to questioning of his right to the assistance of counsel, and
    (5) whether or not such defendant was without the assistance of counsel when questioned and when giving such confession.

The presence or absence of any of the above-mentioned factors to be taken into consideration by the judge need not be conclusive on the issue of voluntariness of the confession.

The passage of Section 3501 was a congressional protest against what many viewed as a movement to end interrogation as an investigative tool, at least as it pertained to suspects with the knowledge and experience to ask for a lawyer. Critics argued that the *Miranda* rules would tend to block federal agents from interrogating the more educated, affluent, or savvy, and result in successful questioning of only those with less education, fewer resources, and less intelligence. In a way, *Miranda* would foster inequality in the criminal justice process.

For three decades, the Justice Department did not attempt to utilize Section 3501. Some officials claimed it was unconstitutional, although political considerations were more likely the reason for its neglect. Eventually, however, the Justice Department attempted to utilize the statute, and the issue of its constitutionality reached the Supreme Court in 2000 in *Dickerson v. United States*, 530 U.S. 28. In *Dickerson*, the Justice Department argued that Section 3501 supported the admissibility of an un-Mirandized, voluntary confession. In addition, Professor Cassell filed an *amicus curiae* (friend of the court) brief in which he argued that Section 3501 required the overruling of *Miranda*.

The Court's Response

Dickerson pertained to a defendant who had been indicted for three bank robberies, using a firearm in the course of committing a crime of violence, and conspiracy. The defendant moved to suppress a confession he gave to FBI agents, claiming that he had not received *Miranda* warnings. The U.S. Fourth Circuit Court of Appeals ruled that, although the evidence was contradictory as to when the warnings were given to the defendant, the confession itself was voluntary. Because the defendant's statement was voluntary, Section 3501 controlled and therefore the confession was admissible.[12]

The Fourth Circuit's decision was a direct challenge to the *Miranda* rules, and because of the important questions in the case the Supreme Court granted a writ of certiorari. The Court reversed the Fourth Circuit and suppressed the confession and the evidence derived from the confession. The holding was comprised of two parts: (1) "In sum, we conclude that *Miranda* announced a constitutional rule that Congress may not supersede legislatively," and (2) "Following the rule of *stare decisis*, we decline to overrule *Miranda* ourselves."

The first part of the holding addressed important questions regarding the separation of powers and the supremacy of powers between the judicial and the legislative branches of government. The Court rejected the proposition that Congress, by passing Section 3501, could overrule a Supreme Court decision on constitutional issues:

> We hold that *Miranda*, being a constitutional decision of this Court, may not be in effect overruled by an Act of Congress, and we decline to overrule *Miranda* ourselves.

In the second part of the holding, the Court gave the following reasons for adhering to *stare decisis* even though the majority of the Court, had it been deciding *Miranda* in 1966, would have ruled differently from the Warren Court:

> Whether or not we would agree with *Miranda*'s reasoning and its resulting rule, were we addressing the issue in the first instance, the principles of *stare decisis* weigh heavily against overruling it now.... *Miranda* has become embedded in routine police practice to the point where the warnings have become part of our national culture.

The Court's decision not to overturn or modify *Miranda* was clearly influenced by the Court's territorial imperative to defend its constitutional authority; however, although the

Court reaffirmed *Miranda*, it has continued to demonstrate its concern with the consequences of the rule.

The Court's pronouncement in *Dickerson* that "*Miranda* is a constitutional decision" implied that law enforcement officers could be liable in a civil action for deprivation of constitutional rights under 42 U.S.C. § 1983 if they violated the *Miranda* requirements. Three years later, the Court backtracked on the implication that *Miranda* warnings were a constitutional right, a violation of which could warrant a civil lawsuit. In *Chavez v. Martinez*, 538 U.S. 760 (2003), the plaintiff, Martinez, sued the police for interrogating him while he was in the hospital without giving him *Miranda* warnings. Two police officers, Salinas and Pena, who were investigating narcotics dealing, had stopped Martinez. Officer Salinas frisked him and discovered a knife in his waistband. A scuffle followed, and the officers claimed that Martinez grabbed Officer Salinas' gun and pointed it at them. Officer Pena shot Martinez five times.

Within minutes, Sergeant Chavez arrived on the scene with paramedics. "Chavez accompanied Martinez to the hospital and then questioned Martinez there while he was receiving treatment from medical personnel. The interview lasted a total of about 10 minutes over a 45-minute period, with Chavez leaving the emergency room for periods of time to permit medical personnel to attend to Martinez." During the interview, Martinez admitted that he took the gun from the officer's holster and pointed it at the police. He also admitted that he used heroin regularly.

Martinez was never charged with a crime, and his answers were never used against him in any criminal prosecution. The shooting left him blind and paralyzed, and he filed a 42 U.S.C. § 1983 civil rights suit. One of the claims in the suit was that Sergeant Chavez's actions violated his Fifth Amendment rights. He claimed that interrogating him without *Miranda* warnings was a constitutional violation.

The Supreme Court rejected the application of the Fifth Amendment to these circumstances, stating:

> We fail to see how, based on the text of the Fifth Amendment, Martinez can allege a violation of this right, since Martinez was never prosecuted for a crime, let alone compelled to be a witness against himself in a criminal case.... We conclude that Martinez's allegations fail to state a violation of his constitutional rights.

Chavez v. Martinez has apparently contradicted the contention that *Dickerson* established *Miranda* warnings as an enforceable constitutional right.

Severing a Branch of the Poisonous Tree

In 2004, the Court turned its attention to the effect of *Miranda* violations on the admissibility of derivative physical evidence. In *United States v. Patane*, 542 U.S. 630 (2004), the Court broke the fruits-of-the-poisonous-tree connection between a *Miranda* violation and the exclusion of physical evidence under the Fourth Amendment right against unreasonable searches and seizures. This might be viewed as the other side of *New York v. Harris*, 495 U.S. 14 (1990), in which the Court broke the connection between a Fourth Amendment search and seizure violation and the alleged mandate to exclude a resultant confession.

Patane was a routine case in which the police, while arresting the defendant for violating a court-imposed restraining order, questioned him about his possession of a Glock semiautomatic pistol. As the police began to give the defendant *Miranda* warnings, he interrupted, asserting that he knew his rights. The police did not attempt to complete the warnings and began to question him. The defendant divulged that the gun was in his bedroom, and he gave the police permission to retrieve it.

The lower court suppressed the gun as it was derived from the questioning that followed the incomplete *Miranda* warnings. The Supreme Court reversed the decision and ruled that, because the confession was voluntary, the proper Fifth Amendment remedy was to exclude the use of the confession at trial, but that it was unnecessary to exclude the physical evidence derived from the confession. The Court reiterated and clarified the mandate that physical evidence obtained from a coerced, involuntary confession would still require suppression. However, the Court's reasoning appeared to abrogate the doctrine that un-Mirandized questioning creates a presumption of coercion that renders a confession involuntary. It now seems that there are at least two categories of involuntary confessions: the first category results from undue physical or psychological coercion; and the second from a technical *Miranda* omission. The former requires suppression of physical evidence derived from the confession; the latter does not.

Notes

1 *Frazier v. United States*, 419 F.2d 1161, 1176 (1969).
2 *Oregon v. Bradshaw*, 462 U.S. 1039 (1983).
3 *Shatzer v. Maryland*, 405 Md. 585 (2008).
4 *New York v. Quarles*, 467 U.S. 649 (1984).
5 *Oregon v. Elstad*, 470 U.S. 298 (1985).
6 *People v. Harris*, 124 A.D.2d 472 (1986).
7 *People v. Harris*, 72 N.Y.2d 614 (1988).
8 *New York v. Harris*, 495 U.S. 14 (1990).
9 *Commonwealth v. Upton*, 394 Mass. 363 (1985); *People v. Elwell*, 50 N.Y.2d 231 (1980).
10 *People v. Harris*, 77 N.Y.2d 434 (1991).
11 Cassell, Paul G., The statute that time forgot: 18 U.S.C. § 3501 and the overhauling of Miranda, *Iowa Law Review*, 85, 175, 1999
12 *United States v. Dickerson*, 166 F.3d 667 (4th Cir. 1999).

References

Edwards v. Arizona, 451 U.S. 477 (1981).
Maryland v. Shatzer, 129 S.Ct. 1043, decided February 24, 2010.
Michigan v. Mosely, 423 U.S. 96 (1975).

Chapter 17

The Right to Counsel

The Sixth Amendment provides fundamental protections for individuals accused of crimes:

> In all criminal prosecutions, the accused shall enjoy the right to a speedy and public trial, by an impartial jury of the State and district wherein the crime shall have been committed, which district shall have been previously ascertained by law, and to be informed of the nature and cause of the accusation; to be confronted with the witnesses against him; to have compulsory process for obtaining witnesses in his favor, and to have the Assistance of Counsel for his defense.

In the landmark case of *Gideon v. Wainwright*, 372 U.S. 335 (1963), the Supreme Court expanded and solidified the right to assistance of counsel, ruling that people charged with a crime who are unable to afford a lawyer are entitled to have one paid for by the state. In *Gideon*, the defendant was tried in Florida for breaking and entering to commit a crime. The trial judge rejected his request for an attorney, and the defendant was convicted and sentenced to five years in prison. Reversing the conviction, the Supreme Court stated: "Lawyers in criminal courts are necessities, not luxuries."

Clearly, most defendants require an attorney to competently exercise the other Sixth Amendment rights. When necessary, an attorney can press the court for a speedy and public trial, challenge a court's jurisdiction, scrutinize indictments and other charging documents for validity and sufficiency, question and cross-examine adversarial witnesses, and prepare and present favorable witnesses and evidence. When necessary, an attorney can appeal an improper court ruling or jury verdict. Without an attorney, most defendants would be unable to accomplish these tasks.

The explicit and implicit mandates of *Gideon* were instrumental to the burgeoning of the defendants' rights revolution. The vast increase in the number of attorneys appointed to represent indigent defendants naturally led to a vast increase in legal challenges to questionable law enforcement practices in such areas as search and seizure, interrogations, and lineups. In the area of right to counsel, *Gideon* left unanswered questions and raised new issues for defense attorneys to address:

1. Does the right to counsel begin at a defendant's trial or at an earlier stage of the criminal proceedings?
2. Is a defendant entitled to an attorney from the point of their arraignment or after their indictment?

DOI: 10.4324/9781003415091-21

3. Is a defendant entitled to an attorney when the police bring them in for questioning or to stand in a lineup?
4. If a defendant has an attorney, whether retained privately or paid for by the state, must the police communicate with them only through their attorney?

In *Massiah v. United States*, 377 U.S. 201 (1964), the Court established the important precedent that, in addition to a defendant's trial, the explicit Sixth Amendment right to counsel applies to the post-indictment stage of a criminal prosecution. Just as a defendant is afforded a counsel at trial, an indicted defendant should be afforded counsel during any questioning by the police after their indictment. This was not a surprise announcement, as in a civil action it is black-letter law that an attorney for one party to a lawsuit may deal only with the attorney for the other party.

The most contentious issue in *Massiah* was whether covert, undercover police contacts with an indicted defendant violated the right to counsel. The defendant, a merchant seaman and a member of the crew of the SS *Santa Maria*, was arrested for smuggling three and a half pounds of cocaine aboard that ship from South America to the United States. He and several others were indicted for violating federal drug laws. Massiah retained an attorney, was arraigned, and was released on bail. The federal agents did not attempt to directly question him, but they sent one of the other defendants, Colson, who had agreed to cooperate with the government, to engage the defendant in conversation about the crimes. Colson installed a radio transmitter in his car and engaged the defendant in a conversation that the agents overheard. During the conversation the defendant made incriminating statements, which were used to convict him. The Warren Court reversed the conviction, ruling that an indicted defendant's right to counsel is violated when government agents deliberately elicit statements from the defendant in the absence of counsel.

In *Escobedo v. Illinois*, 378 U.S. 478 (1964), the Court addressed the issue of the right to counsel during a pre-arraignment custodial interrogation. The police, while interrogating Escobedo about a murder, prevented his attorney from being present during the interrogation and told Escobedo that his lawyer "didn't want to see him."[1] Subsequently, Escobedo confessed to the murder. The Supreme Court suppressed the confession, ruling that his Sixth Amendment right to counsel had been violated. The significance of the decision was the extension of the Sixth Amendment right to counsel from the post-arraignment, post-indictment stage of a criminal prosecution to the pre-prosecution arrest stage. Moreover, the decision implied that the Court would rule in the future that a confession prompted by interrogation could be deemed voluntary only when an attorney had been present to advise the suspect.

Escobedo raised concerns that police would no longer be able to conduct investigative interrogations, but *Escobedo* lost much of its authority as a precedent when the Court, in *Miranda v. Arizona*, 384 U.S. 436 (1966), failed to follow its lead and declined to apply an absolute or automatic Sixth Amendment right to counsel during pre-arraignment custodial interrogations. *Miranda* instead established only a conditional Fifth Amendment right to counsel during station house custodial interrogations. In contrast to *Massiah*, according to which defendants cannot waive their Sixth Amendment right to counsel unless their counsel is present, under *Miranda* defendants can waive their Fifth Amendment right to counsel even without the presence of counsel representing them. In effect, after the *Miranda* decision, *Escobedo* no longer established an automatic right to counsel during pre-arraignment custodial interrogations.

In 1986, *Escobedo* was further modified, and practically nullified, by *Moran v. Burbine*, 475 U.S. 412 (1986). In *Moran*, police in Cranston, Rhode Island, arrested the defendant for a local burglary. An attorney called the detective division and was informed that the defendant would not be questioned regarding the burglary. While the defendant was in custody, he was implicated in an unrelated murder that had occurred several months earlier in Providence, Rhode Island. The murder victim was Mary Jo Hickey, who "was found unconscious in a factory parking lot in Providence, Rhode Island. Suffering from injuries to her skull apparently inflicted by a metal pipe found at the scene, she was rushed to a nearby hospital. Three weeks later she died from her wounds."

During the evening in which the defendant was in custody, detectives from Providence arrived and advised the defendant of his *Miranda* rights. They did not tell him that an attorney had called to represent him regarding the Cranston burglary, and they proceeded to question him about the Providence murder. The defendant, in writing, waived his right to remain silent and his right to counsel and gave three full written confessions to the murder.

The defendant was convicted in Rhode Island of murder in the first degree. He filed a writ of habeas corpus in federal court, where the U.S. First Circuit Court of Appeals reversed the conviction and suppressed the confession, ruling that "the deliberate or reckless failure to inform a suspect in custody that his counsel, or counsel retained for him, is seeking to see him, vitiates any waiver of his Fifth Amendment right to counsel and privilege against self-incrimination."[2]

The Supreme Court disagreed, reversed the First Circuit Court of Appeals, reinstated the conviction, and allowed the confession to stand, finding that the First Circuit's conclusion was "untenable as a matter of both logic and precedent." The Court stated:

> Events occurring outside the presence of the suspect and entirely unknown to him surely can have no bearing on the capacity to comprehend and knowingly relinquish a constitutional right. Under the analysis of the Court of Appeals, the same defendant, armed with the same information and confronted with precisely the same police conduct, would have knowingly waived his Miranda rights had a lawyer not telephoned the police station.... But we have never read the Constitution to require that the police supply a suspect with a flow of information to help him calibrate his self-interest in deciding whether to speak or stand by his rights....
>
> Granting that the deliberate or reckless withholding of information is objectionable as a matter of ethics, such conduct is only relevant to the constitutional validity of a waiver if it deprives a defendant of knowledge essential to his ability to understand the nature of his rights and the consequences of abandoning them. Because respondent's voluntary decision to speak was made with full awareness and comprehension of all the information *Miranda* requires the police to convey, the waivers were valid.[3]

These landmark cases—*Gideon, Massiah,* and *Miranda*—established several clear bright-line rules for criminal procedure, but they also created several other contentious legal issues:

1. When the police elicit information from a represented defendant by indirect communications, under what circumstances will a court deem the communications to be the equivalent of direct questioning in violation of the right to counsel?
2. May the police, through undercover agents or jailhouse informants, continue to gather evidence against a represented defendant?
3. May the police question a suspect in one case who is represented by counsel in another case?
4. When a suspect has counsel in a particular case, does the representation last forever, and are the police precluded from ever approaching or questioning the suspect?

Indirect Questioning

The Supreme Court addressed the issue of indirect, circuitous communication with a represented defendant in *Brewer v. Williams*, 430 U.S. 387 (1977), a case that mirrored every parent's nightmare. On Christmas Eve, 1968, the Powers family attended a wrestling match in a YMCA in Des Moines, Iowa. While the parents watched their son's team, their ten-year-old daughter, Pamela, made a trip to the restroom. She never returned. Robert Williams, a former mental patient who had a room in the YMCA, raped and murdered the little girl.

After the crime, Williams was seen leaving the building and carrying a bundle. The police immediately began searching for him and the girl, without success. Two days later, aided by an attorney, Williams surrendered to the police in Davenport, Iowa, 160 miles from Des Moines. The attorney advised the detectives not to question Williams on the automobile trip back to Des Moines. However, knowing Williams was a former mental patient and deeply religious, one of the officers, Detective Leaming, began a conversation with Williams, saying:

> I want to give you something to think about while we're traveling down the road.... They are predicting several inches of snow for tonight, and I feel that you yourself are the only person that knows where this little girl's body is... and if you get a snow on top of it you yourself may be unable to find it. And since we will be going right past the area where the body is on the way into Des Moines, I feel that we could stop and locate the body... of this little girl who was snatched away from them on Christmas Eve and murdered.... After a snow storm we may not be able to find it at all.

Although the speech did not contain direct questions, it had religious overtones, in that it encouraged Williams to show them where the little girl's body was dumped so the parents could give her a Christian burial. Williams responded and led them to the body.

At his trial, Williams was convicted, but the Supreme Court ruled that the burial speech was an unlawful interrogation in violation of the defendant's Fifth Amendment right against self-incrimination and Sixth Amendment right to counsel. Because the unlawful interrogation led to the discovery of the body, under the fruits-of-the-poisonous-tree doctrine the evidence of the body and any evidence on or around the body had to be excluded from evidence. Williams' conviction was reversed.

Brewer v. Williams, along with several *Miranda*-related decisions, raised the level of criticism of the courts and generated complaints that law enforcement was being unduly constrained. The Rehnquist Court, to modify some of the Court's more extreme holdings, began applying exceptions to the general doctrines of the Warren Court.

Inevitable Discovery Exception

In *Nix v. Williams*, 467 U.S. 431 (1984), the Court applied the *inevitable discovery* exception to the fruits-of-the-poisonous-tree doctrine. *Nix* stemmed from a retrial of *Brewer v. Williams*. At Williams' retrial, his admissions in response to the interrogation were excluded from evidence, but the evidence of the body of the victim, Pamela Powers, was admitted. Williams was convicted again.

He appealed the admission of the evidence of the body, and the case, now entitled *Nix v. Williams*, again reached the Supreme Court. The Court upheld the second conviction, reasoning that the evidence of the body was admissible because the police and citizens had mounted an extensive search party to look for the body and would have inevitably discovered the body, even without the assistance of the defendant's confession. The Court explained the inevitable discovery doctrine as follows:

> The core rationale consistently advanced by this Court for extending the exclusionary rule to evidence that is the fruit of unlawful police conduct has been that this admittedly drastic and socially costly course is needed to deter police from violations of constitutional and statutory protections. This Court has accepted the argument that the way to ensure such protections is to exclude evidence seized as a result of such violations notwithstanding the high social cost of letting persons obviously guilty go unpunished for their crimes. On this rationale, the prosecution is not to be put in a better position than it would have been in if no illegality had transpired.
>
> By contrast, the derivative evidence analysis ensures that the prosecution is not put in a *worse* position simply because of some earlier police error or misconduct. The independent source doctrine allows admission of evidence that has been discovered by means wholly independent of any constitutional violation. That doctrine, although closely related to inevitable discovery doctrine, does not apply here; Williams' statements to Leaming indeed led police to the child's body, but that is not the whole story. The independent source doctrine teaches us that the interests of society in deterring unlawful police conduct and the public interest in having juries receive all probative evidence of a crime are properly balanced by putting the police in the same, not a worse, position than they would have been in if no police error or misconduct had occurred. When the challenged evidence has an independent source, exclusion of such evidence would put the police in a worse position than they would have been in absent any error or violation. There is a functional similarity between these two doctrines in that exclusion of evidence that would inevitably have been discovered would also put the government in a worse position, because the police would have obtained that evidence if no misconduct had taken place. Thus, while the independent source exception would not justify admission of evidence in this case, its rationale is wholly consistent with and justifies our adoption of the ultimate or inevitable discovery exception to the exclusionary rule.
>
> If the prosecution can establish by a preponderance of the evidence that the information ultimately or inevitably would have been discovered by lawful means—here the volunteers' search—then the deterrence rationale has so little basis that the evidence should be received. Anything less would reject logic, experience and common sense.

Problem

Nine-year-old Jessica L. went to bed in her family home, where she lived with her parents. The next morning, the family woke and found her missing from her bed. The parents called the police and a full-scale search was immediately undertaken to find the missing girl, with newspapers and television used to publicize her photograph. Jessica's mother told the police that Jessica's favorite teddy bear was also missing.

The police checked their database for known sex offenders living in the area. The database revealed that a registered sex offender, James Joseph, who had a previous conviction for a sex crime against a child for which he had served five years in prison, was living in a trailer home across the street from Jessica's house.

Detectives Smart and Swift went to the trailer but no one was there. After several days, they located Joseph at his place of employment and asked him to accompany them to the police station. Joseph agreed. At the police station, the detectives conducted a recorded interview of Joseph.

At first, he said he knew nothing about Jessica's disappearance but he was aware that she was missing and had been taken from her bed. His statement that she had been taken from her bed raised the detectives' suspicion because that information had not been publicized. They continued to question him, and he told them that he had seen Jessica many times. He said she was a very nice girl, and she was very attached to her large white teddy bear. The detectives each had a strong feeling that Joseph was involved in Jessica's disappearance, and they decided to advise him of his *Miranda* rights. He waived his right to remain silent and agreed to continue speaking with them. When they questioned him about his prior sex crime conviction, he became extremely nervous. He began shifting in his chair and clenching his fists.

Detective Swift said, "We know you took Jessica. Tell us where she is."

"I think I should talk to a lawyer," Joseph said.

The detectives ignored his statement and continued the interrogation. They believed a chance existed that Jessica was still alive and that Joseph knew where she was located. They felt Joseph was on the verge of opening up and if they stopped the questioning for Joseph to get a lawyer, they would lose the chance to learn of Jessica's whereabouts.

Under further questioning, Joseph admitted that he had kidnapped and raped Jessica, kept her locked in a closet for three days, then buried her alive. He said, "I dug a hole and put her in it, buried her. I pushed. I put her in plastic baggies. She was alive. I buried her alive." He explained that about 3:00 AM on the morning of the kidnapping, he simply entered Jessica's house and took her. He said, "I got high on drugs. I went over there and took her out of her house. I walked back into her room. I just told her to come with me and be quiet. I sexually assaulted her. I went out there one night and dug a hole and put her in it and buried her. She was still alive. I buried her alive, she suffered. I don't know why I did it."

Based on the information, the police dug up the shallow grave in the yard behind Joseph's trailer and found Jessica's body. They found her body kneeling and clutching the white teddy bear, her hands tied with speaker wire, and her fingers poking through the garbage bags in which she had been buried alive. She had been raped and had died of suffocation.

All of the facts of the case indicated that Joseph's confession was reliable and truthful. The details he provided before the body was found matched the physical evidence found in the grave. The body was found buried in his backyard, and a mattress in his trailer home had bloodstains that matched Jessica's DNA.

Joseph was charged with first-degree murder, sexual battery on a child, kidnapping, and burglary. His attorney moved to suppress the confession because of the violation of Joseph's right to counsel. He also moved to suppress Jessica's body and the other physical evidence because that evidence was the fruit of the poisonous tree of the unlawfully obtained confession.

Questions

1. When the detectives had Joseph accompany them to the police station, did that constitute an arrest?
2. When the detectives first began questioning Joseph, were they required to give him *Miranda* warnings?
3. Was Joseph's statement, "I think I should talk to a lawyer," an unequivocal request for a lawyer that required the detectives to cease questioning him or was it an equivocal statement that the detectives could ignore?

4. When Joseph said that he thought he should talk to a lawyer, was it a violation of his Fifth Amendment rights for the detectives to continue questioning him?
5. When Joseph said that he thought he should talk to a lawyer, was it a violation of the *Miranda* rule for the detectives to continue questioning him?
6. Is there a difference between a violation specifically written in the Fifth Amendment right and a violation of the *Miranda* rules?
7. Should the public safety exception to *Miranda* apply to the statements obtained after Joseph requested an attorney?
8. Assuming that the continuation of questioning violated Joseph's rights, should his confession be suppressed?
9. Assuming that the continuation of questioning violated Joseph's rights, should the body and other physical evidence that was recovered be suppressed as fruits of the poisonous tree?
10. Should the inevitable discovery exception be applied to the body and the physical evidence?

Jailhouse Informants

In *United States v. Henry*, 447 U.S. 264 (1980), the Court addressed the issue of government informants covertly eliciting statements from incarcerated defendants who are represented by counsel. In *Henry*, federal agents used a prison inmate who was a paid informant to obtain incriminating statements from the defendant. The Court reinforced the deliberate elicitation rules espoused in *Massiah v. United States*, 377 U.S. 201 (1964), and *Brewer v. Williams*, 430 U.S. 387 (1977), holding that the statements had to be suppressed because the agents intentionally created a situation likely to induce the represented defendant to make incriminating statements without the assistance of counsel.

In *Kuhlman v. Wilson*, 477 U.S. 436 (1986), the Court again addressed the issue of government informants. Police do not easily forgo effective tactics for gathering evidence, and they typically adjust their tactics to comply with or circumvent court rulings. In *Kuhlman*, the police placed a paid jailhouse informant in the defendant's cell; however, to avoid the *Henry* ruling, they instructed the informant not to ask questions and only to passively listen to the defendant's unsolicited statements. They told him to "keep his ears open." The Court ruled that deliberate elicitation had not occurred and the defendant's overheard incriminating statements were admissible.

In *Illinois v. Perkins*, 496 U.S. 292 (1990), the Court addressed covert questioning of a defendant about a crime unrelated to the charge for which the defendant had legal representation. In *Perkins*, a police undercover agent, posing as an inmate, was placed in a suspect's jail cell. The suspect had been incarcerated for an unrelated crime of aggravated battery for which he had counsel. He had not been charged and did not have counsel in connection with a murder that the agent was investigating. The Court held that the right to counsel was offense-specific; therefore, the defendant's incriminating statements regarding the murder were admissible because his right to counsel had not yet attached to that charge. Also, the Court rejected the argument that *Miranda* warnings were required, reasoning that the "questioning" did not occur in a "police-dominated atmosphere," and warnings were "not required when a suspect is unaware that he is speaking to a law enforcement officer and gives a voluntary statement.... *Miranda* was not meant to protect suspects from boasting about their criminal activities in front of persons whom they believe to be their cellmates."

Offense-specific Variations

Perkins established that the Sixth Amendment right to counsel that attaches during an arraignment or indictment is offense-specific. This automatic attachment becomes of significant importance when a represented defendant is unaware that he is in contact with a police agent, and it must be distinguished from the circumstance in which a defendant in custody knowingly invokes his right to have an attorney present during any police interrogation. The latter circumstance is not offense-specific but all-inclusive.

In *Arizona v. Roberson*, 486 U.S. 675 (1988), the Supreme Court held that a defendant in custody who has expressed his desire to deal with the police only through counsel can be questioned further neither about the initial crime nor about unrelated crimes until counsel has been made available to him. At Roberson's arrest at the scene of a burglary and after receiving *Miranda* warnings, he stated that he "wanted a lawyer before answering any questions." Three days later, while Roberson was still in custody, another officer gave him new *Miranda* warnings and questioned him about a second burglary. Roberson made incriminating statements regarding the second burglary.

The Supreme Court suppressed the statements and rejected the contention that the second set of *Miranda* warnings was sufficient to protect an in-custody defendant's rights, as the mere repetition of the warnings would not overcome the presumption of coercion created by the prolonged police custody. *Roberson*, wherein the defendant expressly requested an attorney, is distinguishable from cases in which a court assigns an attorney to a defendant. The Supreme Court has consistently ruled that when the right to counsel attaches not by the defendant's affirmative invocation of the right, but by operation of law, such as at an arraignment, the right to counsel is offense-specific.[4]

In *McNeil v. Wisconsin*, 501 U.S. 171 (1991), the defendant, charged with armed robbery, was represented by a public defender at a bail hearing. While in jail on that charge, police questioned him about an unrelated murder. He was advised of his *Miranda* rights, signed forms waiving them, and made incriminating statements regarding the murder. Convicted of the murder, he appealed on the grounds that his statements should have been suppressed because they were taken in violation of his right to counsel.

The Court upheld the conviction, ruling that the assignment of a counsel at a bail hearing does not satisfy the minimum requirement of a statement that could be reasonably construed as an expression of desire to deal with the police only through counsel. The assignment of counsel by a court was not comparable to the absolute and affirmative requests for counsel recognized in *Edwards v. Arizona*, 451 U.S. 477 (1981), and *Arizona v. Roberson*, 486 U.S. 675 (1988).

On May 26, 2009, the Roberts court attempted to further clarify when and how the assignment of counsel at an arraignment affects a subsequent interrogation. In *Montejo v. Louisiana*, 129 S.Ct. 2079 (2009), the Court overturned *Jackson v. Michigan*, 475 U.S. 625 (1986), and lifted some restrictions on when defendants can be interrogated without their lawyers being present. *Jackson* had held that once a defendant affirmatively asked for the assignment of a state-paid counsel at an arraignment or a similar proceeding, the police were forbidden to interrogate the defendant without his lawyer being present, even when the defendant voluntarily waived his right to an attorney at the interrogation.

Montejo addressed the problem that in some states an attorney is automatically assigned to represent an indigent defendant without a request from the defendant, while in other states an indigent defendant is required to affirmatively request the appointment of an attorney. Consequently, under *Jackson*, defendants who were automatically assigned counsel would not have the same right to counsel protections as defendants who were required to affirmatively request an attorney and who did so.

In *Montejo*, the defendant was arrested for murder and robbery. He was read his *Miranda* rights, and while being interrogated he repeatedly changed his story, at first blaming another person, then admitting that he had shot the victim during a botched burglary. At a preliminary hearing, a judge ordered that a public defender be appointed. Then, at some point afterwards, without his appointed attorney present, the defendant was given his *Miranda* rights again and he agreed to accompany detectives to locate the murder weapon, which he had thrown in a lake. During the trip, he wrote a letter of apology to the victim's widow.

At Montejo's trial, the letter of apology was admitted into evidence. He was convicted, and he appealed on the grounds that because of a violation of his right to counsel the incriminating letter should have been suppressed. However, the Louisiana Supreme Court upheld the conviction, ruling that the *Jackson* rule did not apply to him because in Louisiana lawyers are assigned automatically to indigent defendants and Montejo had not specifically requested counsel at the preliminary hearing.

The Supreme Court affirmed the Louisiana ruling on similar reasoning, but went further by overruling *Jackson* entirely, because *Jackson* mandated an unworkable standard that led to arbitrary and anomalous distinctions between defendants in different states and "when the marginal benefits of the *Jackson* rule weighed against its substantial costs to the truth-seeking process and the criminal justice system, we readily conclude that the rule does not pay its way." The Court emphasized that it was not abrogating a defendant's right to the presence of counsel at critical stages of a prosecution as per *Massiah*, but it was only overturning the *Jackson* rule that a represented defendant could not voluntarily waive that right.

Right to Counsel for Factually-related Cases

In contrast to the offense-specific limitations on the right to counsel that the Supreme Court applied in *Perkins* and *McNeil*, several state courts have expanded the right to counsel to cases factually related to the represented case. For example, in 1997, the New York Court of Appeals in *People v. Cohen*, 90 N.Y.2d 632 (1997), held that legal representation in one case would be automatically applied to a factually-related case.

In *Cohen*, the defendant was a suspect in the burglary of Thompson's Garage in Lake George, New York. Three guns had been stolen in the burglary. Cohen retained counsel in that matter, and the counsel advised the police not to question his client. A few weeks after the burglary, an unrelated robbery and murder took place at a Citgo gas station mini-mart on the Northway in Lake George. In the robbery, a Citgo employee was shot and killed with a .22 caliber gun. Subsequently, the police received information from an informant implicating Cohen in both crimes. The police executed a search warrant, and they recovered the three guns taken in the Thompson's Garage burglary as well as a .22 caliber revolver that was a ballistic match to the bullet that killed the Citgo employee. They asked Cohen to come with them to the police station, advised him of his *Miranda* rights, and interrogated him without his counsel present. Cohen confessed, and he was arrested for and convicted of the Citgo murder and robbery. However, the New York Court of Appeals suppressed the confession and reversed the conviction, holding that Cohen's legal representation in the Thompson burglary investigation applied to the Citgo murder case, and the interrogation violated Cohen's right to counsel. At his retrial, in which his confession was not admissible, Cohen was acquitted of all charges.

In 2001, the Supreme Court in *Texas v. Cobb*, 532 U.S. 162 (2001), rejected the factually-related doctrine and issued a decision contrary to the holding in *Cohen*. The Court, while overturning a Texas court ruling, clarified and reiterated its *McNeil v. Wisconsin* ruling that a defendant's right to counsel that has attached in one case does not attach to other offenses, even offenses "closely related factually."

In *Cobb*, in December 1993, a complainant, Lindsey Owings, reported that his home had been burglarized and that his wife Margaret and their 16-month-old daughter, Kori Rae, were missing. The defendant, Raymond Levi Cobb, lived across the street, and in July 1994 he was charged with the burglary. At his arraignment, an attorney was appointed for him, and he was released on bail.

In November 1995 Cobb told his father that he had killed the wife and daughter, and the father turned him in to the police. Cobb was arrested on a warrant for the murders of Margaret and Kori Rae. After *Miranda* rights and a short period of questioning, he confessed to killing the wife and daughter. He explained that while he was committing the burglary Margaret caught him stealing a stereo, and he stabbed her in the stomach with a knife. He then dragged her body to a wooded area a few hundred yards from the house. He stated:

> I went back to her house and I saw the baby laying on its bed. I took the baby out there and it was sleeping the whole time. I laid the baby down on the ground four or five feet away from its mother. I went back to my house and got a flat edge shovel. That's all I could find. Then I went back over to where they were and I started digging a hole between them. After I got the hole dug, the baby was awake. It started going toward its mom and it fell in the hole. I put the lady in the hole and I covered them up. I remember stabbing a different knife I had in the ground where they were. I was crying right then.

After his confession, Cobb led the police to the location where he had buried the victims' bodies. He was convicted of murder and sentenced to death. However, the Texas Court of Criminal Appeals reversed his conviction on the grounds that his right to counsel had attached at the burglary arraignment, and because the murders were "factually interwoven with the burglary," the right to counsel had also attached to the murder charges. The Texas Court held that the right attached even though Cobb had not yet been charged with the murders; therefore, the police were precluded from questioning Cobb without his counsel.

The Supreme Court reversed the Texas Court of Criminal Appeals, rejected that court's "factually interwoven" analysis, and reinstated Cobb's conviction. The Supreme Court held that the attachment at arraignment of the right to counsel is offense-specific. It does not attach for all future prosecutions. At the time Cobb confessed, he had been charged with the burglary but not with the murders. Burglary and murder are not the same offense; therefore, the police were not barred from questioning him about the murders, and his confession was admissible. The Court emphasized, "It is critical to recognize that the Constitution does not negate society's interest in the ability of police to talk to witnesses and suspects, even those who have been charged with other offenses."

Of note was the Court's discussion of *Brewer v. Williams*, 430 U.S. 387 (1977), the Christian burial speech case in which the defendant's confession was suppressed because the police violated his right to counsel by questioning him while they were transporting him from Davenport, Iowa, where he had been arraigned on the charge of abduction of a child, to Des Moines, Iowa, where he would be charged with the murder. The Court clearly indicated that under its more recent interpretation that the right to counsel is offense-specific, *Brewer* might have been decided differently. In *Brewer*, because the defendant had been charged with abduction only and had not yet been charged with the murder, his right to counsel had attached only to the abduction charge. The questioning by the police might not have infringed the defendant's right to counsel regarding the murder charge, and the Court might have been able to allow the confession into evidence.

Interminable Right to Counsel

Similar to the offense-specific right to counsel question is the "interminable right to counsel" question. The New York Court of Appeals addressed this and related issues in *People v. West*, 81 N.Y.2d 370 (1993). Should an attorney's admonition to the police not to question his client last forever? What if the attorney dies, is disbarred, or resigns from the case? What if the discovery of new evidence initiates a new police investigation? Are the police forever barred from instituting a follow-up investigation?

People v. West was an offspring of *Massiah* but went much further. It was a murder case: Kenneth West was convicted by a jury for the execution-style shooting of Sylvester Coleman, a stranger to him, outside a New York City apartment on West 116th Street in Manhattan. West, in the presence of his associates, "shot Coleman in the head in a fit of anger because Coleman had parked on the street in a place West had 'reserved' for his own use to sell drugs." Shortly after the murder, the police apprehended West and placed him in a lineup. At the lineup, West's attorney appeared and told the police not to question his client. The lineup was inconclusive, and West was released.

Three years later, one of West's associates, Michael Davenport, was arrested for unrelated charges. He admitted that he was one of the gunmen in the Coleman shooting and agreed to testify against West; however, because a defendant cannot be convicted on the uncorroborated testimony of an accomplice, the police needed additional evidence before they could arrest West. Davenport's brother, Mark, was also an associate of West. In order to help his brother, Mark agreed to surreptitiously tape-record conversations with West to obtain incriminating and corroborating statements.

The strategy was successful, and while being tape-recorded West made incriminating statements about the shooting. The taped statements figured prominently in West's trial, and he was convicted; however, the New York Court of Appeals reversed the conviction. The Court held that the taped conversations were equivalent to police questioning, and because three years earlier West's attorney had advised the police not to question his client the surreptitiously taped statements were taken in violation of the defendant's right to counsel. Therefore, the taped statements had to be suppressed.

In response to a strong dissenting opinion, the majority stated:

> We do not hold that the right to counsel is interminable. This is not a case where the police, at the time they arranged for the secret tape recordings, had any reason to believe that a known attorney–client relationship in the matter had ceased. If indeed it had been shown that defendant's lawyer had died, been disbarred, withdrawn, or terminated the relationship because of a conflict of interest, the case would be a different one.

The Court suggested that the police had the burden to determine whether the attorney–client relationship had terminated. How they would go about doing so, the Court did not make clear. Should the police have asked West whether he still had counsel on the case? Doing so might have alerted him that the investigation had been renewed, and might have put him on guard. Should the police have asked the lawyer? The same result would likely follow.

Critics point out that the *West* decision has created a category of unequal citizenship. In New York, persons who once retain an attorney in connection with a case are in effect immune from further police efforts to obtain additional evidence to prove the case; in contrast, persons without an attorney can be subjected to overt or covert police efforts to obtain additional evidence.

Exceptions to *Miranda*, the Right to Counsel, and the Fruits-of-the-Poisonous-Tree Doctrine

- *New York v. Quarles*, 467 U.S. 649 (1984)
  Public safety.
- *Nix v. Williams*, 467 U.S. 431 (1984)
  Inevitable discovery.
- *Murray v. United States*, 487 U.S. 533 (1988)
  Independent source.
- *Oregon v. Bradshaw*, 462 U.S. 1039 (1983)
  Waiver—When defendant initiates new contact with the police, his or her previously invoked right to counsel may be waived and statements may be admissible.
- *Oregon v. Elstad*, 470 U.S. 298 (1985)
  Attenuation—A voluntary un-Mirandized statement does not necessarily taint a subsequent Mirandized statement.
- *New York v. Harris*, 495 U.S. 14 (1990)
  Attenuation—Time and location changes allow admission of a Mirandized statement made subsequent to a Fourth Amendment violation.
- *United States v. Patane*, 542 U.S. 630 (2004)
  Miranda violations do not require suppression of physical evidence subsequently obtained in accordance with the Fourth Amendment.
- *Maryland v. Shatzer*, 129 S.Ct. 1043 (2010)
  Break in custody can abrogate the *Edwards* rule that, once a defendant requests an attorney during custodial interrogation, the police cannot initiate any further attempts at interrogation unless the attorney is present. An imprisoned defendant is not in custody in the context of police interrogation; therefore, because he is not in custody, he can waive his right to counsel during a re-interview three years after an initial interrogation in which he invoked his right to counsel.

Interconnectivity of Rights

The following scenario examines how the application of the exclusionary rule might result in different outcomes depending on how a constitutional right is applied to a particular defendant's case.

Problem

In Atlanta, Georgia, three twenty-year-old young men, Vinny Johnson, Johnny "Bag a Donuts" Fatsom, and Henry Malevento were driving around in Vinny's car. Malevento suggested that they rob a florist shop to get some money to buy cocaine. Vinny did not want to do it, but agreed to drive Malevento and Fatsom to the florist shop. Malevento and Fatsom went inside, where they both took out guns, announced a stickup, and told everyone not to move or they would shoot them.

Mr. Florentino, the owner of the florist, and his daughter, Maria, were behind the counter. Two customers were in the store. Florentino gave the money from the cash register, $200, to Fatsom, who said to Malevento, "Let's go." However, Malevento liked the look of Maria and decided to rape her. When he tried to force her into the back room, Mr. Florentino came to his daughter's defense. Malevento shot Mr. Florentino in the heart, killing him. Maria screamed and pleaded for someone to help her father, but no one moved.

Just as Malevento fired the shot, two more customers came into the store. One of the customers, Mrs. Church, knew Fatsom. She had been his den mother when he was a boy scout. She shouted, "Johnny, what are you doing?" Fatsom told Malevento, "She knows me. She knows my mother. What are we gonna do? We're in big trouble now. My mother's gonna kill me."

Malevento told Fatsom to get all the customers into the back room and to tie them up, which he did. Malevento tried to drag Maria into the back room, but she wouldn't let go of her father, so he shot her in the head, killing her. Then he told Fatsom to shoot all the customers. "I can't do that," Fatsom said.

"You have to," Malevento said. "That woman knows you. It's either them or us."

"I don't care," Fatsom said. "I just can't do it."

Malevento said, "You wimp," and went in the back room and shot all four customers in the head, killing them all.

As the two robbers ran out of the store, got into Vinny's car, and drove away, a dog walker noticed them and made a note of the license plate number.

Within an hour, based on the plate number, the police had identified Vinny as a suspect, and five detectives staked out his house. Vinny had dropped off his two friends, and was then driving home. As he parked in front of his house, the detectives stopped and questioned him. Vinny immediately began crying and blurted out that he didn't know anyone was going to be shot, but he did not say anything else. The detectives arrested him, gave him *Miranda* warnings, and took him to the station house. They also searched the car, and under the front seat found the gun that Malevento had used to shoot the six people.

No fingerprints were found on the gun, but a ballistics comparison test showed that it was the gun used in the killings.

No fingerprints or other physical evidence identifying the perpetrators of the crime were found in the store.

At the station house, Vinny gave a truthful videotaped confession, identified Malevento and Fatsom, and admitted they had all agreed to rob the florist. He also said that Malevento and Fatsom had said they were going to get out of town as soon as possible.

The detectives immediately went to Fatsom's house. When no one answered the door, they broke into the house without a warrant to search for him. They found him hiding in a closet, and found a gun hidden in his sock drawer and $200 in a jewelry box. The detectives questioned him and he admitted that he had been at the florist shop, but then lied, saying he had stayed outside in the car while Vinny and Malevento went in. He said he did not know they were going to commit a robbery. He was arrested and taken to the police station where he was given *Miranda* warnings. He repeated his story, and gave a videotaped statement.

Fatsom's fingerprints were found on the gun from the sock drawer, but a ballistics comparison test showed it was not the gun used in the killings. Later, the $200 was analyzed at the police laboratory and fingerprints belonging to Mr. Florentino were found on several of the bills.

Other detectives went to Malevento's house. They knocked on the door. Malevento answered through the door, but refused to open it. The detectives decided to surround the house and to get a search warrant. While the detectives were waiting outside, Malevento called his lawyer, who called police headquarters and told a police clerk there that he represented Malevento and the police should not question him.

When the search warrant arrived, the detectives broke down the door, entered the house, and arrested Malevento. He did not resist. The detectives searched the house, but did not find any incriminating evidence. At the station house, after *Miranda* warnings, they interrogated Malevento, but he would not admit anything, saying, "You've got nothing on me, no witnesses, no evidence, no nothing."

The detectives put Malevento in a lineup, and had the dog walker try to identify him. However, the dog walker could not. After the lineup, the detectives lied to him and told him that he had been positively identified. Suddenly, Malevento broke down and confessed. He admitted killing all six people, and said he didn't care. He said he wanted to die, the sooner the better.

The dog walker was also unable to identify either Vinny or Fatsom.

Vinny, Fatsom, and Malevento were indicted for the robbery and the six murders. They were each tried separately because of recent Supreme Court rulings prohibiting the use of hearsay statements of one accomplice as evidence against another accomplice. At their trials, all of the defendants chose to remain silent and none testified against the others.

Before the trials, all the lawyers brought motions to exclude their clients' confessions or admissions and to exclude any physical evidence that had been seized. During these motions and at the trials, the following questions were raised. How would they be answered?

Questions

1. Did the detectives have reasonable suspicion to stop and question Vinny in front of his house?
2. During the stop and question did they have to give him *Miranda* warnings?
3. Could the admissions that Vinny blurted out be used against him in court even though he had not been given *Miranda* warnings?
4. Did Vinny have standing to challenge the constitutionality of the car search?
5. Based on the automobile exception, was it lawful for the police to search Vinny's car even without a search warrant?
6. Could the gun found in Vinny's car be used as evidence against him?
7. Could Vinny's videotaped confession be used against him?
8. If the court ruled that the detectives lawfully entered Fatsom's house under the exigent circumstances exception to the warrant requirement in order to capture him before he fled, would it necessarily follow that the $200 found in the jewelry box and the gun found in the sock drawer would be admissible evidence?
9. Would Fatsom's statements to the detectives while inside his house be inadmissible against him because he was not given *Miranda* warnings?
10. In Fatsom's case, would the court exclude the gun found in his sock drawer and the $200 found in the jewelry case because the detectives had no right to search for such small items when they were searching for him?

11. At Fatsom's trial, if the judge ruled that neither the gun nor the $200 was admitted into evidence, and the only evidence admitted against him was his station house statement wherein he claimed he was outside and did not know Vinny and Malevento were going to commit a robbery, could Fatsom be properly acquitted on the basis of the beyond a reasonable doubt standard?

12. Would Malevento's confession be inadmissible against him because his lawyer called police headquarters to advise that his client should not be questioned?

13. In Malevento's case, did he have standing to move to bar the gun found in Vinny's car from being used as evidence against him?

14. Were Malevento's Fourth Amendment rights violated by the search of Vinny's car?

15. At Malevento's trial, since neither Vinny nor Fatsom testified against him and no evidence or foundation connected the gun to him, could the gun be admitted into evidence against him?

16. At Malevento's trial, based on the standard of beyond a reasonable doubt, and according to the fact pattern above, which was that no one identified him at or near the crime scene, his statements and confession were excluded because they were obtained in violation of his right to counsel, neither the confession of Vinny nor the self-serving statements of Fatsom could be introduced against him, and no physical evidence (neither the gun nor the money) could be connected to him, could he properly be acquitted?

17. At Vinny's trial, since his car was seen fleeing from the crime scene, since he made incriminating statements and a videotaped confession that he knew there was going to be a robbery, and since the murder weapon was found under the front seat of his car, could he be lawfully convicted of the robbery and all six murders in that he had acted in concert with Malevento and Fatsom and was liable for their conduct?

Notes

1 *Escobedo v. Illinois*, 378 U.S. 478 (1964), at 481.
2 *Moran v. Burbine*, 753 F.2d 178 (1986).
3 *Moran v. Burbine*, 475 U.S. 412 (1986).
4 *Moran v. Burbine*, 475 U.S. 412 (1986); *Illinois v. Perkins*, 496 U.S. 292 (1990); *Texas v. Cobb*, 532 U.S. 162 (2001).

References

Arizona v. Roberson, 486 U.S. 675 (1988).
California v. Beheler, 463 U.S. 1121 (1983).
Chavez v. Martinez, 538 U.S. 760 (2003).
Davis v. United States, 512 U.S. 452 (1994).
Edwards v. Arizona, 451 U.S. 477 (1981).
New York v. Quarles, 467 U.S. 649 (1984).
Nix v. Williams, 467 U.S. 431 (1984).
Oregon v. Mathiason, 429 U.S. 492 (1977).

Chapter 18

Evidence and Due Process

Under our constitutional system of law, the values of fairness and liberty place the burden on the prosecution in a criminal trial to present sufficient evidence to support a reasonable finding of guilt. A defendant does not have to present evidence to counteract the prosecution's evidence but may do so.

The right to remain silent and the concomitant right that precludes the government from using a defendant's silence against him or her is a modern development. Through the classical, medieval, and monarchical periods, a defendant was obliged to present a defense. During Greek and Roman times, a defendant had to present a defense or lose by default. In the Middle Ages, various forms of defense were required; a defendant might have put forth compurgators or witnesses to vouch for him, suffered an ordeal to prove his innocence, or engaged in trial by combat. Monarchies required defendants to submit to interrogations and, in some instances, to torture.

In the United States, where citizens have inalienable rights to life, liberty, and property, the prosecution alone has the burden of proof, and the evidence presented must be credible and reliable. A prosecution cannot be based on mere possibilities, suspicion, or speculation; we require substantive evidence.

Evidence means testimony, writings, material objects, or other things offered to prove the existence or nonexistence of a fact. Its purpose is to establish the truth of a proposition, and for that reason it must comply with strict rules of admissibility in order to bar the use of improper, misleading, or prejudicial material. Common-law and statutory rules embody protections to ensure the reliability of evidence so that erroneous verdicts are not reached.

Proving a case by presenting evidence in a courtroom is inherently difficult because a case is only a reconstruction of a past event. Time is irreversible and any reconstruction of a past event can, at best, be only an approximation. Defendants who counter the arguments of a prosecution with alternative theories and alternative reconstructions also face a difficult task, but in most cases it is better than remaining passive. The clash of adversaries challenging the other side's evidence refines the process and allows judges and juries to see a more complete picture. Ultimately, the law of evidence is a discipline to ascertain truth and justice, and to be sufficient the evidence presented must convince a reasonable judge or jury of the truth of the proposition.

Relevant, Material, and Competent

Judges determine whether evidence is admissible at a trial, and, to be admissible, evidence must be relevant, material, and competent. Relevant evidence logically tends to prove or disprove one or more of the facts in issue. It includes evidence with any tendency to increase

DOI: 10.4324/9781003415091-22

or decrease the likelihood that a fact in controversy is true, and it may have only a tenuous connection to the matter at hand. For example, in the prosecution of a defendant for the murder of his girlfriend, the defendant offered a defense that the victim committed suicide. He offered proof that years prior to the death the victim had told a counselor that she had thoughts of suicide. The court ruled that the victim's statement was relevant and should have been admissible.[1]

Congress enacted the Federal Rules of Evidence in 1975 and defined relevant evidence as follows:

> Relevant evidence is evidence having any tendency to make the existence of any fact that is of consequence to the determination of the action more probable or less probable than it would be without the evidence.[2]

In a criminal case (as opposed to a civil case), relevant evidence can even include character and reputation evidence.

Material evidence is relevant evidence that affects a fact that is of consequence to the determination of the case or that must be proved. The Federal Rules of Evidence do not define material evidence but incorporate the concept into the definition of relevant evidence by including the phrase "any fact that is of consequence." An example of a material fact in a felonious assault case would be that the victim suffered a serious physical injury, an element of the crime. An example of an immaterial fact would be when, in a prosecution for statutory rape of a minor, the defendant offered proof that he reasonably thought the minor was of age. Such proof would be immaterial because statutory rape is a strict liability crime that does not require knowledge of the minor's age. It would also be immaterial that the minor in fact consented to the sexual intercourse, because a minor cannot legally give such consent.

For evidence to be admissible, it must be introduced by competent testimony. Competent evidence can be given by persons who satisfy all of the following:

1. Have personal knowledge of the subject matter of the testimony.
2. Are capable of observing and remembering the subject matter.
3. Are capable of understanding the nature of an oath or affirmation.
4. Are capable of expressing themselves so that they can be understood by the judge or jury.

Under common-law rules that existed into the nineteenth century (and in some cases even into the twentieth century), parties, spouses of parties, or other persons with an interest in the case were considered incompetent to testify because it was assumed their testimony would be tainted.[3] Furthermore, because oaths were indispensable to support an accusation, felons and atheists could not testify, as they were deemed disreputable or incapable of taking an oath. In medieval times, oaths had great religious significance. They were often taken while holding religious relics, and it was believed that a witness who lied under oath would be subject to irreversible, eternal damnation. The following is a typical admonition given to a witness:

> If you have lied or concealed the truth in this matter, your soul will be damned in perpetuity, and your body will be exposed to shameful abuses in a gaping Hell.[4]

After the Middle Ages, it was satisfactory for witnesses, with their hand on a Bible, merely to take an oath to tell the truth, the whole truth, and nothing but the truth. In recent years, it is not necessary to swear on the Bible, but only to affirm to tell the truth.

In addition to the personal competency of the witness, competency of the evidence is a requirement. Hearsay evidence is inadmissible unless an exception applies, and opinion evidence by an ordinary witness about technical or scientific matters is incompetent and inadmissible. Physical evidence that cannot be authenticated is incompetent and inadmissible. Authentication requires testimony that lays a foundation as to where and how the object was obtained and that the object is what it is claimed to be. For some objects, a chain of custody must be established to prove that the object was not tampered with or altered between its discovery and its presentation in court.

To offer written documents into evidence, it must be shown that they are genuine and authentic. Some methods of proof are testimony of the person who wrote the document or of a person who witnessed the act of writing or signing, testimony by a handwriting expert, or testimony by a person well familiar with the handwriting of the writer.

Relevant, material, and competent evidence, although generally admissible, might nevertheless be kept out of a trial for important public policy reasons. For example, the doctor–patient, attorney–client, and clergy–penitent privileges for confidential communications are deemed more important than the use of these communications at a trial. The purpose of these privileges is to provide protection to the privileged person who is seeking professional advice or assistance. If such persons could not be sure that their confidential communications to the professional would be protected, they might be discouraged from seeking assistance or they might be less than truthful with the professional.

The marital privilege is designed to support the institution of marriage. At common law, married persons were considered one entity and their interests coincident. In the twentieth century, the marital privilege has been codified by statutes. Although the privilege varies between states, a husband or wife cannot be required to disclose confidential communications made by one to the other during marriage. In a trial, the spouse against whom the testimony is offered is the holder of the privilege and can prevent the witness-spouse from divulging confidential communications between them.

In some states, the privilege survives divorce for confidential communications made during the marriage; in other jurisdictions, the privilege dies with divorce.[5] The marital privilege does not prevent all testimony by one spouse against the other:

1. It does not prevent testimony regarding nonconfidential communications made by one spouse to the other, such as a communication made in the presence of a third party.
2. It does not prevent testimony regarding what one spouse witnessed the other spouse do on a particular occasion, for it applies only to utterances, not to acts.
3. It does not apply to conversations between spouses about crimes in which they are joint participants.
4. It does not apply to divorce proceedings.
5. It does not apply during criminal proceedings in which one spouse is charged with committing a crime against the other spouse or their children.

In *People v. Mills*, 1 N.Y.3d 269 (2003), the privilege was inapplicable to a threatening communication made by one spouse to the other during the course of physical abuse, even though the communication pertained to an unrelated incident that had occurred some 20 years earlier and was the subject of a separate prosecution. In *Mills*, the defendant was on trial for pushing a boy off a pier into the water and leaving the boy to drown. His brother had been a witness to the incident but did not report it at the time. Many years later, the defendant had an affair with the brother's wife. To get even with the defendant, the brother came forward with what he had witnessed. To successfully prosecute the defendant, corroborating evidence was required because, first, the brother's testimony might be impeached by his bias, and, second, because he was present during the drowning, he might be considered an accomplice, and accomplice testimony requires corroboration.

To corroborate the brother's testimony, the prosecution called the defendant's wife to the stand, and she testified that during an argument, as the defendant was choking her, he said, "I could kill you just like I did with that kid."

The defendant was convicted of the crime, and he appealed on the grounds that under the marital privilege the wife should not have been allowed to testify to the communication between them. However, the New York Court of Appeals ruled that the marital privilege did not apply because the communication occurred during an assault. The Court also ruled that the evidence was sufficient to sustain the conviction.

Too Prejudicial

Some otherwise admissible evidence might be kept out of a trial because it is too prejudicial to the defendant. The fact that a defendant on trial for burglary was convicted of similar burglaries in the past would be relevant, but allowing a jury to hear such evidence might unjustifiably sway the jury to convict the defendant because of his past, rather than on the basis of the current evidence. Also, evidence that may be relevant proof in the current case but which implies, or would lead a jury to believe, that the defendant committed a crime in the past may be too prejudicial to the defendant and may influence the jury to convict on the basis of the implied crime.

In *People v. Feldman*, 296 N.Y. 127 (1947), the defendant, Benjamin Feldman, a pharmacist, was charged with poisoning his wife Harriet with strychnine, causing her death. A substantial amount of circumstantial evidence was presented against the defendant, but no direct evidence. The defendant had brought medicine that he had assisted in preparing to his wife's hospital bedside. Shortly after taking that medicine, Harriet died. Before dying and while suffering from the severe symptoms of strychnine poisoning, she cried out "Don't touch my feet."

The prosecution presented circumstantial evidence showing that Feldman had the motive, means, opportunity, and skill to obtain and administer the poison. Furthermore, the prosecution called the victim's sister to testify about a conversation that occurred in the hospital after the death. The sister testified that her mother, who had lived with Feldman and Harriet, had died in the same manner and with the same symptoms as Harriet, and had cried out before dying, "Don't touch my feet," just as Harriet had. Concerned about the possibility of a hereditary disease in the family, the sister had asked Feldman to consent to an autopsy, but he had adamantly refused.

This conversation about his refusal to allow the autopsy was admitted into evidence in an attempt to prove Feldman's evasive conduct and consciousness of guilt, which could be considered circumstantial evidence of guilt. Feldman was convicted, but on his appeal the Court of Appeals reversed the conviction, stating:

> The danger of undue emphasis being attached to the testimony outbalances any legitimate probative force it could have had. The vice of the testimony with special reference

to the decedent's outcries "Don't touch my feet," was that—in light of other evidence that such outcries were characteristic symptoms of strychnine poisoning—it implied, and the jury were permitted so to conclude, that the decedent and her mother—with whom the defendant had lived—had died of strychnine poisoning.

Leaving the jury with the impression that Feldman also poisoned the victim's mother was too prejudicial and might have led the jury to convict him not on evidence pertaining to the charged murder, but on speculative evidence about the uncharged murder.

Circumstantial Evidence

Circumstantial evidence, if strong enough, can establish guilt beyond a reasonable doubt. Circumstantial evidence is not based on actual personal knowledge or observation of the fact in controversy. It is personal knowledge or observation of known facts from which the existence of the unknown fact in controversy can reasonably be inferred, because according to the common experience of humankind such inference usually follows. A simple example is a person who goes to sleep for the night while the weather is clear and dry. The person awakes and observes that the ground is wet but that it is not raining. The person did not witness the rain, but reasonably infers that it rained during the night. In court, the witness can testify to the direct observation of the wet ground but, technically, cannot testify that it rained during the night. It is the fact finder's province (the judge or jury) to infer that it rained. Testimony from a witness that he saw a defendant with a pistol in his hand running from the scene of a shooting is not direct evidence of who committed the crime but is circumstantial evidence from which a judge or jury could reasonably infer that the defendant committed the crime.

For police investigating a crime, circumstantial evidence may be the basis for probable cause to arrest. Actions by a suspect (such as flight, hiding, evasion, destruction of evidence, threats against witnesses, resisting arrest, and contradictory explanations) can be useful circumstantial evidence to establish or support probable cause. Physical evidence left by a suspect at a crime scene (e.g., fingerprints, blood, hair, or DNA) may provide circumstantial evidence of a suspect's identity. Evidence removed from a crime scene (e.g., fibers from a carpet or clothing, soil, vegetable matter, paint, or glass particles) may provide circumstantial evidence to associate a suspect with the crime. Matching shoeprints at a crime scene to a suspect's shoes or bullets from a crime scene to a suspect's gun may also provide significant circumstantial evidence linking a suspect to the crime.[6]

Some types of circumstantial evidence (such as motive, opportunity, and the skills to commit the crime) are not sufficient to establish probable cause to make an arrest but may be more useful during a trial as supplemental evidence to establish guilt. If the police were to arrest a suspect only because he had the motive, opportunity, and skills to commit a particular crime, the charges would most likely be dismissed at a preliminary hearing or as a result of a written motion for dismissal. A grand jury would be unlikely to indict without other legally sufficient evidence; however, combining motive, opportunity, and skill with other significant physical evidence might be sufficient to support an arrest and an indictment.

It is incumbent on criminal justice professionals to make proper assessments of available evidence. Evidence has varying degrees of probative value. A police officer cannot assume that one piece of circumstantial evidence provides sufficient probable cause to make an arrest. Building a case based on circumstantial evidence is like building a stone wall—the wall is built one stone at a time, but a sufficient number of stones are necessary to support the structure.

Proof is essentially a high degree of probability, and the more pieces of evidence that lead to the same factual conclusion, the greater the probability that the conclusion is correct. In a case in which a defendant denies being at a crime scene, one hair strand found at the crime scene that is similar in type and color to the defendant's would not establish probable cause that the defendant had been there. Add a cotton fiber from clothing that is similar to the fibers of a shirt worn by the defendant and the probabilities that the defendant had been present increase somewhat, but the evidence would still not be enough to warrant an arrest. Add a shoeprint at the crime scene that matches the type and size of shoes worn by the defendant, and the probabilities increase further. Even these three items taken together, however, would not necessarily be enough proof to warrant an arrest of the defendant. At some point, were enough similar items added to the body of evidence, probable cause might be established.

Increasing the quality and distinctiveness of items of physical evidence greatly enhances the probability of the defendant's presence at a crime scene. Shoeprints left at a crime scene by a relatively new, widely distributed, and common-size shoe that matches the type and size of the shoes worn by a suspect provides what is termed *class evidence*. Such class evidence by itself would not be enough to reasonably conclude that the suspect made the shoeprint. Many people could have the same type and size of shoe; however, were the shoes old and worn, it is possible that an expert could determine that the shoeprint matched the suspect's shoes to a higher degree of probability because the idiosyncrasies of the suspect's walk made the shoeprint *individualized evidence*. A person's walk will cause the soles and heels of his shoes to wear out in a distinctive and individualized manner. Such individualized evidence has a higher probative value than class evidence and would lend support to a finding of probable cause.

Blood types—such as types A, B, or O—are class evidence with minimal probative value for establishing identity because so many people have the same blood types, whereas DNA evidence found in blood can be individualized and has much greater probative value. Fingerprints left at a crime scene that are matched to a suspect may have an extremely high degree of probative value. In fact, fingerprint experts may testify that they have matched the fingerprints to a reasonable degree of scientific certainty because no two persons in the world have the same fingerprint patterns (except, perhaps, identical twins).

By itself, however, the presence of a fingerprint, a shoeprint, or even DNA at a crime scene might be insufficient to establish probable cause. For example, fingerprints may have been left at a burglary crime scene by a person who had lawful access to the location. For the fingerprints to be significant, it must be shown that the person left the fingerprints at the time of the crime.

In those cases in which only a limited number of persons had access to a burglarized location, the police will take elimination fingerprints from them so that any fingerprints found from persons without lawful access may be identified. When the police successfully match fingerprints to a suspect, they may follow up by questioning the suspect. Denial by the suspect of ever being in the burglarized location increases the significance of the evidence. The fingerprints will prove the suspect lied, and lies are powerful circumstantial evidence. When a person lies about a crime, it is reasonable to infer that he or she has a guilty mind about the crime, which is circumstantial evidence of guilt.

Character Evidence

Character can be circumstantial evidence of guilt or innocence. Character is "a generalized description of one's disposition, or of one's disposition in respect to a general trait, such as honesty, temperance, or peacefulness."[7] Whereas in ancient and medieval times, determinations of guilt or innocence could be based on a person's character, American jurisprudence disfavors *trial by character*. As a rule, the prosecution cannot prove its case by showing the defendant's bad character or proclivity to commit crime. Prosecution evidence should focus the fact finders' attention on what people have done, not on their past lives or reputation. Thus, certain categories of evidence are barred.

Neither prior convictions or wrongful acts nor bad character or reputation evidence may be shown as part of the prosecution's direct case. On the other hand, in the interests of fairness, defendants can introduce evidence of their good reputation to prove their good character; however, if a defendant "opens the door" by presenting evidence of his or her good reputation or character, then the otherwise barred evidence of bad character can be introduced by the prosecution to rebut the defendant's evidence.[8]

Good character evidence can be given, by a witness who has knowledge of the defendant's reputation in the community, as to the particular trait in issue prior to the event in issue. The defendant's reputation after the incident is inadmissible. If the defendant is charged with larceny, the requirement of relevancy will be met by evidence of reputation for honesty. If charged with homicide or assault, the evidence may pertain to reputation of the defendant's peaceable nature. Reputation in the community may include the area in which the defendant resides or other areas in which he is known, such as a school, job, organization, or profession.

The prosecution may cross-examine defense character witnesses about their knowledge of particular reports or rumors derogatory to the qualities in question. This is an area subject to abuse, and the judge should ensure that the prosecutor has a good-faith basis for believing the things he is asking about.

Credibility

Defendants who take the witness stand in their own defense are subject to cross-examination not only about the evidence they present but also about their credibility. The credibility of every witness, including a defendant, is always relevant, and they may be subjected to wide-ranging cross-examination about their life, convictions, and prior inconsistent statements. "The price a defendant must pay for attempting to prove his good name is to throw open the entire subject which the law has kept closed for his benefit and to make himself vulnerable where the law otherwise shields him."[9]

Furthermore, a defendant who testifies to material facts may open the door for the prosecutor to contradict the testimony with evidence that otherwise would not have been admissible. In *United States v. Brettholz*, 485 F.2d 483 (1973), the defendant was convicted of unlawful possession with intent to distribute cocaine after he was arrested at a residence in which the police found one quarter of a kilogram of cocaine. In his defense, Brettholz maintained that he had gone to the house only to buy marijuana.

To prove his intent to distribute the cocaine, the prosecutor called a cooperating witness/accomplice who testified that Brettholz had sold cocaine to him on ten prior occasions. The court ruled that because intent was placed in issue by the defendant, the trial court did not err by admitting the prior uncharged crimes for the purpose of proving the defendant's intent.

It must be noted that the prosecution would not have been allowed to introduce the ten prior crimes on its direct case-in-chief but was allowed to do so only to counteract the evidence offered by the defense.

The MIMIC Rule

The MIMIC rule encapsulates the exceptions to the general rule that a prosecutor cannot introduce evidence of a defendant's prior criminal acts to prove the charged crime. MIMIC stands for the exception that uncharged crimes, wrongs, or bad acts of the defendant may be introduced into evidence, not to prove his or her character or proclivity to commit crimes, but for the purposes of showing:

- Motive
- Intent
- Mistake, or, rather, absence of mistake or accident
- Identity
- Common plan or scheme

The above exceptions were identified and explored in the famous case of *People v. Molineux*, 168 N.Y. 264 (1901), and in 1975 the Federal Rules of Evidence added:

- Opportunity
- Preparation
- Plan
- Knowledge[10]

Below are examples of where the admission into evidence of an uncharged crime was approved.

In *Bey v. Bagley*, 500 F.3d 514 (2007), the proprietor of a store was found murdered. At the crime scene, the victim's pants were found neatly folded next to his body. The defendant's fingerprint was recovered at the store, but because the defendant denied committing the crime the evidence against the defendant was inconclusive. However, the defendant had confessed to a similar crime in which the murdered victim was found with his pants near his body and neatly folded in a similar fashion. At the defendant's trial for the murder of the proprietor, evidence of the other store proprietor's murder was introduced, including evidence of the similarities between the crimes. This evidence was introduced to prove the identity of the defendant. Under the theory that people are creatures of habit and that criminals tend to exhibit a *modus operandi* in the manner in which they commit crimes, the unusual manner in which the defendant committed the first crime was circumstantial evidence to identify the defendant as the perpetrator of the second crime.

In *Huddleston v. United States*, 485 U.S. 681 (1988), the defendant was charged with and convicted of selling stolen goods and possessing stolen property, to wit: a shipment of Memorex videotapes. At the trial, the prosecution presented evidence that a trailer containing 32,000 videotapes with a manufacturing cost of $4.53 per tape was stolen from a trucking yard, and that several days later Huddleston offered to sell a large number of Memorex tapes for between $2.75 and $3.00 per tape. To prove the defendant knew the tapes were stolen, the court allowed the prosecution to introduce evidence that, shortly before these events, Huddleston offered to sell a number of new televisions for $28 apiece and that not long after the charged events Huddleston tried to sell a large number of stolen appliances.

The Supreme Court upheld the conviction and the admission of the prior uncharged crimes into evidence as circumstantial evidence that Huddleston did not have the stolen tapes by mistake. Furthermore, the Court ruled that the amount of evidence needed to support the introduction of the uncharged crimes need not be a preponderance of the evidence, but only sufficient relevant evidence from which a jury could reasonably conclude that the items in question were stolen property.

Although prior crimes and wrongs may sometimes be admissible under the MIMIC exceptions and to impeach the credibility of a defendant who testifies on his own behalf, a court, in its discretion, may rule that the otherwise admissible evidence should be excluded because the prejudicial effect of the evidence outweighs its probative value.

Presumptions

The prosecution has the burden of proving each and every element of a crime, including the defendant's culpable state of mind. Proof might be established by testimony of what the defendant said while committing a voluntary act, by prior statements, or by later admissions or confessions. However, when such statements are not available, the prosecution must nevertheless prove the defendant's state of mind. Without the ability to read the defendant's thoughts, this is a heavy burden. To aid the prosecution, the law invokes the fundamental presumption that a person intends the natural and probable consequences of his or her acts.[11] When it is shown that a defendant pointed a gun at someone and pulled the trigger, the trier of the fact, judge or jury, is allowed to presume that the defendant intended to commit murder. If death resulted, the defendant could be convicted of murder; if death did not result, the defendant could be convicted of attempted murder.

Presumptions can be rebutted; therefore, in the above example, if the defendant presented evidence that proved that he thought the gun was unloaded, he could successfully rebut the presumption that he intended to kill. Even if a death resulted, the defendant might be acquitted of intentional murder, although he could be guilty of reckless manslaughter for his actions.

The presumption that a person intends the natural and probable consequences of his acts is a fundamental proposition of all systems of law, as it emanates from a commonsense understanding of human activity. Other presumptions have been developed for practical purposes and do not carry the same strength of argument. Anglo-American common law adopted the presumption that a person who has the recent and exclusive possession of stolen property is the thief.[12] This presumption helps police and prosecutors, for example, to prove that a defendant caught driving a stolen car was the person who committed the larceny of the car even though the police did not see him steal the car. Of course, the defendant might rebut this presumption by contrary evidence.

A statutory presumption that most states employ is that all persons in a vehicle found to contain unlawful controlled substances are presumed to have known that the substances were present. This allows the police to arrest, and the prosecutor to charge, all persons in the vehicle without having to independently prove their knowledge of the presence of the drugs. Again, this presumption can be rebutted, and it does not apply when the drugs are found on the person of one occupant or one of the occupants is licensed to possess them.

Most presumptions in law are permissible only, meaning that a judge or jury may adopt the presumption but are not required to adopt it. The apprehension of a person in possession of recently stolen property may allow a judge or jury to presume he stole it but does not require that they conclude that he stole the property.[13] The judge or jury can simply decide not to apply the presumption even in the absence of rebutting evidence.

Mandatory presumptions require a judge or jury to apply them until they are rebutted by contrary evidence. The presumption of innocence is mandatory, and judges and juries must adhere to it until it is overcome by evidence that proves guilt.

A conclusive presumption in law cannot be disregarded. For example, a child less than seven years old cannot be guilty of a crime; therefore, once it is established that the child is less than seven, a jury cannot disregard the presumption and cannot find the child guilty.

Problem

Shortly after midnight, John Johansen called 911 from his home and reported that his wife, Beatrice, had shot herself. When the police and paramedics arrived, they found Beatrice partially clothed and lying on a sofa in the living room. A six-shot, .38 caliber revolver was lying next to the sofa on the floor below her right hand. A bullet entrance wound to her right temple was visible. They checked for life signs, but she was dead.

When Detective Smart from the homicide squad arrived, Johansen told him that his wife, to whom he had been married for 20 years, had just turned 50 and had been quite depressed about getting old. She had begun to drink a lot, and the previous night had consumed most of a bottle of wine. At about 10:00 PM, he had gone upstairs to their bedroom, but Beatrice had stayed downstairs in the living room. He fell asleep but was later awakened by a "bang." He was not sure what the noise was and tried to go back to sleep; however, something troubled him, so he went downstairs and found his wife lying unconscious. He saw the gun and immediately called the police. It was a licensed firearm, and he usually kept it in the nightstand on his side of their bed. He had not seen or touched the gun for several months.

When the crime scene technicians arrived, they photographed the living room and all the other rooms of the house. In the kitchen, they found a half-full glass of white wine on the countertop and an empty bottle of wine in the trashcan. They dusted several items for fingerprints, including the wine glass and the wine bottle, which had discernable fingerprints. The gun did not have any discernable fingerprints, only smudges, and it contained five live bullets and one spent bullet shell.

The technicians swabbed Johansen's hands and the hands of the deceased for gunshot residue (GSR). These swabs were taken to the crime laboratory and examined by two separate experts. Both experts concluded that the swabs taken from Johansen's hands did not contain GSR, while the swabs taken from Beatrice's hands did contain GSR, and, in fact, the swabs indicated that both of her hands had traces of GSR.

The next day, Detective Smart conducted a follow-up interview with Johansen at his home, which was located in a wooded, suburban area. Johansen stated that it was a surprise that his wife had committed suicide. Their marriage had been a relatively happy one, and they did not have any financial or health problems. He kept the gun loaded for protection and had a box of bullets that he kept in a closet. He had not fired the gun since he had purchased it more than five years ago.

Detective Smart asked Johansen to give him the box of bullets, and Johansen complied. "You'll get the gun and the bullets back when the investigation is complete," Smart said. "That's fine," Johansen said.

When Smart returned to the police station, he counted the bullets in the box. Forty-three bullets were present, which seemed odd; because the box held 50 bullets and the revolver held six bullets, it seemed to him that the box should have contained 44 bullets.

Smart also thought that it was odd that Beatrice had traces of GSR on both hands when the bullet wound was to her right temple and the gun was found below her right hand. It was possible that she held the gun with two hands and placed it to her right temple, but he speculated that if that were the case, the gun would not have fallen so neatly below the right hand.

The body was taken to the medical examiner's office for an autopsy to determine cause of death. An examination of the bullet entrance wound revealed that it was not a contact wound. A burn mark from the gun's muzzle flash and burnt gunpowder were spread in concentric circles around the wound, which indicated that the gun was fired at a right angle, approximately seven inches from the victim's temple. The examining physician noted that it would be possible for the victim to have fired the gun in this way while holding it with two hands, though this would be from a difficult, unwieldy position. The cause of death was a gunshot wound to the head. The toxicology report indicated that the victim did not have alcohol in her blood.

Beatrice's fingerprints were taken at the morgue, and Johansen's fingerprints had been on file since his pistol license application. The identification section matched the fingerprints on the wine glass and the wine bottle to Johansen. The victim's fingerprints were not found on either the glass or the bottle.

Detective Smart spent much of the next two weeks conducting a background investigation. He found that Johansen had a life insurance policy on his wife that was worth a million dollars. He interviewed Beatrice's co-workers at the bank where she was employed. They were all surprised by her apparent suicide, and all said she was a very happy and upbeat person who enjoyed her job.

Phone records from Johansen's home and his cell phone revealed more than 100 calls to Ms. Patricia Hilton. Smart drove to Hilton's residence, knocked on the door, and attempted to interview her. She was about 35 years old, brunette, and attractive. When Smart asked her whether she was acquainted with Johansen, she slammed the door in his face.

The next day, Smart conducted another follow-up interview with Johansen, this time at the police station. After some preliminary questions, Smart said, "We know you were having an affair with Patricia Hilton. Why don't you tell us about it?"

"What are trying to imply?" Johansen said. "My wife committed suicide, that's all. If I did or didn't have an affair, it's none of your business."

"Did Mrs. Johansen find out about it?"

"Find out about what?"

"Your affair with Ms. Hilton."

Johansen exhaled. "Okay. I had an affair. It was over a long time ago. It doesn't mean I killed my wife."

"I didn't say it did, but I have to ask. That's my job."

"Okay, I understand. But there's no need to drag her into this."

"All right, I won't ask you anymore about that now. But what I need to get straight is what happened on the night of the incident. When you and your wife were together before you went up to bed, what were you doing?"

"Nothing. Just talking, I guess."

"Did you argue?"

"No."

"Did you have anything to eat or drink together?"

"No. She drank by herself."

"On the night of the shooting, do you remember how much she had been drinking?"

"Quite a lot, and she could have had more after I went up to bed."

"You didn't pour her a drink?"

Johansen stood up. "Listen, I don't like the way this is going. Furthermore, I don't like your accusations. If you want to talk to me, talk to my lawyer. Can I leave?"

"Yes. You can leave."

After the interview with Johansen, Detective Smart met with District Attorney James Hart to convince him that they had enough probable cause to arrest Johansen for the murder of his wife. Smart maintained that the shooting was not a suicide. Where the gun was lying was too contrived. If Beatrice had been holding the revolver with two hands on the right side of her head, the gun would not have fallen where it was found. Furthermore, most people would simply hold the gun in their right hand and press the barrel against their temple. For someone to shoot herself from a distance of seven inches did not make sense. Also, women who commit suicide rarely shoot themselves in the head.

Smart believed Johansen had a motive, perhaps two motives—the affair and the insurance. He had the opportunity and the murder weapon. More importantly, Johansen had lied. He had said the affair was long over, but the phone records showed recent contact with Ms. Hilton. He said his wife was depressed, but her co-workers said she was happy and upbeat. He said his wife had been drinking heavily, but the toxicology report found no alcohol in her blood. His fingerprints were on the wine bottle, and he was probably the one doing the heavy drinking. They must have been arguing, probably over the affair with Hilton. In his intoxicated condition, his scheme to kill her and make it look like suicide seemed feasible.

Smart's primary argument was that a bullet was missing. Six bullets were in the gun, but only 43 bullets were in the box of 50 bullets, rather than 44. He proposed that Johansen had shot his wife in the temple. After she had died, he had placed the gun in her hands to get her fingerprints on the gun, and he had fired another bullet so the gunpowder residue would be on her hands. He could easily have aimed out of the window into the woods around the house, and the bullet would never be found. All he had to do was to get rid of the extra spent shell and replace it in the revolver with one of the bullets from the box. Then he would have thoroughly washed his hands to get rid of any gunpowder residue. If his fingerprints were on the gun, it would not matter because it was his gun.

Questions

1. Can probable cause be established on circumstantial evidence alone?
2. Were the facts that it was Johansen's gun and that he had the means and opportunity to kill his wife sufficient evidence, by themselves, to establish probable cause to arrest?
3. Were Johansen's possible motives—the life insurance on his wife and his affair with Hilton—sufficient evidence, by themselves, to establish probable cause to arrest?
4. Were Johansen's statements about his wife's depression and heavy drinking, which were contradicted by her co-workers and the toxicology finding of no alcohol in her blood, sufficient evidence, by themselves, to establish probable cause to arrest?
5. Was the fact that it was not his wife's fingerprints but Johansen's fingerprints that were found on the wine bottle and glass sufficient evidence to establish probable cause to arrest?
6. In combination, were all the circumstantial evidence facts, noted above in questions 2, 3, 4, and 5, sufficient to establish probable cause to arrest?
7. Should the fact that gunpowder residue was found on Mrs. Johansen's hands and none was found on Mr. Johansen's hands outweigh the other circumstantial evidence in this case?

8. Assuming that enough probable cause existed to support a lawful arrest for murder, should the district attorney present this circumstantial evidence case to a grand jury, obtain an indictment, and bring the case to trial?
9. If the district attorney strongly believed in Johansen's guilt and presented his evidence to the grand jury, could the grand jury decline to indict Johansen?
10. At a trial, would it be likely that a jury on the basis of the evidence described above could convict Johansen by finding him guilty beyond a reasonable doubt?
11. If the district attorney believed Johansen was guilty but also believed a jury would acquit him, should he proceed to trial or wait in the expectation that other evidence may be developed?
12. If the district attorney decided not to proceed with charges, because he either did not find probable cause or did not believe he could obtain a conviction, what additional investigative steps could be taken?

Notes

1 *State v. Jaeger*, 973 P.2d 404 (1999).
2 Federal Rules of Evidence, Rule 401.
3 *Funk v. United States*, 290 U.S. 371 (1933).
4 Quoted in Whitman, James, *The Origins of Reasonable Doubt*, Yale University Press, New Haven and London, 2008, at p. 76.
5 *People v. Williams*, 579 N.Y.S.2d 256 (1991); *United States v. Taylor*, 92 F.3d 1313 (1996).
6 *People v. Campbell*, 146 Ill.2d 363; 586 N.E.2d 1261 (1992).
7 McCormack, Charles, *Handbook on the Law of Evidence*, West Publishing, St. Paul, MN, 1954, Section 162, p. 540.
8 *Robbins v. State*, 88 S.W.3d 256 (2002).
9 *Michelson v. United States*, 335 U.S. 469 (1948).
10 Federal Rules of Evidence, Rule 404(b).
11 *State v. Noble*, 425 So.2d 734 (La. 1983); *Henderson v. State*, 544 N.E.2d 507 (1989); *State v. Avcollie*, 178 Conn. 450 (1979); *Commonwealth v. Chester*, 587 A.2d 1367 (1991).
12 *Wright v. West*, 112 S.Ct. 2482 (1992).
13 *Sandstrom v. Montana*, 442 U.S. 510 (1979).

References

Beck v. Ohio, 379 U.S. 89 (1964).
Commonwealth v. Hall, 590 N.E.2d 1177 (Mass. App. 1992).
Costello v. United States, 350 U.S. 359 (1956).
Holland v. United States, 348 U.S. 121 (1954).
People v. Campbell, 586 N.E.2d 1261 (Ill.1992).

Chapter 19

Identifications and Due Process

To convict a defendant, the prosecution must prove beyond a reasonable doubt that the defendant was the person who committed the crime. This is a difficult burden to meet even when the victim knows the suspect. For crimes committed by strangers, the difficulty for the prosecution increases substantially.

When an unknown robber attacks or threatens a victim at random, often the only evidence available to convict the criminal is a visual identification by the victim or other witnesses to the crime. The witness, whether a victim or a bystander, might not have had an adequate opportunity to observe the criminal or might not accurately remember the criminal's description due to the stress of the situation, the lighting conditions, or the speed of the encounter. Many victims focus their attention on the threatening weapon, rather than the appearance of the assailant. Bystanders, while witnessing part or all of an encounter, might not have realized a crime was being committed and might not have been paying close attention.

For law enforcement, obtaining a proper and fair identification of a suspect is critical to a successful prosecution. A positive identification of a defendant can be persuasive to juries; however, research has shown that identification testimony is often unreliable and that even the most confidently made identifications are susceptible to error.[1] The power of suggestion and other psychological factors sometimes motivate witnesses to make positive identifications when a more objective approach might cause them to hesitate. Verbal and nonverbal behavior of the police, whether intentional or not, can influence an identification. By merely conducting a lineup or presenting a photo array of potential suspects, the police send a signal to the witness that the suspect is among the persons presented, and some witnesses will feel compelled to make a choice. To counteract such pressures, law enforcement officers must recognize these dangers and take precautions to minimize them.[2]

False identifications are a leading cause of wrongful convictions, and the tragic consequences caused by the false conviction of an innocent person is compounded by the failure to apprehend and convict the guilty person who committed the crime. To avoid false identifications, the police and the courts have developed standardized precautionary measures.

Lineups

Lineups are the preferred method of having victims or witnesses identify a suspect who was unknown to them before the crime. When the suspect was known before the crime, a lineup is not required.[3] Certainly, if a member of the victim's family or a friend assaults the victim,

DOI: 10.4324/9781003415091-23

a lineup is unnecessary. Lineups are designed to reduce the risk of false identifications and prosecution of the wrong person. They should be conducted as close in time as possible to the occurrence of the crime for the following reasons:

1. The recollections of a witness may fade as time passes.
2. A prompt identification procedure may benefit the suspect, as it may lessen the possibility of mistaken identification.
3. It will permit the earlier release of an innocent suspect.
4. A prompt identification procedure will assist the police in determining how or whether to continue the investigation.

In a lineup, the suspect appears before the witness with five other persons of similar age, sex, race, and physical characteristics. If a suspect is wearing a suit, all persons standing in the lineup should wear a suit. If the suspect is dressed in a distinctive manner that cannot be replicated by the other participants in the lineup, the officer administering the lineup must devise methods to minimize unfairness; for example, if the suspect has an unusual hairstyle, all participants may have to wear hats.

Sometimes, depending on what occurred during the crime, the individuals in the lineup might be asked to walk, turn sideways, wear particular items of clothing, or repeat words that were spoken during the crime, such as "This is a stickup" or "Put your hands up." If one individual is asked to do or say something, the others must do or say the same thing.

The police must ensure that witnesses view the lineups separately and that they do not influence one another.[4] Police must also carefully avoid influencing the identification by unintentional cues through body language, tone of voice, or other actions indicating agreement or disagreement with a witness's choice.

In 1999, the National Institute of Justice issued guidelines to ensure the highest level of integrity in the eyewitness identification process.[5] The guidelines are designed to eliminate even inadvertent suggestion. Guidelines, of course, must be adjusted for particular circumstances, and many law enforcement agencies have employed additional safeguards when necessary.

Following are some of the standard safeguards that should be employed:

1. A police officer conducting a lineup should have all the identifying witnesses interviewed prior to the lineup.
2. Each witness's description of the suspect should be obtained and recorded.
3. If there is more than one witness, each should be interviewed separately.
4. The officer must make sure that no person who will be viewed is seen prior to the lineup by any of the witnesses.
5. Witnesses should be told that it is possible that the suspect may not be in the lineup so that they will not feel compelled to identify anyone.
6. When a crime involves multiple suspects, only one suspect may be in each lineup.
7. When a crime involves multiple suspects who are to be viewed by the same witness in a series of lineups, the fillers in the lineups must be changed for each lineup.
8. No witnesses may be told that another witness did or did not make an identification of someone.
9. The officer should make a complete record of the procedure, either by videotaping or photographing, in addition to notes and official records.

Show-ups

When the police apprehend a suspect shortly after a crime and in its vicinity, a lineup is not always required. In some circumstances, the police may conduct a *show-up*, in which they promptly bring the suspect to a witness for a one-on-one identification. Although this procedure is inherently suggestive, it is acceptable for both policy and practical reasons. First, the immediate on-the-scene identification provides the great advantage of expeditiously exonerating an innocent person, and, second, when the suspect is exonerated, it allows the police to continue searching for the guilty criminal, who may still be in the area. Courts have deemed these benefits to outweigh the risks of suggestiveness that occur when a witness sees a single suspect in police custody.[6]

Unless an emergency exists, a show-up should not be conducted at a police station. To present a suspect in a police facility is far too suggestive, and taking a suspect to a police station nullifies an important rationale for a show-up—the facilitation of the prompt release of an innocent person.[7] The police should not conduct a show-up when they have to physically restrain a suspect in the presence of the witness. To do so would be overly suggestive and would likely taint not only the show-up identification but also any subsequent identification.

Point-outs During a Canvas

After a serious crime, police often ask the victim or a witness to drive around an area and to observe pedestrian traffic in an effort to spot the suspect. This can be done immediately after the crime or at a later time. When the witness spontaneously recognizes a suspect in a public place, the suggestiveness that may be inherent in a show-up is avoided and the identification will be admissible in court.[8]

Photographs

Identification of suspects by photographs is a useful investigative tool. When the suspect is unknown, the police will ask the witness to view mug shots or computerized photographs of persons fitting the description of the suspect. In cases in which the police have identified a potential suspect who is not in custody, they will show the witness a photograph of the suspect along with photographs of persons of similar descriptions. This "six-pack" photo array should simulate a fair lineup. The factors that affect the fairness of a photo array are similar to those that affect a corporeal lineup, including the degree to which the defendant resembles the other persons displayed. Looking at a photograph is not the same as seeing a suspect in person, and often it is necessary to have a witness who has identified a suspect from a photograph then view the suspect in a lineup to confirm the identification.

At a trial, testimony about a prior photographic identification should not be admissible during the prosecution's direct case. Courts have ruled that mentioning to a jury that the witness saw the defendant's photograph in a police mug shot file or database is prejudicial, as jurors are likely to assume that the photograph was available because the defendant had a criminal record.[9]

Courts have made exceptions and have allowed evidence of a prior photograph identification when the defendant has changed his or her appearance between the time of the identification and the trial and also when a defense counsel "opens the door" by challenging the suggestiveness of the photo array procedure.

In-court Identifications

During a criminal trial when a witness is asked to look around the courtroom and iden tify the person they saw committing the crime, the witness almost invariably points to the defendant sitting at the defense table. This identification is important evidence; however, the question often arises whether the witness is making the identification on the basis of observing the defendant at the time and place of the crime or, alternatively, on the basis of observing the defendant at a later time in person or in a photograph.

A witness who sees a photograph of a person and decides that the photograph is of the person who committed the crime absorbs the image of the photograph into his memory. Similarly, a witness who views and identifies a person at a show-up or lineup absorbs the appearance of that person into his memory.[10] Furthermore, "Once a witness has picked out the accused at the lineup, he is not likely to go back on his word later on, so that in practice the issue of identity may... for all practical purposes be determined there and then, before the trial."[11]

In circumstances in which the viewing of photographs, a show-up, or a lineup was conducted improperly, the witness may have been led to identify the wrong person. Such improper procedures will taint identifications, and a court might preclude the witness from making the in-court identification.

In making its decision, the court will balance any suggestiveness against other facts that support the reliability of the in-court identification, such as:

1. The witness's opportunity to view the criminal at the time of the crime.
2. The witness's degree of attention.
3. The accuracy of the witness's prior description of the criminal.
4. The level of certainty demonstrated by the witness at the confrontation.
5. The length of time between the crime and the confrontation.[12]

If a court rules that the in-court identification is reliable, it will admit the testimony and allow the jury to evaluate its credibility. If the court rules that the identification is unduly tainted by suggestibility, the testimony will be inadmissible, and the prosecution will have to prove its case through other evidence.

Bolstering In-court Testimony with Prior Identifications

Although a witness may not testify during the prosecution's direct case regarding a prior photograph identification of the defendant, a witness may testify to a prior corporeal show-up or lineup identification. These prior corporeal identifications bolster the witness's in-court identification of the defendant. The witness may testify that, on the basis of present recollection, the defendant is the person he observed on a first incriminating occasion. He may also testify that he observed the defendant on another occasion (show-up or lineup) and recognized him as the person he observed on the first or incriminating occasion.[13]

Problems arise when a witness who has made prior identifications is unable to identify the defendant in court. This often occurs when defendants have changed their appearance between the time of arrest and the trial or because the witness's memory has faded. To address this problem, some states have enacted statutes that abrogate hearsay rules and allow testimony from third persons, usually a police officer who conducted a show-up or a lineup, to establish that the witness identified the defendant at the show-up or lineup.[14] Consequently, to establish the defendant's identification as the person who committed the crime, the witness will testify that at a prior show-up or lineup he saw an individual and recognized him as the criminal, and a police officer will testify that at the show-up or lineup the witness promptly declared his recognition of the defendant as the criminal. Such testimony will constitute evidence sufficient to establish identification.

Right to Counsel at Lineups

A right to counsel does not exist at a show-up, the display of a photo array, or an investigative lineup.[15] A Sixth Amendment right to counsel, however, does exist at a post-arraignment or post-indictment lineup, and such a lineup cannot be held without the attorney present or without a waiver of the right.[16]

The presence of an attorney at a lineup helps the court to reconstruct the procedures that were employed and to determine whether they were in accordance with fairness and due process. Because a defendant who is compelled to stand in a lineup is not likely to be in a position or frame of mind to observe and remember actions that may have created unfair suggestibility, he must rely on his attorney to do so. The Supreme Court described the attorney's function in *United States v. Wade*, 388 U.S. 218 (1967):

> [T]he confrontation compelled by the State between the accused and the victim or witnesses to a crime to elicit identification evidence is peculiarly riddled with innumerable dangers and variable factors which might seriously, even crucially, derogate from a fair trial. The vagaries of eyewitness identification are well-known; the annals of criminal law are rife with instances of mistaken identification.... A major factor contributing to the high incidence of miscarriage of justice from mistaken identification has been the degree of suggestion inherent in the manner in which the prosecution presents the suspect to witnesses for pretrial identification.... Suggestion can be created intentionally or unintentionally in many subtle ways.... But as is the case with secret interrogations, there is serious difficulty in depicting what transpires at lineups and other forms of identification confrontations.... In any event, neither witnesses nor lineup participants are apt to be alert for conditions prejudicial to the suspect. And if they were, it would likely be of scant benefit to the suspect since neither witnesses nor lineup participants are likely to be schooled in the detection of suggestive influences.... Thus, in the present context, where so many variables and pitfalls exist, the first line of defense must be the prevention of unfairness and the lessening of the hazards of eyewitness identification at the lineup itself. The trial which might determine the accused's fate may well not be that in the courtroom but that at the pretrial confrontation, with the State aligned against the accused, the witness the sole jury, and the accused unprotected against the overreaching, intentional or unintentional, and with little or no effective appeal from the judgment there rendered by the witness—That's the man."

Because of the need for expeditious police investigation of serious crimes, courts have not mandated a right to counsel at pre-arraignment or pre-indictment investigative lineups. Nevertheless, when a suspect's attorney can be present without delay at an investigative lineup, he or she should be allowed to observe and make suggestions in the same manner as at a post-arraignment lineup.[17]

Confirmatory Identifications by Police Officers

When a suspect is arrested on the basis of observations by a police officer, lineups are not generally required unless a substantial period of time has elapsed between the observation of the suspect in connection with the crime and the arrest of the suspect. When one police officer has made an observation of the suspect during a crime and another police officer apprehends the suspect a short time later, a full lineup is not required, and a one-on-one confirmatory identification is allowable instead. Most often, this occurs when an undercover police officer buys unlawful drugs from a suspect and other backup officers arrest the suspect a short time after the "buy." Usually, the undercover officer, in order to keep his identity concealed, will surreptitiously view the suspect to confirm that the backup officers arrested the right suspect. In *People v. Wharton*, 74 N.Y.2d 921 (1989), the New York Court of Appeals allowed this type of identification, stating in that case:

> It is not disputed that the identification was made by a trained undercover officer who observed defendant during the face-to-face drug transaction knowing defendant would shortly be arrested. Thus, there is evidence in the record to support the determination of the courts below that the officer's observation of defendant at the station house approximately three hours later was not of a kind ordinarily burdened or compromised by forbidden suggestiveness, warranting a lineup procedure or *Wade* hearing. The viewing by this trained undercover narcotics officer occurred at a place and time sufficiently connected and contemporaneous to the arrest itself as to constitute the ordinary and proper completion of an integral police procedure. Additionally, as we have observed in this kind of situation, it lent assurance that an innocent person was not being detained by reason of a mistaken arrest. The undercover officer's participation in the criminal apprehension operation at issue was planned, and he was experienced and expected to observe carefully the defendant for purposes of later identification and for completion of his official duties.

The Court indicated that merely labeling an identification procedure as a "confirmatory" police identification would not automatically preclude the need for lineup. For example, when one police officer has made a brief or limited observation of a suspect in connection with a crime and another police officer apprehends the suspect a substantial time later at a different location, fairness dictates that the first officer should view the suspect in a lineup.

Corroboration

Common-law doctrines have long recognized that certain types of proof are inherently unreliable and, therefore, that corroborative evidence is required before a conviction will stand. At common law and current statutory law:

1. A conviction cannot be obtained solely upon a defendant's confession to a crime without corroborative evidence that such crime occurred.
2. A conviction cannot be obtained upon the testimony of an accomplice unsupported by corroborative evidence tending to connect the defendant with the commission of the crime.
3. A conviction cannot be obtained solely on the basis of unsworn testimony.

The law has not yet established a requirement that a conviction on the basis of a stranger-on-stranger identification must be supported by independent corroborating evidence against the defendant. Such a stringent rule would immunize a great number of criminals from conviction, because in many crimes the only available evidence is a visual identification. Nonetheless, in stranger identification cases, although not absolutely required, corroborative evidence should be sought. In such cases, without sufficient corroborative evidence, police and prosecutors should use extreme caution before proceeding with charges, and judges and juries should do the same before rendering a guilty verdict.

Sufficient corroboration might come from other independent witnesses or from incriminating statements or actions by the suspect. It might come from physical evidence found on the suspect or left by the suspect at the crime scene. Certainly, a robbery victim's wallet or credit card found on the person of a suspect is rather incriminating evidence that, if unexplained, would provide overwhelming corroboration of a visual identification. Unexplained bloodstains, later determined to be from the victim, found on the clothing of a suspect would be strong corroborating evidence. Other types of physical evidence (e.g., fingerprints, shoeprints, hair follicles, or clothing or rug fibers) either left at or taken from the crime scene might also provide the necessary corroboration of the suspect's identity.

Identifications without Eyewitnesses

In homicides or other crimes in which the victim is unable to identify the assailant, physical evidence may be the only means of identifying and convicting the perpetrator. When evidence such as fingerprints, DNA, blood, saliva, semen, hair, or bite marks are left by a suspect at a crime scene, the police might be able to identify the suspect through such evidence. If the suspect's fingerprints or DNA are already included in official databases, the police may be able to make the identification without confronting the suspect. If a match cannot be found in the databases, the police will have to obtain a sample of identifying material from the suspect to compare to the material found at the crime scene.

Self-incrimination by Physical Evidence

Can a suspect be compelled to give a sample of bodily material or demonstrate a physical characteristic for identification purposes? The answer is yes. But why does the Fifth Amendment right against self-incrimination *not* protect a suspect against such compulsion?

The Fifth Amendment protects against compelled testimony, disclosure of a person's own criminal activities, and communication of a person's thoughts. It does not protect against compelled disclosure of physical evidence, including the physical appearance and makeup of a suspect's body. If it did, a suspect could refuse to stand in a lineup or be fingerprinted. In 1910, in *Holt v. United States*, 218 U.S. 245, the Supreme Court declared:

> The prohibition of compelling a man in a criminal court to be a witness against himself is a prohibition of the use of physical and moral compulsion to extort communication from him, not an exclusion of his body as evidence when it may be material.

In the seminal case of *Schmerber v. California*, 384 U.S. 757 (1966), the Supreme Court reinforced the distinction between testimonial and physical evidence. In *Schmerber*, the defendant was arrested and taken to hospital after an automobile accident. At the hospital, a police officer directed the hospital physician to take a blood sample from the defendant in order to ascertain his blood alcohol level. The blood was extracted and the evidence used in court to convict the defendant of driving under the influence of alcohol. On appeal, the defendant asserted that taking the blood without his consent violated his Fourth Amendment privacy rights, the warrant requirement, and his Fifth Amendment right against self-incrimination.

In upholding the conviction, the Court dismissed the Fourth Amendment claims, stating that because alcohol in blood dissipates rapidly there was no time to secure a search warrant and under the exigent circumstances exception it was reasonable to have a physician draw the blood.

The Court also dismissed the Fifth Amendment claim, stating:

> We hold that the privilege protects an accused only from being compelled to testify against himself, or otherwise provide the state with evidence of a *testimonial* or *communicative* nature, and that the withdrawal of blood and use of analysis in question in this case did not involve compulsion to these ends.

Schmerber involved the seizure of a suspect to recover evidence of a crime (alcohol in the defendant's blood). In addition, the *Schmerber* principle—seizing physical evidence does not violate the Fifth Amendment—has been applied to the seizure of other identification material, such as drawing a defendant's blood to match his DNA with DNA found at a crime scene.

The legal justification for compelling a suspect to provide identification material need not be as stringent as the legal requirements of probable cause to arrest or seize evidence. When law enforcement has a reasonable basis for a legitimate investigative inquiry, a person may be compelled to stand in a lineup; to submit to photographs, fingerprints, and measurements; and to give blood, hair, handwriting, and voice samples. The police may use reasonable physical force to fingerprint and photograph a person who is under arrest. When the person offers unusual resistance or refuses to provide samples, a court order may be obtained. A court order may also be required to obtain samples by more intrusive means, such as taking x-rays or taking body tissue or fluids for forensic analysis, and if the person refuses to comply with the court order the court may hold him in contempt.

Identification evidence can be obtained at any stage of a criminal prosecution, even during a trial. In the O.J. Simpson criminal trial, the judge ordered Simpson to try on a bloody glove that was found at the murder scene. Had he refused, he could have been held in contempt and his refusal could have been used to draw an adverse inference of guilt against him. Simpson tried it on, and the glove did not fit (perhaps because he tried to put it on over a surgical glove). In any event, the principle was demonstrated that suspects may lawfully be compelled to present their physical characteristics for identification purposes.

In *United States v. Dionisio*, 410 U.S. 1 (1973), law enforcement officers obtained wiretap evidence of illicit transactions during an investigation of an illegal gambling ring. To match the voices recorded by the wiretaps with the voices of the suspects under investigation, a grand jury subpoenaed 20 persons, including the defendant, to give voice exemplars. The defendant refused to comply with the subpoena, claiming that to compel him to provide the exemplar would violate his Fifth Amendment right against self-incrimination. The Supreme Court disagreed and ruled that he must comply because the evidence sought was not testimonial or communicative but merely a physical characteristic. The spoken words sought from the defendant were not wanted for their content, but for a spectrograph analysis of the voice timbre. Matching the defendant's voice with a voice recorded on the wiretap provided a positive identification.

Handwriting analysis by a qualified expert has been deemed the equivalent of fingerprints and photographs for the purposes of identifying a suspect. As an Oregon court noted, "It seems now to be a well accepted fact that handwriting is almost as individualistic and identifying as are fingerprints,"[18] and courts have allowed local police investigators, the Internal Revenue Service, and grand juries to compel suspects to submit handwriting samples.[19] In *Gilbert v. California*, 388 U.S. 263 (1967), the Supreme Court held that a suspect could be compelled to provide handwriting samples even though to do so would incriminate him. The Court explained that handwriting patterns are not testimony but are physical characteristics. In addition, suspects can be compelled to repeat the writing sample numerous times in order to counteract deception.

Suspects might disguise their handwriting for a time, but good investigative techniques can uncover the deception. To obtain a valid identification, handwriting experts or investigators taking a writing sample should employ the following techniques:

1. Provide the suspect with the same type of paper and writing instrument as used for the writing in question.
2. Direct the suspect to use the same writing style, whether print or script, that was used in the writing in question and to write the same words and execute the same signature.
3. Remove each page of the writing from the suspect's sight as soon as it is completed.
4. If the writing in question is short (e.g., a forged check), have the suspect repeat it 10 to 20 times.
5. If the writing in question is long, dictate the entire text to the suspect word for word and obtain at least three full copies.
6. Have the suspect speed up, slow down, or alter the slant of the writing.
7. Have the suspect provide a sample with the other hand.
8. Obtain unrelated samples of the suspect's writing to compare to the samples provided.

Bite marks can also be used to identify a suspect. Like handwriting, adult human teeth patterns are unique. Combinations of factors in the form and arrangement of teeth can identify an individual's bite mark.[20] A suspect will sometimes leave a bite mark on an object at a crime scene, such as a piece of food or a Styrofoam or plastic cup, which might later be used to prove his presence at the crime scene. In violent rape and murder cases, it is not uncommon for the criminal to have bitten the victim, and crime scene technicians will photograph the bite mark for later comparison with the dental records of a suspect.

When useful dental records are not available, courts can compel suspects to submit to dental examinations and to provide impressions. The infamous serial killer Ted Bundy, who was suspected of more than 100 murders of young women across the country, was compelled by court order to provide a dental impression in connection with the investigation of two murders in Florida. Bite marks on one of the victims were positively matched to Bundy. He was convicted of the murders and executed. A problem for investigators occurs when a suspect who is not in custody refuses to consent to an immediate dental examination. When this occurs, a detective may obtain a subpoena, but the suspect would then have time to alter his teeth before the examination. The better strategy for an investigator is to surprise the suspect with a search warrant that includes a court order for him to submit to the examination.

When a suspect refuses or physically resists efforts to obtain identification evidence, the police may use reasonable force to attempt to secure the evidence. At trial, a defendant's refusal and resistance can be used as evidence against him from which a jury may draw an adverse inference regarding the suspect's guilt.

The state's ability to forcibly extract evidence from a suspect is not unlimited. In *Winston v. Lee*, 470 U.S. 753 (1985), the prosecutor sought a court order to compel a robbery suspect to undergo surgery to remove a bullet lodged in his collarbone. In that case, Ralph Watkinson was closing his shop for the night.

> As he was locking the door, he observed someone armed with a gun coming toward him from across the street. Watkinson was also armed, and when he drew his gun the other person told him to freeze. Watkinson then fired at the other person, who returned his fire. Watkinson was hit in the legs, while the other individual, who appeared to be wounded in his left side, ran from the scene.... Approximately 20 minutes later, police officers responding to another call found respondent eight blocks from where the earlier shooting occurred. Respondent was suffering from a gunshot wound to his left chest area.

The police arrested the respondent, Lee, and sought the court order to extract the bullet, which would prove that Lee was the robber who had shot Watkinson. After several hearings and court rulings that weighed the risks of the surgery against the benefits of obtaining the evidence, the Supreme Court ultimately decided against allowing the surgery:

> In weighing the various factors in this case, we therefore reach the same conclusions as the courts below. The operation sought will intrude substantially on respondent's protected interests. The medical risks of the operation, although apparently not extremely severe, are a subject of considerable dispute; the very uncertainty militates against finding the operation to be "reasonable." In addition, the intrusion on respondent's privacy interests entailed by the operation can only be characterized as severe. On the other hand, although the bullet may turn out to be useful to the Commonwealth in prosecuting respondent, the Commonwealth has failed to demonstrate a compelling need for it. We believe that in these circumstances the Commonwealth has failed to demonstrate that it would be "reasonable" under the terms of the Fourth Amendment to search for evidence of this crime by means of the contemplated surgery.

The Court did not reach Lee's Fifth Amendment self-incrimination claim because it resolved the case under the Fourth Amendment's reasonable standard, and the safety concerns took precedence. If the bullet could have been removed without risk, the Court could have compelled the defendant to undergo surgery for its removal. In weighing the risks of surgery against the benefit of obtaining the evidence, the Court implied that it was not a necessity to obtain the bullet because other evidence was available to convict the defendant. The Court did not indicate what its ruling would have been had the bullet been the only available evidence.

Problem

The owner of a jewelry store, Stan Goldman, and his assistant manager, Joyce Garnett, were getting ready to close the store when two men wearing baseball caps and dark sunglasses entered the store. One of the men was about 6 feet, 2 inches tall. He put a gun to Goldman's temple and ordered him to open the safe. The other man, who was of average height and had a mustache, grabbed Garnett from behind, placed a knife to her throat, and told her not to move or say anything.

Goldman opened the safe. Then, as the taller robber reached inside, Goldman produced a gun that had been hidden under the safe and began firing. The robber fired back and a bullet struck Goldman in the head, killing him. Garnett bit the other robber's hand, and she managed to get away and run into the back room as the robbers fled from the store. She immediately called 911.

Detective Able and other police officers responded to the store and obtained a description of the robbers from Garnett. Then, while investigating the crime scene, they received a call that a man with bullet wounds was in the emergency room of a nearby hospital. Detective Able went to the hospital where he was informed that the wounded patient, Larry Smith, was in a critical condition, with one bullet lodged near his spine and another bullet lodged near his elbow.

A nurse pointed to a man in the waiting room and told Detective Able that this man had brought the wounded man into the emergency room. The man in the waiting room was about 5 feet, 9 inches in height and had a mustache. When he began to leave, Detective Able stopped, questioned, and frisked him. He did not discover any weapons. The man identified himself as John Dunkel. He denied knowing or bringing the wounded man into the emergency room but could not give an explanation for his own presence.

Within five minutes of Detective Able's arrival, other detectives brought Garnett to the hospital for a show-up. She said that Dunkel fit the description of the man who had grabbed her, but she had not gotten a good look at his face and could not positively identify him.

Garnett was then brought to the bedside of Mr. Smith. After she was told that he had been shot, she positively identified him as the robber with the gun who had shot the storeowner. Smith was arrested and a police officer was assigned to guard him while he was in the hospital. Smith refused to consent to an operation to remove the bullets.

As Detective Able continued to question Dunkel, he noticed a bite mark on his wrist. Able asked Dunkel to accompany him to the police station so he could take a photograph of the bite mark, but Dunkel refused. Able then arrested Dunkel and took him to the police station, where three detectives had to hold Dunkel down while photographs were taken of the bite mark.

Able conferred with Assistant District Attorney Smart, who had been assigned to the case. Smart was concerned about the legality of the arrest and the forcible taking of photographs. He obtained a court order directing Dunkel to submit to additional photographs. These were taken the following day when the bite marks had darkened and were more visible.

Smart was also concerned about the legality of the hospital bedside identification of Smith. To improve the case, he applied for a court order mandating that Smith submit to surgery to remove the bullets so they could be matched to Goldman's gun and used to identify Smith as the robber.

During pretrial hearings, a forensics expert testified that he had examined the photographs of the bite mark on Dunkel's wrist and matched them against dental records of Garnett. He concluded that the bite mark was made by Garnett's teeth.

The defense attorney contended that, because Dunkel had not been positively identified, there was no probable cause for the arrest. On that basis, he moved to preclude the expert's testimony and to suppress the two sets of photographs as they were forcibly taken during an unlawful arrest of Dunkel.

The defense attorney further moved to suppress the hospital bedside identification of Smith as overly suggestive because Garnett had been told of the gunshot wounds. He also contended that, because no emergency existed, the police should have waited until Smith's release from the hospital to conduct a proper lineup. In addition, he asked the judge to preclude any in-court identification of Smith by Garnett, as that identification would be the tainted product of the improper hospital identification.

The defense attorney also filed a motion in opposition to the district attorney's request for a court order requiring Smith to submit to surgery to remove the two bullets. The defense claimed that the surgery would create an unreasonable risk to the defendant and, therefore, would be a violation of his substantive due process rights.

Questions

1. Should the court suppress Garnett's hospital identification of Smith as too suggestive?
2. If the court decided that Garnett's hospital bedside identification of Smith was too suggestive, should the court preclude Garnett from making an in-court identification of Smith during the trial?
3. Should the court order Smith to submit to the surgery, either for one bullet or for both?
4. If the court suppressed Garnett's identification of Smith, should that influence the court's decision whether to order Smith to submit to surgery?
5. Was it lawful for Detective Able to stop, question, and frisk Dunkel?
6. Was the show-up, in which Garnett viewed Dunkel at the hospital, a violation of the latter's due process rights?
7. Was it lawful for Detective Able to arrest and forcibly take photographs of Dunkel?
8. Assuming the court ruled that the arrest and seizure of Dunkel were unlawful, should the court preclude the forensics expert from testifying about the bite mark evidence?
9. If the court ruled that the police took the first set of bite mark photographs illegally, could it, nevertheless, admit the second set of photographs into evidence?
10. Should the court allow Garnett to make an in-court identification of Dunkel even though at the hospital she had said that she could not positively identify him?
11. Should the court allow Garnett to testify about the general description of her assailant?
12. Assuming that Garnett could not positively identify either Smith or Dunkel at their trial, could the jury still convict them?

Notes

1 Cutler, Brian and Penrod, Steven, *Mistaken Identification: The Eyewitness, Psychology, and the Law*, Cambridge University Press, New York, 1995.
2 *Stovall v. Denno*, 388 U.S. 293 (1967); *Neil v. Biggers*, 409 U.S. 188 (1973).
3 *People v. Rodriguez*, 79 N.Y.2d 445 (1992).
4 *Gilbert v. California*, 388 U.S. 263 (1967).
5 National Institute of Justice, *Eyewitness Evidence: A Guide for Law Enforcement*, U.S. Department of Justice, Washington, D.C., 1999.
6 See *Stovall v. Denno*, 388 U.S. 293 (1967); *People v. Hicks*, 68 N.Y.2d 234 (1986).
7 *People v. Riley*, 70 N.Y.2d 573 (1987).
8 *Holland v. Maryland*, 122 Md. App. 532; 713 A.2d 364 (1998).
9 *People v. Grajales*, 8 N.Y.3d 861 (2007); *People v. Caserta*, 19 N.Y.2d 18 (1966).
10 Mayer, Connie, Due process challenges to eyewitness identifications based on pretrial photographic arrays, *Pace Law Review*, 13, 825, 1994.
11 Williams, Glanville and Hammelmann, H.A., Identification parades, Part I, *Criminal Law Review*, 479, 482, 1963.
12 *Neil v. Biggers*, 409 U.S. 188 (1973).
13 Federal Rules of Evidence, Rule 801(d)(1)(c); California Evidence Code § 1238; New York Criminal Procedure, Article 60.30; New Jersey Evidence Rule 63(1)(c).
14 New York Criminal Procedure, Article 60.25.
15 *Kirby v. Illinois*, 406 U.S. 682 (1972).
16 *United States v. Wade*, 388 U.S. 218 (1967).

17 Some states grant rights more extensive than the U.S. Constitution requires by providing a right to counsel before arraignment or indictment but after an accusatory instrument has been filed, such as an affidavit for an arrest warrant: *People v. Hawkins*, 55 N.Y.2d 474 (1982). In such a case, a defendant's right to counsel has already attached when he is arrested under the warrant. Therefore, if the police question him or place him in a lineup, he would have the right to the presence of his attorney. Conversely, a defendant arrested without a warrant would not have an automatic right to the presence of an attorney at a lineup between the time of his arrest and his arraignment.

18 *State v. Fisher*, 242 Or. 419 (1966).

19 *United States v. Mara*, 410 U.S. 19 (1973); *Trimble v. Hudman*, 291 Minn. 442 (1971); *United States v. Euge*, 444 U.S. 707 (1980).

20 *ABFO Bitemark Guidelines*, American Board of Forensic Odontology, Colorado Springs, CO, 2009.

References

Cupp v. Murphy, 412 U.S. 291 (1973).
Gilbert v. California, 388 U.S. 263 (1967).
Kirby v. Illinois, 406 U.S. 682 (1972).
Neil v. Biggers, 409 U.S. 188 (1973).
People v. Hicks, 68 N.Y.2d 234 (1986).
Schmerber v. California, 384 U.S. 757 (1966).
Stovall v. Denno, 388 U.S. 293 (1967).
United States v. Wade, 388 U.S. 218 (1967).

Chapter 20

The Right of Confrontation

The right of defendants to confront their accusers is exercised through cross-examination of witnesses, whether the witnesses are accusatory or neutral. Cross-examination is the principal means by which the defendant's attorney challenges the reliability and credibility of the prosecution's witnesses, and the cross-examiner is permitted to explore and test the perception, memory, bias, interest, and credibility of the witnesses. To impeach the credibility of a witness, the examining attorney may use the following methods:

1. Showing that the witness has been convicted of a crime.
2. Questioning the witness about his or her prior immoral, vicious, or criminal acts that tend to show that the witness is not worthy of belief.
3. Showing that the witness is biased for or against a party.
4. Showing that the witness has made prior statements inconsistent or contradictory to his or her current testimony.
5. Showing the witness' bad reputation for truth and veracity.

The attorney may attempt to introduce such evidence through cross-examination or by presenting extrinsic evidence through other witnesses.

Hearsay

In a criminal trial, a problematic issue for all parties and the court is the reconciliation of the traditional hearsay rules and exceptions with the defendant's right to confront witnesses. Hearsay is a contraction of the old English phrase, "I heard it said." By legal definition, hearsay is a statement that was made outside of court that is offered in court for the truth of its content. For example, if a police officer takes the witness stand to testify that an alleged crime victim told him that the defendant had robbed him, the officer would not be able to so testify because the statement was made out of court and is being introduced for the truth of its content. The crime victim is the person who should take the witness stand to testify against the defendant.

The Federal Rules of Evidence define hearsay as follows:

Hearsay is a statement, other than one made by the declarant while testifying at the trial or hearing, offered in evidence to prove the truth of the matter asserted.[1]

DOI: 10.4324/9781003415091-24

The declarant is the person who made the statement outside of court. Even if the declarant takes the witness stand, he or she may not testify to his or her own out-of-court hearsay statements.

The law deems hearsay incompetent and refuses to admit hearsay for the following reasons:

1. No ability for the judge or jury to observe the declarer's demeanor when he or she spoke.
2. No ability to test the declarer's perception, memory, sincerity, or communication skills.
3. No ability to cross-examine the declarer.
4. Declarer not being under oath.

Non-hearsay

The hearsay rule does not mean that witnesses cannot testify to anything that other persons have said. It is only when the purpose of the testimony is to establish the truth of the content of the other person's statement that the issue comes into play. When the statement is offered for other purposes, such as to prove the speaker's state of mind, it is not hearsay and it is admissible. For example, a witness may testify that he heard the speaker say, "I am Napoleon Bonaparte." The statement is admitted not for the truth of its content but to show that the speaker was mentally deranged.

Courtroom testimony overwhelmingly involves testimony about out-of-court statements that are introduced for purposes other than the truth of their content. Such statements are classified as non-hearsay and may include:

1. Words of legal significance, such as:
   Slander
   Libel
   Contract (offer/acceptance)
   Guarantee
   Criminal threats (robbery, extortion, harassment)
   Fraud
   Misrepresentation
2. Circumstantial evidence of the state of mind of the declarer, such as:
   Malice
   Hatred
   Love
   Premeditation
   Motive
   Fear
   Affection
3. Statements about the state of mind of the hearer to establish:
   Knowledge
   Notice
   Self-defense against aggressor
4. Statements about the insanity of the speaker
5. Prior inconsistent statements for impeachment of credibility
6. Statements made by co-conspirators in furtherance of the conspiracy[2]

An example of an admissible out-of-court statement for the purposes of establishing a defendant's state of mind or motive to commit murder would be his statement prior to the murder, "My wife is cheating with Joe." Such a statement would be admissible, not to prove that the wife was actually cheating but for evidence of the defendant's motive to kill Joe.

A convenient method of ascertaining whether an out-of-court statement is hearsay or non-hearsay is to identify it by its grammar. The basic types of sentences are:

1. Declarative (assertion).
2. Interrogative (question).
3. Imperative (command).
4. Subjunctive (conditional).

Hearsay must be an assertion of fact for the truth of its content and generally must be a declarative sentence, such as "John threw the rock." Hearsay generally cannot be interrogative (e.g., "What time is it?"); imperative (e.g., "Put your hands up or I'll shoot"); or subjunctive (e.g., "I think I'll go to the movies later").

Hearsay Exceptions

The general hearsay rule has many exceptions that allow certain types of hearsay statements into evidence for practical necessity and because they have an inherent reliability or a circumstantial guarantee of trustworthiness. The terminology used to describe these admissible statements is not uniform; the Federal Rules of Evidence labels many such statements as non-hearsay, while many courts refer to the same statements as exceptions. Most of these exceptions have been in existence for centuries and predate the Sixth Amendment confrontation clause. Nevertheless, courts have ruled that because the exceptions continued in use after ratification of the Constitution the Framers did not intend to abrogate them, and in most cases these exceptions do not violate the confrontation clause. One argument in support of the continued use of the exceptions is that the in-court testifying witness can be cross-examined, thereby satisfying the confrontation clause.

Dying Declarations

An early hearsay exception is the dying declaration, which has a long history dating back to the Middle Ages. When the victim of a fatal assault who is on the verge of death states who inflicted the wound, the out-of-court statement is admissible in court for the truth of its content. As a practical matter, without the admission of dying declarations many murders would be difficult to prove, because the only persons present during the crime might have been the victim and the murderer.

Dying declarations originated during the deeply religious medieval period, when people believed that upon death a person went to either heaven or hell. If one lied on his deathbed, he would go to hell. For that reason, dying declarations were deemed reliable and trustworthy. The predicate for a dying declaration was that the declarant must have known he was going to die, knew his death was imminent, and had no hope of recovery.

Dying declarations can be used to implicate only the murderer. They cannot be used as a confession of the victim to their own crimes and cannot be used to exonerate other persons of their crimes.

Confessions

Out-of-court confessions are admissible for the same reasons of practicality, inherent reliability, and trustworthiness. Confessions are direct acknowledgements of guilt, and people do not ordinarily confess to crimes that they did not commit because, as a general rule, self-interest prevents them from doing so.

Sometimes people confess in open court, but that is not hearsay because they testify to what they did and saw. A hearsay confession occurs when a defendant confesses outside of court to another person or a police officer, then during trial remains silent or denies that he confessed. At the trial, the person who heard the confession may testify to the out-of-court statement for the truth of its content—that is the confession exception.

There are noted differences between a deathbed statement in which the dying person confesses to a crime and an admissible out-of-court confession. The dying person who states that he committed a certain crime will suffer no adverse penal, financial, or other punishments for the statement, whereas a person who expects to live, yet confesses, may suffer adverse consequences. The dying person may falsely take the blame for a crime in order to exonerate a friend or relative who has committed or may be accused of the crime. While occasionally a person who expects to live may falsely take the blame for a crime to exonerate another, this is a rarity and, furthermore, the person's confession and its credibility can be more thoroughly challenged through investigation and the adversarial process.

A person's hearsay confession can be used as evidence only against the confessor; it cannot be used against others. For example, if co-defendants are tried together and one confessed to the police while the other did not, the first defendant's confession is only admissible against him. It is not admissible against the second defendant.

In *Bruton v. United States*, 391 U.S. 123 (1968), the U.S. Supreme Court held that, in a joint trial of two defendants with only one jury, allowing the jury to hear one defendant's out-of-court confession was too prejudicial against the other defendant who did not confess. Furthermore, merely instructing the jury to disregard the first defendant's confession as it pertained to the second defendant was not sufficient to mitigate the prejudice. To handle such a situation appropriately, the defendants would have to be tried separately or one trial could be held, but it would have two juries—one for each defendant. In a joint trial, before the confession of the first defendant was introduced, the jury for the second defendant would leave the court.

Admissions

An admission is not a direct acknowledgement of guilt but a statement that is inconsistent with or adverse to the defendant's position at trial. For example, during a trial, a defendant might offer an alibi that he or she was out of town when the crime occurred. However, if the defendant had told a friend that he or she was, in fact, in town and in the vicinity of the crime, the defendant has made an admission, and the friend may testify to the defendant's out-of-court statement for the truth of its content. The admission is not direct evidence of guilt, but it is relevant evidence that can be used to build a circumstantial evidence case of guilt. In co-defendant joint trials, one defendant's admissions can be introduced into evidence. Because an admission is not as directly damaging as a confession, a separate trial or jury is not required. Any potential prejudice to the co-defendant may be mitigated by an instruction to the jury to apply it only to the defendant who made the statement.

Excited Utterances and Spontaneous Statements

Statements made by persons during or immediately after a startling event or a serious injury may be admissible as a hearsay exception. Such statements are deemed reliable and trustworthy because the declarant was under the stress of excitement caused by the event and had no time to reflect and possibly fabricate a story. Consequently, a person who heard the statement may testify to the out-of-court statement for the truth of its content. For example, if immediately after a car accident, the driver exits the car and shouts, "I'm sorry, I wasn't looking," that statement would be admissible to prove the driver's liability. The following are other examples:

- Statements of witnesses or victims made during or immediately after shootings, stabbings, or other sudden violent occurrences
- Statements made during calls to 911 and other telephone calls where the caller was speaking under the stress of danger or excitement
- Statements made by rape or domestic violence victims immediately after the crime

The classic example of a spontaneous statement occurred in *People v. Del Vermo*, 192 N.Y. 470 (1908). In that case, three young men, including the defendant Del Vermo, were walking abreast of each other. One of the young men, Page, was teasing Del Vermo about his wife when suddenly he fell to the ground. The other young man had not seen what happened, but when he asked Page what happened, Page replied, "Del Vermo stabbed me."

Page died, but there was no direct evidence against Del Vermo; therefore, the prosecution introduced Page's last statement as evidence, and Del Vermo was convicted. He appealed the trial court's admission of the statement, claiming that there was no indication that Page was excited when he made the statement, and his statement was not a dying declaration because there was no evidence he knew was going to die. However, the court ruled that it was a spontaneous statement made without time to fabricate an answer and ruled that it was admissible, stating, "What the law distrusts is not after-speech, but after thought."

Sometimes a higher value is placed on out-of-court excited utterances than on in-court testimony. In *People v. Fratello*, 92 N.Y.2d 565 (1998), the defendant, Frank Fratello, was charged with attempted murder and other crimes arising out of the shooting of Guy Peduto during a car chase. Peduto received serious head and body wounds, and after he was shot he lost control of his vehicle and crashed into two parked cars. Less than a minute after the crash and while lying in his vehicle and suffering from bullet wounds, Peduto told a good Samaritan that Fratello shot him. He also told a responding police officer that Fratello shot him.

Apparently, between the shooting and Fratello's trial, Peduto and Fratello resolved their differences, and at the trial Peduto refused to testify for the prosecution against Fratello. When Fratello called Peduto to testify for the defense, Peduto testified that he did not know who shot him. To contradict this testimony, the prosecution called the good Samaritan and the police officer to testify to Peduto's out-of-court statements, which were admitted as excited utterances. The jury convicted Fratello, obviously believing the reliability of the excited utterances more than Peduto's in-court testimony.

The trial judge is the gatekeeper who determines what evidence shall be admissible, and often the proper decision is a matter of discretion and judgment made on the basis of the facts and circumstances of the particular case. Issues pertaining to hearsay arise in almost all trials, and appellate courts give great deference to trial court decisions.

Generally, appellate courts will not reverse a verdict unless the trial judge's ruling was an abuse of discretion.[3]

Other hearsay exceptions include:

- Business records
- Past recollection recorded
- Reputation evidence
- Present sense impressions
- Statements of personal and family history
- Prior testimony
- Declarations against interest

The above list is not all-inclusive.[4]

Prior Inconsistent Statements

Prior inconsistent statements are non-hearsay. Although they are out-of-court statements, they are not admissible for the truth of their content but only to impeach the credibility of the witness. Moreover, the prior statement need not be relevant to the primary trial question in controversy. For example, a witness may testify that he was within 10 feet of a crime when it was committed and clearly saw everything that happened. The witness can then be confronted with a prior statement in which he said that he was about 50 feet from the crime. The jury does not have to decide whether 10 feet or 50 feet was more accurate, because under the premise that when a person gives two or more inconsistent accounts he is not credible, that witness's testimony may be disregarded.

To be clear, there is no equivalency between prior inconsistent and prior consistent statements. As a general rule, prior consistent statements are not admissible to bolster a witness's credibility. The exception occurs when a witness gives testimony and then is accused of the recent fabrication of that testimony. An example might be as follows: A complaining witness on April 1 reports to the police that on February 1 she was raped by Larry. At Larry's trial, she testifies consistently with her report. In defense, Larry's attorney introduces evidence implying that Larry had been the complainant's boyfriend, but he broke up with her on Valentines' Day, February 14. The attorney implies that the complainant made the false rape charge to get even with him. Under these circumstances, the prosecutor in rebuttal could introduce testimony that immediately after it happened the complainant had told her girlfriend that Larry had raped her. Although this prior consistent statement is hearsay, it would be admissible as an exception in order to contradict the allegation that the complainant recently fabricated the rape charge.

Defendant's Prior Inconsistent Statements

Quite often in criminal procedure and evidence law, two competing policy interests conflict, and eventually the conflict must be resolved by the Supreme Court. Many courts have faced the dilemma of protecting defendants' right to counsel or *Miranda* rights while having to allow vigorous cross-examination of defendants who take the witness stand.

Cross-examination has been called the greatest single engine for the ascertainment of truth, and a major instrument of cross-examination is to confront witnesses with their prior inconsistent statements. Doing so has the dual effect of placing stress on the witness while showing the jury that the witness has given different accounts of the same incident or subject matter. However, when the witnesses are defendants who gave prior inconsistent statements that were taken in violation of *Miranda* or their right to counsel, a conflict exists between the policy of excluding such statements from evidence and allowing their use to impeach credibility.

The Supreme Court has addressed aspects of this dilemma several times during the last four decades. In *Harris v. New York*, 401 U.S. 222 (1971), the defendant had given an un-Mirandized incriminating statement to the police in which he admitted some involvement in narcotics dealing. While that statement could not be used against the defendant during the prosecution's direct case because of the *Miranda* violation, when the defendant chose to testify and told a contradictory story in which he denied any involvement in narcotics, the prosecution was allowed to cross-examine him and to impeach his credibility by using the prior un-Mirandized inconsistent and incriminatory statement. The Supreme Court stated:

> The impeachment process here undoubtedly provided valuable aid to the jury in assessing petitioner's credibility, and the benefits of this process should not be lost, in our view, because of the speculative possibility that impermissible police conduct will be encouraged thereby. Assuming that the exclusionary rule has a deterrent effect on proscribed police conduct, sufficient deterrence flows when the evidence in question is made unavailable to the prosecution in its case in chief.
>
> Every criminal defendant is privileged to testify in his own defense, or to refuse to do so. But that privilege cannot be construed to include the right to commit perjury.... Having voluntarily taken the stand, petitioner was under an obligation to speak truthfully and accurately, and the prosecution here did no more than utilize the traditional truth-testing devices of the adversary process.

In *Oregon v. Hass*, 420 U.S. 714 (1975), the Court reached a similar result. In *Hass*, the defendant had been advised on his rights. He asked for counsel but was questioned nevertheless. He made incriminating statements that were suppressed for use during the prosecution's direct case, but the defendant took the witness stand and his prior inconsistent statement, though taken in violation of his Fifth Amendment right to counsel, was admissible to impeach him. The Court stated that "inadmissibility would pervert the constitutional right into a right to falsify."

In *United States v. Havens*, 446 U.S. 620 (1980), a testifying defendant was allowed to be impeached on cross-examination by the admission of physical evidence that had been suppressed because of a Fourth Amendment search and seizure violation. The Court stated:

> In terms of impeaching a defendant's seemingly false statements with his prior inconsistent utterances or with other reliable evidence available to the government, we see no difference of constitutional magnitude between the defendant's statements on direct examination and his answers to questions put to him on cross-examination that are plainly within the scope of the defendant's direct examination.

The Court's ruling that a defendant's direct testimony and his cross-examination testimony are subject to the same impeachment rules prevents a defendant from limiting the prosecution to impeachment only on subject matter the defendant brought out on direct examination. If the prosecutor, on cross-examination, can elicit a false statement from the defendant, the prosecutor can then introduce evidence to contradict the statement.

In *Kansas v. Ventris*, 129 S.Ct. 1841, decided April 29, 2009, the Court built upon the impeachment exception for statements obtained in violation of *Miranda* warnings and extended the exception to statements obtained in violation of the *Massiah* Sixth Amendment right to counsel. In *Ventris*, Donnie Ray Ventris and Rhonda Theel entered the home of Ernest Hicks. One or both of the pair shot and killed Hicks. They also stole his truck, approximately $300 in cash, and his cell phone. After they were arrested and charged with the murder and robbery, Theel agreed to testify against Ventris. In exchange for reduced charges, she agreed to identify him as the shooter.

While Ventris was in jail awaiting trial, the police planted an informant in his cell. They instructed the informant to "keep his ears open and listen" for incriminating statements. According to the informant, in response to his statement that Ventris appeared to have "something more serious weighing in on his mind," Ventris divulged that he had shot a man and taken his keys, his wallet, about $350, and a vehicle.

At the trial, the prosecution conceded that Ventris' statement was obtained in violation of *Massiah* and it was not introduced during the prosecution's direct case; however, when Ventris took the stand and blamed the robbery and shooting entirely on Theel, the prosecution called the informant to testify to Ventris' prior contradictory statement in which he admitted to the shooting. The purpose of the informant's testimony was to impeach Ventris' credibility.

Ventris was not convicted of the murder, but he was convicted of burglary and robbery. He appealed those convictions on the grounds that the informant's statement should have been suppressed completely for all purposes. The Kansas Supreme Court agreed and reversed the convictions, because "once a criminal prosecution has commenced, the defendant's statements made to an undercover informant surreptitiously acting as an agent for the State are not admissible at trial for any reason, including impeachment of the defendant's testimony."

The Supreme Court, in a seven-to-two decision, reversed the Kansas Supreme Court, unequivocally ruling that such statements may indeed be used for impeachment purposes. The Court reiterated several of its prior pronouncements, quoting that "it is one thing to say that the Government cannot make an affirmative use of evidence unlawfully obtained. It is quite another to say that the defendant can turn the illegal method by which evidence in the Government's possession was obtained to his own advantage and provide himself with a shield against contradiction of his untruths."[5] Simply, a defendant cannot use the exclusionary rule as a license to commit perjury.

Ventris has apparently simplified the impeachment exception by eliminating the distinctions between statements obtained in violation of *Miranda* and those taken in violation of *Massiah*, and it has reaffirmed the Court's position that the introduction of illegally obtained evidence during a trial is not absolutely barred by the Constitution, particularly when barring the evidence would not provide a substantial deterrent to police misconduct. The Court's seven-to-two adoption of the impeachment exception establishes that the truth-seeking process is more important than the exclusionary rule.

Nonetheless, it is important to note that involuntary statements may not be used for any purpose, including impeachment. This black-letter law was established in *New Jersey v. Portash*, 440 U.S. 450 (1979), and *Mincey v. Arizona*, 437 U.S. 385 (1978). Therefore, even when a defendant waives the right to remain silent or the right to have an attorney present but the defendant is coerced or inappropriately manipulated to give an involuntary statement, such statement cannot be used even for impeachment, as it has no evidentiary value.

Prior Testimony

The prior testimony hearsay exception has been allowed for reasons of practicality, reli ability, and trustworthiness. When a witness who has given testimony under oath in a prior proceeding and was subjected to cross-examination is unavailable to testify at a current trial, the prior testimony may be read into the record. The unavailability must be for a sub- stantial reason, such as:

* Death
* Disease or injury
* Distance (out of the jurisdiction)
* Detained in prison (out of jurisdiction)
* Declined to testify under the Fifth Amendment privilege
* Deterred by threats

If the criteria are met, the prior testimony may be admitted for the truth of its content; however, the cross-examination or the opportunity for cross-examination during the prior testimony must have been meaningful. In *Pointer v. Texas*, 380 U.S. 400 (1965), a witness had testified at a preliminary hearing against a defendant who had been charged with rob- bery. The defendant was 18 years old and did not have an attorney. Although he tried to conduct some cross-examination of witnesses during the hearing, he was ill equipped to do so. Later, at the defendant's trial, the primary witness was unavailable because he had moved to California; consequently, the prosecutor introduced the witness's prior testimony into the record.

Pointer was convicted and appealed. The Supreme Court reversed the conviction, ruling that the Sixth Amendment confrontation clause applied to the states through the Fourteenth Amendment. The Court ruled that the opportunity for cross-examination of the prior testi- mony was not meaningful and did not meet constitutional standards.

Declarations against Interest

A declaration against interest is a statement made by a third party that may be relevant evidence either against a defendant or in favor of a defendant. The rules for admission of declarations against interest are not uniform for all courts. Generally, statements are admis- sible that at the time of their making were so far contrary to the declarant's pecuniary, pro- prietary, or penal interest that a reasonable person in his or her position would not have made the statement unless he believed it to be true.

For a statement against interest to be admissible, the declarant must be unavailable on the same grounds as those for prior testimony. In addition, unavailability for statements against interest can be established by unavailability due to the marital privilege. Declarations against interest by an unavailable third party, when offered by the prosecution against a defendant, also face the Sixth Amendment right to confrontation hurdles established in *Pointer v. Texas*, 380 U.S. 400 (1965).

In *Crawford v. Washington*, 541 U.S. 36 (2004), the Supreme Court strengthened con- frontation clause protections. In *Crawford*, the defendant, Michael Crawford, was charged with assault and the attempted murder of Kenneth Lee, a man he believed had attempted to rape his wife, Sylvia, who had told Crawford about the attempted rape and led him to Lee's residence.

The police interrogated Crawford and Sylvia and took tape-recorded statements from each. Crawford claimed self-defense and stated that he stabbed Lee because Lee threatened him with a knife; however, Sylvia stated that she did not see a knife in Lee's hand when Crawford stabbed him.

At Crawford's trial, although the prosecution could not call Sylvia to testify because of the marital privilege, they introduced her tape-recorded statement that contradicted Crawford's self-defense claim. Her statement was admitted as a declaration against interest because she led Crawford to Lee and she potentially could be charged as an accomplice. Crawford was convicted.

The Supreme Court reversed the conviction because the introduction of Sylvia's statement violated the confrontation clause. Her statement was testimonial in nature, akin to testimony at a prior legal proceeding, which, as per *Pointer v. Texas*, would only be admissible if there had been an opportunity for cross-examination.

Justice Antonin Scalia, writing for the majority, equated statements taken during official police interrogations to other testimonial proceedings. *Crawford* reinforced the premise that the opportunity for cross-examination is the necessary predicate for the introduction of testimonial statements against interest by unavailable witnesses, including statements taken at the following:

1. Prior preliminary hearings.
2. Prior grand jury hearings.
3. Prior trials.
4. Police interrogations.

Because police station interrogations would not involve cross-examination by an attorney for a potential defendant, hearsay declarations against interest made during police interrogations will not be admissible at trials.[6]

Not all statements given to the police are testimonial, and statements encompassed by other hearsay exceptions (e.g., excited utterances) can be admissible without violating the confrontation clause. In *Washington v. Davis*, 126 S.Ct 2266 (2006), the Supreme Court, with Justice Scalia writing for the majority, distinguished statements made by a caller to 911 about occurring domestic violence from statements taken by the police for the purposes of a report after the violence had been controlled. The former was admissible because it was non-testimonial but pertained to an ongoing emergency, while the latter was inadmissible because it was testimonial in that the report was prepared after the fact for the purposes of a potential prosecution.

A different approach is applicable to declarations against interest when they are offered by the defense to exculpate the accused. Contrary to the limits placed on the introduction of testimonial hearsay by the prosecution, when similar statements are introduced by the defense, they are more likely to be deemed admissible. Several landmark cases have established that statements against penal interests, even without an opportunity for cross-examination of the declarant, may be admissible when offered on behalf of an accused. In *Washington v. Texas*, 388 U.S. 14 (1967), *People v. Brown*, 26 N.Y.2d 88 (1970), *Chambers v. Mississippi*, 410 U.S. 284 (1973), *Crane v. Kentucky*, 476 U.S. 683 (1986), and *Holmes v. South Carolina*, 547 U.S. 319 (2006), courts have proclaimed the right of defendants to present a complete defense. The right mandates the admissibility of defense evidence when such evidence is sufficiently relevant, trustworthy, and probative. Such evidence should only be excluded where it is speculative or remote or does not tend to prove or disprove a material fact in issue. To be sure, such statements must be examined with caution, and, generally, they are not admissible unless corroborating circumstances clearly indicate the trustworthiness of the statement.[7] Caution is necessary, because otherwise defendants could routinely offer unverifiable and fallacious evidence of third-party guilt.

In *Holmes v. South Carolina*, the defendant was convicted of murder, sexual assault, and robbery. At his trial, substantial forensic evidence was introduced against him. In his defense, he sought to introduce proof that another man, Jimmy McCaw White, had committed the crime. Four witnesses were to testify that at various times White, to some degree, had acknowledged that he had committed the crime. However, the trial court would not allow the third-party guilt evidence to be taken, and a South Carolina appellate court upheld the verdict, ruling, "Where there is strong evidence of an appellant's guilt, especially where there is strong forensic evidence, the proffered evidence about a third party's alleged guilt does not raise a reasonable inference as to the appellant's own innocence."

The Supreme Court, in the majority opinion written by Justice Samuel Alito, vacated the South Carolina judgment, ruling that the defendant's evidence should have been admitted and that the South Carolina judgment violated the defendant's right to have a meaningful opportunity to present a complete defense.

Problem

A police officer was called to a family dispute. When he arrived, a woman ran toward him screaming, "My husband tried to choke me to death." The officer noticed red marks around the woman's throat. As the officer investigated the woman's complaint, he found the husband in another room, sitting in a chair, smoking a cigarette, and watching a football game. The officer asked the husband what had happened, and the husband answered, "I didn't choke her. She choked me."

After a brief investigation, the officer arrested the husband. Later, at the police station while filling out paperwork, the woman called the officer over and made a second statement to him, "I pretended to be dead so he would stop." The husband was charged with attempted murder and assault; however, at the trial the woman refused to testify against her husband, and the prosecution called the officer to the witness stand.

After the officer's direct examination by the prosecutor, the defense attorney cross-examined the officer and through him sought to introduce the husband's out-of-court statement that the wife had choked him. After the officer testified, the husband took the witness stand and claimed self-defense. He testified that he and his wife had had an argument but no physical contact had occurred between them. He testified she accused him of choking her because she was jealous of his relationship with another woman. After the husband's testimony, the police officer was recalled to the witness stand as a rebuttal witness.

Questions

Regarding the officer's direct examination by the prosecutor, which of the following would be correct?

1. The officer would be allowed to testify about his observation of the red marks on the woman's throat but not about any of her out-of-court statements.
2. He would be allowed to testify about both of the woman's out-of-court statements because she was in an excited state when she made the statements.

3. He would be allowed to testify about his observation of the red marks and about the woman's first out-of-court statement.
4. He would be allowed to testify about his observation of the red marks and about the woman's second statement because she had calmed down by the time she made that statement.

Regarding the officer's cross-examination by the defense attorney, which of the following would be correct?

5. The officer would be allowed to testify about the husband's statement because it was a spontaneous statement.
6. The officer would be allowed to testify about the husband's statement because it was an excited utterance.
7. The officer would not be allowed to testify about the husband's statement because it was in response to a question.
8. The officer would not be allowed to testify about the husband's statement because it was self-serving and made after the husband had had an opportunity to reflect or to contrive.

Regarding the officer's rebuttal testimony, which of the following would be correct?

9. The officer would be allowed to testify about the husband's statement because it was a spontaneous statement.
10. The officer would be allowed to testify about the husband's statement because it was an excited utterance.
11. The officer would be allowed to testify about the husband's statement because the wife had refused to testify.
12. The officer would be allowed to testify about the husband's statement because it was not offered for the truth of the fact asserted in the statement but to impeach the husband's credibility by showing that he had made a prior inconsistent statement.

Notes

1 Federal Rules of Evidence, Rule 801(c).
2 *United States v. Tellier*, 83 F.3d 578 (1996).
3 *People v. Marks*, 6 N.Y.2d 67 (1959).
4 Federal Rules of Evidence, Rules 803 and 804.
5 *Walder v. United States*, 347 U.S. 62 (1954); *Harris v. New York*, 401 U.S. 222 (1971); *Oregon v. Hass*, 420 U.S. 714 (1975); *Stone v. Powell*, 428 U.S. 465 (1976); *Michigan v. Harvey*, 494 U.S. 344 (1990).
6 See *Lilly v. Virginia*, 527 U.S. 116 (1999), for a comparable ruling.
7 Federal Rules of Evidence, Rule 804(b)(3).

Chapter 21

Government Surveillance

According to *Webster's Dictionary*, *eavesdropping* refers to the rain-water that drips from the eaves of a house, and *eavesdropper* refers to a person who stands under the eaves to listen secretly to the private conversations of others inside the house.[1] Throughout history, overheard conversations have provided evidence for criminal prosecutions. To provide evidence of a criminal conspiracy or other unlawful activity, a witness might testify to incriminating conversations he overheard while eavesdropping at an open door or window. When the witness testifying is a government agent, Fourth Amendment protections are implicated. If the government agent is lawfully present at a place where he or she can hear the conversation with the naked ear, no search occurs. The reasoning is analogous to the plain view doctrine. Here, it is the plain hearing doctrine because people who speak loudly or purposefully enough to be heard by others knowingly expose their conversation to the public.[2]

It is another matter when the agent is not lawfully in place or uses enhanced listening devices to overhear a private conversation. For the first 200 years of our nation, the bright-line rule that courts used to judge Fourth Amendment questions was whether government agents physically trespassed on private property to search personal papers or effects. Essentially, the rule was no physical trespass, no violation; however, with the advent of modern technology, it was inevitable that the trespass rule had to be reexamined.

In 1928, the U.S. Supreme Court conducted a major reexamination of the trespass rule in *Olmstead v. United States*, 277 U.S. 438, a case in which wiretapping and eavesdropping by federal agents was challenged as unconstitutional. In *Olmstead*, the defendant was convicted of conspiracy to violate the National Prohibition Act. Evidence was obtained against him by intercepting his telephone conversations by means of a wiretapping device that federal agents had placed on a telephone pole outside his house. The wiretapping was a violation of Washington state law, but a comparable federal law had not been enacted at that time. The question for the Court was whether this interception of the defendant's conversations by federal agents violated the Fourth Amendment right against unreasonable search and seizure. The Court's majority ruled that it was not a violation because no physical invasion of the house or the curtilage around the house had occurred, and also because the telephone wires and the conversations passing through them were within the public sphere and not protected as private. The majority stated, "The language of the Amendment cannot be extended and expanded to include telephone wires reaching to the whole world from the defendant's house or office. The intervening wires are not part of his house or office any more than are the highways along which they are stretched."

Olmstead has been most remembered for its marvelous dissenting opinions, one by Justice Oliver Wendell Holmes and another by Justice Louis Brandeis. Holmes' dissent produced one of the most famous quotations of legal literature: "It is less evil that some criminals should

DOI: 10.4324/9781003415091-25

escape than that the government should play an ignoble part." Brandeis' dissent included prophecy of government intrusiveness and omnipresence long before George Orwell's novel *1984*, which dramatized totalitarian government as "Big Brother." Brandeis wrote:

> When the Fourth and Fifth Amendments were adopted, "the form that evil had theretofore taken," had been necessarily simple. Force and violence were then the only means known to man by which a Government could directly effect self-incrimination. It could compel the individual to testify—a compulsion effected, if need be, by torture. It could secure possession of his papers and other articles incident to his private life—a seizure effected, if need be, by breaking and entry. Protection against such invasion of "the sanctities of a man's home and the privacies of life" was provided in the Fourth and Fifth Amendments by specific language.... Subtler and more far-reaching means of invading privacy have become available to the Government. Discovery and invention have made it possible for the Government, by means far more effective than stretching upon the rack, to obtain disclosure in court of what is whispered in the closet.

Brandeis believed that the language of the Amendments had to be expanded to encompass protections for private thoughts and expressions:

> The makers of our Constitution undertook to secure conditions favorable to the pursuit of happiness. They recognized the significance of man's spiritual nature, of his feelings and of his intellect. They knew that only a part of the pain, pleasure and satisfactions of life are to be found in material things. They sought to protect Americans in their beliefs, their thoughts, their emotions and their sensations. They conferred, as against the Government, the right to be let alone—the most comprehensive of rights and the right most valued by civilized men. To protect that right, every unjustifiable intrusion by the Government upon the privacy of the individual, whatever the means employed, must be deemed a violation of the Fourth Amendment.

Irrespective of the dissenting opinions of Holmes and Brandeis, the Court's majority upheld the use of the evidence against Olmstead and retained the physical trespass rule, and this decision stood until 1967.

Further technological advances since *Olmstead* caused the Court and Congress to reconsider the rule. Police have obtained even more sophisticated eavesdropping and surveillance devices that have made it possible to invade a person's privacy without a physical trespass. They have electronic tracking devices, telescopic lenses and cameras, heat sensors, metal detectors, and drug-sniffing dogs to obtain evidence without having to trespass physically. Doors and walls can no longer ensure a person's privacy.

Congress, partly in response to *Olmstead*, enacted the Federal Communications Act of 1934, which addressed telephonic communications and provided:

> No person not being authorized by the sender shall intercept any communication and divulge or publish the existence, contents, purport, effect or meaning of such intercepted communications to any person.

This statute had a limited effect on law enforcement conduct. It was interpreted to mean that since intercepted telephonic communications could not be divulged, the contents of an intercepted communication could not be used as evidence in a federal court. It did not definitely prohibit wiretapping; consequently, wiretapping by federal agents and local police continued for intelligence gathering purposes, but not for use in court. Moreover, eavesdropping by other electronic means (e.g., bugging a room or vehicle) was not addressed by the Federal Communications Act, and the trespass doctrine remained the primary method of regulating such law enforcement conduct.

Cases decided in the four decades after *Olmstead* demonstrated the unsatisfactory nature of the trespass rule and the difficulty of applying it. In *Goldman v. United States*, 316 U.S. 129 (1942), the Court held that the use of a Dictaphone placed against an office wall to hear private conversations conducted in the room on the other side of the wall did not violate the Fourth Amendment because no physical trespass occurred. Conversely, in *Silverman v. United States*, 365 U.S. 505 (1961), the Court held that a "spike-mike" inserted under the baseboard of a wall until it made contact with a heating duct in Silverman's room did violate the Amendment because it constituted a trespass.

Goldman, Silverman, and many similar cases highlighted the unsoundness of the trespass rule and caused the Warren Court to overrule it in *Katz v. United States,* 389 U.S. 347 (1967). *Katz* replaced the trespass doctrine with the reasonable expectation of privacy doctrine. In *Katz,* federal agents, investigating the defendant for illegal gambling, placed a listening and recording device on the exterior of a public telephone booth that they knew he used regularly to make gambling calls. Under the trespass rule, the interception of Katz's conversations (not over the phone wires, but in the phone booth) would not have been a violation for two reasons: first, Katz did not own the phone booth, and second, the device was not placed inside the phone booth.

Discarding the trespass rule, the Court abandoned *Olmstead* and *Goldman* and declared:

> The Fourth Amendment protects people, not places. What a person knowingly exposes to the public, even in his own home or office, is not a subject of Fourth Amendment protection. But what he seeks to preserve as private, even in an area accessible to the public, may be constitutionally protected.

Closing the phone booth door established Katz's expectation of privacy; therefore, as the Court stated:

> The Government's activities in electronically listening to and recording the petitioner's words violated the privacy upon which he justifiably relied while using the telephone booth and thus constituted a "search and seizure" within the meaning of the Fourth Amendment. The fact that the electronic device employed to achieve that end did not happen to penetrate the wall of the booth can have no constitutional significance.

The agents investigating Katz's activities needed a search warrant to lawfully intrude upon his privacy. Without a warrant, his verbal statements or tangible evidence derived from his statements would be suppressed.

The *Katz* expectation of privacy doctrine has affected search and seizure law well beyond wiretapping and eavesdropping issues. To challenge the admissibility of evidence, defendants must show that they have standing to do so, which in many cases requires them to show that they had an expectation of privacy in the area searched or the property seized. For example, visitors to an apartment cannot challenge the constitutionality of a search of the apartment unless they can show they had a reasonable expectation of privacy in relation to the apartment,[3] and passengers in a vehicle cannot challenge a search of the vehicle unless they can show their reasonable expectation of privacy in relation to the vehicle.[4]

Although *Katz* added privacy protections for some, it had the unintended consequence of reducing privacy protections for others. An expectation of privacy must be both personal and reasonable, and courts have held that a person would be foolish to expect privacy in police cars, interrogation rooms, jail visiting areas, or prisons.[5]

Omnibus Crime Control and Safe Streets Act of 1968

In response to *Katz*, Congress enacted Title III of the Omnibus Crime Control and Safe Streets Act of 1968,[6] which included authorization for eavesdropping warrants for both wiretapping and listening devices in private locations. Most states passed similar laws, many of which provided greater protection for individuals than the federal law.

Eavesdropping in the legal context is knowingly and without lawful authority engaging in the following conduct:

(a) Entering into a private place with intent to listen surreptitiously to private conversations or to observe the personal conduct of any other person or persons therein; or (b) Installing or using outside a private place any device for hearing, recording, amplifying, or broadcasting sounds originating in such place, which sounds would not ordinarily be audible or comprehensible outside, without the consent of the person or persons entitled to privacy therein; or (c) Installing or using any device or equipment for the interception of any telephone, telegraph or other wire communication without the consent of the person in possession or control of the facilities for such wire communication. Such activities are regulated by state and federal statutes, and commonly require a court order.[7]

The eavesdropping statutes, while designed to aid law enforcement, also instituted broad protections for individual privacy. The mandates of Title III and state statutes include the following:

1. Nonconsensual government interceptions of wire or oral communications require an eavesdropping warrant issued by a court of competent jurisdiction.
2. The time, place, type, and extent of the interceptions are to be under the control and supervision of the court.
3. Eavesdropping warrants shall be issued only for investigation of certain major types of serious crimes.
4. The identity of the individual whose communications are to be intercepted and the nature of the communications sought to be intercepted must be described with particularity.
5. Eavesdropping warrants shall be issued only when other conventional investigative techniques are not available or practicable.
6. The information obtained by the interceptions shall not be misused.
7. Warrants shall be issued only for limited time periods, and extensions must be approved by the court.
8. Persons whose conversations were overheard must be notified of the interception within 90 days of the termination of the warrant, unless such notification would jeopardize an ongoing criminal investigation.

Title III allows federal agents to intercept communications without a warrant when one party to the conversation consents, such as when one party wears a secreted recording device or transmitter during a face-to-face conversation or when one party allows agents to overhear or record his or her telephone calls. The party consenting to the interception may be an undercover officer or a civilian.

Title III prohibits state law enforcement officers from engaging in nonconsensual law enforcement wiretapping and bugging unless authorized under a state statute at least as restrictive as federal law.[8] Title III allows state law enforcement officers to intercept communications without a warrant when one party to the conversation consents, unless prohibited by state law.

States impose strict civil and criminal sanctions for violations of eavesdropping laws; however, exceptions apply in express or implied consent situations. For example, employees may consent to an employer monitoring their telephone conversations with customers or clients, and prisoners know their phone calls may be monitored by prison authorities.[9]

The development of electronic mail, computer-to-computer data transmissions, cellular phones, paging devices, and videoconferencing has limited the effectiveness of the 1968 law. In 1986, Congress amended Title III in response to technological advances in the communications industry. The amended Act adjusted the warrant or consent requirements for these new and advanced communication tools. For example, the widespread use of cellular phones and the tactical replacement of phones by professional criminals led to a change in the law. Under the 1968 law, a warrant had to identify the particular telephone the suspect was expected to use, and interceptions were limited to the identified phone; however, under the 1986 law, interceptions are allowed for any cellular phone that the suspect uses.

Strict Requirements

Title III and state wiretap and eavesdropping warrants are far more intrusive than the conventional search warrant for physical evidence. Conventional search warrants are normally executed during a designated ten-day period. They are executed once; additional searches require additional warrants. The police officers search through a home, office, or other premises for contraband or evidence of a crime; when they are finished, they leave. In contrast, wiretap and eavesdropping warrants are not one-time events but are of a continuing nature, intruding into a person's private conversations and private life for extended periods of time. Such intrusions pose a greater threat to privacy than a one-time physical search. For this reason, courts apply strict standards for the issuance and implementation of Title III warrants.

In addition to the Fourth Amendment probable cause and particularity requirements, a court may not issue a Title III warrant unless conventional investigative methods have been tried and failed, appear unlikely to succeed, or are too dangerous.[10] To obtain a wiretap or eavesdropping warrant, the government must demonstrate that it has made a good-faith effort to utilize standard investigative methods, such as those listed below:

1. Visual surveillance.
2. Examination of public records.
3. Interviewing witnesses.
4. Use of standard search warrants.
5. Use of informants.
6. Infiltration by undercover officers.
7. Use of pen registers and/or trap-and-trace devices (see below).

Which of these methods must be attempted depends on the circumstances of each case, but reasonable efforts by other means must be tried or considered before resorting to the extraordinary means of secretly listening to private conversations. Wiretap and eavesdropping warrants raise heightened privacy concerns because much of the overheard conversations will most likely be irrelevant to the suspected criminal activity, and many of the conversations might involve individuals who are not engaged in any criminal activity. To use the overheard conversations as evidence in court, the prosecutor must meet strict standards. Not only will the obtained evidence be excluded when it was seized in violation of the Fourth Amendment, but it will also be excluded when the procedures followed fail to comply with strict statutory rules. For example, if the overheard conversations were not recorded, time sheets were not maintained, or the listening by the agents was not minimized to avoid non-criminal conversations, then all of the evidence collected might be excluded because the agents did not follow the mandated rules.

E-mail and Text Messages

Title III and state eavesdropping statutes regulate the interception of communications during transmission. Because e-mails and text messages are only in transmission for seconds, eavesdropping warrants are impracticable to implement; however, once an e-mail or text message reaches its intended destination, it becomes a stored communication and can be accessed. Stored communications are regulated by the Stored Wire and Electronic Communications and Transactional Records Act.[11] This Act provides less privacy protection than Title III. During the first 180 days of storage, government investigators can access the records through a conventional search warrant, requiring only probable cause, not the stricter standards of Title III. Moreover, after 180 days of storage, upon notification to the subscriber, the custodian of the records can be compelled to disclose the records through an administrative subpoena, grand jury subpoena, or court order. The standard to compel disclosure of post-180 day records is the same as for any subpoena: a simple showing that the contents of the records are relevant to an ongoing criminal investigation.

Pen Registers and Trap-and-Trace Devices

Pen register devices identify and record the telephone numbers dialed from a particular phone; trap-and-trace devices identify and record telephone numbers calling into a particular phone. Investigators typically use such caller and receiver identification information to develop probable cause for arrests or other searches. Because these devices do not capture the contents of a call, they are not regulated by Title III. Telephone users do not have a reasonable expectation of privacy for the phone numbers they dial because they know the telephone company must record the information for billing and other business purposes. Without an expectation of privacy, Fourth Amendment protections do not apply.

In 1987, to provide some control over the use of pen register and trap-and-trace devices and some protection for subjects of investigations, Congress enacted the Electronic Communications Privacy Act (ECPA),[12] which made it illegal to install these devices without a court order. The standard for obtaining such a court order is far below constitutional probable cause requirements. The applicant need only provide the judge with the name of the law enforcement agency conducting the investigation and a certification that the information sought is relevant to an ongoing criminal investigation.

Tracking a Person's Movements

The location of a person's cell phone can be tracked by the signals sent between the phone and cellular receiving towers. Whether law enforcement officers need a warrant or subpoena to obtain real-time information of cell phone movements has not been settled, but records of past calls and locations may be obtained under the Stored Wire and Electronic Communications and Transactional Records Act.[13] Such information has proved extremely useful for law enforcement (in the California trial of Scott Peterson for murdering his wife and child, phone records contradicted his alibi testimony) and for defendants (one of the students accused in the 2007 Duke University rape case proved his alibi through Automated Teller Machine records).

Electronic beepers and global positioning systems (GPS) enable law enforcement officers to track the movements of vehicles. Most courts have held that as long as the law enforcement agent attaches the beeper or GPS device inside a container while it is in a public place or to the outside of a vehicle (usually to the undercarriage) while it is parked in a public place, no search or seizure occurs.

In *United States v. Knotts*, 460 U.S. 276 (1983), the Supreme Court held that it was not a Fourth Amendment violation when government agents who were investigating an illegal drug laboratory placed a beeper in a five-gallon drum of chloroform to track the container's movements. The agents then followed the vehicle that transported the drum by monitoring the signals received from the beeper. The drum was tracked to Knotts' cabin. He was arrested and filed a motion for suppression of the chloroform evidence on the grounds that his privacy rights had been violated. The Supreme Court held that a person's public movements are not protected by the Fourth Amendment, as "a person traveling in an automobile on public thoroughfares has no reasonable expectation of privacy in his movements from one place to another."

The tracking device could be viewed merely as an enhancement of an officer's ability to observe a vehicle in a public place, similar to the use of binoculars. As the Court stated, "Nothing in the Fourth Amendment prohibited the police from augmenting the sensory faculties bestowed upon them at birth with such enhancement as science and technology afforded them in this case."[14]

Conversely, the New York Court of Appeals in *People v. Weaver*, 12 N.Y.3d 433 (2009), held that the government's use of a GPS tracking device violated the right to privacy. The majority four-to-three opinion was written by Chief Judge Jonathan Lippman and was his first major criminal procedure opinion since his appointment as New York's Chief Judge. He outlined the facts of the case as follows:

> In the early morning hours of December 21, 2005, a State Police Investigator crept underneath defendant's street-parked van and placed a global positioning system (GPS) tracking device inside the bumper. The device remained in place for 65 days, constantly monitoring the position of the van. This nonstop surveillance was conducted without a warrant.
>
> The GPS device, known as a "Q-ball," once attached to the van, operated in conjunction with numerous satellites, from which it received tracking data, to fix the van's location. The Q-ball readings indicated the speed of the van and pinpointed its location within 30 feet. Readings were taken approximately every minute while the vehicle was in motion, but less often when it was stationary.... To download the location information retrieved by the Q-ball, the investigator would simply drive past the van and press

a button on a corresponding receiver unit, causing the tracking history to be transmitted to and saved by a computer in the investigator's vehicle.

[The defendant] was eventually charged with and tried in a single proceeding for crimes relating to two separate burglaries—one committed on July 2005 at the Latham Meat Market and the other on Christmas Eve of the same year at the Latham K-Mart.

The prosecution sought to have admitted at trial GPS readings showing that, on the evening of the Latham K-Mart burglary at 7:26, defendant's van traversed the store's parking lot at a speed of six miles per hour.

Over the defendant's objection, the trial court admitted the electronic surveillance evidence. That evidence combined with testimony of the defendant's accomplice resulted in his conviction for the burglaries. Weaver appealed, and the New York Court of Appeals reversed the conviction, ruling that the evidence obtained from the GPS should be suppressed.

Justice Lippman distinguished the *Knotts* case from *Weaver*. In *Knotts*, the beeper was used to track a single trip from the place where the chloroform was purchased to the cabin; however, in *Weaver*:

[W]e are not presented with the use of a mere beeper to facilitate visual surveillance during a single trip. GPS is a vastly different and exponentially more sophisticated and powerful technology that is easily and cheaply deployed and has virtually unlimited and remarkably precise tracking capability. With the addition of new GPS satellites, the technology is rapidly improving so that any person or object, such as a car, may be tracked with uncanny accuracy to virtually any interior or exterior location, at any time and regardless of atmospheric conditions. Constant, relentless tracking of anything is now not merely possible but entirely practicable, indeed much more practicable than the surveillance conducted in *Knotts*. GPS is not a mere enhancement of human sensory capacity; it facilitates a new technological perception of the world in which the situation of any object may be followed and exhaustively recorded, over, in most cases, a practically unlimited period....

One need only consider what the police may learn, practically effortlessly, from planting a single device. The whole of a person's progress through the world, into both public and private spatial spheres, can be charted and recorded over lengthy periods.

Judge Lippman pointed out that the *Knotts* court had reserved for another day the question of whether the Fourth Amendment would be implicated if "twenty-four-hour surveillance of any citizen of this country were possible, without judicial knowledge or supervision."[15] He differentiated the voluntary use or submission to GPS technology from the government's secret use of such technology:

It would appear clear to us that the great popularity of GPS technology for its many useful applications may not be taken simply as a massive, undifferentiated concession of personal privacy to agents of the state. Indeed, contemporary technology projects our private activities into public space as never before. Cell technology has moved presumptively private phone conversation from the enclosure of Katz's phone booth to the open sidewalk and the car, and the advent of portable computing devices has re-situated transactions of all kinds to relatively public spaces. It is fair to say, and we think consistent with prevalent social views, that this change in venue has not been accompanied by any dramatic diminution in the socially reasonable expectation that our communications and transactions will remain to a large extent private. Here, particularly, where there was no voluntary utilization of the tracking technology, and the technology was surreptitiously installed, there exists no basis to find an expectation of privacy so diminished as to render constitutional concerns *de minimis*.

Though a citizen has a lesser expectation of privacy while traveling in his vehicle on public highways, a residual expectation of privacy exists. In this case, the prolonged invasion of privacy was inconsistent with even the slightest reasonable expectation of privacy. Not only did a Fourth Amendment violation occur, but even if a warrant had been obtained it would not have been justified under these circumstances. Judge Lippman explained his divergence from federal law:

> In reaching this conclusion, we acknowledge that the determinative issue remains open as a matter of federal constitutional law, since the United States Supreme Court has not yet ruled upon whether the use of GPS by the state for the purpose of criminal investigation constitutes a search under the Fourth Amendment.... Thus, we do not presume to decide the question as a matter of federal law. The very same principles are, however, dispositive of this matter under our State Constitution. If, as we have found, defendant had a reasonable expectation of privacy that was infringed by the State's placement and monitoring of the Q-ball on his van to track his movements over a period of more than two months, there was a search under Article I, Section 12 of the State Constitution. And that search was illegal because it was executed without a warrant and without justification under any exception to the warrant requirement. In light of the unsettled state of federal law on the issue, we premise our ruling on our State Constitution alone.

The conflict between the Supreme Court ruling in *Knotts* and the New York Court of Appeals ruling in *Weaver* called for a resolution because of the importance of the issue, and how it was resolved would affect the future tenor and nature of our society. The Supreme Court addressed the issue in two cases: *United States v. Jones*, 565 U.S. 400 (2012), and *Carpenter v. United States*, 585 U.S. 19 (2018).

In *Jones*, the defendant came under suspicion of trafficking in narcotics. Drug enforcement agents installed a GPS tracking device on the undercarriage of his vehicle while it was parked in a public parking lot. For 28 days, the agents used the device to monitor the vehicle's movements, and using the cell site location information (CSLI) acquired, they obtained an indictment of the defendant, who was convicted of conspiracy to distribute narcotics. He appealed.

The Supreme Court ruled that the acquisition of Jones' CSLI from the telephone carrier constituted an unlawful search and seizure that infringed on the defendant's reasonable expectation of privacy, a Fourth Amendment right that had been established in *Katz v. United States*. The Court said that CSLI is so comprehensive, although merely turning on your cell phone results in sharing your location information, that there is a reasonable expectation of privacy in the information. Consequently, the government must obtain a warrant to search for such information.

In *Carpenter*, four men were arrested for a series of armed robberies of Radio Shacks and T-Mobile stores in Detroit. One of the men provided the cell phone numbers of fifteen accomplices, including Carpenter, the alleged ring leader. The FBI subpoenaed Carpenter's cell phone records from his service providers.

Cell phones automatically search for and contact the nearest cell site, which is usually located on a tower, light post, flag pole, church steeple, or the side of a building. Once the cell phone contacts the tower, the telephone company stamps the event and makes a near-precise record of the location of the cell phone at a particular time and date.

Using the data provided by the telephone company, the FBI was able to place Carpenter near four of the six armed robberies, and they charged him with six counts of robbery and weapons possession.

Carpenter moved to suppress the information derived from the cell phone records, claiming that, to get the records, the agents violated his reasonable expectation of privacy in those records. The Federal District Court denied the motion, and Carpenter was convicted and sentenced to 116 years in prison. His appeal to the Sixth Circuit Court of Appeals was denied, and he then appealed to the Supreme Court.

Reversing the Sixth Circuit, the Supreme Court held that law enforcement must obtain a warrant to obtain cell site location information. Exceptions can be made when there is an emergency requiring real-time information in such cases as bomb threats, active shootings, hostage situations, or child abductions.

The government had argued that, since the information was maintained by a third-party cell phone service provider, the "third-party doctrine" applied. That doctrine holds that business records voluntarily shared with third parties such as banks, utilities, and so on, are not protected by the Fourth Amendment and could be obtained without a warrant.

The Court rejected that argument, noting that in the United States cell phones constantly track our whereabouts. They are ubiquitous, "almost a feature of human anatomy... Carrying one is indispensable to participation in modern society... Nearly three-quarters of smart phone users report being within five feet of their phones most of the time."

The time-stamped location information from cell sites is stored with third-party providers for years. The Court stated: "Although such records are generated for commercial purposes, that distinction does not negate Carpenter's anticipation of privacy in his physical location." The time-stamped location data "provides an intimate window into a person's life, revealing not only his particular movements, but through them his familial, political, professional, religious and sexual associations... While individuals regularly leave their vehicles, they compulsively carry cell phones with them all the time. A cell phone faithfully follows its owner beyond public thoroughfares and into private residences, doctor's offices, political headquarters, and other potentially revealing locales."

The Court's ruling apparently does not affect the third-party business-records doctrine as it pertains to telephone call numbers, credit card purchases, and bank transactions. Law enforcement can still obtain information from those sources by means of a subpoena. The basis for obtaining a subpoena usually requires only a "legitimate investigative purpose," which is a lower standard than the probable cause required for a warrant. Obtaining cell site location information requires the higher standard of a warrant because citizens have a reasonable expectation of privacy that their every movement over long periods of time will not be recorded by the government.

X-rays, Metal Detectors, Thermal Imaging, and Video

Searches by screening devices at airports, subways, courthouses, prisons, and other public facilities to detect weapons, explosives, or other dangerous items are generally considered reasonable and do not violate the Fourth Amendment. Persons entering these facilities do not have a reasonable expectation of privacy regarding minimally intrusive screening. In addition, voluntary consent to be searched is an exception to the warrant requirement, and a person who wishes to avoid a search can choose not to enter the public facility.

On the contrary, a person in his home or private premises has an expectation of privacy, and law enforcement officers cannot invade the home by means of enhanced technological devices. In *Kyllo v. United States*, 533 U.S. 27 (2001), the Supreme Court ruled that the Fourth Amendment was violated when the police aimed a thermal imaging device, or heat sensor, at the suspect's home from a public street. The police did so to determine whether the amount of heat emanating from the house indicated the presence of high-intensity lamps customarily used to grow marijuana. The thermal imaging device indicated that Kyllo's garage roof and a side wall were hot compared to the rest of his house. On the basis of this and other information, the police obtained a search warrant, and when they entered the house they found marijuana plants. Kyllo appealed his conviction, asserting that a search warrant is generally required to use a heat sensor to explore activities inside a home not visible from the outside. The government countered that the thermal imaging was not a search because it detected only heat radiating from the home's external surfaces. The Court rejected the government's argument and sided with Kyllo, stating that to allow such thermal imaging without a warrant would leave the homeowner at the mercy of advanced technology that could discern all human activity in the home.

Although a search warrant is not required to place the outside of a home under normal visual surveillance,[16] search warrants are required to train video cameras on the interiors of homes, private offices, and other locations where a person reasonably has an expectation of privacy. The Fourth Amendment was violated by a surveillance camera mounted on a telephone pole and trained on a suspect's backyard that was screened from ground-level view by a fence.[17]

Dogs

In *Illinois v. Caballes*, 543 U.S. 405 (2005), the Supreme Court upheld the warrantless search of the defendant's car trunk after a police drug-sniffing dog alerted to the presence of marijuana. The Court stated that a "dog sniff conducted during a concededly lawful traffic stop that reveals no information other than the location of a substance that no individual has any right to possess does not violate the Fourth Amendment." Using the dog to sniff around the vehicle was not a violation of the Fourth Amendment, and the dog's alert provided the probable cause to conduct the vehicle search. *Caballes* may have far-reaching ramifications. In the age of terrorism, newly developed chemical detection devices, designed to identify not only drugs but also explosives, poisonous gases, and nuclear materials, are undoubtedly going to be utilized as a first line of defense. When alerts are obtained from a dog, a chemical detection device, or a radiation Geiger counter, the Court has given a green light for the police to act quickly.

Problem

On a Saturday afternoon, U.S. Drug Enforcement Agents Trapp and Herring, while conducting an investigation of unlawful drug dealing in New York City, followed a suspect, Louis Sniffen, from his Park Avenue apartment to the Museum of Modern Art on Fifth Avenue. The agents observed Sniffen, who was a middle-aged man, meet a young woman on the steps of the museum. The woman was approximately 25 years old and had long black hair. Sniffen spoke to the woman briefly, handed her a leather-bound notebook, then departed and walked directly back to his apartment.

During the following weeks, the agents continued their surveillance of Sniffen, and on three occasions he met the same woman on the steps of the museum. On the first occasion, the steps were crowded with people, and Agent Herring sat on the steps near the suspects in an attempt to overhear their conversation. Although he was unable to discern most of what they said, Herring heard the woman say "twenty-five thousand" as she handed the leatherbound notebook back to Sniffen.

On the second occasion, the steps were less crowded. Agent Herring placed a shoulder bag close to the suspects and then sat about 20 feet away. The shoulder bag contained a recording device to capture the suspects' conversation, but Herring was unable to discern anything in their conversation. Later, when the agents listened to the recorded conversation, it proved mostly unintelligible because of the surrounding street sounds, but one statement by Sniffen was heard clearly enough. He said, "Make sure they don't cut the coke more than once. It has to have a good level of potency, or we'll lose our customers."

On the third occasion, it was raining and only a few people were walking on the steps. The agents parked a surveillance van on Fifth Avenue across from the museum from which they directed a video-recording camera and a parabolic microphone/audio recorder at the suspects. The camera had a telescopic lens that provided close-ups of the suspects, and the microphone had enhanced capabilities to pick up the conversation of the suspects unencumbered by surrounding sounds.

The microphone captured most of the suspects' conversation, although some words were garbled. Also, the agents had a lip-reading expert view the video-recording to ascertain what the suspects had said. The expert provided a transcript of their conversation, which generally matched the captured conversation on the audio recording and clarified some of the garbled words.

The following was the most pertinent part of the conversation between Sniffen and the woman, who was subsequently identified as Laura Diavlos:

Diavlos: "Only eighteen thousand."
Sniffen: "They had twenty-five worth."
Diavlos: "They said the packages arrived a day late, so they should make it up next week."
Sniffen: "Make sure they account for every package."
Diavlos: "I'll tell them."

The agents continued their investigation and were able to connect Diavlos with a ring of cocaine dealers who sold the drugs on the streets and in apartments. Agent Trapp, posing as a drug dealer, bought cocaine from members of the ring. He asked to buy a larger amount of cocaine, and a meeting was arranged with Diavlos. At the meeting in a Lower Eastside apartment, Trapp wore a hidden recording device, and Diavlos was recorded saying that she would sell him "a kilo of the best cocaine around for thirty thousand dollars." Trapp said he would bring the money the next day, and they agreed to consummate the sale. The agents immediately obtained a search warrant for the apartment, and the next day they executed the warrant while Diavlos was present inside the apartment. They recovered ten kilos of cocaine and $15,000 in cash. They also recovered the leatherbound notebook, which contained accounting entries that clearly related to unlawful cocaine trafficking.

The agents obtained a search warrant for Sniffen's apartment, but when they executed it they did not recover any evidence in connection with the drug dealing. Nevertheless, Sniffen was indicted with Diavlos in federal court for possession and sale of cocaine, as well as conspiracy to sell cocaine. Evidence in the indictment included the three museumstep conversations between Sniffen and Diavlos and the conversation between Diavlos and Agent Trapp.

The defendants moved to suppress all three of the overheard museum-step conversations on the grounds that the recordings were obtained without a warrant in violation of their Fourth Amendment rights. Also, they alleged that the warrantless interception of the second and third conversations by the agents violated Title III, 18 U.S.C. §§ 2510 et seq., which prohibits warrantless electronic interceptions of "any oral communications uttered by a person exhibiting an expectation that such communication is not subject to interception under circumstances justifying such expectation."

On the same grounds, Diavlos moved separately to suppress the conversation with Trapp recorded in the Lower Eastside apartment.

Questions

1. Should any or all of the three museum-step conversations between Sniffen and Diavlos be suppressed because their interception violated the Fourth Amendment and/or Title III?
2. During their first conversation, did they have a reasonable expectation of privacy that their conversation could not be overheard by the unaided ear of a bystander, namely Agent Herring?
3. During their second conversation, did they have a reasonable expectation of privacy that their conversation could not be overheard and recorded by the electronic recording device in Herring's shoulder bag?
4. During their third conversation, did they have a reasonable expectation of privacy that their conversation could not be overheard and recorded by a telescopic camera and a parabolic microphone?
5. Assuming the defendants had an expectation of privacy in their conversations, must that expectation be recognized by society as reasonable?
6. Did Trapp violate Diavlos' Fourth Amendment rights by secretly recording their conversation with an electronic recording device?
7. Assuming that it was a violation for the agents to intercept one or more of the museum-step conversations, should the evidence recovered in the Lower Eastside apartment be suppressed as fruits of the poisonous tree?

Notes

1 *Webster's New World Dictionary*, 2nd College Edition, Simon & Schuster, New York, 1980.
2 *United States v. Jackson*, 588 F.2d 1046 (5th Cir. 1979).
3 *Minnesota v. Carter*, 525 U.S. 83 (1998).
4 *Rakas v. Illinois*, 439 U.S. 128 (1978).
5 *United States v. Turner*, 209 F.3d 1198 (10th Cir. 2000); *United States v. Harrelson*, 754 F.2d 1153 (5th Cir. 1985).
6 18 U.S.C. §§ 2510–2521.
7 *Black's Law Dictionary*, West Publishing, St. Paul, MN, 1979.
8 *Berger v. New York*, 388 U.S. 41 (1967).
9 *United States v. Willoughby*, 860 F.2d 15 (2d Cir. 1988).
10 18 U.S.C. § 2518(3)(c).
11 18 U.S.C. §§ 2701 et seq.
12 18 U.S.C. §§ 3121 et seq.
13 *United States v. Forest*, 355 F.3d 942 (6th Cir. 2004).
14 *United States v. Knotts*, 460 U.S. 276 (1983), at p. 282.
15 *United States v. Knotts*, 460 U.S. 276 (1983), at p. 283.
16 *California v. Ciraolo*, 476 U.S. 207 (1986).
17 *United States v. Cuevez-Sanches*, 821 F.2d 248 (5th Cir. 1987).

References

18 U.S.C. § 2510 (2); 18 U.S.C. §§ 2511 et seq.
Berger v. New York, 388 U.S. 41 (1967).
Katz v. United States, 389 U.S. 347 (1967).
Kee v. City of Rowlett, Texas, 247 F.3d 206 (2001).
Lewis v. United States, 385 U.S. 206 (1966).
Lopez v. United States, 373 U.S. 427 (1963).
People v. Edwards, 71 Cal.2d 1096 (1969).
United States v. McIntyre, 582 F.2d 1221 (1978).
United States v. White, 401 U.S. 745 (1971).

Chapter 22

Terrorism and the Patriot Act

The September 11, 2001, terrorist attack killed almost three thousand American civilians and destroyed the Twin Towers of the World Trade Center in New York, part of the Pentagon in Washington, D.C., and four commercial airliners with all of their passengers. Was this attack an act of war requiring a warlike response, or was it an enormous crime requiring a massive increase in criminal justice resources and authority? That question has been the subject of intense debate since the attack.

Terrorism is the name given to sneak-attack warfare waged against civilian populations for the purpose of forcing changes in the political policies that the leaders of those populations impose and practice. Based on this definition, a warlike response against an identified enemy would seem appropriate; however, in the contemporary permutation of terrorist warfare, the enemy is not easily identified. Undercover enemy agents are in the midst of our population, and to identify them we must utilize enhanced criminal investigative techniques.

Two months after the September 11th attack, Congress passed the USA Patriot Act, which included several amendments to existing federal laws.[1] Prior to the Patriot Act, several federal laws authorized enhanced criminal investigative techniques, but they included stringent restrictions on government action. The most notable enhanced investigation statute was Title III of the Omnibus Crime Control and Safe Streets Act of 1968. This required law enforcement agents to obtain warrants to conduct electronic surveillance in connection with criminal investigations;[2] however, Title III did not require warrants for electronic surveillance conducted by the executive branch for national security purposes.

In 1968, the consensus of legal and political opinion was that the President's authority as Commander in Chief allowed him to authorize warrantless searches in connection with national security activities. Later, after the Watergate scandals and President Nixon's resignation in 1974, Congress passed the Foreign Intelligence Surveillance Act (FISA) and created FISA courts. The Act requires the executive branch in national security matters to obtain a warrant from a FISA court for domestic searches or surveillance. Nevertheless, although the FISA warrant requirement is a restraint on the government, a benefit for the government is the limited information that must be provided to the FISA court. Probable cause is not required, only a reasonable national security need, and the government does not have to fully disclose its evidence and intelligence sources as it would were it applying for a Title III eavesdropping warrant or a conventional search warrant.

The Patriot Act expanded the government's ability to obtain domestic FISA warrants or orders. While foreign intelligence affecting national security was previously the sole purpose for a FISA warrant, under the Patriot Act, foreign intelligence need only be "a significant purpose of the surveillance." Furthermore, the potential targets of the warrants, formerly confined to agents of a "foreign power," were expanded to include persons associated

DOI: 10.4324/9781003415091-26

with "a group engaged in international terrorism or activities in preparation therefor."[3] Consequently, American citizens who were not associated with a foreign power could be the targets of FISA warrants.

The Patriot Act also authorized so-called sneak-and-peek warrants "to search for and seize any property or material that constitutes evidence of a criminal offense in violation of the laws of the United States." These warrants allow a physical or electronic intrusion by government agents into homes and personal records, such as records from libraries, telephone companies, credit card companies, hospitals, schools, advocacy organizations, and Internet service providers. They are distinguished from conventional warrants in that they do not require a timely notification to the target that the intrusion has occurred.[4] Delayed notifications are allowed so that ongoing investigations will not be jeopardized; however, a cost associated with delayed notification is the inability of the targeted person to challenge the legality of the government action in a court of law.

Some critics argue that in the panic after the 9/11 attacks, both Congress, by enacting the Patriot Act, and the executive branch, by the manner in which it applied the Act and other procedures, have undermined the privacy and due process rights guaranteed by the Constitution. These critics approach the issues from a criminal justice perspective, and they maintain that full constitutional protections should be applied to suspected terrorists captured outside of a war zone.

Others approach the issues from a warfare perspective. They argue that the terrorist organizations that have emerged, although not officially connected to a foreign power, are nevertheless as dangerous and formidable as a foreign military, perhaps more so. The proponents of the warfare approach argue that during World War II the executive branch did not need to obtain prior court approval before intercepting coded radio transmissions between American citizens and the German or Japanese governments. They argue that speed is essential in the battle to prevent terrorist attacks and that FBI and other government agents assigned to anti-terrorism duties must act as though American soil is the battlefield. The goal is to prevent attacks by whatever means necessary.

Proponents of the warfare approach also argue that trials for persons charged with war crimes can be delayed until the war is over. Because, in most wars, prisoners of war are not released until the end of hostilities, to prevent them from returning to the battlefield, it follows that captured terrorists should be held in custody until the end of hostilities to prevent them from returning to terrorism. These proponents argue that if criminal trials are required for unlawful enemy combatants with the proof beyond a reasonable doubt standard for convictions, many enemy combatants will be released without trials or after acquittals.

Proponents of the criminal justice approach argue that treatment of captured terrorist suspects and the investigative methods used to build cases against them must comport with traditional due process protections. To dispense with due process protections even for terrorists, they argue, will lead to a diminishment of due process protections for all citizens. Arbitrary arrests, indefinite detentions, harsh interrogations, and torture for terrorists might be applied against innocent persons.

If history is any teacher, the conflict between the warfare and the criminal justice approaches will be resolved by our checks-and-balance system. During periods of crisis—World War I, the Bolshevik scare of the 1920s, World War II, and the suspected Communist infiltration of American institutions in the 1950s—the government enacted and stringently enforced laws that impinged on constitutional protections. Then, after the passing of each crisis, Congress rescinded some of the laws, law enforcement agencies redirected their priorities, and courts ameliorated some of their earlier rulings and positions.[5]

Recently, in a series of decisions, the Supreme Court has determined that captured domestic terrorists must be afforded full due process rights,[6] and that foreign terrorists held at the U.S. military prison in Guantanamo Bay, Cuba, although classified by the military as unlawful enemy combatants, are entitled to at least the right of habeas corpus and the right to petition the federal district court in Washington, D.C., regarding their status.[7] Conversely, enemy combatants held on the Bagram airbase in Afghanistan are not entitled to such habeas corpus relief. The distinction between the bases at Guantanamo Bay and at Bagram is simply that Guantanamo was deemed a territory under *de facto* United States sovereignty, while Bagram was the sovereign territory of another nation outside the jurisdiction of United States courts.[8]

Other decisions have supported expanded government authority. In August 2008, the Foreign Intelligence Court of Review, which oversees the FISA court and hears appeals from that court, upheld the Protect America Act of 2007,[9] which authorizes warrantless searches for national security purposes, and ruled that the Fourth Amendment requirement for warrants does not apply to the collection of foreign intelligence involving Americans. The Court stated:

> Our decision recognizes that where the government has instituted several layers of serviceable safeguards to protect individuals against unwarranted harms and to minimize incidental intrusions, its efforts to protect national security should not be frustrated by the courts.[10]

On June 21, 2010, the Supreme Court in *Holder v. Humanitarian Law Project*, 130 S.Ct. 2705 (2010), upheld convictions based on a ban against providing material support to terrorist organizations.[11] The appellants had provided expert advice and assistance to organizations designated by the U.S. Secretary of State as terrorist organizations. The defendants challenged their convictions on the grounds that the statute was too vague and violated free speech and free association rights. The Court rejected their appeals and upheld the statute as applied to the defendants. Although the defendants claimed that their support was only for nonviolent activities of the terrorist organizations, the Court held that material support for nonviolent activities may save the resources of the terrorist organization for use in violent activities.

Questions pertaining to the treatment of captured suspected terrorists and the methods of interrogation used against them have not yet been decided by the high court. How far the Court or Congress will delve into the methods of ongoing anti-terrorism activities remains to be seen. In actual practice, captured terrorists held in secret for intelligence purposes or to avoid alerting other members of their terrorist organizations have little recourse to the courts until after their capture is officially acknowledged. Additionally, government use of harsh interrogation methods or even torture does not generally come to the public's attention unless the government prosecutes or releases the suspect.[12] Many people find it shocking even to suggest that torture by the U.S. government could ever be considered legal. To most Americans, our country stands for freedom and the proposition that individuals have inalienable rights. We believe our country would never resort to the barbaric practices employed in other times and places. However, the threat of nuclear, biological, or chemical weapons in the hands of terrorists who have no compunction about killing thousands of people raises the proposition that we have a right to self-defense.

Respected legal scholars have proposed authorizing judicial torture warrants for ticking time bomb situations;[13] however, the fact that no major follow-up terrorist attacks have occurred since 9/11 has lessened the urgency of such proposals. As of now, the decision-making burden remains with operational actors, whether law enforcement, military, or intelligence agents. These actors must make crucial decisions without prior approvals or standard policies, and they are subject to after-the-fact judgment and potential civil and criminal liability.

Problem

At 8:30 AM, in New York City, a school bus carrying 12 children between the ages of 9 and 11 was hijacked by a group of men wearing black ski masks and carrying automatic weapons. The bus driver was shot in the head and left in the bus, while the children were taken away in other vehicles.

At 8:50 AM, someone called the police to report that the school bus was blocking a street. When the police responded, they found the bus driver who had died from his wound. They also found a cardboard placard with words written in magic marker: "Release Abdul Abdullah or All Will Die—Instructions Will Follow."

The police quickly ascertained that the bus had been bound for a private elementary school where a substantial number of children of foreign diplomats were enrolled. Dozens of FBI, Homeland Security, and State Department officials responded to the incident, and a joint headquarters was established by the New York City Police Department (NYPD) with 100 detectives assembled to work on the case.

At 10:00 AM, the body of a young girl, whose throat had been cut, was thrown from a car in front of the Israeli embassy. A note was pinned to the girl's school uniform. It demanded the release of Abdul Abdullah from an Israeli prison and his safe passage into the Palestinian-controlled Gaza Strip. The note stated that if he were not released by noon, more children would be killed. By 10:15 AM, the demands in the note had been relayed to the joint headquarters, and the NYPD Chief of Detectives immediately ordered that teams of detectives be stationed outside each foreign embassy in the city. Noon passed without the release of Abdullah, and at 1:00 PM, a team of detectives in a squad car parked down the block from the British embassy observed a sports utility vehicle (SUV), occupied by three men wearing ski masks, speeding toward the embassy. When the SUV stopped in front of the embassy and a body was thrown to the sidewalk, the detectives drove around the front of the SUV, cutting it off before it could drive away. Two men leaned from the SUV windows and began firing automatic weapons at the squad car. The detectives drove to the end of the block to get away from the firing, and left their vehicle blocking the intersection as other police units began to arrive.

The men in the SUV tried to back out of the block, but they were hemmed in by traffic. A shootout followed. One police officer was killed. One of the masked suspects was killed, another wounded, and a third captured when his weapon ran out of ammunition.

The captured suspect was immediately taken to the FBI New York headquarters for interrogation. He said he would not talk without a lawyer, and the FBI agents conferred about whether they should keep interrogating him without a lawyer present because of the imminent danger to the other children. Eventually, they decided to continue interrogating him, but the suspect refused to respond to their questions.

At 4:00 PM, the body of a 10-year-old boy was thrown from the roof of a 10-story apartment building in the Riverdale section of the Bronx. The body landed a short distance away from a synagogue. A cardboard placard was tied to the body. It read, "Free Abdullah." More detectives and FBI agents were assigned to the case, and every piece of evidence was investigated. The SUV had apparently been leased by someone using a fraudulent name, but no immediate leads were developed to identify the terrorists or locate the children.

The State Department conferred with the government of Israel. Although Israel stated that they would release Abdullah if the United States requested them to do so, they recommended against it. To give in to the kidnappers would lead to more terrorism. At the Justice Department in Washington, D.C., high-level discussions took place at which a Justice Department attorney suggested that this was an international terrorist incident being perpetrated by "a group engaged in international terrorism." Legally, the CIA could be employed to utilize harsh or enhanced methods of interrogation on the captured suspect to obtain information about the children. A decision was made not to employ such methods.

Meanwhile, the wounded suspect had been taken to a hospital where a bullet was surgically removed from his leg, but another bullet that had lodged close to his spine was not removed. The suspect was taken to a secure room in the intensive care unit, and eight NYPD detectives were assigned to guard him—four to stay with the suspect, and four to guard against a potential attack on the hospital by other terrorists to either rescue or kill the suspect.

At 9:00 PM, a package was delivered to the New York Times Building. The ear of a child was found in it, along with a note which read: "At 9:00 AM tomorrow, unless Abdullah is released, the beheading of the children will begin—one each hour. Your government will receive their heads." The message delivered to *The New York Times* was a temporary relief for most of the detectives working on the case as it gave them some time and breathing room, and the information was eagerly passed around.

At the hospital, sometime after midnight, Detectives Strayer and Powers were taking their four-hour turn guarding the wounded suspect in his room when they heard about the new message. Strayer was not relieved. He suddenly went to the suspect's bed and began choking him. The suspect stared in disbelief.

"Where are the kids, you son of a bitch?" Strayer demanded.

The suspect could not talk while being choked.

Detective Powers grabbed Strayer. "Are you crazy? Cut it out."

"I'll cut it out when he tells me where the kids are." Strayer squeezed tighter. "Are you going to tell me where they are?"

The suspect tried to catch his breath. He pointed to his chest, indicating pain.

"You want me to help you? You want me to call the doctor?"

The suspect nodded his head, and Strayer loosened his grip.

"Where are the kids?"

The suspect was able to whisper breathlessly, "I don't know."

Strayer began choking him again.

"Stop it. You're going to kill him," Powers said

"So what? They'll think he died from the bullet wound."

"But they'll find your finger marks around his throat."

"You're right." Strayer let go of the suspect's throat. He propped a chair against the door so no one could come into the room, then he wheeled the bed over to the basin sink.

"Grab his legs," he told Powers, and the two detectives lifted the suspect over the sink and placed his head under the faucet. Strayer turned the faucet on, running water onto the suspect's face and into his mouth. The water began to fill the sink.

The suspect tried to shout, but could not.

Powers said that he thought that they used a towel when waterboarding someone. He took a pillow case from the bed, tied it around the suspect's head, and ran more water on the suspect. The detectives repeated this several times and each time asked the suspect to tell them where the children were. With each repetition, the suspect panicked more. He was able to scream once, but no one came to his aid.

"Don't bother screaming. There's nobody here but us," Strayer said. "Now where are the children, or we're going to drown you."

"Okay. Okay." The suspect tried to catch his breath. "But you can't tell anyone I told."

"Fine," Strayer said. "Where are they?"

"An apartment building, Riverdale, in the Bronx, two blocks from the synagogue."

"What's the address?"

"I don't know."

"Tell me the address or I'm going to give you more water."

"I don't know. It's on the corner."

"What apartment?"

"Please. Don't tell that I told."

"I won't tell a soul."

"They're in a storage room, next to the super's apartment."

Strayer and Powers threw the suspect back on the bed just as a nurse tried to open the door.

She pushed the door open. "What's going on?"

"He had to throw up. So we moved him closer to the sink."

The nurse looked skeptical but said nothing else.

Strayer and Powers had the other detectives guard the suspect while they called the Chief of Detectives at headquarters with the information.

Before dawn, the storage room was located and raided. Two terrorists were killed and two were captured, and nine children were rescued. One had lost his ears, but the others were not physically injured.

Questions

1. Did the FBI agents who continued interrogating the captured suspect without a lawyer present for him violate the suspect's constitutional rights?
2. Did the Justice Department officials act correctly not to allow the use of enhanced interrogation methods on the captured suspect because to do so would have violated his constitutional rights?
3. Did the Justice Department officials act correctly in disapproving the use of enhanced interrogation methods on the captured suspect because, although the children's lives were at stake, the threat did not amount to a threat against national security?
4. Did the Justice Department officials have an obligation to use enhanced interrogation methods in an effort to rescue the kidnapped children?
5. Did Strayer violate the wounded suspect's constitutional rights by choking him and subjecting him to the waterboarding?
6. If so, what constitutional right did he violate?
7. Could the suspect's statements be used against him were he prosecuted in a court of law?
8. Had Strayer given the suspect *Miranda* warnings, could the suspect's statements be used against him?
9. Could Strayer and Powers be sued for civil damages?
10. Could Strayer and Powers be charged with criminal assault and coercion?

11. If so, would the charges be constitutional violations or common-law crimes?
12. If placed on trial, could Strayer and Powers admit what they did but claim justification for their actions?

Notes

1 50 U.S.C. §§ 1801 et seq.
2 18 U.S.C. §§ 2510–2522.
3 50 U.S.C. § 1801.
4 18 U.S.C. § 3103(b).
5 Strauss Feuerlicht, Roberta, *America's Reign of Terror: World War I, the Red Scare, and the Palmer Raids*, Random House, New York, 1971.
6 *Rumsfeld v. Padilla*, 542 U.S. 426 (2004); *Hamdi v. Rumsfeld*, 542 U.S. 507 (2004).
7 *Rasul v. Bush*, 542 U.S. 466 (2004); *Hamdan v. Rumsfeld*, 548 U.S. 557 (2006); *Boumediene v. Bush*, 553 U.S. 723 (2008).
8 *Jalatzai v. Gates*, U.S. Circuit Court of Appeals for Washington, D.C., decided May 21, 2010, Judge David Sentelle.
9 18 U.S.C. § 1803.
10 Risen, James and Lichtblau, Eric, Court affirms wiretapping without warrants, *The New York Times*, January 16, 2009.
11 18 U.S.C. § 2339B.
12 Priest, Dana and Gellman, Barton, U.S. decries abuse but defends interrogations; 'stress and duress' tactics used on terrorism suspects held in secret overseas facilities, *The Washington Post*, December 26, 2002.
13 Dershowitz, Alan, Reply: torture without visibility and accountability is worse than with it, *University of Pennsylvania Journal of Constitutional Law* 6, 326, 2003.

References

Chavez v. Martinez, 538 U.S. 760 (2003).
Dershowitz, Alan, Reply: torture without visibility and accountability is worse than with it, *University of Pennsylvania Journal of Constitutional Law*, 6, 326, 2003.
Graham v. Connor, 490 U.S. 386 (1989).
Parry, John, What is torture, are we doing it, and what if we are? *University of Pittsburgh Law Review*, 64, 237, 2003.
Tennessee v. Garner, 471 U.S. 1 (1985).

Case Index

Aguilar v. Texas, 378 U.S. 108 (1964) 44, 99
Alabama v. White, 496 U.S. 325 (1990) 158–9
Apodaca v. Oregon, 406 U.S. 404 (1972) 40
Arizona v. Evans, 514 U.S. 1 (1995) 102
Arizona v. Gant, 129 S.Ct. 1710 (2009) 182–3
Arizona v. Hicks, 480 U.S. 321 (1987) 129
Arizona v. (Lemon Montrea) Johnson,
  129 S.Ct. 781 (2009) 186–7
Arizona v. Roberson, 486 U.S. 675 (1988) 226
Ashcraft v. Tennessee, 322 U.S. 143 (1944) 199

Baldwin v. New York, 399 U.S. 66 (1970) 40
Benton v. Maryland, 395 U.S. 784 (1969) 45
Berghuis Warden v. Thompkins, 130 S.Ct. 2250
  (2010) 209–10
Berkemer v. McCarty, 468 U.S. 420 (1984)
  211–12
Bey v. Begley, 500 F.3d 514 (2007) 241
Brendlin v. California, 127 S.Ct. 2400, 168
  L.Ed.2d 132 (2007) 187, 189
Brewer v. Williams, 430 U.S. 387 (1977) 222,
  225, 228–9
Brigham City, Utah v. Stuart, 547 U.S. 398, 126
  S.Ct. 1943 (2006) 134–7
Brown v. Illinois, 422 U.S. 590 (1975) 154
Brown v. Mississippi, 297 U.S. 278 (1936)
  35–7, 40
Bruton v. United States, 391 U.S. 123
  (1968) 263
Byford v. State, 994 P.2d 700 (2000) 70–1

California v. Acevedo, 500 U.S. 565 (1991) 181
California v. Carney, 471 U.S. 386 (1985) 180
California v. Greenwood, 486 U.S. 35
  (1988) 174–7
Carpenter v. United States, 585 U.S. 19
  (2018) 280–1
Carroll v. United States, 267 U.S. 132
  (1925) 179–80
Chambers v. Maroney, 399 U.S. 42 (1970)
  122, 180

Chambers v. Mississippi, 410 U.S. 284
  (1973) 269
Chavez v. Martinez, 538 U.S. 760 (2003) 217
Chicago v. Morales, 527 U.S. 41 (1999) 16–17
Chimel v. California, 395 U.S. 752 (1969) 45,
  129–31, 138, 182
Clark v. Arizona, 548 U.S. 735 (2006) 67
Coates v. City of Cincinnati, 402 U.S. 611
  (1971) 16
Coker v. Georgia, 433 U.S. 584 (1977) 72
Colorado v. Spring, 479 U.S. 564 (1987) 212–13
Crane v. Kentucky, 476 U.S. 683 (1986) 269
Crawford v. Washington, 541 U.S. 36
  (2004) 268–9
Culombe v. Connecticut, 367 U.S. 568
  (1961) 197
Cupp v. Murphy, 412 U.S. 291 (1973) 134

Davis v. Mississippi, 394 U.S. 721 (1969)
  121, 154
Davis v. United States, 160 U.S. 469
  (1895) 80–1
Davis v. United States, 512 U.S. 452 (1994) 210
Delaware v. Prouse, 440 U.S. 648 (1979)
  183, 188
Dennis v. United States, 341 U.S. 494
  (1951) 21–2
Dickerson v. United States, 530 U.S. 28 (2000)
  216–17, 217
District of Columbia v. Heller, 554 U.S. 570
  (2008) 22, 46–7
Doyle v. Ohio, 426 U.S. 610 (1976) 44
Draper v. United States, 358 U.S. 307
  (1959) 123
Dunaway v. New York, 442 U.S. 200 (1979)
  121, 154, 211, 213
Duncan v. Louisiana, 391 U.S. 145 (1968)
  39–40, 45

Edwards v. Arizona, 451 U.S. 477 (1981)
  208–9, 211, 226

Escobedo v. Illinois, 378 U.S. 478 (1964) 44, 220
Ewing v. California, 538 U.S. 11 (2003) 75

Fletcher v. Weir, 455 U.S. 603 (1982) 44
Florida v. J.L., 529 U.S. 266 (2000) 159
Florida v. Royer, 460 U.S. 491 (1983) 117–21
Franks v. Delaware, 438 U.S. 154 (1978) 102
Frisbee v. Collins, 342 U.S. 519 (1952) 116
Furman v. Georgia, 408 U.S. 238 (1972) 70

Gamble v. United States, 587 U.S. (2019), 139 S.Ct. 1960 79
Georgia v. Randolph, 547 U.S. 103 (2006) 167–9, 173
Gideon v. Wainwright, 372 U.S. 335 (1963) 44, 219–20, 221
Gilbert v. California, 388 U.S. 263 (1967) 255
Goldman v. United States 274
Gregg v. Georgia, 427 U.S. 153 (1976) 70
Griffin v California, 380 U.S. 609 (1965) 40, 43–4, 44

Harris v. New York, 401 U.S. 222 (1971) 266
Hayes v. Florida, 470 U.S. 811 (1985) 154
Herring v. United States, 129 S. Ct. 695 (2009) 101–2
Holder v. Humanitarian Law Project, 130 S.Ct. 2705 (2010) 288
Holmes v. South Carolina, 547 U.S. 319 (2006) 269, 270
Holt v. United States, 218 U.S. 245 (1910) 253
Huddleston v. United States, 485 U.S. 681 (1988) 241–2
Hudson v. Michigan, 547 U.S. 586 (2006) 102, 107–8
Husty v. United States, 282 U.S. 694 (1931) 180

Illinois v. Caballes, 543 U.S. 405 (2005) 282
Illinois v. Gates, 426 U.S. 213 (1983) 99–100, 102, 104, 108, 159
Illinois v. Perkins, 496 U.S. 292 (1990) 225, 227
Illinois v. Rodriguez, 497 U.S. 177 (1990) 168, 172, 173–4
Illinois v. Wardlow, 528 U.S. 119 (2000) 162
In re Gault, 387 U.S. 1 (1967) 45
In re Hodari D., 216 Cal. App. 3d 745 (1989) 177
In re Winship, 397 U.S. 358 (1970) 81, 82, 83

Jackson v. Michigan, 475 U.S. 625 (1986) 226–7
Johnson v. United States, 333 U.S. 10 (1948) 97

Kansas v. Ventris, 129 S.Ct. 1841 (2009) 267
Katz v. United States, 389 U.S. 347 (1967) 45, 274–5, 280
Keeler v. Superior Court, 470 P.2d 617 (Cal. 1970) 15–16

Kennedy v. Louisiana, 129 S.Ct. 1 (2008) 73
King v. Parratt, 4 Car.& P. 570 (1831) 198, 199
Klopfer v. North Carolina, 386 U.S. 213 (1967) 44
Kuhlman v. Wilson, 477 U.S. 436 (1986) 225
Kyllo v. United States, 533 U.S. 27 (2001) 282

Leland v. Oregon [343 U.S. 790 798 (1952)] 81, 82

Malloy v. Hogan, 378 U.S. 1 (1964) 40, 44
Mapp v. Ohio, 367 U.S. 643 (1961) 39, 44, 88, 89, 152
Maryland v. Buie, 494 U.S.325 (1990) 138
Maryland v. Shatzer, 129 S.Ct. 1043 (2010) 209, 230
Maryland v. Wilson, 539 U.S. 408 (1997) 186
Massachusetts v. Sheppard, 468 U.S. 981 (1984) 102
Massiah v. United States, 377 U.S. 201 (1964) 45, 220, 221, 225, 229, 267
McDonald v. Chicago, 130 S.Ct. 3020 (2010) 45–7
McNeil v. Wisconsin, 501 U.S. 171 (1991) 226, 227
Michigan Department of State Police v. Sitz, 496 U.S. 444 (1990) 188
Michigan v. Long, 463 U.S. 1032 (1983) 183, 187
Michigan v. Mosley, 423 U.S. 96 (1975) 208, 210
Michigan v. Tucker, 417 U.S. 433 (1974) 208, 211
Michigan v. Tyler, 436 U.S. 499 (1978) 109
Mincey v. Arizona, 437 U.S. 385 (1978) 133–4, 267
Minnesota v. Dickerson, 508 U.S. 366 (1993) 155
Miranda v. Arizona, 384 U.S. 436 (1966) 39, 40, 44, 90, 121, 139, 148, 150, 196–7, 200, 201, 207–18, 220, 221, 222, 224–5, 226, 227, 228, 230, 231
Montejo v. Louisiana, 129 S.Ct. 2079 (2009) 226–7
Moran v. Burbine, 475 U.S. 412 (1986) 44, 220–1
Morisette v. United States, 342 U.S. 246 (1952) 51
Muehler v. Mena, 544 U.S. 93, 100–1001 (2005) 187
Mullaney v.Wilbur, 421 U.S. 684 (1975) 80, 81
Murray v. United States, 487 U.S. 533 (1988) 91, 230

New Jersey v. Portash, 440 U.S. 450 (1979) 267
New Jersey v. T.L.O., 469 U.S. 325 (1985) 111–12

New York State Rifle & Pistol Association v. Bruen, 597 U.S. (2022), 142 S. Ct. 2111 (2022) 47
New York v. Belton, 453 U.S. 454 (1981) 182–3
New York v. Harris, 495 U.S. 14 (1990) 213–15, 217, 230
New York v. Quarles, 467 U.S. 649 (1984) 211, 230
Nix v. Williams, 467 U.S. 431 (1984) 222–3, 230

Olmstead v. United States, 277 U.S. 438 (1928) 272–4
Oregon v. Bradshaw, 462 U.S. 1039 (1983) 230
Oregon v. Elstad, 470 U.S. 298 (1985) 212, 230
Oregon v. Hass, 420 U.S. 714 (1975) 266

Palko v. Connecticut, 302 U.S. 319 (1937) 38–9
Parker v. Gladden, 385 U.S. 363 (1966) 44
Patterson v. New York, 432 U.S. 197 (1977) 66, 79–80, 81–2
Payton v. New York, 445 U.S. 573 (1980) 89, 116, 213, 214
Pennsylvania v. Mimms, 434 U.S. 106 (1977) 186
People v. Armitage, 194 Cal. App.3d. 405 (1987) 54
People v. Brengard 15
People v. Brown, 26 N.Y. 2d 88 (1970) 269
People v. Burger, 67 N.Y.2d 338 (1986) 109
People v. Cohen, 90 N.Y.2d 632 (1997) 227–8
People v. DeBour, 40 N.Y.2d 210 (1976) 160–1, 162
People v. Del Vermo, 192 N.Y. 470 (1908) 264
People v. Dlugash, 41 N.Y.2d 725 (1977) 67–8
People v. Feldman, 296 N.Y. 127 (1947) 9, 237–8
People v. Fratello, 92 N.Y.2d565 (1998) 264
People v. Harris, 72 N.Y.2d 614 (1988) 214–15
People v. Hernandez and Santana, 82 N.Y.2d 309 (1993) 56
People v. Joseph, 130 Misc.2d 377, 496, N.Y.S.2d 328 (1985) 16
People v. Keta, 79 N.Y.2d 474 (1992) 109
People v. Kibbe, 35 N.Y.2d 407 (1974) 54–5
People v. Mills, 1 N.Y.3d 269 (2003) 236–7
People v. Molineux, 168 N.Y. 264 (1901) 241
People v. Moore, 74 N.Y.2d 224 (2006) 161–2
People v. Weaver, 12 N.Y. 3d 433 (2009) 278–80
People v. West, 81 N.Y.2d 370 (1993) 229–30
People v. Wharton, 74 N.Y.2d 921 (1989) 252
Pointer v. Texas, 380 U.S. 400 (1965) 44, 268, 269
Powell v. Alabama, 287 U.S. 45 (1932) 34–5

Rakas v. Illinois, 439 U.S. 128 (1978) 189
Ramos v. Louisiana, 590 U.S. .(2020), 140 S.Ct. 1390 (2020) 40
Riley v. California, 573 U.S. 373 (2014) 131
Rivera v. Delaware, 429 U.S. 877 (1976) 81, 82
Robinson v. California, 370 U.S. 660 (1962) 44, 50
Rochin v. California, 342 U.S. 165 (1952) 37–8

Schenk v. United States, 249 U.S.47 (1919) 21
Schmerber v. California, 384 U.S. 757 (1966) 253–4
Schneckloth v. Bustamonte, 412 U.S. 218 (1973) 165
Silverman v. United States, 365 U.S. 505 (1961) 274
Silverthorne Lumber Co. v. United States, 251 U.S. 385 (1920) 86, 89–90, 91
Solem v. Helm, 463 U.S. 277 (1983) 75
South Dakota v. Oppermann, 428 U.S.364 (1976) 188
Spinelli v. United States, 393 U.S. 410 (1969) 45, 99
State v. Wilson, 685 So.2d 1063 (1993) 72–3

Tennessee v. Garner, 471 U.S. 1 (1985) 124
Terry v. Ohio, 392 U.S. 1 (1968) 45, 119, 120, 152–3, 154, 158, 162, 183, 187, 190
Texas v. Cobb, 532 U.S. 162 (2001) 227–8

United States v. Banks, 540 U.S. 31 (2003) 107
United States v. Brettholz, 485 F.2d 483 (1973) 240–1
United States v. Buswell, 406 U.S. 311 (1972) 108
United States v. Cortez, 449 U.S. 411 (1981) 162–3
United States v. Dionisio, 410 U.S. 1 (1973) 254
United States v. Drayton, 536 U.S. 194 (2002) 165
United States v. Frazier, 408 F.3d 1102 (8th Cir. 2005) 44
United States v. Grubbs, 547 U.S. 90 (2006) 105
United States v. Havens, 466 U.S. 620 (1980) 266
United States v. Henry, 447 U.S. 264 (1980) 225
United States v. Jones, 565 U.S. 400 (2012) 280
United States v. Knights, 534 U.S. 112 (2001) 111
United States v. Knotts, 460 U.S. 276 (1983) 278, 279
United States v. Leon, 468 U.S. 897 (1984) 100–1, 102, 108, 174
United States v. Lopez, 514 U.S. 549 (1995) 77
United States v. Matlock, 415 U.S. 164 (1974) 168, 169–70, 172–3
United States v. Montoya de Hernandez, 473 U.S. 531 (1985) 154

United States v. Morrison, 529 U.S. 598 (2000) 77

United States v. O'Brien, 391 U.S. 367 (1968) 22

United States v. Patane, 542 U.S. 630 (2004) 217–18, 230

United States v. Robinson, 414 U.S. 218 (1973) 182, 183

United States v. Ross, 456 U.S. 798 (1982) 181

United States v. Velarde-Gomez, 269 F.3d 1023 (9th Cir. 2001) 44

United States v. Wade, 388 U.S. 218 (1967) 45, 251

United States v. Watson, 423 U.S. 411 (1976) 116

United States v. Weeks, 232 U.S. 383 (1914) 85, 86, 89

Victor v. Nebraska, 511 U.S. 1 (1994) 8, 24

Virginia v. Moore, 553 U.S. 164 128 S.Ct. 1598, 170 L.Ed.2d 539 (2008) 184

Wainwright v. Greenfield, 474 U.S. 284 (1986) 44

Warden v. Hayden, 387 U.S. 297 (1967) 132, 138

Washington v. Davis, 126 S.Ct. 2266 (2006) 269

Washington v. Texas, 388 U.S. 14 (1967) 44, 269

Welsh v. Wisconsin, 466 U.S. 740 (1984) 132–3, 136

Whren v. United States, 517 U.S. 806 (1996) 187–8

Wilson v. Arkansas, 514 U.S. 927 (1995) 106–7

Winston v. Lee, 470 U.S. 753 (1985) 256

Wolf v. Colorado, 338 U.S. 25 (1949) 25–6, 86, 87–8, 89

Wong Sun v. United States, 371 U.S. 471 (1963) 45, 90–1

Wyoming v. Houghton, 526 U.S. 295 (1999) 181

Subject Index

18 U.S.C. § 242 78
18 U.S.C. § 249 65
18 U.S.C. § 922(g) 78–9
18 U.S.C. § 3501 215–16

42 U.S.C. § 1983 217

abandoned property 174–7
abandonment, induced 177
accomplices: death of accomplice 57; liability of 56–7
actus reus 50–1, 53
administrative warrants 108–10
admissions 162, 197, 204, 212, 222–3, 241–2, 263, 268
affidavit 97–8, 101, 102, 103–4, 105, 126, 175
affirmation 97–8
affirmative defenses 8, 66–7, 80, 81–2, 83
Aguilar-Spinelli test 99–100, 108
alibis 66, 263, 278
amicus curiae 216
Anti-Drug Abuse Act (1988) 71
anticipatory warrants 104–5
Arbery, Ahmaud 65
arraignment 7, 195
arrests 4, 5–6, 114–27, 147–8; arrest warrants 116–17; authority to arrest 114; citizen's arrest 64–6, 114; confidential informants 123, 124–5; elements of 117–21; good judgement and discretion 121–2; hearsay 121–2; probable cause for 5, 7, 23, 24–5, 65, 89, 92, 101, 114, 115–16, 116–17, 119, 120, 121–3, 123, 130, 145–6, 152, 184, 211, 214, 238, 246; and prosecution 126; in a suspects home 89, 90–1; and use of force 123–4
arson 12, 55, 57, 62, 63, 64, 70, 109
assault 11, 12, 15, 49, 64, 129; and domestic violence 126; intentional 53, 55; by the police 77–8, 79, 114; and self-defense 60–1; sexual assault 204–5, 224, 235, 270
Athenian code 11–12
attenuation 91, 212, 214, 230

attorneys 219–33
automobiles *see* searches of vehicles and occupants

Bagram, Afghanistan 288
bail 7, 27–8, 126
Bail Reform Act (1984) 27–8
be on the lookout (BOLO) bulletin 123
Bentham, Jeremy 50
Bill of Rights 3, 38, 40, 85, 179, 195; summary of 20–30
Bills of Attainder 18, 20
bite marks 253, 255, 257, 258
Black, Conrad 18, 51
Blackstone, William 9, 14
blood samples and types 29, 239, 253–4
Brandeis, Louis 272–3
bribery 18, 52, 76
Bundy, Ted 255
burden of production 66
Burger, Warren 207

capital punishment *see* death penalty
Cardozo, Benjamin 86
Cassell, Paul G. 215, 216
causation 53–5
caveat emptor 17
cell phones 131, 276, 278, 280–1
cell site location information (CLSI) 280, 281
Central Park jogger case 205–7
Cicero, Marcus Tullius 12
citations, traffic 184, 186
civil negligence 63
civil rights 33–4; state violations of 35–7
Civil Rights Act (1871) 46
Civil Rights Act (1964) 37
Code of Hammurabi 11, 13
Coke, Sir Edward 61
commerce clause 76–7
common law 14–16, 20, 57, 61, 80, 83, 106, 114, 123–4, 159, 235

Comprehensive Drug Abuse Prevention and Control Act (1970) 76
computer data transmission 276
computer files 131
confessions 196–8; coerced confessions 35–7, 41; as evidence of guilt 38–9; false confessions 198–9; *Miranda* rights 196, 207, 208, 215–16; non-hearsay 261–2; out-of-court confessions 263; suppression of 208, 211, 213–15, 216, 218, 220; voluntary and involuntary nature of 199, 202–3, 215–16
confrontation rights 260–71; admissions 263; confessions 262; cross-examination 260, 265–6, 267; declarations against interest 268–70; defendant's prior inconsistent statements 265–7; dying declarations 262; exceptions to hearsay 261–2, 264–5; excited utterances and spontaneous statements 263–4; hearsay 260–1, 269; non-hearsay 261–2; prior testimony 268; witness prior inconsistent statements 265
Congress 3, 4, 18, 20, 21, 28–9, 33, 73, 76–7, 235, 273, 275; attempt to overrule *Miranda* 215–17
consent searches 165–78; abandoned property 174–7; good-faith mistakes 173–4; induced abandonment 177; third-party consent 167–73; voluntary consent 165–7
Continuing Criminal Enterprise Act 76–7
Corpus Juris Civilis 12–14
counsel, right to 27, 34–5, 203, 208–9, 219–33, 266; exceptions to 230; and factually-related cases 227–9; and indirect questioning 222; inevitable discovery exception 222–5; interconnectivity of rights 230–3; interminable right to counsel 229–30; jailhouse informants 221, 225; at lineups 251; *Miranda* rights 203, 220, 221; offense-specific variations 226–7
courts 4, 14–15; dual court system 34; standards 7–8
crimes 10–11, 21; common-law crimes 15–16; and punishments 60–84; white-collar crime 17–18
criminal law principles 49–59; accomplice liability 56–7; *actus reus* 50–1, 53; causation 53–5; death of accomplice 57; felony murder 55–6; *mens rea* 51–3, 55, 72; strict liability crimes 57–8
criminal negligence 51, 52, 60, 63
Criminal Procedure Law 140.15 (4) (New York) 89
cross-examination 43–4, 260; of defendants 240, 265, 266; of witnesses 260, 265–6, 268, 269
custodial interrogation 199–206; and a break in custody 209, 230

dangerous instruments 60–1
deadly physical force 63–4, 65, 106, 124
deadly weapons 60–1
death penalty 14, 28, 34–5, 51, 57, 69–73
Declaration of Independence 3
defense attorneys 4, 5, 27, 104, 126, 187, 219–20, 257–8, 270, 271
dental examinations 255
detention 154; of vehicle drivers and passengers 186–7
Devlin, Lord Patrick 196
DNA 92, 205, 224, 238, 239, 253, 254
dogs 282
domestic violence 171–2, 264, 269
double jeopardy 25, 38–9, 77–8
drunk driving 58, 132–3, 144, 188, 211–12, 253–4
due process of law 3, 8–9, 16, 18, 20, 23; applying due process to the States 34–8; cornerstone right 25–6; due process protections 33–48; and evidence 234–46; federalism and the dual court system 34; Fifth Amendment 199; Fourteenth Amendment 40, 45–6, 79–80, 81, 82–3, 199; and identifications 247–59; right to bear arms 45–7; right to remain silent and presumption of innocence 41–4; selective incorporation of federal rights into the Fourteenth Amendment 38–9; self-incrimination 40–3; and terrorism 287–8; and trial by jury 39–40; unanimous verdicts 40
duress defenses 66
dying declarations 262

eavesdropping 272, 273, 274; legal context 275; strict requirements for warrants 276–7; warrants 275, 277, 286; without a warrant 275–6
Eighth Amendment 3–4, 27–8, 70, 73, 75
electronic beepers 278
Electronic Communications Privacy Act (ECPA) 277
electronic eavesdropping 23
electronic mail 276, 277
emergencies 89, 110, 116, 121, 131–2, 134, 136–7; emergency aid doctrine 135
Enron scandal (2001) 17–18
entrapment defenses 66
evidence: and affirmative defenses 66–7; character evidence 240; circumstantial 197–8, 237, 238–9, 245–6, 261; class evidence 239; confessions as evidence 196–9; confidential communications 236; corroborative evidence 252–3; credibility 240–1; and due process 234–46; exculpatory evidence 121; fingerprints 239, 253; forcible extraction of 37–8, 255–6; of guilt 43–4; hearsay 26, 121–2, 236, 260–1, 262, 264–5, 269;

inadmissible 85–6, 88, 89–91, 100, 107; independent source doctrine 223; individualized evidence 239; legally sufficient evidence 7; marital privilege 236–7; MIMIC rule 241–2; opinion evidence 236; physical evidence 236, 239, 253–6; preponderance of 8; presumptions 242–3; prima facie evidence 8; relevant, material, and competent evidence 234–7; reliability of 234; suppression of 115, 116, 121, 134, 182–3, 213–15, 216, 218; too prejudicial 237–8; wiretapping 254; and wiretapping/eavesdropping 277; written documents 236

evolving standards of decency 70–1, 73

ex post facto laws 18, 20

exclusionary rule 5, 100–1, 101–2, 106, 107, 152, 184, 211, 213, 214, 267; and evidence resulting from unlawful police conduct 223; and the Fourth Amendment 85–93

exigent circumstances 89, 116, 128, 133–7, 180

extortion 69, 74–5, 76, 261

extreme emotional disturbance defenses 62, 67, 79–80, 81–2

factual impossibility 67–8

factually-related cases 227–9

fairness 50

false pretenses 74

Federal Communications Act (1934) 273–4

federal crimes 76–7

Federal Rules of Evidence 235, 241, 260–1, 262

Feldman, Benjamin 9

Felon in Possession of a Firearm Act (FPF) 78–9

Fifteenth Amendment 33–4

Fifth Amendment 3–4, 25–6, 34, 40–1, 43, 70, 195, 196, 199, 202, 203, 211, 217, 220, 221, 222, 225, 253, 254, 256, 273

fingerprints 239, 253

firearms *see* guns and firearms

Firearms Control Act (2023) (New York) 47

First Amendment 3, 21–2

Foreign Intelligence Court of Review 288

Foreign Intelligence Surveillance Act (FISA) (1974) 286–7

forgery 52

Fourteenth Amendment 3, 33–4, 34, 40, 70, 124, 188, 268; due process clause 37–8, 40, 45–6, 79–80, 81, 82–3, 199; selective incorporation of federal rights 38–9

Fourth Amendment 3–4, 23–5, 35, 37, 38, 97, 106, 108, 111, 112, 119, 124, 128, 132, 135, 136, 137, 152, 160, 165, 167, 168, 171, 174, 175–6, 177, 179, 180, 183, 184, 187, 211, 213, 217, 254, 256, 272, 273, 274, 277, 278–80, 279, 282, 288; and the exclusionary rule 85–93

Frankfurter, Felix 87, 197, 199

free speech 21, 22

freedom 3, 10

French Revolution 14

frisking *see* stop, question and frisk

fruits-of-the-poisonous-tree doctrine 86, 90, 91, 189, 211, 213–15, 217–18, 222; exceptions to 230; and inevitable discovery exception 222–3

Gang Congregation Ordinance (Chicago) 16–17

global positioning systems (GPS) 278–80

good-faith exception 101–2

good-faith mistakes 173–4

government surveillance 272–85, 277; dogs 282; email and text messages 277; pen registers and trap-and-trace devices 277; stored communications 277; strict requirements for eavesdropping/wiretapping warrants 276–7; surveillance devices 273, 274, 275; tracking a person's movements 278–81; x-rays, metal detectors, thermal imaging, and video 281–2; *see also* terrorism

Guantanamo Bay, Cuba 288

guns and firearms 22, 45–7, 78–9, 153, 160–2, 183, 186–7, 213, 217–18

habeas corpus 20, 34, 221, 288

handwriting 236, 254, 255

hazardous materials 58

hearsay 26, 121–2, 236, 250–1, 260–1, 262, 263, 264–5, 269

heat of passion 62–3

Hobbs Act (1946) 76

Holmes, Oliver Wendell 15, 21, 86, 272–3

homicide *see* murder

honest services statute 18

honor killings 63

hot pursuits 7, 129, 132–3, 135, 138, 140

hue and cry 195–6

identifications 247–59; bite marks 255; bolstering un-court testimony with prior identifications 250–1; confirmatory identifications by police officers 252; corroboration 252–3; in-court identifications 250; and court orders 254; false identifications 247, 251; forcible extraction of evidence 255–6; handwriting 255; lineups 247–8; photographs 249; point-outs during a canvas 249; right to counsel at lineups 251; self-incrimination by physical evidence 253–6; show-ups 249; without eyewitnesses 253

immunity from prosecution 41

indecency 17

independent source doctrine 223

individual rights 3, 4, 9, 20, 23, 128

inevitable discovery exception 222–5

informants: anonymous tips 158–9, 161; confidential 99–102, 102–4, 123, 124–5; jailhouse informants 221, 225, 267

innocence: inconsistent with innocence standard 197–8; presumption of 25, 41, 242
insanity 67, 80–1
intent 51–2; specific intent and voluntary acts 52–3; transferred intent 53, 55
interrogation *see* questioning and interrogation

Jefferson, Thomas 3
judges 14; as gate keepers 7
juries 7, 21, 26, 27, 39–40; and the death penalty 70
justification defenses 63–4, 66
Justinian Code 12–14

Kant, Immanuel 49
kidnapping 55, 56, 62, 63, 64, 71, 76, 116, 224, 289–90, 291
King, Rodney 77–8
knock-and-announce rules 106–9, 137

larceny 52–3, 74–5
law enforcement agencies 4–5, 9
legality principle of 16
lineups 247–8, 251
Lippman, Jonathan 278–80
little fish to big fish investigation 99
loitering laws 16–17

Madison, James 3, 21, 23, 27, 28–9
Magna Carta, 1215 3, 23
malice aforethought 12, 16, 61–2, 79, 80
malum in se 11
malum prohibitum 11
manslaughter 29, 51, 63, 80, 81–2; as homicide 62, 63
marital privilege 236–7, 268, 269
mens rea 51–3, 55, 72
mental state 51–3, 67, 261–2
metal detectors 281–2
Mill, John Stuart 50
MIMIC rule 241–2
minors 58; rape of 58, 72–4
Miranda rights 207–18, 224, 225, 232, 265, 266; and attenuation 212, 214; and confessions 196, 207, 208, 215; Congressional attempt to overrule *Miranda* 215–17; exceptions to 211–13, 230; fruits-of-the-poisonous-tree doctrine 213–15, 217–18; and public safety 211; and questioning 200, 202–6; questions raised by *Miranda* 207–11; and right to consult counsel 203, 220, 221; and rights to counsel 208–10, 226–7; and self incrimination 195–206; suppressing confessions to enforce the Fourth Amendment 211; and traffic enforcement 211–12; voluntary waiver of the right to remain silent 212–13
mistake of fact 67–8
mobile homes 180

modus operandi 241
murder 51, 81–2; felony murder 55–6, 62; first and second degree 69–70, 72; as homicide 61–2; honor killings 63; of unborn children 15–16; year-and-a-day rule 15, 61
Murphy, Frank 87–8

Napoleonic Code 14
National Prohibition Act 272
negative defenses 66
Ninth Amendment 28
non-hearsay 126, 261–2

oaths 97–8, 235–6
Omnibus Crime Control and Safe Streets Act (1968) 215–16; Title III 275–6, 277, 286
Organized Crime Control Act (1970) 76
Orwell, George 273
out-of-court statements 261–2

paging devices 276
parole 75, 110, 111
pat-down 110, 153, 154, 165, 186, 187
Patriot Act *see* USA Patriot Act (2001)
peace officers 64
pen registers 277
penal law 60
physical force: and arrests 64–5; and frisking 156; justifiable 63–4
plain feel doctrine 155
plain hearing doctrine 272
plain view doctrine 88, 128–9, 132, 134, 138, 140, 145, 155, 166, 171, 173, 181, 272
plea bargains 7, 126
police 9, 16; assaults by 77–8, 79, 114; confirmatory identifications of suspects 252; establishment of 196; evidence and misconduct 223; knowledge of law 4–5, 6, 24–5; and probable cause 23–5; questioning and interrogation 196–7, 198, 199–207; uncommon encounters with citizens 142–51; undercover activities 252; and undercover contacts 220, 221; violation of citizens' rights 85–8, 90–1; walking away/fleeing from 161–2; withholding of information 221; *see also* search warrants
pornography 104, 105
posses comitatis 195–6
premeditation 61–2, 71, 72, 81, 261
presumption 185–6, 242–3; of coercion 218, 226; and guilt 83; of innocence 8, 25, 41, 43, 79–80, 243; of intention 74; and malice aforethought 80
prisons 111
privacy 28, 112, 128, 131, 175–6, 273, 274, 287; and enhanced technological devices 282; expectation of 274–5; and searches/seizures 274–5; and vehicles 181, 188–9, 278–80

private thoughts and expressions 273
probable cause 4, 23–4, 243; and the *Aguilar-Spinelli* test 99–100, 104, 108; arrests 5, 7, 23, 24–5, 65, 89, 92, 101, 114, 115–17, 119, 120, 121–3, 123, 130, 145–6, 152, 184, 211, 214, 238, 246; circumstantial evidence 238–9; exceptions to 128, 132, 138, 153; individualized evidence 239, 245–6; search warrants 7, 23–4, 90, 97, 98, 101, 102, 104, 105, 108, 109; searches of students 112; totality of the circumstances test 163; traffic violations 187; vehicle searches 179, 180, 181, 182, 189–90, 282
probation 111
Prohibition 179–80
proof beyond reasonable doubt 8, 9, 25, 82–3, 196
proof, burden of 79, 88, 234, 239, 242
prosecutions 4, 6–7, 126; and double jeopardy 77–8; immunity from 41, 124
Protect America Act (2007) 288
proximate cause 53–5
public safety 211, 230
punishment 10, 11, 14, 27–8; and crimes 60–84; theories of 49–50

questioning and interrogation 195–6; after a break in custody 208–9; covert questioning 225; indirect questioning 222; *Miranda* rights 200, 202–6, 208–9; police methods 198, 199–207; police practices, supervision of 199; of suspected terrorists 288; taped statements 230; *see also* stop, question and frisk

Racketeer Influenced and Corrupt Organizations statute (RICO) 76
Raleigh, Sir Walter 26
rape 26, 56, 58, 62, 64, 72–4, 121, 202, 204–5, 235, 255, 264, 278; and the death penalty 34–5, 72–3; false charges 265
rationalism 14
Rawls, John 49
reachable-area searches 130
reasonable cause to believe 115
reasonable suspicion 7, 25, 45, 92, 111, 112, 150–1, 153–4, 155, 166, 177; inquiries on less than reasonable suspicion 159–63; traffic stops 183, 187, 188, 189, 190
recklessness 51, 52, 63
renunciation 66
right to bear arms 22, 45–7
right to remain silent 41–4, 208, 209–11, 234; voluntary waiver of 212–13
rule of law 3, 15

schools 111–12
Scottsboro Boys case 34–5

search warrants 5–6, 23–4, 85–8, 91, 97–113, 117, 276; administrative warrants 108–10; anticipatory warrants and controlled deliveries 104–5; border and airport searches 110; and cell site location information 281; challenges to 100–1, 102; confidential informants 99–102, 102–4; knock-and-announce rules 106–9; oath or affirmation 97–8; obtaining 97; prison, parole and probation supervision 111; probable cause for 7, 23–4, 90, 97, 98, 101, 102, 104, 105, 108, 109; procedures and statutory rules 105–6; schools and students 111–12; sneak-and-peak warrants 287; special needs searches 110; stored communications 277; and surveillance devices 274; telephonic applications 98; truthfulness 102; and vehicle mobility 179–80; *see also* consent searches
searches of vehicles and occupants 179–91; closed containers 181; detention of drivers and passengers 186–7; with dogs 282; incidental to arrest 182–3; inventory searches 188; mobile homes 180; mobility and the automobile exception 179–80; occupants 181; and privacy 181; roadblocks and safety checks 188; standing to challenge searches 188–9; stop and frisk 183; traffic stops 183–6; traffic violations as a pretext to stop, frisk, or search 187–8
searches without warrants 7, 128–41, 155, 286, 288; emergency exceptions 131–2; exigent circumstances 133–7, 180; hot pursuits 132–3, 138; open fields 140; plain view doctrine 128–9; protective sweeps 138; searches incidental to a lawful arrest 129–30; telephone and computer files 131; *see also* consent searches
Second Amendment 22, 45, 46, 47
seizures 23, 159–60, 161, 165, 177, 273; of vehicles 179–91; violations 85–8
self-defense 46–7, 61, 63, 106
self-incrimination 25, 40–3, 43, 195–206, 221, 222, 273; confessions 196–8; false confessions 198–9; and physical evidence 253–6
Seventh Amendment 27
shocks the conscience 38–9, 43
Simpson, O.J. 254
Sixth Amendment 3–4, 26–7, 40, 219, 220, 222, 226, 251, 262, 268
Skilling, Jeffrey 18
slavery 33
social control 10–19, 49; constitutional requirements 16–17
stare decisis 14, 216
state constitutionalism 214–15
state of mind 13
statements: declarations against interest 268–70; impeachment exceptions 267; involuntary

statements 267; out-of-court statements
261–2; against penal interest 269–70; prior
inconsistent statements 265–7; spontaneous
statements 263–4; taped statements 230, 269
statutes 15–16; constitutional requirements
16–17; eavesdropping 275; honest services
statute 18
stigma 10
stop, question and frisk 7, 25, 152, 185;
anonymous tips 158–9, 161; in and around
vehicles 183, 187, 187–8; force, use of 156;
frisking 154–5, 157; inquiries on less than
reasonable suspicion 159–63; reasonable
suspicion 153–4; time and place 154
Stored Wire and Electronic Communications
and Transactional Records Act 277, 278
Story, Joseph 198
strict liability crimes 57–8
strip searches 110, 111
students 111–12
sufficient danger of substantive evil 22
suspicion see reasonable suspicion

Tenth Amendment 28
terrorism 286–92; warfare approach to 287
text messages 277
thermal imaging 281–2
Third Amendment 22
third-party doctrine 281
Thirteenth Amendment 33
three strikes 75–6
torture 35–7, 41, 195, 273, 288–9, 290–1
totality of the circumstances 162–3
traffic offenses 58, 183–4, 187–8
traffic stops 183–6; and Miranda rights
211–12
transactional immunity 41
trap-and-trace devices 277

treason 21
trespass 52, 272, 274
trials: by jury 21, 26, 27, 39–40; public 26
Twelve Tables 12

undercover contacts 220, 221
Uniform Code of Military Justice 73
U.S. Constitution 3–4, 18, 20–1, 34, 179, 203,
287; as a living document 28, 73
U.S. Supreme Court 34, 70, 71, 73
USA Patriot Act (2001) 286–7
use immunity 41
utilitarianism 49–50

vagrancy laws 16
vehicles: searches of 179–91, 282; tracking
278–9
verdicts: guilty 8; not guilty 8; unanimous
verdicts 40
video 281–2
voluntary acts 50–1; and manslaughter 63;
and specific intent 52–3

Warren Court 22, 39, 40, 99, 121, 202, 220,
274; criminal procedure decisions 44–5
Weyhrauch, Bruce 18
white-collar crime 17–18
William the Conqueror 14
wiretapping 23, 254, 272, 274, 275, 276; strict
requirements for warrants 276–7
witnesses 26; credibility 240–1, 260;
cross-examination 260, 265–6, 267;
and self-incrimination 41–3
writ of certiorari 34, 35, 38, 109, 216

x-rays 281–2

year-and-a-day rule 15, 61